PHILOSOPHY OF MIND IN THE NINETEENTH CENTURY

Between the publication of Kant's *Critique of Pure Reason* in 1781 and Husserl's *Ideas* in 1913, the nineteenth century is a pivotal period in the philosophy of mind, witnessing the emergence of the phenomenological and analytical traditions that continue to shape philosophical debate in fundamental ways. The nineteenth century also challenged many prevailing assumptions about the transparency of the mind, particularly in the ideas of Nietzsche and Freud, whilst at the same time witnessing the birth of modern psychology in the work of William James.

Covering the main figures of German idealism to the birth of the phenomenological movement under Brentano and Husserl, *Philosophy of Mind in the Nineteenth Century* provides an outstanding survey to these new directions in philosophy of mind.

Following an introduction by Sandra Lapointe, fourteen specially commissioned chapters by an international team of contributors discuss key topics, thinkers, and debates, including:

- German idealism,
- Bolzano,
- Johann Friedrich Herbart,
- Ernst Mach,
- Helmholtz,
- Nietzsche,
- William James,
- Sigmund Freud,
- Brentano's early philosophy of mind,
- Meinong,
- Christian von Ehrenfels,
- Husserl, and
- Natorp.

Essential reading for students and researchers in philosophy of mind, continental philosophy, and the history of philosophy, *Philosophy of Mind in the Nineteenth Century* is also a valuable resource for those in related disciplines such as psychology, religion, and literature.

Sandra Lapointe is Associate Professor of Philosophy at McMaster University, Canada. A Commonwealth Alumna and Fellow of the Humboldt Foundation, she has published extensively in the history of nineteenth- and twentieth-century philosophy of logic, language, and mind. She is a founding associate editor of the *Journal for the History of Analytical Philosophy* and the founding president of the Society for the Study of the History of Analytical Philosophy.

The History of the Philosophy of Mind
General Editors: Rebecca Copenhaver and Christopher Shields

The History of the Philosophy of Mind is a major six-volume reference collection, covering the key topics, thinkers, and debates within philosophy of mind, from Antiquity to the present day. Each volume is edited by a leading scholar in the field and comprises chapters written by an international team of specially commissioned contributors.

Including a general introduction by Rebecca Copenhaver and Christopher Shields, and fully cross-referenced within and across the six volumes, *The History of the Philosophy of Mind* is an essential resource for students and researchers in philosophy of mind, and will also be of interest to those in many related disciplines, including Classics, Religion, Literature, History of Psychology, and Cognitive Science.

VOL.1 PHILOSOPHY OF MIND IN ANTIQUITY,
edited by John E. Sisko

VOL.2 PHILOSOPHY OF MIND IN THE EARLY AND
HIGH MIDDLE AGES,
edited by Margaret Cameron

VOL.3 PHILOSOPHY OF MIND IN THE LATE MIDDLE AGES
AND RENAISSANCE,
edited by Stephan Schmid

VOL.4 PHILOSOPHY OF MIND IN THE EARLY MODERN
AND MODERN AGES,
edited by Rebecca Copenhaver

VOL.5 PHILOSOPHY OF MIND IN THE NINETEENTH CENTURY,
edited by Sandra Lapointe

VOL.6 PHILOSOPHY OF MIND IN THE TWENTIETH AND
TWENTY-FIRST CENTURIES,
edited by Amy Kind

PHILOSOPHY OF MIND IN THE NINETEENTH CENTURY

The History of the Philosophy of Mind,
Volume 5

Edited by Sandra Lapointe

LONDON AND NEW YORK

First published 2018
by Routledge
2 Park Square, Milton Park, Abingdon, Oxon OX14 4RN

and by Routledge
711 Third Avenue, New York, NY 10017

Routledge is an imprint of the Taylor & Francis Group, an informa business

© 2019 selection and editorial matter, Sandra Lapointe; individual chapters, the contributors

The right of Sandra Lapointe to be identified as the author of the editorial material, and of the authors for their individual chapters, has been asserted in accordance with sections 77 and 78 of the Copyright, Designs and Patents Act 1988.

All rights reserved. No part of this book may be reprinted or reproduced or utilised in any form or by any electronic, mechanical, or other means, now known or hereafter invented, including photocopying and recording, or in any information storage or retrieval system, without permission in writing from the publishers.

Trademark notice: Product or corporate names may be trademarks or registered trademarks, and are used only for identification and explanation without intent to infringe.

British Library Cataloguing-in-Publication Data
A catalogue record for this book is available from the British Library

Library of Congress Cataloging-in-Publication Data
Names: Lapointe, Sandra, editor.
Title: Philosophy of mind in the nineteenth century / edited by Sandra Lapointe.
Description: New York : Routledge, 2018. | Series: The history of the philosophy of mind ; Volume 5 | Includes bibliographical references and index.
Identifiers: LCCN 2017060256 | ISBN 9781138243965 (hardback : alk. paper) | ISBN 9780429508134 (e-book)
Subjects: LCSH: Philosophy of mind—History—19th century.
Classification: LCC BD418.3 .P4845 2018 | DDC 128/.209034—dc23
LC record available at https://lccn.loc.gov/2017060256

ISBN: 978-1-138-24396-5 (Vol V, hbk)
ISBN: 978-0-429-50813-4 (Vol V, ebk)

ISBN: 978-1-138-24392-7 (Vol I, hbk)
ISBN: 978-0-429-50821-9 (Vol I, ebk)
ISBN: 978-1-138-24393-4 (Vol II, hbk)
ISBN: 978-0-429-50819-6 (Vol II, ebk)
ISBN: 978-1-138-24394-1 (Vol III, hbk)
ISBN: 978-0-429-50817-2 (Vol III, ebk)
ISBN: 978-1-138-24395-8 (Vol IV, hbk)
ISBN: 978-0-429-50815-8 (Vol IV, ebk)
ISBN: 978-1-138-24397-2 (Vol VI, hbk)
ISBN: 978-0-429-50812-7 (Vol VI, ebk)
ISBN: 978-1-138-92535-9 (6-volume set, hbk)

Typeset in Times New Roman
by Apex CoVantage, LLC

CONTENTS

Notes on contributors   vii
General introduction   x
REBECCA COPENHAVER AND CHRISTOPHER SHIELDS

Introduction to volume 5   1
SANDRA LAPOINTE

1 **Representation, consciousness, and mind in German idealism**   23
CLINTON TOLLEY

2 **Bolzano's philosophy of mind and action**   42
SANDRA LAPOINTE

3 **Johann Friedrich Herbart on mind**   60
CHRISTOPH LANDERER AND WOLFGANG HUEMER

4 **Ernst Mach's contributions to the philosophy of mind**   77
ERIK C. BANKS

5 **Helmholtz's physiological psychology**   96
LYDIA PATTON

6 **Nietzsche's philosophy of mind**   117
MATTIA RICCARDI

CONTENTS

7 William James's naturalistic account of concepts and his 'rejection of logic'   133
HENRY JACKMAN

8 Sigmund Freud on brain and mind   147
BETTINA BERGO

9 Brentano's early philosophy of mind   168
ROBIN D. ROLLINGER

10 Meinong and mind   186
PETER SIMONS

11 'Apprehending a multitude as a unity': Stumpf on perceiving space and hearing chords   198
MARK TEXTOR

12 Christian von Ehrenfels on the mind and its metaphysics   214
CARLO IERNA

13 Edmund Husserl: from intentionality to transcendental phenomenology   232
PAUL M. LIVINGSTON

14 Natorp's two-dimensional mind   249
ALAN KIM

Index   269

CONTRIBUTORS

Erik C. Banks was Professor of Philosophy at Wright State University, Dayton, Ohio. After graduating from City University of New York Graduate Center, he spent a year as a Fulbright Scholar at the Max Planck Institute for the History of Science in Berlin. His area of specialization was the History and Philosophy of Science, with emphasis on Ernst Mach. He was the author of two books, most recently The Realistic Empiricism of Mach, James, and Russell: Neutral Monism Reconceived (2014), and numerous articles. Erik Banks passed away suddenly in August 2017.

Bettina Bergo is author of some fifty articles on phenomenology and psychology. She has translated three works of Levinas as well as Didier Franck's *Nietzsche and the Shadow of God* (Northwestern 2012). Bergo is the author of *Levinas between Ethics and Politics*, among others, and co-editor of several collections.

Wolfgang Huemer is Professore Associato at the University of Parma. His research focuses mainly on the philosophy of mind, the philosophy of language, and the philosophy of literature. He is author of *The Constitution of Consciousness: A Study in Analytic Phenomenology* (Routledge, 2005) and numerous articles. He has co-edited several volumes on the philosophy of literature, on the relation between analytic philosophy and phenomenology and on Austrian philosophy.

Carlo Ierna is currently lecturer in modern philosophy at the University of Groningen. In 2012 he was awarded a prestigious Dutch NWO VENI grant for his research on the idea of philosophy as science in the School of Brentano. In 2014, he was Visiting Fellow in Philosophy at Harvard. His recent publications deal mainly with the philosophy of mathematics in the School of Brentano.

Henry Jackman is an associate Professor of Philosophy at York University in Canada and works primarily on issues in the Philosophy of Language and the History of American Pragmatism. He is currently president of the William James Society.

CONTRIBUTORS

Alan Kim teaches Greek philosophy at Stony Brook University. He has published widely on nineteenth- and early twentieth-century German psychology and philosophy, as well as on Plato. His book *Plato in Germany: Kant, Natorp, Heidegger* appeared in 2010. He is currently completing a monograph on Socratic ethics, and is the volume editor of the Brill Companion to German Platonism, a history of the reception of Plato in Germany from Cusanus to Gadamer (forthcoming 2018).

Christoph Landerer is currently working as principal investigator on a research project on Eduard Hanslick at the Austrian Academy of Sciences. His interests include Hanslick, Nietzsche, Herbart, and Austrian intellectual history. He is co-author of a new English translation of Eduard Hanslick's *Vom Musikalisch-Schönen* (with Lee Rothfarb), forthcoming at Oxford University Press (2018).

Sandra Lapointe is Associate Professor of Philosophy at McMaster University. A Commonwealth Alumna and a Fellow of the Humboldt Foundation, she has published extensively in the history of nineteenth- and twentieth-century philosophy of logic, language and mind. She is a Founding Associate Editor of the *Journal for the History of Analytical Philosophy* and the founding President of the Society for the Study of the History of Analytical Philosophy.

Paul M. Livingston is professor of philosophy at the University of New Mexico in Albuquerque. He is the sole author of four books, the most recent of which is *The Logic of Being: Realism, Truth, and Time* with Northwestern University Press (2017).

Lydia Patton is a philosopher of science and historian of philosophy of science working at Virginia Tech. She works on the development of scientific theories and methods, on the use of scientific models, and on the history of philosophy of science, especially the semantic view. Her work appears in venues including *Synthese*, *The Monist*, and *Historia Mathematica*, and a book co-edited with Walter Ott, *Laws of Nature* will appear in 2018 with Oxford University Press.

Mattia Riccardi is currently lecturer in philosophy at the University of Bonn, Germany. He works primarily on Post-Kantian Philosophy and Philosophy of Mind.

Robin D. Rollinger is a Researcher at the Institute of Philosophy of the Czech Academy of Sciences. He has written several books and numerous articles on Franz Brentano, his students (including Edmund Husserl), and phenomenology. In addition, he is the editor of two volumes of the complete works of Husserl (*Husserliana*). At present he is writing a book on Brentano's logic and translating Carl Stumpf's *Tone Psychology* into English.

Peter Simons is Emeritus Professor of Philosophy at Trinity College Dublin. He works in metaphysics and ontology and their applications, the history of Central European and early analytic philosophy and logic, with emphasis on

Bolzano, Brentano, Meinong, Frege, and Polish logic. He is the author or co-author of five books, the most-cited being *Parts* (1987), and some 300 articles. He is a Fellow of the British Academy and Member of the Academia Europaea, the Royal Irish Academy, and the Polish Academy of Sciences.

Mark Textor is Professor of Philosophy in King's College London. He works on philosophy of language and mind (often from a historical perspective). He is the author of *Bolzanos Propositionalismus*, *Frege on Sense and Reference* and *Brentano's Mind*.

Clinton Tolley is an Associate Professor of Philosophy at the University of California, San Diego, where he is also an affiliated member of the German Studies Program and the Interdisciplinary Program with Cognitive Science. He has published numerous articles on modern European philosophy, focusing especially on Kant, German Idealism, and other currents in post-Kantianism. With Sandra Lapointe, he co-translated and co-edited *The New Anti-Kant* (Palgrave, 2014). He is currently at work on a book on Kant's philosophical psychology.

GENERAL INTRODUCTION

Rebecca Copenhaver and Christopher Shields

How far back does the history of philosophy of mind extend? In one sense, the entire history of the discipline extends no further than living memory. Construed as a recognized sub-discipline of philosophy, philosophy of mind seems to have entered the academy in a regular way only in the latter half of the twentieth century. At any rate, as an institutional matter, courses listed under the name 'Philosophy of Mind' or 'The Mind-Body Problem' were rare before then and seem not to have become fixtures of the curriculum in Anglo-American universities until the 1960s.[1] More broadly, construed as the systematic self-conscious reflection on the question of how mental states and processes should be conceived in relation to physical states and processes, one might put the date to the late nineteenth or early twentieth century.

One might infer on this basis that a six-volume work on *The History of Philosophy of Mind* extending back to antiquity is bound to be anachronistic: we cannot, after all, assume that our questions were the questions of, say, Democritus, working in Thrace in the fifth century BC, or of Avicenna (Ibn-Sînâ), active in Persia in the twelfth century, or of John Blund, the Oxford- and Paris-trained Chancellor of the see of York from 1234–1248, or, for that matter, of the great German philosopher and mathematician Leibniz (1646–1716). One might on the contrary think it *prima facie* unlikely that thinkers as diverse as these in their disparate times and places would share very many preoccupations either with each other or with us.

Any such immediate inference would be unduly hasty and also potentially misleading. It would be misleading not least because it relies on an unrealistically unified conception of what *we* find engaging in this area: philosophy of mind comprises today a wide range of interests, orientations, and methodologies, some almost purely *a priori* and others almost exclusively empirical. It is potentially misleading in another way as well, heading in the opposite direction. If we presume that the only thinkers who have something useful to say to us are those engaging the questions of mind we find salient, using idioms we find congenial, then we will likely overlook some surprising continuities as well as instructive discontinuities across these figures and periods.

Some issues pertinent to mental activity may prove perennial. Of equal importance, however, are the differences and discontinuities we find when we investigate questions of mind assayed in earlier periods of thought. In some cases, it is true, we find it difficult to determine without careful investigation whether difference in idiom suffices for difference in interest or orientation. For instance, it was once commonplace to frame questions about mental activity as questions about the soul, where today questions posed about the nature of the soul and its relation to the body are apt to sound to many outmoded or at best quaintly archaic. Yet when we read what, for instance, medieval philosophers investigated under that rubric, we are as likely as not to find them reflecting on such core contemporary concerns as the nature of perception, the character of consciousness, the relation of mental faculties to the body, and the problem of intentionality – and to be doing so in a manner immediately continuous with some of our own preoccupations.

That said, even where upon examination we find little or no continuity between present-day and earlier concerns, this very difference can be illuminating. Why, for instance, is the will discussed so little in antiquity? Hannah Arendt suggests an answer: the will was not discussed in antiquity because it was not discovered before St. Augustine managed to do so in the third century.[2] Is she right? Or is the will in fact discussed obliquely in antiquity, enmeshed in a vocabulary at least initially alien to our own? On the supposition that Arendt is right, and the will is not even a topic of inquiry before Augustine, why should this be so? Should this make us less confident that we have a faculty rightly called 'the will'? Perhaps Augustine not so much discovered the will as *invented* it, to give it pride of place in his conception of human nature. A millennium later Thomas Aquinas contended that the will is but one power or faculty of the soul, as an intellectual appetite for the good (*ST* I 82, resp.). Is he right? Is the will as examined by Augustine and Aquinas the same will of which we ask, when we do, whether our will is free or determined?

A study of the history of philosophy of mind turns up, in sum, some surprising continuities, some instructive partial overlaps, and some illuminating discontinuities across the ages. When we reflect on the history of the discipline, we bring into sharper relief some of the questions we find most pressing, and we inevitably come to ask new and different questions, even as we retire questions which we earlier took to be of moment. Let us reflect first then on some surprising continuities. Three illustrations will suffice, but they could easily be multiplied.

First, consider some questions about minds and machines: whether machines can be conscious or otherwise minded, whether human intelligence is felicitously explicated in terms of computer software, hardware, or functional processes more generally. Surely such questions belong to our era uniquely? Yet we find upon reading some early modern philosophy that this is not so. In Leibniz, for instance, we find this striking passage, known as 'Leibniz's mill':

> Imagine there were a machine whose structure produced thought, feeling, and perception; we can conceive of its being enlarged while maintaining the same relative proportions, so that we could walk into it as we can walk into a mill. Suppose we do walk into it; all we would find there

are cogs and levers and so on pushing one another, and never anything to account for a perception. So perception must be sought in simple substances, not in composite things like machines. And that is all that can be found in a simple substance – perceptions and changes in perceptions; and those changes are all that the internal actions of simple substances can consist in.

(*Monadology* §17)

Leibniz offers an argument against mechanistic conceptions of mental activity in this passage, one with a recognizably contemporary counterpart. His view may be defensible or it may be indefensible; but it is certainly relevant to questions currently being debated.

Similarly, nearly every course in philosophy of mind these days begins with some formulation of the 'mind-body problem', usually presented as a descendant of the sort of argument Descartes advanced most famously in his *Meditations*, and defended most famously in his correspondence with Elisabeth of Bohemia. Centuries before Descartes, however, we encounter the Islamic polymath Avicenna (Ibn-Sînâ) wondering in detail about the question of whether the soul has or lacks quantitative extension, deploying a striking thought experiment in three separate passages, one of which runs:

One of us must suppose that he was just created at a stroke, fully developed and perfectly formed but with his vision shrouded from perceiving all external objects – created floating in the air or in space, not buffeted by any perceptible current of the air that supports him, his limbs separated and kept out of contact with one another, so that they do not feel each other. Then let the subject consider whether he would affirm the existence of his self. There is no doubt that he would affirm his own existence, although not affirming the reality of any of his limbs or inner organs, his bowels, or heart or brain or any external thing. Indeed he would affirm the existence of this self of his while not affirming that it had any length, breadth or depth. And if it were possible for him in such a state to imagine a hand or any other organ, he would not imagine it to be a part of himself or a condition of his existence.

(Avicenna, '*The Book of Healing*')

Avicenna's 'Floating Man', or 'Flying Man', reflects his Neoplatonist orientation and prefigures in obvious ways Descartes' more celebrated arguments of *Meditations* II. Scholars dispute just how close this parallel is,[3] but it seems plain that these arguments and parables bear a strong family resemblance to one another, and then each in turn to a yet earlier argument by Augustine,[4] more prosaically put, but engaging many of the same themes.

The point is not to determine who won the race to this particular argument, nor to insist that these authors arrive at precisely the same finish line. Rather, when we study each expression in its own context, we find illuminating samenesses and differences, which in turn assist us in framing our own questions about the character of the quantitative and qualitative features of mind, about the tenability of solipsism, and about the nature of the human self. One would like to know, for instance, whether such a narrow focus on the internal states of human consciousness provides a productive method for the science of mind. Or have our philosophical forebears, as some today think, created impediments by conceiving of the very project in a way that neglects the embodied characteristics of cognition? From another angle, one may wonder whether these approaches, seen throughout the history of the discipline, lead inexorably to Sartre's conclusion that 'consciousness is a wind blowing from nowhere towards objects'.[5] One way to find out is to study each of these approaches in the context of its own deployment.

For a final example, we return to the birthplace of Western philosophy to reflect upon a striking argument of Democritus in the philosophy of perception. After joining Leucippus in arguing that the physical world comprises countless small atoms swirling in the void, Democritus observes that *only* atoms and the void are, so to speak, really real. All else exists by convention: 'by convention sweet and by convention bitter, by convention hot, by convention cold, by convention colour; but in reality atoms and void' (DK 68B9). This remark evidently denies the reality of sensible qualities, such as sweetness and bitterness, and even colour. What might Democritus be thinking? By judging this remark alongside his remaining fragments, we see that he is appealing to the variability of perception to argue that if one perceiver tastes a glass of wine and finds it sweet, while another perceiver tastes the same glass and finds it bitter, then we must conclude – on the assumption that perceptual qualities are real – that either one or the other perceiver is wrong. After all, they cannot both be right, and there seems little point in treating them as both wrong. The correct conclusion, Democritus urges, is that sensible qualities, in contrast to atoms and the void, are not real. The wine is neither sweet nor bitter; sweetness and bitterness are wholly subjective states of perceivers.

Readers of seventeenth- and eighteenth-century British philosophy will recognize this argument in Locke and Berkeley. Locke presents the argument to support his distinction between primary and secondary qualities: primary qualities being those features of objects that are (putatively) *in* objects, independently of perception, such as number, shape, size, and motion; secondary qualities being those features of objects subject to the variability of perception recognized by Democritus. Locke struggles with the reality of secondary qualities, sometimes treating them as ideas in our minds and other times as dispositions of the primary qualities of objects that exist independently of us. Democritus, by contrast, aligning the real with the objective, simply banishes them to the realm of convention. And Berkeley appeals to the same phenomenon on which Locke founds his famous distinction – the variability of perception – to argue that the distinction is unsustainable and thus embraces the anti-Democritean option: the real is the ideal.

We may ask which if any of these philosophers deserves to be followed. As an anecdotal matter, when beginning philosophy students grasp the point of arguments from the variability of perception, they become flummoxed, because before having their attention focussed on the phenomenon of variability, most tend to think of sensible qualities as intrinsic monadic properties of the external objects of perception. This issue in the philosophy of perception, straddling as it does different periods and idioms, remains a live one, proving as vivid for us as it was for Democritus and Locke.

When we find similar philosophical arguments and tropes recurring in radically different periods and contexts throughout the history of philosophy, that is usually at least a strong *prima facie* indication that we are in an area demanding careful scrutiny. Unsurprisingly, arguments concerning the nature of perception and perceptible qualities offer one telling illustration. Still, we should resist the temptation to find continuities where none exists, especially where none exists beyond the verbal or superficial. We should moreover resist, perhaps more strongly still, the tendency to minimize or overlook differences where they appear. One of the intellectual joys of studying the history of philosophy resides precisely in uncovering and appreciating the deep discontinuities between disparate times and contexts.

On this score, examples abound, but one suffices to illustrate our point. The title of a widely read article written in the 1960s posed a provocative question: 'Why Isn't the Mind-Body Problem Ancient?'.[6] This question, of course, has a presupposition, namely that the mind-body problem is in fact *not* ancient. It also seems to betray a second presupposition, namely that there is *a* mind-body problem: a single problem that that engages philosophers of the modern era but that escaped the ancients. This presupposition raises the question: what *is* the single, unified, mind-body problem that the ancients failed to recognize? In fact, when we turn to the range of questions posed in this domain, we find a family of recognizably distinct concerns: the hard problem, the explanatory gap, mental causation, and so on. Not all these questions have a common orientation, even if they arise from a common anxiety that the mind and the body are at once so dissimilar that inquiring into their relationship may already be an error, and yet so similar in their occupation and operation as to obliterate any meaningful difference.

We might call this anxiety *categorial*. That is, it has seemed to various philosophers in various eras that there is some basic categorial distinction to be observed in the domain of the mental, to the effect that mental states belong to one category and physical states to another. That by itself might be true without, however, there being any attendant problem. After all, we might agree that there is a categorial distinction between, say, biological properties and mathematical properties, and even that these families of properties are never co-instantiable. After all, no number can undergo descent with modification, and no animal can be a cosine. That is hardly a problem: no one expects numbers to be biological subjects, and no one would ever mistake an organism for a mathematical function. The problem in the domain of the mental and physical seems to arise only when we assume that some objects – namely ourselves – exhibit both mentality and physicality, and do so in a way that is systematic and unified. Bringing these thoughts together we arrive at a mind-body problem: if mental and physical properties are categorially exclusive while we ourselves are mental and physical at once, we must be what we cannot be, namely subjects of properties that cannot coincide.

In this sense, Cartesian dualism might be regarded as a solution to the mind-body problem, at least *this* mind-body problem, one which simply concedes its conclusion by affirming that minds and bodies are irredeemably different sorts of substances displaying different sorts of properties. Needless to say, this 'solution' invites a series of still more intractable problems concerning the interaction of these postulated disparate substances, about the location of the mental, and so forth. Even so, when the Cartesian expedient is rejected on these or other grounds, the old problem re-emerges, in one guise yielding an equally desperate seeming sort of solution, namely the total elimination of the mental as ultimately not amenable to a purely physicalistic characterization.[7] Eliminativism, no less than Cartesianism, solves the mind-body problem effectively by concession.

One should accordingly look afresh at the problem as formulated. In fact, when one asks *what* these purportedly mutually excluding properties may be, several candidates come to the fore. Some think properties such as *being conscious* are mental and cannot possibly be physical, perhaps because conscious states are ineliminably subjective, whereas all physical properties are objective, or because mental properties are essentially qualitative, whereas physical properties are only quantitative. Descartes' own reasons, though disputed, seem to have been largely epistemic: possibly one can doubt the existence of one's body, whereas it is impossible, because self-defeating, to doubt the existence of one's own mind or mental states (*Meditation* II). If these property-differences obtain in these domains and are in fact such as to be mutually exclusive, then we do now have the makings of a mind-body problem.

Returning, then, to the question pertinent to our study of the ancient period, we may ask: do the ancients draw these sorts of categorial distinctions? If so, why do they fail to appreciate the problems we find so familiar and obvious? Or do they in fact fail to draw these categorial distinctions in the first place? If they do not, then one would like to know why not. One can imagine a number of different options here: one could fault the ancients for failing to pick up on such starkly categorial differences; one could credit them for astutely avoiding the conceptual muddles of Cartesianism. Some argue, for instance, that Aristotelian hylomorphism embraces a framework of explanation within which Cartesian questions simply cannot arise, thereby obviating an array of otherwise intractable problems.[8] Although we do not attempt to litigate these issues here, one can appreciate how an investigation into ancient approaches to philosophy of mind yields palpable benefits for some modern questions, even if and perhaps precisely because such questions were not ancient.

Needless to say, we never know in advance of our investigations whether the benefits of such study will be forthcoming. To make such discoveries as can be made in this area, then, we need ask a set of questions similar to those we asked regarding the mind-body problem, *mutatis mutandis*, for other philosophical problems in the mental domain, broadly construed, as they arise in other periods of philosophy beyond ancient philosophy as well.

If we proceed in this way, we find that the study of the history of philosophy of mind offers the contemporary philosopher perspectives on the discipline which, however far below the surface, may yet guide our own inquiries into the mental and physical, and into the character of mental and physical states and processes. This is, of course, but one reason to engage the studies these six volumes contain. Other researchers with a more purely historical orientation will find a wealth of material in these pages as well, ranging across all periods of western philosophy, from antiquity to that part of the discipline that resides in living memory. Our historical and philosophical interests here may, of course, be fully complementary: the history of philosophy of mind takes one down some odd by-ways off some familiar boulevards, into some dead-ends and cul-de-sacs, but also along some well-travelled highways that are well worth traversing over and again.

Notes

1 A perusal of the course offerings of leading universities in the US tends to confirm this. To take but one example, which may be multiplied, a search of the archives of the University of Notre Dame lists one course in 'Philosophy of Mind' offered as an advanced elective in 1918 and 1928, 1929, but then no further course until 1967, when 'The Mind-Body Problem,' began to be offered yearly off and on for two decades. In the 1970s, various electives such as 'Mind and Machines' were offered intermittently, and a regular offering in 'Philosophy of Mind' began only in 1982. This offering continues down to the present. While we have not done a comprehensive study, these results cohere with archive searches of several other North American universities.
2 Arendt sees prefigurations in St. Paul and others, but regards Augustine as 'the first philosopher of the will and the only philosopher the Romans ever had' (1978, vol. ii, 84).
3 For an overview of these issues, see Marmura (1986).
4 On the relation between Descartes and Augustine, see the instructive treatment in Matthews (1992).
5 Sartre (1943: 32–33).
6 Matson (1966). Citing Matson's question, King (2007) went on to pose a continuing question of his own: 'Why Isn't the Mind-Body Problem Medieval?'. In so doing, King meant to oppose Matson, who had claimed that the one should not assume that medieval philosophers, although writing in a recognizably Aristotelian idiom, similarly failed to engage any mind-body problem. After all, he noted, in addition to their Aristotelianism, they accepted a full range of theistic commitments alien to Aristotle.
7 Eliminativism about the mental has a long and chequered history, extending at least as far back as Broad (1925) (who rejects it), but has its most forceful and accessible formulation in Churchland (1988).
8 Charles (2008) has advanced this sort of argument on behalf of hylomorphism.

Bibliography

Arendt, Hannah. 1978. *The Life of the Mind*, vols. i and ii. New York: Harcourt Brace Jovanovich.
Broad, C. D. 1925. *The Mind and Its Place in Nature*. London: Routledge & Kegan.

Charles, David. 2008. "Aristotle's Psychological Theory". *Proceedings of the Boston Area Colloquium in Ancient Philosophy* **24**: 1–29.

Churchland, P. M. 1988. *Matter and Consciousness*. Cambridge, MA: MIT Press.

King, Peter. 2007. "Why Isn't the Mind-Body Problem Medieval?" In *Forming the Mind: Essays on the Internal Senses and the Mind/Body Problem From Avicenna to the Medical Enlightenment*, 187–205. Berlin: Springer.

Marmura, Michael. 1986. "Avicenna's Flying Man in Context". *The Monist* **69** (3): 383–395.

Matson, Wallace. 1966. "Why Isn't the Mind-Body Problem Ancient?" In *Mind, Matter, and Method: Essays in Philosophy and Science in Honor of Herbert Feigl*, 92–102. St. Paul: University of Minnesota Press.

Matthews, Gareth. 1992. *Thought's Ego in Augustine and Descartes*. Ithaca: Cornell University Press.

Sartre, Jean-Paul. 1943. "Une Idée fondamentale de la phénomenologie de Husserl: L'intentionalité". In *Situations I*. Paris: Gallimard.

INTRODUCTION TO VOLUME 5**

Sandra Lapointe

1. Prelude

The aim of this volume is to provide a picture of the wealth of work that went toward the philosophical study of mind in the nineteenth century. While the disciplinary specialities in whose purview the study of mind falls today are all relatively new, the problems that define the field have a long history. The views of past philosophers range over phenomena – what they called 'representation', 'sensation', 'perception', 'emotion', 'thinking', 'judgement', 'cognition', 'intention', 'action' – that continue to fuel contemporary mind research. To the extent that these terms are still in use, there are often important differences between the contemporary use and that of our predecessors. Such differences extend to the plethora of terms that have been used to refer to the object domain to which these phenomena belong over the centuries, in the current occurrence over the modern era: 'Geist', 'Seele', 'Gemüt', 'mind' 'soul', 'spirit', 'esprit', 'âme'. Assuredly, historians ought to proceed with cautiousness. In what follows, if we speak of the 'study of mind', it should be assumed to be in full awareness of the complexity of the historical occurrences at hand and with the understanding that each theory is at least provisionally best understood in its own context. At the same time, what follows also assumes that historical research will reveal theoretical overlaps, anticipations and innovations that are crucial to understanding how contemporary philosophy of mind was shaped.

For the purpose of this book, 'nineteenth century' refers to the period that extends from the publication of Immanuel Kant's *Critique of Pure Reason* (1781) to that of Edmund Husserl's *Ideas* (1913). Little of substance rests on these chronological boundaries, which are somewhat arbitrary. There are good reasons to reserve judgement regarding periodization: this issue is potentially controversial and, to the extent that it is significant, it deserves to be dealt with systematically, on its own. Overlaps with the volume that precedes in this series and the one that follows are meant to signify agnosticism as regards what might be distinctive of nineteenth-century philosophy as a possible "actor category". No general claim is made, at least not in this introduction, as to whether or in what way philosophy in the nineteenth century perpetuates or breaks from philosophy in the periods that precede or follow. The sole motivation as far as the editor is concerned for dedicating (only) one volume to the period that extends between Kant and Husserl was the necessity to exercise restraint – and respect the word limit.

Periodization aside, the table of contents reflects editorial choices not unlikely to thwart most readers' expectations. This is not accidental. The editorial approach in this volume follows two somewhat iconoclastic lines. (i) It seeks to emphasise the cross- or inter-disciplinary nature of the topic under study and of the resulting theories, most of which belong neither entirely to philosophy nor to psychology as we conceive of these disciplines today. (ii) It encourages deliberate critical distance vis-à-vis what is usually taken to be the philosophical canon. (i) and (ii) epitomise a position that challenges many standard assumptions that underlie philosophical history. These are assumptions that often remain implicit. The main ones are discussed in the next two sections.

2. The philosophical canon and the history of the study of mind

Whether or not this is desirable, the idea that there exists a finite list of canonical authors, i.e. philosophers whose works merit examination more than others', is constitutive of our understanding of philosophical history and – clandestinely or not – it contributes to shaping our views concerning the past. At least as far as Western philosophy is concerned, narratives are usually premised on the idea that the last 200 years have seen at least two traditions arise – continental and analytical – that are deemed predominant today. These narratives rest on two conceptions of the philosophical canon that are assumed to be at once autonomous and complementary.

As regards the continental tradition, narratives that are considered to be authoritative often focus on the significance, in Germany and beyond, of post-Kantian Idealism. According to most of these narratives, nineteenth-century philosophy developed in two stages: first with the rise of Idealist systematic philosophy in Hegel, Fichte and Schelling, in the first half of the century; then, in the second half, after Hegel's death, with the efforts of the young Hegelians (e.g. Feuerbach), Marx, Kierkegaard and Nietzsche toward transforming or rejecting Hegel's philosophy. The more or less direct upshots of these efforts are usually assumed to be at the root of the philosophical traditions that shaped continental philosophy in the twentieth century: Marxism, phenomenology and existentialism, being among the most prominent ones.[1]

On the other side, while there are more or less discordant opinions on the exact place and time of analytical philosophy's putative birth, it is generally assumed that it is in large part under the initial impetus of philosophers from Britain (e.g. Moore and Russell in Cambridge) and Austria (Wittgenstein and the Logical Empiricists in Vienna) that it came to dominate large parts of philosophical practice in North America and Europe in the twentieth century. Over the course of the last three or four decades, historians of 'early' analytical philosophy have sought to enhance this account by looking at multiple sources of analytical thought in the nineteenth century, explaining e.g. how work by arithmeticians and geometers – from Bolzano and Frege to Peano and Hilbert – anticipated or contributed to making possible the exponential developments that followed in logic and semantics and the foundations of mathematics in the twentieth century.

The two narratives are, for most general purposes, firmly established; they in any case reflect a conception of the past that continues to shape philosophical identities today. There are however important problems with these narratives, all of which should incite us – and the historian of philosophy of mind in particular – to resist the conceptions of the canon that transpire from both sides.[2] One particular problem concerns the relation between the two putative canons and, by extension, between the two putative traditions they portray.[3] The continental and analytical traditions, although they are considered to be complementary, are also usually understood to be hermetic, each narrative camp claiming the prerogative over the study of a distinctive set of thinkers. Overlaps are exceptional. As a result, it is typically assumed that the connections between the two camps, e.g. between post-Kantian German idealism and early analytical philosophy were minimal and/or even antagonistic. Such conjectures concerning the nature of the continuity – or lack thereof – between the two main intellectual currents in nineteenth- and twentieth-century philosophy however are not only poorly documented, they often project on past philosophers antipathies that are retroactive and largely anachronistic.

Contrary to the picture standard narratives tend to brush, much significant continuity exists between philosophers that are assumed to belong to the two different traditions. If historical narratives are to be accurate, these need to be acknowledged. Early analytical philosophers – Bolzano is a good example – while they indeed radically rejected crucial aspects of Kantian (and post-Kantian) treatment of certain philosophical problems, did not start anew, with a blank slate. The extent of the continuity and rupture with their predecessors varies in each case, and the finesse of each individual case should be the topic of circumspect philosophical and historical work. This is not just a matter of 'filling the gaps' but of reassessing the storyline we use to position ourselves and understand our origins. Sweeping claims such as: 'Bolzano rejected (Kantian) Idealism' – something similar can be said about the claim: 'Russell and Moore rejected (British) Idealism' – are eminently elusive. Bolzano (or Russell or Moore) did not reject every single claim Kant put forward in the *Critique of Pure Reason*. Which precise aspect of Kant's *opus magnum* epitomises an 'idealist' – as opposed to an 'empiricist', or 'subjectivist', or 'realist', or 'dualist', or even 'constructivist' – position depends on parameters that fluctuate with each new interpretive perspective, a state of affairs that creates pervasive ambiguities. Bolzano (or Russell or Moore) may have rejected some aspects of Kant (or Hegel or Bradley's) work but, whether those aspects of Kant's thought that are associated with Idealism are effectively the ones that were rejected by Bolzano (or Russell or Moore) – and, if so, whether they were rejected for the very reason that they support Idealism – is a question that is vastly underdetermined and the answer is anything but straightforwardly affirmative.[4]

Likewise, even if we can indeed document the existence of more or less cultivated enmities, a manifold of antagonisms between individual figures – say between Bolzano and Kant or between Carnap and Heidegger – does not immediately translate into one overarching antagonism between the two putatively distinct traditions. Assuredly, entire schools may have been targeted by an author or groups of authors on the basis of methodological or doctrinal disagreements that were considered to be fundamental. But the situation then was no different than it is in the discipline today: disagreements (and agreements) were more or less punctual, ideological, superficial and definitive. For instance, early analytic philosophers did not think of Brentanian phenomenology as the foe Ryle would later – rather ideologically – make it to be. While the young Russell, for one, may have had qualms with some of Brentano's students, e.g. Meinong's specific treatment of existence and the semantics of putatively empty terms, he also admired the work of others, e.g. Edmund Husserl's *Logical Investigations*. We may even speculate that his familiarity and punctual sympathies for the Austrian brand of 'descriptive psychology' was residual of his teachers' own intellectual sympathies: G. F. Stout's *Analytic Psychology* is informed in substantial ways by Brentano's *Psychology from an Empirical Standpoint*.

The point is the following: standard accounts of the history of philosophy in the nineteenth century are not merely 'gappy'. Rather, they misleadingly project an all-encompassing chiasm where there originally was none. This is partly the consequence of the fact that the conception of the canon on which standard (analytic and continental) narratives rest is driven by more or less clandestine assumptions – e.g. as to what is philosophically significant and what is not, or as to what constitutes an adequate theoretical or methodological commitment – that are rooted in hermeneutic circumstances as well as other kinds of epistemic limitations that ought to be themselves subject to scrutiny. For this reason, at least, resorting to standard conceptions of the philosophical canon, from Kant (or Bolzano) to Husserl (or Russell), in historical reconstruction should be the object of caution.

In light of such considerations, one challenge for the current project was to develop an editorial perspective that would be inclusive enough to carve a new space for the abundant theoretical efforts that went toward the study of mind in the period that precedes and overlaps with what is usually conceived to be the birth of both analytical and continental philosophy, in the decisive decades of the nineteenth and early twentieth centuries. In what follows, we put on an equal footing the theories of authors that range from Freud, Nietzsche and Husserl to Bolzano, Mach and Helmholtz. To the extent that the objective is to offer insights into a history of the study of mind that rests on a better-informed alternative to standard conceptions of the canon, the first step is to withhold as much as possible judgement as to the relative place of each author in the development of the study of mind over the period under study. The present introduction thus does not venture to speculate much about the existence of overarching intellectual continuities between the authors the volume examines, or about their respective place within the development of philosophy of mind at large.

Indeed, in spite of the quite detailed analyses each individual chapter provides and the breadth of authors who are discussed, the present book does not presume to offer a complete picture of the nineteenth century. The table of contents could have been more comprehensive. For instance, it could have more consistently stressed the relevance of early psychological theories to the history of the philosophical study of mind. It could have included articles on Jakob Friedrich Fries (1773–1843), Friedrich Eduard Beneke, (1798–1854), Gustav Fechner (1801–1887), Friedrich Albert Lange (1828–1875), Wilhelm Wundt (1832–1920) and others. Likewise, it ought to have better reflected the diversity of nineteenth-century philosophical thought by including, e.g. discussion of Schopenhauer and Kierkegaard as well as Lotze and Frege, to name only a few. It should have dedicated at least a chapter to the history of the study of mind in Britain – the absence of articles on John Stuart Mill and Henry Maudsley is not deliberate – in particular about the influence of Cantabrigian "analytic psychologists" such as G. F. Stout (1860–1944) and James Ward (1843–1925) on G. E. Moore, Bertrand Russell and others in the last decade of the nineteenth century.[5] But this is the first book so far to be dedicated to the study of mind in the nineteenth century and, just like a child's first steps, it should indicate the potential for future advances.

3. Philosophy, psychology and the study of mind

Assuredly, future histories of philosophy would be at best patchy if they overlooked psychologists', in particular neuroscientists' and cognitive researchers' contribution to the philosophical study of mind at the turn of the twenty-first century. The emergence in the last couple of decades of new philosophical specialities such as the philosophy of cognitive sciences and neurophilosophy are evidence for the fact that psychology and philosophy continue to entertain a complex and intimate relationship. Current research projects on sensation, perception, cognition, emotions, communication and action bring, e.g. philosophers, psychologists, neuroscientists and anthropologists together: specialists of various provenances inform each other's research in ways that raise important questions about the topology of disciplinary boundaries. Interestingly, something similar holds for the nineteenth century. Consider, e.g. the fact that the full original subtitle of the eminent British journal *Mind* when it was founded at the end of the nineteenth century was *A Quarterly Review of Psychology and Philosophy*. The name is not an accident: it testifies to the close connection the two fields – under the common designation of 'mental sciences' in Cambridge – were held to entertain at the time. Consider, in turn, the range of factors relevant to a satisfactory reconstruction of the theoretical issues and contextual factors that contributed in the second half of the nineteenth century to the rise of psychology as a discipline independent from philosophy. This episode, which assuredly has numerous geographical segments, belongs no more and no less to the history of philosophy than it does to the history of psychology at large.

Few would think that the study of mind is the exclusive prerogative of either philosophers or psychologists and, as such, the history of the study of mind should cut across disciplinary boundaries. However, developing a cross-disciplinary historical approach supposes that we can discriminate the disciplines involved and this, as it occurs, is not uncomplicated. Nineteenth century theories of sensation, perception, judgement, emotions, intentions, action etc., tend to resist non-arbitrary classifications as 'philosophical' or 'psychological'. The main reason for this is not only that current disciplinary and sub-disciplinary labels and divisions – between what belongs to philosophy and what belongs to psychology – are too recent to be projected back without complications, but also the fact that they remain in flux. The problem, to be clear, is twofold. On the one hand, the use of contemporary classifications to describe the study of mind in the nineteenth century is potentially anachronistic, and while anachronism is not necessarily objectionable it raises for the philosophical historiographer questions that have yet to be systematically addressed. On the other hand, our conceptions of the precise scope and methods of the disciplines that are involved in the study on mind and, in particular, of their theoretical boundaries do not appear to be definitive and/or hermetic. Think of the plethora of new labels and classifications that have emerged and evolved over the course of the last 50 years alone for the purpose of characterising the relentless developments in mind research. Attending to this is important. In principle, any meaningful attempt to delimit the scope of what counts as belonging to the history of philosophy of mind as opposed to the history of psychology broadly construed is bound to be informed by assumptions concerning the division of knowledge or delimitation of disciplinary frontiers in the study of mind. We face important challenges if these assumptions themselves continue to change.[6]

Our understanding of disciplinary boundaries unsurprisingly depends on the kinds of conceptual resources and investigative methods we consider to be adequate given our purposes as researchers. In the study of mind, the latter have completely transformed over the last 200 years. Among other things, the successes of empirically based research have contributed to establishing new methodological standards and paradigms. In part driven by the ever-increasing range of application of experimental methods, problems traditionally associated with the 'philosophical science' were gradually appropriated by research programs that went on to progressively claim disciplinary and institutional autonomy. The resulting reorganisation of knowledge over the last two centuries has been radical. In this respect, the nineteenth century is a crucial juncture when it comes to understanding the many factors that contributed to shaping what, in the century that followed, became the dominant conceptions of disciplinary boundaries and specialities, as well as standard views on the methodological differences between philosophy and psychology.

Nineteenth-century mind-researchers developed their theories in a context where empirical methods flourished and seemed increasingly relevant, but where disciplinary boundaries were in flux. There were crucial questions regarding the nature of the task at hand, questions that drove researchers to gain clarity and make (more or less deliberate and circumspect) choices pertaining to methodology. In many cases, this resulted in significant pressure on the negotiation of institutional appointments or curricular decisions – interestingly, empirically minded researchers were initially often excluded from academia altogether.[7] Although sociological factors of this sort have no direct bearing on the value of theories or on the determination of their respective scope, there are good reasons to refrain from ignoring them: science happens as a result of human industry and depends on a range of concomitant beliefs agents hold about their research object and practices. At least part of what is at stake for philosophical historians is to understand the context of this type of human endeavour.

The implication here is not that disciplinary boundaries in the study of mind are arbitrary, insignificant or futile. Rather, the suggestion is that historians should not presume of the *immutability* of disciplinary boundaries. In particular, they should not presume of what counts as 'standard' conceptions of philosophy's relative role in the study of mind. Drawing the line between what pertains to philosophy and what pertains to psychology is neither straightforward nor indisputable. One difficulty arises from the fact that while psychology only emerged as an academic discipline independent from philosophy in the last decades of the nineteenth century, the theoretical foundations for the research programs that led to psychology's independence can be found in the works of authors who, a century earlier, unequivocally self-identified as philosophers. The decades that followed almost immediately the publication of the *Critique of Pure Reason* (1781) – Kant's very project was crucial to setting the terms of the debates that would follow – were absolutely decisive, in particular the criticism found in the work of Jakob Friedrich Fries and Friedrich Herbart.[8] For the historian, the task of drawing the line between philosophy and psychology in the theories of these authors and, more generally, of singling out what in the history of the study of mind pertains to philosophy and what pertains to psychology is anything but obvious. And just like what is involved in any other historical task, one's attempt to draw the frontier between philosophy and psychology may be influenced by more or less clandestine – and indeed, existential! – assumptions about the nature of philosophy and/or psychology as one understands it. Whenever this is the case, historians may unwittingly or unwarrantedly disregard or omit certain kinds of problems, methods or data as irrelevant that ultimately are not.

More importantly, in order for historians of philosophy and psychology to have a genuine basis to divorce their respective narratives, they would have to agree on the nature of the methodological differences that exist between the philosophical and the psychological study of mind. Whether such difference can be established unambiguously, and whether they would be undisputed and helpful is not clear. The traditional way of framing methodological differences between what belongs to philosophy of mind and what belongs to psychology, respectively, is to invoke the contrast between 'a priori' (viz. conceptual analysis) and 'empirical' – a term used in different context to mean different things and which can connote at once 'empiricist' and 'experimental' – approaches. While enlightening in certain respects, there are problems – at least four – with this suggestion.

1 In order to be expedient, the distinction requires a satisfactory account of what is involved, respectively, in empirical methods and in (a priori) conceptual analysis at large and in both cases this is generally still up for debate.
2 Even if a satisfactory account of the traditional distinction between a priori and empirical methods were in principle workable, it could turn out that it does not in fact correspond to a distinction in principle between philosophy and psychology. It might be that psychology is at least in part a conceptual exercise and that philosophy needs substantial empirical input or even experimentation. Again, at least the latter is up for debate – and the former, if it is not up for debate, should be.
3 Even if some such methodological distinction were to hold of contemporary philosophy and psychology, it should not be projected back onto the past without further examination. And vice versa. Conceptions of philosophy and psychology have evolved tremendously over the course of the last two centuries and whether all respective methodological commitments were preserved over the years is a question that cannot be answered a priori and whose answer would presumably be negative.
4 To the extent that contemporary philosophers compete for resources – academic funding, institutional appointments – with scientific disciplines whose quantifiable economic impact make them often more likely to attract investment, the strategic value of an approach that would want to capitalise on philosophy's methodological distinctiveness and independence is unclear.

(4) is not a philosophical point, but an 'administrative' one. Nonetheless, I think it ought to be emphasised. Philosophy has a long and complicated history of territorial transactions with the natural sciences in general, and with psychology in particular. In the absence of a clear and workable account of the methodological differences between philosophy and psychology, stressing philosophy's distinctiveness gives additional argument to those inclined to exclude it altogether. In this context, attempting to single out what does and what does not pertain to philosophy in the history of the study of mind, especially over the last 200 years, could contribute to nourishing the unfortunate and mistaken – yet rather widespread – prejudice that contemporary philosophy is irrelevant to the putatively genuinely 'scientific' (or 'naturalistic' or 'empirical') study of mind. The point is not cynical. At the very least, the view that philosophy is distinctive needs to go hand in hand with a careful account of philosophy's place among the sciences and its relevance within large, cross-disciplinary research projects. More importantly it needs to have a clear self-conception of its *collaborative potential* with other disciplines. This holds a fortiori for the study of mind.

4. Post-Kantian idealism and the study of mind

This volume contains 14 chapters devoted to as many authors, with the exception of Chapter 1, which deals with the main figures of German idealism: Kant, Reinhold, Fichte, Schelling and Hegel. There would have been many reasons to devote an individual chapter to each – Volume 4 in this series devotes a chapter to Kant.[9] The decision to devote a single article to post-Kantian Idealism has a twofold motivation. On the one hand, canonical narratives that place Fichte, Schelling, Hegel and their schools at the centre of 19th century intellectual life are not based on a genuinely objective appraisal and circumspect consideration of the comparative philosophical significance of their work with that of the manifold of unsung authors who offered alternative theories or approaches. Assuredly, objectivity and circumspection are typically not what underwrites one's conception of the canon. But even allowing for some partiality, from the perspective of a researcher whose work focuses on the lesser known aspect of nineteenth-century philosophy, the vastly preferential literary attention we continue to pay to German idealism today appears somewhat disproportionate and it seemed fair, considering the pre-existing literature, to make place for theories that are too often left at the margins.

To be clear, this editorial choice is not driven by some negative judgement on the philosophical value of post-Kantian German Idealism. Rather, it is meant to be the expedient of increased philosophical diversity. Assuredly, German Idealism is a 'monument'. But great monuments tend to overshadow much of the landscape. What's more, what turns out to be in the shadow depends on the time of the day, i.e. the position of the sun. Our historical position is part of what determines our perspective on the past and, in turn, limits our capacity to assess the significance and philosophical value of problems and theories with even-handedness. From our standpoint, certain historical factors may be obscured, e.g. those facts that would allow us to comprehend the whims of long-forgotten academic and political fashions and the vagaries of timeworn conceptions of intellectual merit to which our predecessors' literary faiths were tied. The almost complete oversight of Bolzano's monumental work until the late 1960s is in all respects a case in point.

The decision to devote less space than is customary to Idealism, is also motivated by the following consideration. Assuredly, much of what constitutes the theme of German idealism takes the notion of 'mind' or 'spirit' as absolutely central to philosophising. For the Idealists, there is a sense in which philosophy, *all* of philosophy, is about – or more precisely perhaps: 'is' – mind. The way that the Idealists express some of their fundamental claims – e.g. the commitment to the identity of mind and object (in Schelling) or the refusal to see a distinction between what is mind and what is not (in Hegel) – might suggest that they reject some of the most fundamental assumptions of traditional metaphysics and epistemology. But rather than merely rejecting the distinction between subject and object, the relation between body and mind, they more precisely reject the very terms of the traditional debates. This is presumably what explains part of the originality and appeal of German Idealism. But it also makes it difficult to connect German idealists' talk of 'mind' with that of those of their predecessors, contemporaries and successors who, by contrast, understand the study of mind within the parameters of post-Cartesian philosophy to pertain to a range of traditional epistemological and metaphysical problems about the nature and structure of mind, cognition, judgement, perception, awareness, consciousness, sensation, etc.

There is one important respect however, in which German Idealists converge with their contemporaries and successors in the nineteenth century in spite of all other divergences: the eminently post-Kantian flavour of their theories. This is the topic of Clinton Tolley's chapter, the first in the book. Kant's 'cognitive psychology' defined much of the parameters within which subsequent theories of cognition and knowledge, judging (or thinking), perceiving and sensing evolved. As Tolley shows, part of what makes the originality and interest of post-Kantian German Idealism rests in a shared approach to philosophy, the purpose of which Idealists all understood to consist in establishing, a priori, on the basis of something very much akin to Kant's own transcendental deduction, the 'conditions of possibility' of cognition and agency. Through discussion of Reinhold and Fichte, Schelling and Hegel, Tolley documents a shared quest for an ever more fundamental and more satisfactory – more 'radical' at least in the sense that it ought to do away with covert assumptions – basis for an understanding of the conditions that are assumed to make possible what is conceived as the most basic subjective activity such as mere representing and becoming conscious as such.

The doctrines of the German Idealists became influential – if only in a negative manner – well beyond the spheres traditionally associated with their intellectual posterity. Hegel's theory infamously culminates in an attempt to show that the most basic conditions of possibility of representation are something 'purely logical', the so-called 'absolute Idea' or perhaps even theological insofar as Hegel seemed to identify this 'Idea' with God. The desire to avoid such 'absolute idealistic' conclusions is part of what motivated thinkers from Fries, Herbart and Mill to Mach, Brentano and Stout to conceive of the study of the mind on a more austerely empirical basis; the contrast is at any rate patent. Idealism was, for this reason at least, a forceful intellectual current well beyond what it meant for Idealists. This complex state of affairs is an important factor in understanding nineteenth-century philosophy as a whole, and one that remains unfortunately vastly unexplored. Tolley's paper is an important first step in this direction.

5. Antipsychologism and the study of mind

Of all the nineteenth-century authors who were overshadowed by German Idealism and who, as a consequence, have been neglected in extant canonical narratives, no other has greater philosophical merit than Bernard Bolzano. Nonetheless, the inclusion of a chapter devoted to the 'Bohemian Leibniz', which I sign, in a volume on the history of the philosophy *of mind* is likely to be unexpected. The main reason for this is a presumption that has become somewhat pervasive in contemporary philosophical culture, even among Bolzano experts, and according to which the commitment of early analytical philosophers to logical Platonism – a commitment which Bolzano eminently shares with Frege and Husserl among others – is tributary to a form of antipsychologism that leaves no consistent and systematic place for a philosophical investigation of mind.

Such presumption has unfortunately been the source of much confusion ever since the height of the famous controversy around psychologism, at the turn of the twentieth century. To be clear, antipsychologism *in logic* and the concomitant commitment to logical Platonism are rooted in epistemological assumptions that are inconsistent with the idea that semantic properties, i.e. properties that are distinctive of language (whether formal or natural) such as truth, reference and meaningfulness are derivative or reducible to mental or psychological attributes of a speaker. But antipsychologism *in logic* does not amount to antipsychologism *in philosophy*. Assuredly, a philosophical explanation of perception, cognition and agency is directly relevant to what agents do and such an explanation, even a philosophical one, would certainly draw on what empirical mind researchers have to contribute to the topic. The challenge for the antipsychologistic, Platonising logician is thus not to show how philosophical problems at large can be solved without recourse to the study of mind but, more pertinently, to explain how one can think of logical form and meaning as objective and abstract without depreciating the fact that such accounts need to be consistent with what we have to say about thought and language in the philosophy of mind, epistemology and the theory of cognition, which need to draw on empirical or even experimental psychological considerations to deliver acceptable theories.

Although Bolzano himself did not attempt to answer this very question – Edmund Husserl may have been the only nineteenth-century philosopher to take on this task (more on Husserl below) – his approach to the study of mind, cognition, representation and action is based on the assumption that logic ultimately depends on psychology, a feature of Bolzano's theory which is not often mentioned.[10] His inquiry into the cognitive and psychological underpinnings of reasoning – the 'Art of Discovery', 'Theory of Cognition' and 'Doctrine of Method' in the third and fourth volumes of the *Theory of Science* (1837) – are accordingly informed by a philosophy of mind and action that copiously draws from pragmatic considerations. Bolzano's views are nothing short of groundbreaking and prophetic, incorporating aspects of an approach to the analysis of agency and communication that would not begin to be systematically articulated until the second half of the twentieth century. If Bolzano is right, the mind is not so much what produces consciousness – although it does produce it – as what structures our behaviour in a way that makes sense to those who, in order to come up with adequate responses, need to 'interpret' our 'intentions'. In this, he anticipated much of the approach, in pragmatics, associated with post-Gricean linguists and philosophy of mind and language. This is the object of Chapter 2.

6. Philosophical origins of psychology as a science

Although Fries deserves a mention, the greatest impetus toward the emergence of empirical psychology at the beginning of the nineteenth century came from Friedrich Herbart, an eminent and respected contemporary of Bolzano and Hegel, whose theories continued to exercise a vast influence until the end of the nineteenth century in a number of fields including but not limited to nascent experimental psychology. Herbart's most important contribution to the study of mind has its source in a fundamental disagreement with Kant's conception of the epistemological status of psychology. In Chapter 3, Christoph Landerer and Wolfgang Huemer offer a presentation of Herbart's criticisms of Kantian philosophy of psychology and sketch the elements of Herbart's own views. According to Kant, a discipline is not apt to advance to scientific standing unless its object of study is objectively quantifiable. This however is an aptitude Kant denies psychology. Herbart endeavoured to show, against Kant, that psychology could in fact meet the challenge. His argument thrives on a powerful criticism of the discipline that underpins Kant's project of a transcendental philosophy, i.e. the inquiry into the nature and structure of the cognitive, affective and conative 'faculties'. According to Herbart, the 'faculty psychology' that underlies Kantian (and mainstream post-Kantian) epistemologies thrives on hypostatisation, and this is unacceptable. Instead of attempting to determine a priori the structure of putative 'faculties' that are assumed to produce representations and concepts, the investigation of mind ought to be driven by a theory of the representations (*Vorstellungen*) per se. Landerer and Huemer discuss Herbart's tremendous impact after Hegel's death, at a time when philosophers in Germany and beyond eagerly leveraged empirical methods in order to overcome the hegemony of Hegelian idealism. That time was ripe to see psychology prosper, and Herbart's theories shaped the views of philosophers-psychologists well into the second half of the nineteenth century, notably those of Hermann von Helmholtz, Ernst Mach as well as those of many of Brentano's students, among which we find the young Sigmund Freud.

Herbart's legacy in the nineteenth century can be seen in the rapid progress of the idea that psychology can be a science, one based on the study of physiological data and the elaboration of new experimental techniques. But other Herbartian ideas were widely shared among mind researchers. The idea that representations and thought processes can be unconscious is one of them. This idea plays an important role, notably, in the theories of the German physiologist Hermann von Helmholtz. Helmholtz relies on the notion of 'unconscious inference' to provide an empirical – or at the very least an 'empiricist' – account of the mental processes that underlie sensation and perception. Helmholtz's approach and method are representative of those of a range of other German mind researchers in the second half of the nineteenth century, from Johannes Müller and Emil Dubois-Reymond to Gustav Fechner and Wilhelm Wundt: all of them contributed to the emergence of "physiological" and "physical", i.e. experimental psychology in Germany. By contrast to their Kantian and post-Kantian predecessors who saw the task of cognitive psychology as residing first and foremost in providing an account of 'thinking', the early experimental psychologists took *perceiving* as their primary object of inquiry. In this, they operated a broad theoretical shift that would set the stage for ulterior developments of experimental psychology.

Helmholtz himself helped shape the general investigative framework and methods of the broader discipline. In particular, the results of his inquiry into auditory and visual sensation also had substantial impact. In Chapter 4, Lydia Patton leverages her extensive knowledge of Helmholtz and his context to discuss some of the main innovations of this important thinker. A number of elements are distinctive of the type of views Helmholtz defended. For one, Helmholtz saw causality as the elemental framework within which to account for perception and sensation, one that allows to understand sensations as the physiological 'effects' of external physical object that are their 'causes'. As such, sensations – and the perceptions they make possible – are subject to laws. Systematic attempts to implement this approach were new at the time. The conviction that basic perceptual and cognitive relationships, e.g. between a kinaesthetic agent and her spatial environment can be described on the basis of nomological principles *that are not innate* opened the door to an inquiry into physical and physiological developments, correlations and regularities that could be anchored in measurement and experimentation. As Patton explains, Helmholtz pioneered an approach to the study of perception that is based on a number of precepts that continue to inform experimental psychology: (i) perception is 'geared toward representing external object and the environment' and in this respect, at least, it is 'intentional'; (ii) sensation and perception both involves cognitive processing; (iii) perception is a law-governed process that (iv) can be described as the result of causal transaction with the world, on the basis of experimentation. Patton's chapter documents these aspects of Helmholtz's views, with a specific focus on their application in one of his most influential works: the *Physiological Optics* (1867).

When it comes to understanding the context in which early experimental psychology evolved, one should not fail to consider the testimony of those directly concerned. Ernst Mach, for one, not only made some of the most enduring contributions to the field: in his *Lectures on Psychophysics* he also offered a historical perspective on the discipline that is rooted in a fluent knowledge of the literature of the period. In Chapter 5, the late Erik Banks[11] sketched a meticulous overview of some of Mach's main contributions to the theory of perception, assessing them in light of later developments and criticisms. He also offered insight into Mach's treatment of adjacent metaphysical questions. As Banks argued, faced with the task of articulating a unifying metaphysical framework within which the relationship between physics and experimental psychology could be articulated, Mach opted to reject both the existence of a substantial ego and (substance and property) dualism. As Banks explained, in addition to having benefited from Gustav Fechner's influence, Mach credits the elaboration of the resulting position, i.e. 'neutral monism' to another aspect of Herbart's influence, the latter's musings on monadology.[12] Even at the time, recourse to the idea that the world is exclusively constituted by monad-like elements that are neither 'material' nor 'spiritual' ought to have served speculative elegance and theoretical expediency more than it reflected experimental output. Nonetheless, by making place for the idea that mental phenomena occupy a place *in the causal space*, just like any other element of physical reality, the neutral monist disposes of a metatheoretical framework within which she can justify the hegemony of causal analysis. In a monadology, the problem of explaining the connection between mind and body, e.g. by recourse to some metaphysically opaque views on substance parallelism or occasionalism dissolves. Instead, the investigation is geared toward documenting the structure of the putatively causal connections between the various elements of the system. In this respect, neutral monism offered a scientifically motivated alternative to *materialism*. After presenting Mach's version of neutral monism in some detail, Banks's chapter offers two illustrative examples of Mach's ensuing criticism of contemporary psychological and metaphysical assumptions: the problems of introjection and bilocation.

Chapter 6, under the pen of Mattia Riccardi, is devoted to Friedrich Nietzsche. While the inclusion of Nietzsche might seem like a perplexing editorial choice – there is little literature on Nietzsche's view on mind and such concern might seem to lie somewhat outside the purview of his theories – it is in fact in line with the approach preconized throughout the volume. On the one hand, it pushes the boundaries of standard narratives by throwing new lights on the theories of a nineteenth-century philosopher whose orthodox interpretation is perhaps too narrow. On the other hand, while Nietzsche's view on mind and psychology are not exactly expansive, they arguably ought to be taken seriously, as representative of the kind of views that would have been fashionable in some quarters of the German intellectual elite in the second half of the nineteenth century.

Nietzsche is committed to a form of naturalism about the mind which, while it excludes dualism, does not imply physicalism. According to Riccardi, Nietzsche is an epiphenomenalist about reflexive self-consciousness, but one whose views on self-consciousness do not exhaust his views on mind. On Nietzsche's account, reflexive self-consciousness is merely the by-product of the communicative and linguistic practices available to an agent in a given community. The notion that is at the center of Nietzsche's positive views on mind is not however that of consciousness, but that of 'drives', i.e. unconscious inclinations, or dispositions that serve to calibrate affective responses in our interactions with the natural and social world. Riccardi devotes the second part of Chapter 6 to explaining what drives are and how they work, assessing the notion in light of contemporary concerns. For instance, Riccardi reviews a series of responses to the interpretation of Nietzsche's notion of drive that commits him to the homuncular fallacy, i.e. the fallacy that consists in ascribing to a mental entity, e.g. a drive, precisely the type of mental properties they are supposed to explain, e.g. the evaluative dimension of agency.

Nietzsche's views on mind are not only consistent with the views he puts forward in much of his more fervent anthropological writings; it is the basis of his exhortations to go beyond group mentality. Riccardi's chapter thus offers a remarkably interesting 'analytical' perspective on a classical corpus usually associated to the 'continental' tradition, one that illustrates remarkably well the kind of role philosophical views on language and mind can play within a theory aimed at offering insight into existential meaning.

The volume includes a chapter by Henry Jackman on William James, an author whose philosophical views have been mostly unfashionable over the course of the last century, wildly misunderstood, but nonetheless influential.[13] James's theories are fascinating, rooted in a pragmatist perspective on mental life that compares in originality to that of some of the most important schools in Europe at the time, including psychophysiology, Brentanian descriptive psychology and psychoanalysis. Jackman's Chapter 7 focuses on James's account of 'concepts' to throw light on the reasons for James's putative "rejection" of logic. As Jackman maintains, James's argument is rooted in an insight that is both profound and sophisticated about the nature of concepts and rationality: on James's account logic 'fails' to be useful when it comes to understanding rationality, not because we are all deeply irrational, but because there is a gap between concepts (understood by James as anchored in *practical* interactions with the world) and an account of rationality that is modeled on the *theoretical* study of formal inferences. Pragmatism, then, offers a formidably interesting perspective on rationality, one that does not equate rationality with logic but relies on the study of mind to better understand the normative basis of practical and epistemic agency.

By contrast to James's pragmatism, the significance and interest of contribution of Sigmund Freud's psychoanalysis to the study of mind do not need to be emphasised. The purpose of Bergo's Chapter 8 is to paint a picture of Freud as a mind-researcher, focusing on the work he accomplished in the 1880s and 1890s as an experimental psychologist working on neurophysiological anatomy. As Bergo amply documents, Freud's formative years were spent in a context determined by the rise of neurology, materialism, mechanism, as well as Brentanian phenomenology, all of which informed his later theories. She focuses on two of Freud's most representative publications – 'The Brain' (1888) and *On Aphasia* (1891), documenting their origin in the context of Viennese and Parisian experimental psychology and drawing connections with the theories of Freud's mentors, e.g. Ernst Wilhelm von Brücke, Theodor Meynert, and Jean-Martin Charcot – or those of their competitors. There is much to be learned from Bergo's chapter, in particular about the state of neurophysiology at the time – something that will be of interest to the historian of cognitive sciences – but also about the way in which technological and theoretical advances of which Freud had first-hand knowledge in the study of brain contributed to shape Freud's later views, the ones with which we are all familiar, on consciousness, the unconscious, psychological analysis and therapy.

7. Brentanian descriptive psychology

If most contemporary philosophers of mind see the nineteenth century as the cradle of the discipline, it is predominantly on account of the enduring philosophical significance of Franz Brentano's groundbreaking work on "intentionality". Brentano was first to place the study of mind, understood as consciousness, at the heart of the philosophical enterprise, thus carving a space for a new discipline he dubbed 'descriptive psychology'. Though Brentano sees the latter as belonging to 'empirical' psychology, he also argues that it mobilizes *a priori* investigative methods that make descriptive psychology both distinct from and epistemologically more fundamental than its experimental counterpart. In this respect, 'empiricist' might offer a better characterization of his enterprise. Either way, the theories Brentano puts forward in *Psychology from an Empirical Standpoint* (1874) raise a number of important methodological and metatheoretical questions that are not always heeded, e.g.: What was Brentano's conception of the relation between philosophy and psychology? What does Brentano understand 'empirical' to mean? What is the basis for the claim that the data we acquire in 'inner-perception' is *a priori*? What is the role of experimentation in psychology as he conceived of it?

Brentano's influence on the late nineteenth and twentieth centuries is significant. While Brentano's theories shaped one of the common *loci* of contemporary philosophy of mind – the conception of mental states in terms of psychological attitudes that have a (propositional) "content", i.e. that are "directed toward" an object or proposition or that are "intentional" – they impregnated the work of his students even more thoroughly. This is significant. Many of the students he trained in Würzburg (e.g. Carl Stumpf) and Vienna (among others: Alexius Meinong, Anton Marty, Alois Höfler, Christian von Ehrenfels, Kasimierz Twardowski, Benno Kerry and Edmund Husserl) went on to occupy prestigious university positions – in Prague, Berlin, Halle, Graz and Freiburg – and to publish work that would in turn be important in the century that followed. Not only is Brentano the forebear of both Polish analytical philosophy (in Lvov and Warsaw, through Twardowski) and of what will become (so-called: 'transcendental') phenomenology between the wars (through Husserl and, after him, Heidegger), he was also one of the main influence on the 'moral scientists' in Cambridge in the late nineteenth century – through analytic psychologists including Stout and Ward – in the last decades of the nineteenth century. Through them, aspects of Brentano's theories shaped the thought of a number of young British philosophers, including Moore and Russell (Cf. van der Schaar 2013).

In Chapter 9, Robin Rollinger brushes a picture of the 'classical' Brentanian theory of intentionality. His discussion and presentation of Brentano, which rest on his thorough knowledge of the Brentanian school as a whole as well as his familiarity with Brentanian scholarship, sketch a crucial part of the shared theoretical context in which the views of Brentano's students evolved, and thus prepare the ground for Chapters 10 (Meinong), 11 (Stumpf), 12 (Ehrenfels) and 13 (Husserl).

One distinctive feature of Brentanian theories of mind is the fact that while they take the study of mental phenomena to be key to the resolution of traditional philosophical questions (from logic and ontology to ethics and aesthetics), their engagement with the philosophical problems traditionally associated with the study of mind is itself virtually naught. They have nothing to say on the nature of the 'soul' and the possibility of its surviving death. For early phenomenologists, discussion of the mind-body problem was also a non-starter. The same holds, inasmuch as phenomenologists are concerned,[14] as regards debates around materialism, panpsychism or dualism. As Peter Simons stresses in Chapter 10, Alexius Meinong is a particularly good example of the general indifference of the Brentanians toward the traditional 'metaphysics of mind'.

Meinong's indifference in this respect is not the consequence of a general disinterest for ontology. Rather it epitomises the notoriously distinctive approach Brentanians took to questions of existence and ontological fundamentality. The one aspect of Meinong's views that is most likely to be familiar to the reader is presumably the claim, in *Theory of Object* (1904) that there are "non-existent objects" – a conclusion he owes in part to Kasimierz Twardowki's criticism of Brentano in *On the Content and Object of Presentations* (1894). But there are at least three other aspects of Meinong's work that deserve closer attention, all of which are also discussed by Simons. First, Meinong identifies a new category of quasi-doxastic states he calls 'assumptions' (*Annahmen*). The notion has been the topic of recent studies and its interest and significance are neither trivial nor merely historical.[15] Second, Meinong's work is rooted in a conception of the relation between philosophy – understood in a Brentanian vein, as the science of phenomena – and (experimental, physiological) psychology that has much to teach us about the kinds of considerations that led to a redefinition of the respective scope of these two disciplines. Finally, Meinong's work is representative of the broad engagement of Brentanians with affective and normative considerations, an engagement that constitutes a remarkably fertile ground for research in the philosophy of emotions, meta-ethics and the theory of value.

In Chapter 11 Mark Textor examines Carl Stumpf's philosophy of perception. Stumpf, who was one of Brentano's first students and also one of the few who benefited from his supervision in an official capacity, remained active well into the twentieth century, contributing in many ways to the training of Brentano's younger students. After Brentano was demoted, Stumpf "officially" supervised the post-graduate or post-doctoral work of many who worked on various aspects of descriptive psychology with Brentano – including Husserl. Stumpf also contributed to the development of psychology beyond phenomenology. Notably, while the notion of *Gestalt*-quality should be credited to another one of Brentano's students, Christian von Ehrenfels (see *infra*, Chapter 12), Stumpf was instrumental in developing the theory and introducing it to the next generation of researchers in Berlin.

Textor's chapter offers insight into one problem that permeates the entire Stumpfian corpus: how to account for the fact that we perceive certain kinds of objects as unities – as opposed to multiplicities – in spite of the fact that they are composed of "parts" that are recognisably independent of each other. Textor introduces the question in the following terms:

> When we see a yellow patch we see spatial extension and colour together, they, as Stumpf said, appear to us as one unity. Is this so because there is one unity that we perceive? If so, how and why can we say that we perceive two things, colour as well as spatial extension? If, in contrast, we indeed perceive simultaneously colour as well extension, *two* qualities, how come that they appear to us as *one* unity.

Textor's discussion of Stumpf, in addition to being informed by recent research on perception, has the merit of focusing on a problem that can be seen as emblematic of the early phenomenological approach: the application of increasingly sophisticated mereological analyses to the study of perceptual content.

The single most influential contribution by a phenomenologist to modern psychology is likely to be Christian von Ehrenfels's theory of '*Gestalt*-qualities'. Indeed, the conceptual resources it provides for the analysis of the structure of perception continue to inform contemporary research on cognition. In Chapter 12, Carlo Ierna offers insight into the context in which Ehrenfels developed his theory: while Ehrenfels himself credits Mach, whose views were broadly discussed by Brentano's students, a range of other theories, from Stumpf's to Meinong's, form the background of his views. Ierna draws a picture of the influence of Ehrenfels's theory of *Gestalt*-qualities on phenomenology and through phenomenology – in particular through Meinong (in Graz), Marty (in Prague) and Stumpf (in Berlin) – on the next generation of European psychologists: Max Wertheimer, Kurt Koffka, and Wolfgang Köhler. He also seeks to understand the origins of Ehrenfels's somewhat esoteric views on the metaphysics of mind, which just like most of his other writings, and perhaps not entirely unjustly, have not enjoyed much recognition.

When it comes to Edmund Husserl, there seem to be two scholarly factions. On the one hand, there are those who believe that Husserl's work came to fruition in his commitment, most notably in *Ideas* (1913), to a form of transcendental subjectivism that is reminiscent of the traditional Cartesian and Kantian epistemological projects. On the other hand, there are those who believe that Husserl's 'transcendental turn' was an unfortunate concession to the Neo-Kantian *zeitgeist*, one that distracted Husserl from his true purpose as a philosopher of psychology, mathematics and logic. While it's unclear that either camp appreciates the full extent of Husserl's contribution, the first camp is in many ways predominant. In spite of some fair attempts by analytically minded philosophers to do justice to Husserl's philosophy of logic and mathematics, continental commentators have succeeded so far in claiming monopole over Husserlian scholarship. This partly explains why Husserl has few sympathisers outside the narrow circle of scholars interested in so-called "transcendental phenomenology", and why his early work is vastly understudied and underappreciated. In this respect, the 'early' Husserl is at once the most prolific and the most underrated of all of Brentano's students. His *Logical Investigations*, published in two volumes in 1900 and 1901, are the flagship of what is perhaps the single most ambitious philosophical project of the twentieth century, and certainly one of the most interesting.

From today's perspective, the suggestion in the very title of the book that the *Logical Investigations*, especially the second volume, are about logic seems misleading: the book places the phenomenological investigation of mind at the centre stage of an enterprise that aims at A Philosophical Account of Many Things, few of which have to do directly with logic as we know it or even with what is commonly understood to be its philosophy. The six *Logical Investigations* (LI I–VI) span a number of philosophical concerns, including: establishing the objective status of meaning and truth (LI I), giving an account of language use and understanding in communication (LI II), providing a quasi axiomatic definition of formal mereological concepts (LI III), developing a logical syntax (LI IV), offering a new account of intentionality that puts phenomenology on realist grounds (LI V), and explaining what constitutes cognition and truth (LI VI). Independently of any question as to Husserl's relative success, the mere breadth of Husserl's theoretical concerns makes one's attempt to survey what is presumably meant to be a unified theory somewhat unmanageable. Husserl's notoriously impenetrable style and his predilection for clunky neologisms only add to the difficulty. But none of this diminishes the fact that different aspects of Husserl's work, for instance his criticism of psychologism in logic, his views on ontological dependence and grounding, or on intentionality, meaning and communication were deeply insightful and prophetic and would deserve to be studied at least as much as that of some of the better-known authors whose contributions on the same topic pale by comparison. Husserl's broad-ranging theoretical interests – in mathematics, logic, ontology, the study of language and beyond – led to discoveries that radically transformed the Brentanian theory of consciousness and intentionality. Yet, in spite of these and other differences, the study of intentionality remains, for Husserl as for Brentano, at the core of the philosophical project. In Chapter 13, Paul Livingston offers a remarkably accessible discussion of the way in which Husserl's views developed, from his early work in the philosophy of mathematics in the late 1880s to the publication of *Ideas* in 1913.

The last chapter, by Alan Kim on Paul Natorp, is meant to illustrate the Neo-Kantian perspective on the study of mind, in particular their criticism of the attempt by early psychologists and phenomenologists to offer an account of mental phenomena. According to Kim, Natorp's views must be understood in a context that is determined by two broad factors. On the one hand, by the end of the nineteenth century, the study of mind was no longer assumed to fall within the sole purview of traditional philosophy: although authors at the time remained rather vague on the relationship between philosophy and psychology (including phenomenology), psychology was in full growth mode and philosophy relented her dominion on the *psyche*. On the other hand, the second half of the nineteenth century coincides with the rise of anti-psychologism in logic broadly construed. The conjunction of the two factors – the rise of psychology as a discipline and of antipsychologism in philosophy – was a fertile ground for the idea that a foundational philosophical project that aims at establishing philosophy as 'scientific' and 'objective' could not rely on psychology or, indeed, any theory that draws on the study of the *psyche*. This, in essence, is Natorp's position. Natorp's (Kantian) argument against, for instance, (Husserlian) phenomenology's claim to provide a (psychological, subjective) foundation to knowledge as a whole is a remarkable opportunity for a dialogue between different traditions. Kim offers a clear presentation of an author who is almost entirely snubbed by historians of the nineteenth and twentieth centuries whose interests lie beyond Neo-Kantianism. Kim's chapter constitutes, in this respect, the perfect conclusion to a book the purpose of which is to broaden the horizon of philosophical historians and historically minded philosophers.

Notes

** I would like to thank Lydia Patton and Clinton Tolley for their helpful comments on a previous version of this introduction.
1 Beiser (2014a, 7) briefly discusses the historiography of such narratives.
2 See Lapointe (2017) for a critical perspective on the historiography of analytical philosophy.
3 Let us overlook, for the sake of brevity, reservations with the very notion of a canon and in particular, scruples that may come from the fact talk of a canon typically contributes to exclude individual authors whose work is being ignored or downplayed for reasons that have more to do with sociological and political capital than with philosophical value.
4 In the case of Bolzano, there is evidence that the answer to this question is far from clearly affirmative. Bolzano did agree with Kant on some crucial issues. For instance, while rejecting the doctrine of a putatively pure intuition, Bolzano agreed with Kant that arithmetic and geometry are not 'analytic' but 'synthetic', and that they deliver 'a priori' as opposed to 'a posteriori' knowledge. In Bolzano as in Kant, the definition of these notions rests on another eminently Kantian distinction: the distinction between 'concept' and 'intuition'. In light of the fact that Bolzano here adopts conceptual resources that are originally and distinctively Kantian, Bolzano's positions are arguably more aptly described as post-Kantian rather than as anti-Kantian.
5 See Van der Schaar (2013); see also Preti (forthcoming).
6 For the sake of expediency, I'll use the term 'psychology' to refer to the broad range of research projects that draw primarily on empirical and/or experimental methods and data in order to explain cognition and behaviour. I will also speak of 'the study of mind in the nineteenth century', without further qualification, when referring to efforts irrespective of disciplinary boundaries.
7 See Kusch (1999) see also Hatfield (2002) among other relevant work by the same author.
8 See Beiser (2014b) for a discussion of the 'lost tradition' of psychologistic neo-Kantianism.
9 See Andrew Brook, Kant on Mind, Volume IV of this series, Chapter 16.

10 See Bolzano 1837, §13: 'To show how many sciences are auxiliary to logic, one would have to decide first how many sciences there are and what their boundaries are. It is premature to do this, so I shall here content myself with the following: Logic is to teach us rules by which our knowledge can be organised into a scientific whole. To do this, it must also teach us how truth may be found, error discovered, etc. It cannot do the latter without or so attending to the way in which the mind acquires its ideas and knowledge. The proofs of its rules and theories must therefore make reference to the faculty of representation, to memory, the association of ideas, imagination, etc. But the human mind and its faculties are the subject of an already existing science, namely, empirical psychology. From this it follows that logic is dependent at least on psychology, and that it must forego the reputation of being a completely independent science.'

11 Erik Banks untimely passing in the final stage of the editorial process saddened us all. We are thankful to the Chair of the Department of Religion, Philosophy and Classics at Wright State University, Ava Chamberlain, for her support is insuring the chapter would be published.

12 Incidentally, Bolzano himself subscribes to a variant of Leibniz's monadology (see Lapointe, *infra*).

13 Cf. Klein (2016)

14 Here Ehrenfels might have been an unhappy exception.

15 See Textor (2015); see also Mulligan (2015).

Bibliography

Beiser, Frederich (2014a) *After Hegel*, Princeton, Princeton University Press.

Beiser, Frederich (2014b) *The Genesis of Neo-Kantianism, 1796–1880*, Oxford, Oxford University Press.

Bolzano, Bernard (1837) *Wissenschaftslehre*, Sulzbach, Seidel [translation by Paul Rusnock and Rolf George, Oxford, Oxford University Press, 2014].

Freud, Sigmund (1888) "The Brain," in Mark Solms and Michael Saling, Eds. *A Moment of Transition: Two Neuroscientific Articles by Sigmund Freud*. London: Karnac Books, 1990, 39-86.

Freud, Sigmund (1891) *On Aphasia: A Critical Study*. New York: International Universities Press, 1953.

Hatfield, Gary (2002) "Psychology, Philosophy, and Cognitive Science: Reflections on the History and Philosophy of Experimental Psychology" in *Mind & Language*, Vol. 17/3, 207–232

Husserl, Edmund (1913) Ideen zu einer reinen Phänomenologie und phänomenologischen Philosophie (vol. 1), Jahrbuch für Philosophie und phänomenologische Forschung 1/1, 1-323.

Kant, Immanuel (1781) Critik der reinen Vernunft, Riga, Johann Friedrich Hartknoch

Klein, Alexander (2016) "Was James Psychologistic?" in *Journal of the History of Analytical Philosophy*, Vol. 4.5 (https://jhaponline.org/jhap/article/view/2945/2606).

Kusch, Martin (1999) *Psychological Knowledge. A Social History and Philosophy*, London, Routledge.

Lapointe, Sandra (2017) "On the Traditionalist Conjecture" in Preston, Aaron (ed.) *Analytic Philosophy: An Interpretive History*, London, Routledge.

Mulligan, Kevin (2015) "Annehmen, Phantasieren und Entertaining: Husserl und Meinong" in *Themes from Ontology, Mind, and Logic*, Sandra Lapointe (ed.), Grazer Philosophische Studien 91, 245-283.

Preti, Consuelo (forthcoming) *The Metaphysical Basis of Ethics: G.E. Moore and the Origins of Early Analytic Philosophy*, Houndmills, Palgrave Macmillan.

Textor, Mark (2015) "Meaning, Entertaining, and Phantasy Judgement" in *Themes from Ontology, Mind, and Logic*, Sandra Lapointe (ed.), Grazer Philosophische Studien 91, 285-302.

Van der Schaar, Maria (2013) *G.F. Stout and the Psychological Origins of Analytic Philosophy*, Houndmills, Palgrave.

1

REPRESENTATION, CONSCIOUSNESS, AND MIND IN GERMAN IDEALISM

Clinton Tolley

1. Introduction

The German Idealist tradition after Kant has much of interest to say on key questions in the philosophy of mind, though this is not always easy to draw out, given their dense prose and often unelaborated or even merely implicit allusions to their predecessors or to one another. Here I aim to highlight and clarify an important line of thought that emerges in the wake of Kant's 'critique' of our powers of 'cognition' (*Erkenntnis*).

As I will show below (§2), Kant takes cognition to be built up out of several 'steps' (*Stufen*), involving different 'acts' of 'representation' (*Vorstellung*) by our 'mind' (*Gemüt*) and eventually involving 'consciousness' (*Bewußtsein*). Yet, as Kant's successors were quick to point out, Kant seemed to presuppose, problematically, that representation and consciousness themselves were already well understood. They also complained that Kant had said very little about the nature of mental activity in general.

These perceived shortcomings led later Idealists to rethink Kant's analysis of mind from the ground up. As we will see, Reinhold (§3), Fichte (§4), Schelling (§5), and Hegel (§6) can all be viewed as attempting to identify and articulate deeper, philosophically more satisfactory – and when necessary, revisionary – foundations for a distinctively post-Kantian cognitive psychology, by relentlessly insisting on the need for philosophical investigation into the conditions for the possibility of consciousness, representation, and even the mind itself – all of which they felt Kant had left shrouded in darkness.[1]

2. Kant

As Kant's 'Critical' project provides the most significant impetus for the Idealist contributions to philosophy of mind, let me begin by setting out some of the aspects most relevant to subsequent developments. One of the main conclusions of Kant's *Critique of Pure Reason* is that, with respect to key propositions of traditional metaphysics, concerning the existence of God, our own freedom, and our immortality, we have to 'deny *knowledge* [das Wissen aufheben] in order to make room for *faith* [Glaube]' (Bxxx). Kant understands *knowledge* to consist in the '*holding-true*' (*Fürwahrhalten*) of a true proposition or 'judgment' (*Urteil*) for objectively sufficient grounds or reasons (cf. B848f). To establish this epistemological conclusion, Kant's method is to look first to our cognitive *psychology*, i.e., to examine the more primitive mental acts responsible for forming *judgments* about such objects in the first place, by looking at the more familiar process by which we judge about everyday real objects in our '*cognition*' of objects in the mental activity he calls 'experience' (*Erfahrung*).

In preparation for the examination of knowledge in its concluding part, the bulk of Kant's *Critique* is thereby devoted to presenting the 'Doctrine of the Elements' of our cognition. Kant famously claims that these elements arise from two distinct 'stems of human cognition', the mental capacities for *representation* he calls 'sensibility' and 'understanding', respectively (B29). Sensibility is 'the *receptivity* of our mind to acquire representations insofar as it is affected in some way', whereas understanding is 'the capacity for bringing forth representations itself', and thus a kind of '*spontaneity*' (B75). The initial representations that our mind receives through sensibility are '*sensations*' (*Empfindungen*) (B34). Our mind then places sensations in an order or a 'form' so as to yield an '*intuition*' (*Anschauung*) which contains an 'appearance' (*Erscheinung*) of the object (B34). Once in possession of an appearance via intuition, our mind can then become 'conscious' of this intuition – and thereby turn it into something '*for* me' rather than merely being something '*in* me' – by using our capacity for apperception (cf. B131–132), and achieve what Kant calls '*perception*' (*Wahrnehmung*) or 'empirical *consciousness*' of the appearance (cf. B160; B207). After our mind is aware of enough appearances, it is then able to use our understanding to form judgments about the objects of these appearances, through acts of 'synthesis' which bring these appearances under a 'concept' (*Begriff*) of the further object to which they are related (B137). This allows us to '*cognize* an *object by means of* these representations' when the *object* is '*thought* in relation to' its appearances (B74; my ital.). This 'empirical *cognition*' of objects 'through perceptions' is what Kant calls 'experience' (cf. B218; 4:298f).[2]

Kant's Critical project concerning *knowledge* therefore takes its 'elementary' starting point a rich picture of our mind, its capacities, acts, products (representations), and consciousness, and how all of these contribute to the more primitive act of *cognition*.[3] What is much less clear from the *Critique* itself, however, is what Kant thinks the mind itself actually is. One important hint can be found tucked away in remarks Kant wrote up as an afterword for S. T. Sömmerring's 1796 *On the organ of the soul*, a work which discusses the anatomy of the human brain:

> By *mind* [Gemüt] one means only the *capacity* (*animus*) of combining the given representations and effecting the unity of empirical apperception,

not yet the *substance* (*anima*) according to its nature which is entirely distinct from matter and from which one is abstracting here.

(12:32)

Here the human mind is identified with a set of *capacities* (especially our capacity for 'combining' what we apperceive, i.e., our understanding), and is distinguished from whatever *substance* (i.e., *soul*) might be responsible for bearing these capacities. This distinction is important, in light of Kant's ultimate prohibition on knowledge, or even cognition, of our own *soul* as to the features that it has 'in itself' (e.g., immortality), limiting knowledge only to how the soul 'appears' in inner intuition and inner experience. Otherwise Kant's own exposition in the *Critique* would rest on uncertain ground, since it seems to presuppose a considerable amount of cognition and knowledge concerning our own *mind itself* (its capacities, activities), and not merely of its appearances.[4]

One way in which self-cognition of the mind might transpire is through what Kant calls *pure* 'apperception' or '*self*-consciousness', in which 'I am conscious of myself, not as I appear to myself, nor as I am in myself, but only *that* I am' (B157). Kant hesitates about calling this not especially informative type of self-awareness 'cognition', especially since it does not involve any *intuition* of my mind (it is pure 'thinking'; B157). Nevertheless, Kant does think that through such consciousness I am able to at least 'represent the spontaneity of my thought' (B158n).

In any case, Kant thinks that we also can use our mind to cognize itself as to how it appears, since 'I am *also* given to myself in intuition' (B155; my ital.). This occurs through what Kant calls 'inner sense', which is 'that by means of which the mind intuits *itself*, or its inner state', and so is given 'inner appearances' of itself and its own activity (B37; my ital.). The substance (subject, soul) which possesses the mind, by contrast, can never itself be 'given': inner sense 'gives, to be sure, no intuition of the *soul* itself, as an object' (B37)). Nevertheless, Kant does think that inner sense is sufficient for us to arrive at cognition and knowledge of our minds – and even our souls – by way of its appearances; we can, for example, 'prove the persistence of our soul during life' (4:335).

As the connection between soul and 'life' (*Leben*) is echoed elsewhere in Kant's writings (cf. B403), the question arises as to whether, for Kant, everything living is ensouled, and, furthermore, whether everything living or ensouled has a mind in particular. Kant does think that being able to *represent*, and being able to 'act' and 'cause' things on the basis of such representing, is a condition for life (cf. 28:762, 28:247). Kant also associates this 'inner principle in a substance for changing its state' with '*desiring*' (*Begehren*) (4:544). This implies that all animals and (seemingly) even *plants* have representations and desires, since Kant counts both among the living (cf. 7:135; 28:205). Only animals, however, are explicitly described as also being *conscious* of their representations. This comes about through their 'perception' and 'apprehension' (*Auffassung*) of their representations (cf. 11:345;

7:134; 9:64–65), which allows them to be 'acquainted with' (*kennen*) sensible appearances (9:65).

Only humans, though, can become conscious not just of their *representations*, but of *objects (things)* through these representations. In the inner case, this allows humans to be conscious not just of their inner appearances, but of *themselves* as existent objects, in 'apperception'; this capacity for self-consciousness indicates we possess not just a *soul* but '*intelligence*' (cf. 29:878–879; cf. B158). Animals lack not only this inner *self*-consciousness but are also (perhaps surprisingly) not able to genuinely *cognize* the objects of *outer* intuition either (even though they are 'acquainted' with (and conscious of) sensible representations or appearances of these objects (cf. 9:65)). The reason Kant gives for this is once again animals' lack of the capacity for *understanding*, since this enables 'consciousness of an action whereby the representations *relate to a given object* and this relation may be *thought*' (7:397; my ital.).

Kant thereby orders *souls* into a kind of progression (from plants to animals to humans), according to the kind of representations the kind of soul is capable of: whether unconscious representation, conscious representation, or, finally, self-conscious, intelligent representation or cognition. Strikingly, this same threefold progression of representations (unconscious, conscious, cognitive) is something Kant also sees as duplicated *within* the human soul itself, as we saw above, which suggestively echoes the Aristotelian idea that our own mental life depends on partially vegetative and animal activity.[5]

3. Reinhold

Though it set about a revolution in German-language philosophy, even Kant's more sympathetic readers conceded that the *Critique* did not make clear its own presuppositions about the mind and its acts as directly as one might hope. One of the most influential early critics of Kant on this point was Karl Reinhold. Reinhold's main concern was that Kant's analysis of the concept of *cognition* assumes, without any argument, that we understand what *representation* itself is, both because cognition is classified as a *species* of representation, and because cognition involves other representations (intuitions, concepts) as its *constituents*. Reinhold concludes: 'whatever concept of cognition one accepts, it presupposes a concept of representation' (Reinhold 1789 §V 189–190). In fact, Reinhold thought the problem was much worse, since in fact our understanding of *all* of the other things that Kant had identified as 'elements' of cognition presupposes an understanding of representation, since 'representation encompasses ... sensation, thought, intuition, concept, idea, in a word everything which occurs in our consciousness as an immediate effect of sensing, thinking, intuiting, comprehending' (Reinhold 1789 §IX 210). From this Reinhold concludes that Kant's overall position must remain problematically opaque until we get clear on what is meant by 'representation' and 'representational capacity' (Reinhold 1789 §V 188–189; cf. 62f).

To remedy this, the *Critique*'s own analysis must be preceded by an *even more* 'elementary' science, which would *truly* 'establish its foundation [Fundament]' – namely, 'the science of the entire capacity of *representation* as such' (Reinhold 1791 71–72; my ital.). Reinhold himself attempts to provide this more elementary philosophy in his (aptly named) 1789 *Attempt at a New Theory of Human Representation*. Reinhold there gives both an extensional specification of what he means by 'representation' (cf. the list above), as well as the following quasi-intensional one: 'everything which occurs in consciousness as an immediate effect of mental activity' (Reinhold 1789 §IX 210). Reinhold hopes that characterizations like these (compare: 'that to which everything that is and can be object of consciousness must relate') will be sufficient to point us to his subject-matter, which he also claims is 'the most familiar' in our consciousness, even claiming (strikingly) that representation 'is neither capable of or *in need of* an explanation' (Reinhold 1789 §XIII 223–224; my ital.). In fact, Reinhold is so confident that ostensive appeal to what is immediately given to consciousness is sufficient both to convey what representation in general consists in (its nature and structure) as well as to inform us about its basic kinds, that he stakes his whole theory upon it: 'the basis [Grund] on which the new theory could and had to be developed consists solely of *consciousness* as it functions in all people according to basic laws, and what follows immediately from that and will be actually conceded by all thinkers' (Reinhold 1789 66); the 'foundation [Grundlage] of my theory' is something 'necessitated by consciousness' (Reinhold 1789 §§VI-VII 200–201).[6]

Consciousness itself is sufficient, Reinhold thinks, to 'give' us those 'properties' of representation 'through which it is conceived and which belong among the *inner* conditions of representation, insofar as representation is *not conceivable* without these properties' (Reinhold 1789 §XIV 227; my ital.). The first such 'inner condition' on something's being conceivable as a representation is that it is at once related to, but yet itself distinct from, both a subject and an object:

> There is agreement, necessitated by consciousness, that there belongs to representation a representing subject and a represented object, which both must be distinguished from the representation to which they belong.
> (Reinhold 1789 §VII 200)

Because of the distinguishability of the representation from the representing subject and represented object, Reinhold argues that subject and object *themselves* cannot be thought to function as '*inner* constituents' or 'components' of the representation considered 'merely' by itself; rather, the subject and the object 'pertain simply to the *external* conditions of representation' (Reinhold 1789 §XIII 220–221; my ital.). In explaining what he means by 'inner' vs. 'external', Reinhold in effect anticipates something of Husserl's phenomenological method, according to which what is immediately given *in* consciousness can be analyzed without making use of any presuppositions about the existence of anything *outside* of this givenness – including the represented object or even the representing subject:

> It is not being claimed here either that or how *objects* are present *outside* the mind, but only that they must be distinguished from mere representations.
> (Reinhold 1789 201; my ital.)

> In all experiences which are possible to our mind, only representations can occur, and never the representing entity [das Vorstellende] itself, always only the *effects* of the representing subject, never the *subject* itself.
> (Reinhold 1789 161–162; my ital.)

Reinhold insists, therefore, that the 'inner conditions' of representation simply cannot be 'derived' from either reflection on the subject or the object, but only from attending to representation itself, in its primitive givenness to consciousness (Reinhold 1789 §XIII 220–221).

Even so, when Reinhold turns to the positive task of characterizing the 'inner conditions' (constituents) of mere representation, these essential components turn out to '*correspond*' to the represented object and the representing subject, respectively – even while not being identical with them. The correlate of the *object* is what Reinhold calls the '*material*' of the representation (Reinhold 1789 §XV 230). That in the representation which correlates with the *subject* is what Reinhold calls the '*form*' of the representation, and which is singled out both as that 'through which the pure material *becomes* a representation' in the first place (Reinhold 1789 §XVI 235), and also 'that *by means of which* the representation belongs to the mind' (Reinhold 1789 §XVI 237; my ital.). As the correlate of the representing subject, the form of a representation is 'that *in* the representation which *belongs to the mind*' in a special way, in the sense that 'the material could only acquire the form of representation *in* the mind and only *by means of* the capacity for representation' (ibid.; my ital.). The form of a representation, therefore, is the distinctive result of the subject's own exercise of its representational capacity and is what transforms the material into something representational in the first place. The material, by contrast, is 'that by means of which the representation *belongs to the represented (object)*' (Reinhold 1789 §XVI 237; my ital.), in the sense that certain sense-impressions 'belong to' an object in virtue of their causal connectedness to it as its effects (Reinhold 1789 §XVI 242).

In this way, Reinhold takes great pains both to distinguish these internal conditions (constituents) of representations from their external conditions (subject, object), and also to prioritize the former methodologically, due to their immediate occurrence or presence in consciousness. Nevertheless, Reinhold's account of representation ultimately seems to bottom out in something which is itself *external* to any representation and hence *cannot occur in* any consciousness. This comes out most clearly in the Appendix to his *Attempt*, where Reinhold ends up following Kant in positing a necessary real (causally efficacious) relation between our representations and our 'capacities' (*Vermögen*) – namely, the former being effects of the latter's realization in 'powers or forces' (*Kräfte*), which serve as grounds for any actual representing to occur (Reinhold 1789 560). Moreover, what is responsible for initiating the movement from possible representing to actual representing – i.e., the realization of these powers and the 'production' (*Erzeugung*) of actual representations – is a deeper 'drive' (*Trieb*), and ultimately a 'desire' (*Begehren*), *for* representations (Reinhold 1789 561).

Now, the exercise of this originary drive and desire to represent cannot itself be dependent upon any actually existent representation, on pain of circularity (unless Reinhold were to accept innately actual representations, which he does not; cf. Reinhold 1789 §XXXII 312). What is more, because neither the drive, nor the desire, nor the capacities they actualize in forces, are *themselves* representations, none of these can be immediately present 'in' consciousness itself. Hence, by Reinhold's own lights, the appeal to these items as at all explanatory of representation would seem to directly conflict with Reinhold's methodological 'principle of consciousness' – unless Reinhold concedes that there is something 'in' consciousness itself after all (an 'inner condition' of representations themselves) which entails that, to *conceive* of representations at all, we must think of them as related to something beyond themselves.[7] But then Reinhold's own lights seem to have led him to admit (albeit begrudgingly and perhaps belatedly) the ultimate insufficiency of the mere 'facts' contained within consciousness to provide a sufficient ground or foundation for the philosophical account of representation itself – let alone Kant's original topics of cognition and knowledge.

4. Fichte

In this partial concession that the external conditions of representation might not ultimately be so external after all, those who were closely following Reinhold's exposition and development of the Kantian philosophy, such as Fichte, saw Reinhold pointing the way toward deeper, hitherto largely uncharted questions. In his own 1794 work on the 'foundation [Grundlage] for the entire doctrine of science [Wissenschaftslehre]', Fichte pressed directly on just this issue, charging Reinhold with a lack of a truly 'foundational' account of representation and hence 'what can occur in consciousness'. The echoes of Reinhold's own critique of Kant are thus clear enough: whereas Reinhold had complained that Kant had simply presupposed that the genus of representation was understood in order to account for one of its species (cognition), Fichte now complained that Reinhold himself makes similarly unsatisfactory presuppositions about the primitive intelligibility of representation itself:

> Reinhold put forward the principle of representation, and in Cartesian form his basic proposition would run: *repraesento, ergo sum,* or more

properly: *repraesentans sum, ergo sum*.[. . .] But representing is not the essence of being, but a specific determination thereof; and our being has still other determinations besides this, *even if they must pass through the medium of representation in order to reach empirical consciousness*.
(Fichte 1794 I.100)

Representation cannot be a primitive term, thinks Fichte, because it is a species of a still higher genus – namely, *being* in general. Moreover, even with respect to specifically *human being*, Reinhold himself was forced to accept that the activity of representing is only one among many 'determinations' of our being, as is witnessed by his own postulation of a ground for representation in activities (drives, desires) which were not themselves further acts of representing.

In his own 1794 *Grundlage*, Fichte can be seen as trying to systematically account for just those activities which function as pre-conditions for representation and consciousness, and thereby provide a more adequate account of the true 'foundation' for cognition, science, and knowledge itself. Against Reinhold, Fichte argues that the most fundamental characterization of the kind of being which is ultimately capable of representation – what Fichte calls 'the I' (*Ich*) – should not be in terms of representing or consciousness, but rather in terms of something even more basic. This is because (as was already acknowledged by Kant) the I is capable of activity which includes 'no consciousness' and which is such that 'no consciousness *comes about* through this mere act' (Fichte 1797 §4 I.459; my ital.). Rather, there is a layer of activity that 'lies at the *basis* [Grund] of all consciousness and alone makes it possible' (Fichte 1794 §1 I.91; my ital.).

What is this activity like? Fichte accepts Reinhold's thesis that representation (and, hence, the occurrence of consciousness) requires a relation to both the object (what Fichte calls 'the not-I') and to the subject ('the I'). In Fichte's terms, the I's consciousness (and representations) 'only comes about *by contrast with* a not-I, and through the determination of the I within this *opposition*' (Fichte 1797 §4 I.459; my ital.). One thing that Fichte is insisting on, then, is that not every activity by the I already has this particular structure – i.e., that there is pre-conscious, pre-representational activity, in which the I and the not-I are not yet 'contrasted', 'determined', or 'opposed'. But what kind of activity will this be?

In its most basic form, Fichte's proposal would seem to be simply – activity per se; 'The I is originally a *doing* [Tun]' (Fichte 1797 §7 I.496; my ital.), perhaps on the model of Reinhold's mysterious 'drive'. It is hard to see how any *simple* activity, however, could ever function as a genuinely explanatory ground of the *relational* structure present in representation and consciousness. In order to succeed where Reinhold fails, then, Fichte holds that this originary activity must itself contain a *difference* within itself which can serve as the ground for the possibility of the structural components eventually manifest in representation and consciousness. That is, it must somehow already 'contain' some sort of twofold relationality – even if not the specific subject-object relatedness that furnishes the inner constituents of representationality in particular. Fichte's more fleshed-out proposal, therefore, is that the originary activity of the I is itself twofold, consisting, on the *one* hand, of an initial and entirely indeterminate 'going out' (*hinaus gehen*) or 'positing' (*setzen*) of itself; and on the *other*, an equally indeterminate 'reverting back' (*zurückkehren*) into itself due to an equally basic 'op-positing' or 'counter-positing' (*gegensetzen*) (cf. Fichte 1794 1.96–98), in the form of a 'check' (*Anstoss*) which 'reflects' the positing, such that it is 'driven inwards (*nach innen getrieben*); it takes exactly the reverse direction' (Fichte 1794 1.228; cf. 1.272, 1.275).

What this means, concretely, is far from clear, especially as we are now to be looking below the context of representationality and consciousness, and we are hence prohibited at this stage from interpreting 'positing' ('going-forth') and 'counter-positing' ('returning back') as *representing something* to the I, or even having a representation *'in'* the I. Rather, this originary twofold activity itself is intended to function as a pre-condition for even any determinate 'positing *in* the I', let alone any instance of consciousness of a representation of an object ('not-I'). As Fichte sees it, 'it is a *ground of explanation* of all the facts of empirical consciousness, that prior to all positing *in* the I, the I itself is posited'; that is, there is simply the I's going-out (Fichte 1794 1.95; my ital.). Ultimately, 'consciousness is itself a *product* of the I's original act, its own positing of itself' (Fichte 1794 1.107; my ital.). Similarly, oppositing or counter-positing ('reverting back') stands as a pre-condition for representing something to oneself, rather than being itself an instance of it: 'If I am to represent anything at all, I must counter-posit *it* to the one representing' (Fichte 1794 1.105). The idea of the primitive though indeterminate 'check' is 'prerequisite for explaining representation' (Fichte 1794 1.218), but only in that it prefigures the relation to a not-I, since 'representation in general' is 'indisputably the effect' of 'the not-I' in particular being counter-posited (Fichte 1794 1.251).

In fact, neither the originary (absolute, infinite) positing ('going forth'), nor even the originary counter-positing ('reverting back'), *has any 'object'* (*Gegenstand*). This is because such a relatedness would make these acts 'finite' and conditioned by something outside of themselves, something 'standing over and against' (*gegenstehende*) the activity; rather, there is only a 'pure' and free act of 'reverting back [*zurückgehende*] *to itself*' without any external 'resistance' (*Widerstand*) (Fichte 1794 1.256–257; my ital.). In the originary 'reverting back', the I's activity is not 'directed at any object', not even the not-I or the 'check'; this only happens once it finally '*represents*' what it itself counter-posits 'to itself'; only then does it take up an object (Fichte 1794 1.134; cf. 1.159). It is only '*non*-objective' activity of the prior sort which can be 'pure' and 'absolute' in the required sense (Fichte 1794 1.237; my ital.).

All of this helps to explain why it is only much later in Fichte's *Grundlage*, many pages after the introduction of these originary activities, and after many intermediate 'steps' beyond them, that he thinks we have enough on the table to achieve that necessary task which Reinhold was prohibited from even attempting – namely, a true 'deduction of *representation*' as such (Fichte 1794 1.228), and a more general reconstruction of the developmental 'history' of 'human spirit [Geist]' (Fichte 1794 1.222). Strikingly, this takes the form of the derivation of a progression of the species of representations that very closely echoes Kant's original progression noted above (cf. §2), beginning with sensory representation and imagination (Fichte 1794 1.229f), and then on to the 'higher', specifically cognitive, capacities of understanding (Fichte 1794 1.233f) and reason (Fichte 1794 1.244f). Unlike Kant, however, Fichte suggests that it is only once we reach the level of *reason* that we finally arrive at 'the source of all *self-consciousness*' (Fichte 1794 1.244), rather than this being possible through mere *thinking* (Kantian apperception).

If this captures the core of Fichte's attempt to find a better ground for Reinhold's account of the mind, we might wonder (as Fichte did of Reinhold) whether there might be any *further* possible explanation of the nature of this originary activity itself, in particular of why the originary activity is twofold in the first place. That such deeper twofold activity *does* occur is something Fichte takes to be demonstrated (a posteriori) by the sheer *existence* of consciousness and representation, suggesting he is also confident that it must be in place '*if* actual consciousness is to be *possible*' at all (Fichte 1794 1.275; my ital). Nevertheless, Fichte concedes: '*that* this occurs, as a fact, is *absolutely incapable of derivation from the I*' – which he takes to imply, furthermore, that the I itself 'is *not* to exhaust the infinite' (ibid.; my ital.), i.e., the indeterminacy out of which the originary activity itself emerges, since there must be some other ground or reason outside of these acts, conditioning the I in some way so as to elicit or actualize just this activity in the first place.

Ultimately, Fichte thinks that this question about the grounds for actualizing the I's originary activity simply can't be answered within the context of 'theoretical' philosophy *at all* (cf. Fichte 1794 1.218). It is only once we introduce the 'practical' part of philosophy later in the *Grundlage* that Fichte thinks we can begin to provide an answer to the question as to *why* the I ever comes *actually* to act ('go out' and 'come back') in the first place. In this, the shape of this 'practical' answer sounds surprisingly similar to Reinhold's, since Fichte, too, takes the actualization of the I's originary activity to require something in the I *prior to* the act itself, something that Fichte himself (like Reinhold) calls a '*drive*', and which he understands to be a kind of '*striving*' (*Streben*) on the part of the I (Fichte 1794 1.288).[8] Fichte even likewise concedes that 'the action should admit of being regarded as *brought about* [hervorgebracht] by the drive' (Fichte 1794 1.327).

The problem with all of this, however, is that, as per Fichte's own original criticism of Reinhold, this even more originary drive now seems to function as a precondition on the hitherto allegedly foundational activity. To avoid this conclusion, Fichte tries to argue that, conversely, 'the drive should admit of being posited as *determined* [bestimmt] by the action' – even though it is the drive that 'brings about' the action (Fichte 1794 1.328; my ital.). It seems that the activation of the capacity is somehow 'determined' by the originary activity in the sense that this activity is the *end* to be achieved by the striving, as that for the sake of which the drive strives. In this way, Fichte shifts the ultimate ground of the explanation of mind away from something self-standing in immediate consciousness, or even pre-conscious activity, and toward a deeper *teleology*,[9] a pre-active layer of end-oriented drives and strivings.[10]

5. Schelling

For these reasons, Schelling, and Hegel after him, concluded that what Fichte had officially identified as absolute – namely, the originary activity of the I – turned out not to be so absolute after all. Fichte's 'practical' turn to 'strivings' toward 'ends' acknowledged that there was in fact a deeper reason or ground for why the putatively absolute activity itself occurred and had the structure that it did. This acknowledgement, however, simply again pointed up the need for further philosophical investigation to clarify what it was that served as the condition for Fichtean activity. As we will see, in his 1800 *System of Transcendental Idealism* and in his subsequent 'System'-writings (1801 *Darstellung meines Systems*; 1802 *Ferner Darstellung meines Systems*), Schelling follows out Fichte's gesture toward teleology to attempt to show how these acts of the I arise out of *living nature*.

This turn toward organicism, however, was also motivated by a second failing Schelling identified in Fichte's system, this time with consequences upstream, concerning how Fichte's originary derivation of representation and consciousness would ever allow for genuine *knowledge*. Like Kant and Reinhold before him, Fichte had only shown how the development or progression from activity to consciousness took place from the '*subjective*' side of things, only from 'within' the I. Yet, no approach of this sort, thought Schelling, could possibly provide a satisfactory analysis of the 'not-I' or *object* in that 'subject-object' relation which turns out to be constitutive of consciousness and representationality. For Fichte left open the possibility that when the object-term was considered in *itself*, it would turn out to have an *infinitely different kind of being* than the originally active subject which constituted the relation to it. Not only would this in turn leave uncertain the very possibility of the higher unity of I with the not-I that Fichte poses as a practical 'task', Schelling argues that it leaves the door open to a vicious skepticism about the possibility of knowing this object.

This is because, like Kant before him, Schelling takes knowledge to depend on *truth* – since 'one knows only the truth' – yet (also like Kant) Schelling notes that truth itself consists in the 'harmony or *agreement*' (*Uebereinstimmung*) of something 'subjective' (namely: our representations) with something 'objective' (their 'objects') (Schelling 1800 I.3:339). For such agreement itself to be possible, Schelling thinks, there must 'exist a point at which both representation and object are originally *one* . . . at which they are in the most perfect *identity*' (Schelling 1800 3:363–364; my ital.). For this ultimate identity in knowledge to be possible, however, Schelling thinks there must *always already be* an '*originary* identity' between the kind of being that the object represented has, and the kind of being that the representation itself has. But then, since Schelling agrees with Fichte,

Reinhold, and Kant that representationality, or the 'subjective' side of this agreement, is something which is an expression of '*activity*' (*Tätigkeit*), he concludes that the 'agreement' required for knowledge 'is itself unthinkable unless the activity, whereby the *objective world* is produced, is at bottom *identical* with that activity which expresses itself in [*representation* and] volition, and vice versa' (Schelling 1800 3:348; my ital.).

What this 'at bottom identity' amounts to, thinks Schelling, is in one respect like Fichte's originary I, in that it must come before the emergence of the *relation* between representation and object that eventually comes to constitute the conscious perspective of the I. Yet, it is even more like Fichte's pre-active striving beneath the I and its originary activity, in that this identity is to come before anything that is specifically assignable to the I, anything distinctively subjective. Rather, the originary identity is a 'point of *indifference*' which is *neither* subjective *nor* objective. Only in this way can it thereby serve as the ground *both* for the distinctively subjective activity that Fichte had charted out in his *Grundlage*, but *also* for the ultimate, parallel constitution of what is objective – and do so in such a way that leaves open the possibility of harmony and ultimately knowledge itself.

This originary grounding point of indifference is what Schelling calls '*absolute reason*' (*Vernunft*), though Schelling takes care to sharply distinguish this from whatever 'reason' Kant and others might take to be possessed by individual persons, since what is in question here is the ground for all subjectivity whatsoever, including individualized versions. 'Reason' here means instead: 'reason insofar as it is thought of as the total indifference of the subjective and objective' (Schelling 1801 §1), as the entirely impersonal ultimate ground of the very difference between subjective and objective in the first place.

Schelling then poses the following two tasks for post-Fichtean philosophy of mind, if it is to avoid extreme skepticism: *first*, to show how this originary indifference-point could give rise to the specific progression of activities which Fichte had shown to constitute the subjective (the I), and thereby allow for a derivation of representationality and consciousness; and *second*, to show that and how it also gives rise to the very same sort of progression of activity (positing, opposing, etc.) on the side of the object as well, on the side of the not-I, or what Schelling describes as 'nature'.

In the 1800 *System* itself Schelling traces the 'history' of the I's own progression through a broadly Fichtean 'step-wise series' (*Stufenfolge*) of 'epochs' (Schelling 1800 3:331).[11] Schelling, too, insists that we must first go below Descartes' 'I *think*' and Reinhold's 'I *represent*' to an even deeper 'era' of the I, if we are 'to become originally conscious' of the ground for representing and thinking itself: we must 'free ourselves of all representing', in order to allow the proposition 'I *am*' to arise for us, because this 'is without doubt a higher proposition' (Schelling 1800 3:367). What is then revealed is Fichte's truth that, originally, 'the I is pure *act*, pure *doing*' (Schelling 1800 3:368; my ital.).

Yet, while Schelling agrees with the general shape of Fichte's developmental-historical analysis of the I, he aims to go beyond Fichte by attempting to remove the sense that the progression in question (from originary act, through positing, opposing, etc.) is the *unique* property of the I, or what is subjective. He aims to do this by showing how the stages ('epochs') in the I's development can be viewed as closely correlated with the stages in the development of *nature* itself, in the exercise of its various 'potencies' (*Potenzen*) for activity. The first potency is that which is responsible for *matter* as the originary filling of space with gravitational force of attraction and repulsion, manifest, e.g., in magnetism; this then develops into a second 'reflective' potency manifest in *light* and ultimately, electrical and chemical relations as well, and which again include unities of polarity (cf. Schelling 1800 3:433–454); '*organized* nature' or 'life' forms a third potency, which brings about self-maintaining and self-monitoring activity structured as sensibility, irritability, and 'formative drive' (*Bildungstrieb*) (Schelling 1800 3:495f).

Schelling argues that we can see this 'objective' progression as exactly parallel to the three-step series of 'epochs' that we find in subjective history of the I's activity: the first involves bare '*sensing*' (*empfinden*), as like a 'pulse' that runs out and returns to itself, filling the I, though '*without* consciousness' (Schelling 1800 4:462); the second includes the development into an *intelligence*, which allows for sensing '*with* consciousness' (Schelling 1800 4:462), and hence with the further 'reflective' intuition of the I's activity of sensing itself (Schelling 1800 3:454); the third stage involves the self-intuition of the I as being *alive*, i.e., the intelligence '*appearing* to itself' as 'an *organic* individual', whose (Schelling 1800 3:495; my ital.). In this, the I shows itself to be constituted by a progression of activity precisely of a piece with that which generates the nature which it ultimately relates to as 'object'.

What is less clear in the *System*, however, is, first, how both parallel (subjective and objective) progressions can be seen as arising *from one and the same* single originary point of indifference, and second, what exactly it means, once representation is possible on the subjective side, for what is being represented by such representations (the objective) to be *identical with* what is doing the representing (the subjective). It might appear that Schelling does not think he has, or even can have, completed the latter task in the *System* itself, since in the Foreword to his *System*, Schelling claims only to be able to show that 'the same potencies of intuition which are in the I can also be indicated in nature *up to a certain limit*' (Schelling 1800 3:332; my ital.). This alludes to Schelling's further thesis that the progression of the I actually has a further, *fourth* 'epoch', corresponding to the step from I's self-intuition as a living organism to the self-determination of its activity through free *willing* and the '*cognition* of itself as intelligence' in *self-consciousness* (Schelling 1800 3:524–525; my ital.).

Now, if there could be no corresponding fourth 'potency' charted out within nature itself, this would imply that, though there are important parallels between the progression in the I and that in nature, these parallels ultimately run out. This in turn would show the I's potencies (and the mind more generally) to be ultimately of a different kind than nature per se, and Schelling's position would succumb to skepticism as much as Fichte's. Schelling, however, tries to avoid such bifurcation by arguing that we can observe, already in the early stages of nature's potencies, that these phenomena are *themselves* products of the activity of 'an immature [unreife] intelligence' which is merely 'conscious-less' (*bewußtlos*) (Schelling 1800 3:341). For example, a ray of light is described as 'the original seeing' (*das ursprüngliche Sehen*), as 'intuiting itself' (*das Anschauen selbst*) (Schelling 1800 3:430). In other words, recognizing the correlation in progressions is not merely meant to point up ultimately limited parallels but rather really to uncover a deeper identity.

In fact, when the fourth epoch of self-consciousness is finally achieved by the I, Schelling claims that precisely here 'it becomes evident that *nature* is *originally identical* with that which is cognized in us as something intelligent and conscious' (Schelling 1800 3:341), and that it is *nature itself* which thereby reveals itself to be 'an *absolute*, the absolute identity of the subjective and objective, and that which in its highest potency is nothing other than self-consciousness' (Schelling 1800 3:356). In this way, the fourth epoch of the I is at one and the same time *nature's* fourth potency as well; it is absolute reason coming (finally) to know itself.[12]

6. Hegel

Early on a colleague and collaborator of Schelling, Hegel continues to hold onto core features of both Schelling's philosophy of nature and philosophy of mind (or 'spirit', i.e., *Geist*) in his own mature 1817–1830 *Encyclopedia of Philosophical Sciences*. In particular, Hegel accepts Schelling's criticism of Fichte's merely 'subjective' articulation of the activity which gives rise to 'subject-object' relations, and takes over the general shape of Schelling's account of the parallel progression in 'objective' potencies responsible for the correlative relations found in nature itself.

What Hegel takes to follow from the demonstrability of this parallelism, however, is that there must be *more* than just an original identity-*point* which is neither subjective nor objective but which gives rise to both – the point that Schelling had called 'reason'. Rather, the parallel progressions themselves should be viewed as both dual manifestations of a single original identity-*progression* – the *whole sequence of* which is indifferent both to the I (spirit) and to nature, and only the whole sequence of which, Hegel thinks, should merit the name of absolute '*reason*'. Any philosophy of mind must therefore be preceded by a philosophical science of reason itself, one which provides the neutral account of what is common across the progressions in mind and those in nature – i.e., the series of 'determinations' of '*pure* reason', or what Hegel also calls '*thinking*' (*Denken*) and 'the *idea*' (both understood, *à la Schelling*, in a fairly revisionary, non-subjective sense). This, thinks Hegel, is the science of *logic*: 'what is logical' (*das Logische*), for Hegel, is the '*system* of thought-determinations in general, for which *the opposition between subjective and objective* (in its common meaning) *falls away*' (Hegel 1830a §24 8:81). This is equally 'the system of *pure reason*', whose pure 'content' Hegel strikingly identifies with '*the presentation of God as he is in his eternal essence before the creation of nature and a finite spirit* (Hegel 1816 5:44; my ital.). Logic must first present 'the foundation [Grundlage] and the inner simple scaffold [Gerüst]', or pure abstract structure, of the 'forms' and 'steps' (*Stufen*) of 'the idea' – which then will be shown to be 'concretized' in both Nature and Spirit (Hegel 1816 6:257).

Hegel also goes beyond Schelling, however, in holding that not just Logic, but also the Philosophy of *Nature* must come *before* the Philosophy of Spirit. As Hegel sees it, reason as a whole first 'resolves to *release* [entlassen] itself, freely from itself, as *nature*' *first of all*, because 'nature' is 'the moment of . . . its *first* determining and being-other [Anders-sein]' (Hegel 1830a §244, 8:393; my ital.). In this initial 'self-releasing', reason (the idea) becomes 'other' to itself, it '*posits* forth from itself [herauszusetzen] this other' as nature (Hegel 1830b §244 Z, 9:24; my ital.). Only subsequently (in the Philosophy of Spirit) does reason 'then *take it back* into itself [züruckzunehmen]', as ultimately not radically other than itself, since it has been seen (in the philosophy of nature) to be constituted concretely by the very same progression that is manifest in pure reason by itself, as considered in logic (ibid.). With such reconciliation, reason (the idea) finally '*comes to be* subjectivity and spirit' (ibid.; my ital.). For Hegel, then, mind can only be properly understood after and in light of nature (and logic); consequently, Hegel introduces a more explicit ordering than Schelling's: 'actual spirit . . . has external nature as its *most proximate* presupposition, as it has the logical idea as its *first*' (Hegel 1830c §381 Z, 10:18; my ital.).

Even so, the ultimate goal of passing through the Philosophy of Nature remains broadly Schellingian: to make it possible for us (as subjects) to understand how to 'overcome [aufheben] the *division* of nature and spirit, and grant to spirit the *cognition* of *its* essence *in* nature' (Hegel 1830b §247 Z; my ital.). Also like Schelling, Hegel thinks spirit is best led to see its own essence '*in* nature' by having the Philosophy of Nature lead up to an account of specifically '*organic*' or 'living' nature, thereby seeing spirit's prefigurings already in the movements and structures present in mechanics, dynamics, and chemical processes. Here Hegel includes under 'organism' not just animal as well as vegetative life, but going even farther than Kant in also including the *earth*, as the systematic 'totality of unliving, existing, mechanical and physical nature', under the heading of a '*geological* organism' (cf. Hegel 1830b §337). In the details, Hegel's account highlights the extent to which the dimensions of Fichtean originary activity (going forth, returning, and (aiming for) unifying) are continuously manifest throughout the 'natural' progression from earth, to plant, to animals, which thereby shows itself as a progression in '*being self-like*' (*Selbstischkeit*), and in this way sets the stage for the treatment of specifically mental self and its acts of consciousness and representation in the *Philosophy of Spirit*.

Not only does 'nature' thereby stand as a fundamental 'presupposition' for spirit itself (Hegel 1830c §38, 10:17), it also continues to be present 'in' spirit, which leads Hegel to cover a broad range of 'natural' (biological-developmental) phenomena within the first sections of the *Philosophy of Spirit* itself. In this way,

Hegel perhaps strikes the most directly 'Aristotelian' notes among the Idealists (cf. Hegel 1830c §378). These occur in what Hegel calls 'the *soul*' (*Seele*), and more specifically, in what Hegel calls the '*natural* [natürliche] soul'. The natural soul's activity is not much more than a 'simple pulsing' (Hegel 1830c §390 Z, 10:49; cf. Schelling's first 'epoch'), which merely 'lives a life of nature' (*Naturleben*), as something which essentially 'lives along with the universal planetary life, the difference in climates, the changes of seasons and times of day, and so on' (Hegel 1830c §392, 10:52). As with Schelling (and Fichte and Kant), Hegel takes this initial psychical activity to remain entirely 'without consciousness [bewußtlos] and without understanding [verstandlos]' (Hegel 1830c §400, 10:97), features which can only be achieved once the mental acts of 'reflection' and abstraction ('exclusion') are on the scene, and which lead to the achievement of 'the I' properly speaking (Hegel 1830c §412, 10:197).

Once we reach the stage of consciousness, Hegel's account mirrors Kant's own 'progression' within consciousness (cf. §2 above) in key ways (cf. Hegel 1830c §418, §420), moving from simple '*sensory* [sinnliche] consciousness', which has as its object something 'immediate' and 'individual'; to a '*perceiving* [wahrnehmende] consciousness' of the 'essence' of this initial object, by relating what is immediate and individual to something 'universal'; to finally an '*intellectual* [verständige] consciousness', which distinguishes between the immediate object of sensory consciousness and its universal features as 'appearance', and a further 'interior' to the object beyond its appearance, or a way of its being 'in itself' (Hegel 1830c §418 Z, 10:206–207; cf. §422).

As with Fichte, Hegel departs from Kant, however, in holding that it is only much later – after the development of both *self*-consciousness (cf. Hegel 1830c §423) and consciousness of the universal perspective given by *reason* (Hegel 1830c §437) – that enough has developed in the mental life of consciousness in order to introduce the signature theoretical-cognitive mental acts or processes that Kant had originally made the focus of the *Critique*: the specifically *subjective* acts of intuition, attention, imagination, thinking, judgment, and so on (cf. Hegel 1830c §445 Z, 10:245). In fact, it is also only here, well after the introduction of consciousness and self-consciousness, that Hegel himself finally thinks we can find '*representation*' (*Vorstellung*) itself, something which Hegel claims requires not just a mental relation to an object, but *also* 'that I make the reflection that it is I who have' this relation (Hegel 1830c §449 Z, 10:254).[13]

7. Conclusion

We have seen that Reinhold set the course for the later Idealists by insisting that Kant's analysis of *cognition* (cf. §2) must be preceded by an analysis of *representation* and the contents of *consciousness* (cf. §3). Fichte pushed further, insisting that this itself must be preceded by an account of the pre-representational, pre-conscious 'originary' *activity* required for representations and consciousness themselves to come about (cf. §4). Schelling then sought to further ground this originary activity in 'potencies' equally present in 'unconscious' nature (cf. §5). Finally, Hegel radicalized Schelling by first tracing out an even more originary 'logical' progression, of which the development of mind and of nature could both be viewed as manifestations, and then by deepening the account of how the mental (spirit) develops out of, presupposes, and is prefigured in the natural (cf. §6).

These developments in German Idealist philosophy of mind proved to make influential and lasting contributions to an intellectual context which also gave rise, first, to the empirical-experimental psychology of Fries, Herbart, Helmholtz, Mueller, and Brentano (with their varying agendas), and, eventually, led to both the scientific investigation of the unconscious (Freudian psychoanalysis) and the scientific analysis of consciousness itself (Husserlian phenomenology).[14] Tracing out these lines in Idealism therefore perhaps gives clues as to what prospects and problems might face contemporary attempts to unify and systematize logic and the philosophy of nature within a more holistic philosophy of mind. At the very least, it hopefully brings some additional light to the motivations, contents, and context of views developed in a series of notoriously difficult texts.[15]

Notes

1 For treatments of this period covering similar themes, see Förster (2012) and Gabriel (2013).
2 Kant presents this 'progression' (*Stufenleiter*; step-ladder) of our representations explicitly at several points in his writings and lectures (cf. B376f; 9:64–65), and it is also a main theme of the *Critique* itself, especially in the Transcendental Deduction as well as in the subsequent Principles, whose very titles indicate the crucial significance of the transitions from intuition, to perception, to experience (cf. B199f).
3 Cognition is more primitive since it need not involve any epistemic attitude toward the truth or falsity of the judgment in question, let alone require that the judgment in question be true (cf. B83).
4 Kant describes logic, for example – which he understands as the science of understanding, and hence a key component of the *Critique*'s Doctrine of Elements – as a science in which our understanding achieves 'self-cognition' (*Selbsterkenntniß*) (9:14).
5 For more discussion of Kant's philosophy of mind, see Ameriks (2000a); Brook (1994); Kitcher (1990 and 2011); and Longuenesse (1998). See also Brook's contribution to Volume Four of the present series.
6 The foundational role of consciousness is something Reinhold emphasizes even more directly in his next major work; cf. Reinhold (1791 77f). This is complicated, however, by Reinhold's (Kantian) insistence at times that representation itself somehow actually '*precedes* all consciousness', and that consciousness *itself* 'is only possible because of it' (Reinhold 1789 §XIII 223–224; my ital.) – which would seem to limit the explanatory usefulness (or non-circularity) of the appeal to consciousness.
7 For more on Reinhold's account of representationality, see Ameriks (2000b, Chapter 2) and Beiser (1987, Chapter 8).
8 In an even more Reinholdian vein, Fichte also sees this as true not only of the *originary* activity, but of *representational* activity in particular, which likewise only comes about through actualizing a specifically representational 'drive' (cf. Fichte 1794 I.294).
9 Elsewhere Fichte describes teleological-causal activity of this sort in terms of 'striving' and 'tendency' (cf. Fichte 1794 I.261). This would fit nicely with Fichte's related thesis that the genuinely 'absolute' *unifying* of positing and opposing in the I (and the

unifying of the I and the not-I) remains an essentially moral 'task' (*Aufgabe*) set for the I by itself, rather than a 'resolution' (*Lösung*) already present (Fichte 1794 1.105–106).
10 For further discussion of Fichte's account of the foundations of representation and consciousness, see Ameriks (2000b, Chapters 3–5); Breazeale (1995); Martin (1997); and Reid (2003).
11 Schelling even explicitly and approvingly cites Fichte in this regard (Schelling 1800 3:370).
12 For further discussion of Schelling's account of this progression, as well as other themes in his philosophy of mind, see Förster (2012); Nassar (2013); and Redding (1999).
13 For more on Hegel's philosophy of mind with special emphasis on his Aristotelian naturalism, see Ferrarin (2001); and Pinkard (2012). For alternative views on Hegel's Kantianism, see Pippin (1989) and Sedgwick (2012). For complementary treatments of Hegel's philosophy of mind, see also de Vries (1988); Findlay (1970); Gabriel (2013); and Malabou (2005).
14 For more on these, see the later contributions to this volume.
15 I would like to thank audiences at University of Chicago, McMaster University, McGill University, and Universität Bonn, as well as participants in my graduate seminar on German Idealism at UCSD, along with Lydia Patton and Sandra Lapointe, for very helpful discussion and feedback on previous versions of this material.

Bibliography

Primary literature

Fichte. 1794 *Grundlage der gesammten Wissenschaftslehre*. Reprinted in Fichte 1971.
Fichte. 1797. *Zweite Einleitung in die Wissenschaftslehre*. Reprinted in Fichte 1971.
Fichte. 1971. *Fichtes Werke*. I.H. Fichte, ed. de Gruyter. Berlin.
Hegel. 1970. *Werke in 20 Bände*. Frankfurt. Suhrkamp.
Hegel. 1807. *Phenomenologie des Geistes*. Reprinted in Hegel 1970.
Hegel. 1816. *Wissenschaft der Logik*. Reprinted in Hegel 1970.
Hegel. 1830a. *Enzyclopaedia der philosophischen Wissenschaften: Logik*. Reprinted in Hegel 1970.
Hegel. 1830b. *Enzyclopaedia der philosophischen Wissenschaften: Philosophie der Natur*. Reprinted in Hegel 1970.
Hegel. 1830c. *Enzyclopaedia der philosophischen Wissenschaften: Philosophie des Geistes*. Reprinted in Hegel 1970.
Kant. 1787. *Critique of Pure Reason*, 2nd (B) edition. Hartknoch. Riga, Estonia.
Kant. 1900. *Kants gesammelte Schriften*. 'Akademie Ausgabe'. Deutschen Akademie der Wissenschaften zu Berlin. Berlin. (volume #:page #).
Reinhold. 1789. *Versuch einer neuen Theorie des menschlichen Vorstellungsvermögens*. Mauke. Jena.
Reinhold. 1791. *Über das Fundament des philosophischen Wissens*. Johann Michael Mauke. Jene, Germany.
Schelling. 1800. *System des transscendentale Idealismus*. Reprinted in Schelling 1856.
Schelling. 1801. *Ferner Darstellung meines Systems*. Reprinted in Schelling 1856.
Schelling. 1856. *Sämmtliche Werke*. K.F.A. Schelling, ed. Gottascher Verlag. Stuttgart.

Secondary literature

Ameriks, Karl. 2000a. *Kant's Theory of Mind*, 2nd edition. Oxford. Oxford University Press.
Ameriks, Karl. 2000b. *Kant and the Fate of Autonomy*. Oxford. Oxford University Press.
Beiser, Frederick. 1987. *The Fate of Reason*. Cambridge, MA. Harvard University Press.
Breazeale, Daniel. 1982. 'Between Kant and Fichte: Karl Leonhard Reinhold's "Elementary Philosophy"', in *Review of Metaphysics*. Vol. 35, No. 4, pp. 785–821.
Breazeale, Daniel. 1995. 'Check or Checkmate? On the Finitude of the Fichtean Self', in *The Modem Subject: Conceptions of the Self in Classical German Philosophy*. Karl Ameriks and Dieter Sturma, eds. Albany, pp. 87–114.
Brook, Andrew. 1994. *Kant on the Mind*. Oxford. Oxford University Press.
de Vries, Willem. 1988. *Hegel's Theory of Mental Activity*. Ithaca. Cornell University Press.
Ferrarin, Alfredo. 2001. *Hegel and Aristotle*. Cambridge, MA. Cambridge University Press.
Findlay, J. N. 1970. *Hegel: A Re-Examination*. Oxford. Oxford University Press.
Förster, Eckart. 2012. *The Twenty Five Years of Philosophy*. Cambridge, MA. Harvard University Press.
Gabriel, Markus. 2013. *Transcendental Ontology*. London. Continuum.
Kitcher, Patricia. 1990. *Kant's Transcendental Psychology*. Oxford. Oxford University Press.
Kitcher, Patricia. 2011. *Kant's Thinker*. Oxford. Oxford.
Longuenesse, Béatrice. 1998. *Kant and the Capacity to Judge*. Princeton. Princeton University Press.
Malabou, Catherine. 2005. *The Future of Hegel*. London. Routledge.
Martin, Wayne. 1997. *Idealism and Objectivity*. Cambridge, MA. Cambridge University Press.
Nassar, Dalia. 2013. *The Romantic Absolute*. Chicago. Chicago University Press.
Pinkard, Terry. 2012. *Hegel's Naturalism*. Oxford. Oxford University Press.
Pippin, Robert. 1989. *Hegel's Idealism*. Cambridge, MA. Cambridge University Press.
Redding, Paul. 1999. *The Logic of Affect*. Ithaca. Cornell University Press.
Reid, James. 2003. 'On the Unity of Theoretical Subjectivity in Kant and Fichte', in *Review of Metaphysics*. Vol. 57, No. 2, pp. 243–277.
Sedgwick, Sally. 2012. *Hegel's Critique of Kant*. Oxford. Oxford University Press.

2

BOLZANO'S PHILOSOPHY OF MIND AND ACTION*

Sandra Lapointe

Since the 1980s, a number of publications have duly emphasised Bernard Bolzano's significance for analytical philosophy. The increasing attention paid to Bolzano's theories does not come one moment too soon. Bolzano's work is not only monumental; it is also formidably rich and original. Although Bolzano's historical impact on the development of the discipline was modest – a victim of political persecution, he lost his university appointment and was banned from publication – he anticipated in the early 1800s a remarkable number of the theoretical innovations that shaped the subsequent century, from Frege's distinction between *Sinn* and *Bedeutung* to the substitutional accounts of logical consequence and analyticity associated with Tarski and Quine.[1] As such he represents an important aspect of our post-Kantian philosophical heritage and one to which historians ought to do justice.

In spite of the overwhelmingly sympathetic consensus on the significance of Bolzano's contribution to theoretical philosophy, little attention has to this date been paid to his views on mind. Many have been quick to presume that Bolzano's foremost contributions – to mathematics and logic – are rooted in a form of antipsychologistic Platonism *à la Frege* that considers recourse to psychology to be irrelevant and/or pernicious. The prevailing view is that Bolzano contributed little of substance to the philosophy of mind and that most, if not all, of what he has contributed to the field can be found in his *Athanasia* (1827), a treatise on the metaphysics of the soul.[2] The prevailing view however is incorrect, and this for at least three reasons. First, Bolzano considered psychology to be philosophically relevant, arguing that significant aspects of logic in fact depend on it.[3] In particular, and this is the second point, Bolzano had substantive views on what is involved in representing, cognizing, feeling, desiring, willing and acting, and we find a number of proposals, both historically and philosophically interesting, throughout Bolzano's work, including in understudied yet copious passages of his *opus magnum*, the *Theory of Science* (1837). Finally, Bolzano's views on mind are part of a broader account of what it means for living beings to act, and the ideas Bolzano puts forward in *Athanasia* benefit from being considered in light of what he has to say about mental powers in other places. These considerations are indeed tightly linked to his metaphysics of substances and are further discussed in *On the Concept of an Organism* (see Bolzano 1851b) and, perhaps more interestingly, although admittedly succinctly, in the *Paradoxes of the Infinite* (Bolzano 1851a, §50ff).

There is some urgency in understanding Bolzano's views on mind. As Konzelmann-Ziv (2009, 2010) has convincingly argued, Bolzano's views on mind shape his views on rational knowledge as a whole and Bolzano's account of the way in which "mental powers" underpin rationality is consistent with contemporary – and plausible – understandings of the way in which rational knowledge is cognitively and pragmatically constrained. As a result, it would seem that the widespread assumption that Bolzano is committed to a form of ideal rationalism needs to be re-evaluated. We are still far from having gained a cohesive understanding of what would amount to a Bolzanian account of the nature and structure of consciousness, mind and action. Likewise, we have yet to understand where Bolzano's account fits within the broader 19th century – between say, Kant and Husserl. The present chapter is an attempt to go some way toward such an understanding.

The first part of the chapter offers a brief comparison of Bolzanian and Brentanian views on representation and judgement. A brief survey of Brentano's main positions is informative as a theoretical point of comparison for Bolzano's own views. At the very least, it is helpful to have the Brentanian theory in mind when gauging the impact – however humble – Bolzano effectively had on the theories of mind of some of Brentano's students.[4] The comparison however does not fully do justice to Bolzano's views. This is mainly because Bolzano's approach to the philosophy of mind and action has more to share with contemporary theorists' than with any of his predecessors or successors in the 19th century. This claim is likely to arouse perplexity. Bolzano puts forward his views on mind in *Athanasia* (1827), a treatise in which a hefty metaphysics of substance is put to work for the purpose of proving the immortality of the soul, a context which *prima facie* is unlikely to afford much relevance. Those who have discussed Bolzano's views on mind, with few exceptions, have however consistently missed what is most remarkably interesting about them. First, the framework within which Bolzano develops his metaphysics of mind and agency is not dualistic and presents some anticipation of what will later be known as "neutral monism".[5] Second, the conceptual resources that are deployed to make sense of the way in which "body" and "soul" interact in living beings presuppose an understanding of organisms that goes against – or far beyond – much of what Bolzano's contemporaries and successors in the the 19th century wrote on the topic, especially the Idealists. More importantly, Bolzano puts forward an account of rational agency based on a theory of mind that anticipates crucial aspects of contemporary discussions on the role of intentions as "reasons" or "causes" for action. In the second and more substantive part of the paper, I focus on Bolzano's views on the ontology of mind and rational agency.

1. Austrian views on representation and judgement

When it comes to 19th-century contributions to the philosophy of mind, there is little doubt that many influential theories, just like Bolzano who lived in Prague most of his life, came from Austria – or more precisely: the Austro-Hungarian Empire. Two are especially noteworthy and both have their origins in the seminal theories of Franz Brentano, who was appointed Professor in Vienna in 1874. First, we owe to Brentano, and various members of his school, the first fully fledged theories of intentionality. Second, Brentano and his students were among the first to attempt to draw, on the basis of what they conceived to be a putatively "empirical" method, a systematic inventory of the furniture of the mind, proposing classifications of and distinctions between types of mental acts that substantially contributed to psychological debates at the turn of the 19th century and beyond.

The methods and approach at play in Brentano's seminal *Psychology from an Empirical Standpoint* (1874) were arguably neither psychological in the sense in which we understand the term today, nor indeed genuinely empirical. They more accurately pertain to a variety of disciplines whose respective domains and methods remained insufficiently distinguished for most of the modern era and which include: psychology, philosophy of mind, epistemology and the theory of cognition. Part of what makes Brentano's theories unlike contemporary theories is that he relies on what he calls "inner perception", a capacity that is assumed to be distinct from "introspection", but the principles of which are in retrospect eminently unclear. Nonetheless, Brentano's investigation clearly targets the mind understood in terms of "consciousness" as its subject matter and it is one of the first modern psychological theories to do so. The Brentanian theory of mind is, in sum, a descriptive theory of the nature and structure of conscious mental acts or, as he terms it, "mental phenomena". Although the exclusion is not principled, it does exclude questions pertaining to the metaphysical origin of mental phenomena or the cognitive and physiological make-up that underlie their production.

Brentano's theory rests on a number of fundamental principles, three of which seem to be fundamental:[6]

(1) Every mental act has an object toward which it is directed.
(2) There are three classes of mental phenomena: presentations (*Vorstellungen*),[7] judgements, love/hate.
(3) Every mental act either is a presentation (*Vorstellung*) or is based on a presentation.

(1)-(3), together, were the point of departure – and a constant point of reference – for virtually all of Brentano's students.[8] (1), in particular, is the keystone of Brentano's theory of the mental. Put in contemporary terms, it amounts to saying that consciousness is always consciousness "of" or "about" something, i.e. that mental phenomena are distinctively "intentional" and should, as such, be understood to consist of "attitudes" directed toward a "content".[9] Few however, if any, of the Brentanians remained entirely faithful to (1)-(3) and all, in one way or another, sought to improve on various aspects of Brentano's theory. (1) itself was no exception. *In On the Content and Object of Presentation (Vorstellung)*, Kasimierz Twardowski – partly prompted by Alois Höfler and Alexius Meinong (1885) – argued that the Brentanian notion of an "immanent object" is ambiguous and devoted the book – the published version of his *Habilitationsschrift*, which he wrote under the supervision of one of Bolzano's rare pupils, Robert Zimmermann – to resolving the equivocation.[10] According to Twardowski, an adequate understanding of the structure of intentional acts requires that we make a distinction between the "content" (roughly that aspect of a mental act that "presents" the object) and the "object" (toward which the act is "directed"). What is interesting for our purpose is not so much the detail of Twardowski's views as the fact that he credited the distinction between content and object of mental acts to Bernard Bolzano.

That Bolzano's theories ultimately provide their basis to Twardwoski's seminal criticisms of Brentano's theory of intentionality is both ironic and somewhat perplexing. It is ironic to the extent that Brentano himself did not hold Bolzano's views in high esteem and even warned his students against him. And it is perplexing considering that, to be clear, Bolzano's theories do not include an account of intentionality. Bolzano did assume that at least some of our "representations" and "propositions in themselves" (*Vorstellungen, Sätze and sich*) "*have* an object" and, when they do, he calls them 'objectual'. But Bolzanian objectuality and Brentanian intentionality are meant to track different properties. Intentionality is a (presumably: qualitatively distinct) property of conscious mental acts and it is standardly understood to be relational. On Bolzano's account, however, objectuality is not a property of mental acts, e.g. of subjective representations or judgements *per se*. Objectuality is a property of the *objective* representations and propositions, i.e. the representations and propositions in themselves that forms the stuff (*Stoff*) of the latter. And by contrast to intentionality, "having an object" is also not a relational property, a point for which Bolzano explicitly argued. (See Bolzano 1837, §66.4, 299.)

Brentanian intentionality and Bolzanian objectuality also serve different theoretical purposes. In the *Theory of Science*, as we have just suggested, Bolzano distinguishes between:

(i) subjective representations and propositions (*subjektive Vorstellungen, Sätze*)
(ii) representations and propositions "in themselves" (*Vorstellungen, Sätze an sich*) that are the objective "stuff" (*Stoff*) or "content" (*Inhalt*) of (i); and
(iii) the object(s) (*Gegenstände*) that fall in the extension (*Umfang*) of (ii).

The distinction between (i)-(iii) however is not proposed in the context of a discussion of mind. It is first and foremost meant to provide a basis to an objectivist conception of truth in the context of a semantic theory: what we call 'true' are not subjective cognitive episodes, but rather the objective, abstract "content" of the latter – which Bolzano also characterises as the sense (*Sinn*) of the corresponding linguistic statements and equates with (ii). Strictly speaking, only objective representations and, by extension, objective propositions can be said to have an object. A subjective representation or judgement only has objects indirectly, by virtue of its "grasping" an objective representation – its content – that has the attribute of being "objectual" properly speaking.

Of course, in spite of the differences, Bolzanian objectuality (as a property of objective representations and propositions) and Brentanian intentionality (as a property of mental acts) cater to connected concerns. One of these concerns is to explain that we are able to form beliefs and make statements about things presumably "outside" our mind. In this respect, Brentano's claim that *every* presentation and therefore *all* mental phenomena have an object has significant consequences for his logic, that is, for his theory of judgement. If every Brentanian presentation (*Vorstellung*) has an object, then the presentation of a unicorn has an object, which seems to imply that there are unicorns. But Brentano does not want the judgement 'There are unicorns' to turn out as true on his account, and this requires him to refine his views on judgement and inference.[11] It is reasonable to think that similar problems would arise for Bolzano if he turned out to believe both that every objective representation is objectual and that every subjective mental state has an objective content: he would, like Brentano, be committed to an ontology of mind in which psychological attitudes are invariably representational. Bolzano however refuses both commitments.

According to Bolzano, there are "objectless" representations in themselves, and by extension, objectless propositions in themselves (cf. 1837, §66; §130). Whenever I think of a golden mountain, say, when I judge that golden mountains are made of gold, I have a *subjective* representation (*Vorstellung*) of a golden moutain which, while it has as a content, namely the *objective* representation of a golden mountain *in itself* which I happen to grasp through it, fails to be related to something beyond it since, as Bolzano argues, that objective representation is objectless.[12]

Interestingly, the possibility of "objectless" representations posed a crucial challenge to early phenomenologists and once it came to their attention, through Twardowski, Bolzano's claim that some representations lack an object was vehemently discussed by Brentanians. As we have seen, Brentano himself rejected the view (Brentano 1874, pp. 88–91). Those who, like Twardowski, followed Brentano in conceiving of the object of mental acts as essentially "immanent" to consciousness also rejected Bolzano's claim. Meinong, for instance, tried to save the Brentanian doctrine by introducing auxiliary types of "objects" for each type of mental phenomena[13] (cf. Meinong 1917, p. 103).

It is particularly noteworthy that Twardowski's *On the Content and Object of Presentation* and, in particular, the copious references he makes to Bolzano's theory of representation in themselves had a considerable impact on the thought of the younger Edmund Husserl. Husserl, upon reading Twardowski in 1894, was enthused enough to attempt to write a review of the book, which however remained unpublished. Independently, he also set out to discuss the "paradox of objectless representations".[14] Although Husserl did not devote much ink to the problem in the *Logical Investigation*, it played an important role in shaping his views in the crucial years leading toward their publication. As a result, Husserl's approach in 1900-01 is guided by a commitment to epistemological realism that contrasts with the immanentism of other Brentanians: Husserl ultimately proposed so to say a compromise between Brentano and Bolzano. We do not have the letter Husserl sent to Anton Marty (another student of Brentano's) on 7 July 1901, but we know from a draft that he sought to clarify a point he makes in the fifth *Logical Investigation*:

> A representation without a represented object cannot be thought, there are therefore no objectless (*gegenstandlosen*) representations. On the other hand, it is not the case that actual (*wirklich*) objects correspond to all representations; there are therefore objectless representations. The contradiction, it seems, can only be avoided if one distinguishes between the represented object and the actual object: There is no representations without an immanent object – there are representations without actual objects.
> (Husserl 1979, 419f – my translation)[15]

What the quote from Husserl's draft makes clear is that Bolzano's theory of objectless representations is not in principle inconsistent with the claim that intentionality is the mark of the mental: as Husserl puts it, it may be that all (subjective) representation have an "immanent object", while they fail to have an "actual" one. The claim here is incidentally restricted to representations, and this is significant because Husserl did not think that all mental states are intentional.

Incidentally, the latter is a point on which Bolzano would have agreed. In response to one of F. Exner's questions in the well-known correspondence, Bolzano considered whether, by analogy with objective representations and propositions, he thought that putatively "objective" feelings and wishes constitute the "stuff" of subjective feelings and wishes. Bolzano's position on this is negative and categorical:

> Only our *judgments* and *ideas* are the sort of appearances in the mind that are directed toward something that is not an appearance, and of which they can be considered the grasping. A *wish*, a *feeling*, an *act of will* represent nothing, are not graspings of something else.
> (Bolzano 1935, p. 166)

This passage reveals at least two important features that distinguish Bolzano's theory from orthodox Brentanian views. On the one hand, affective states (e.g. sensations and desires), on Bolzano's account, are not representational: contrary to what Brentano assumed, they are not "based on a representation". According to Bolzano, feelings and sensations are a kind of physical states and are individuated as such.[16] On the other hand, the passage above makes clear that Bolzano includes conative states – what he calls 'acts of will' – and indeed actions (*Handlungen*) among mental phenomena (*psychische Erscheinungen*). By the same token, Bolzano offers a classification of mental phenomena that differs in substantial ways from those put forward by Brentano and any of his students.

Brentano's tripartite classification of mental acts, to the extent that it is supposed to be exhaustive, is surprisingly parsimonious: Brentano separates judgments from mere presentations (*Vorstellungen*), but puts affective and conative states together, arguing for the unity of emotions and volitions, in one and the same class of "love and hate" (Brentano 1874, Chapter 8). This classificatory parsimony was questioned by those of Brentano's students who sought to refine Brentano's account of the mental landscape. Meinong, for one, found it essential to at least distinguish emotions from desires, thus dividing all mental or inner phenomena into four mutually exclusive categories: representations, thoughts, emotions and desires (Meinong 1910, pp. 366, 370, 382, Meinong 1921, pp. 14, 28ff.).[17] Husserl, in the *Logical Investigation*, had similar concerns (see, e.g. Husserl 1901, Investigation V §16).

At various places in his work[18] and in different theoretical contexts, Bolzano for his part consistently distinguishes at least six classes of "mental phenomena" (*psychische Erscheinungen*), i.e. appearances – or "events" – in the soul. According to Bolzano, mental phenomena include:

(1) (subjective) representations (*Vorstellungen*)
(2) judgements (*Urteile*)
(3) sensations (*Empfindungen*)
(4) wishes or desires (*Wunschen, Verlangen, Begehren*)
(5) willings or acts of volition (*Wollen, Willensentschließung*).
(6) actions (*Handlungen*)

Bolzano's classification is remarkable on many accounts. We can start by noting the following.

- First, on Bolzano's account, as we have seen, sensations (*Empfindungen*) are not a type of representing and, as such, they are not part of judgings either. As Bolzano puts it, sensations pertain only to the "state" (*Zustand*) of she who senses (*empfindet*) and come in two main kinds: pleasant and unpleasant. Although Bolzano was not first to make this distinction, he emphasises the fact that we can only judge *about* a sensation, and only once we have formed a representation of that sensation (cf. Bolzano 1837, §35, p. 163).
- Second, Bolzano's theory affords for a distinction between (i) mere wishes or desires, (ii) willings or acts of volition and (iii) fully fledged "actions" (*Handlungen*), i.e. actings (*Handeln*) or doings (*Tun*). (Bolzano 1837, §143, p. 68). This distinction which is absent from Brentanian theories is interesting and important. Although Bolzano himself does not discuss particular examples, the distinction provides Bolzano with the conceptual resources to account for

the fact that we can will and intend to act in ways that go against our desires, for instance when our quest for long-term happiness is incompatible with some immediate pursuit or inclination, like smoking a cigarette.

- Third, Bolzano sees actions (*Handlungen*) as types of mental phenomena whose interpretation requires the recognition of other agents' "intentions" (*Absichte*). What's more, he offers what may be the first account of such intentions formulated in terms of complex propositional attitudes that structure practical rationality (Bolzano 1837, §387). This is both historically significant and philosophically interesting, all the more so that on Bolzano's account linguistic understanding and communication are special cases of intentional action: they are interactive behaviours that (typically) involve the manipulation of auditory or symbolic artefacts and whose success ultimately rests on the agents' capacity to ascribe appropriate intentions to each other (Bolzano 1837, §388).

Each of these aspects of Bolzano's theory would deserve to be discussed in detail, something that cannot be undertaken in the context of the present study. In what follows, I focus on the third point: I explain how Bolzano's ontology on mind supports his account of action and rational agency.

2. Mind, body and action

On Bolzano's account, agents may have different kinds of mental phenomena – representations, judgements, sensations, willings etc. – and these, just like the agent that have them, are part of reality (*Wirklichkeit*). I say 'have' and not 'experience' or something of the sort because this is the most accurate way of describing the relation between the agent and her representations, judgments etc: she has them as a substance has its attribute. Let's see this in some detail.

As Bolzano sees it, mental phenomena is part of reality. Bolzano characterizes as *real* (*wirklich*) entities that may cause something, i.e. things that have effects. There are essentially two such kinds of entities. There are, on the one hand, those that are attributes (*Beschaffenheiten*) of some other real entity. Such entities may in turn, but need not, be themselves attributes. Bolzano conceives of attributes as individualised or particular properties comparable to the "accidents" of Aristotelian metaphysics. The real entities that are not attributes of anything else, those that do not exist "in" something else, but only in themselves. Bolzano calls – in agreement with traditional philosophical terminology – 'substances' (Bolzano 1827, p. 21, 283f; Bolzano 1834 I, p. 183; Bolzano 1837 §142, p. 65). On Bolzano's account, mental phenomena belong to the former category: they cannot exist "by themselves", they need something (or someone) *in* which they can exist. In traditional ontological terms this means that a mental phenomena on Bolzano's account are not substances, but "adherences" (*Adherenz*) – what contemporary theorists would call a "trope".[19]

Bolzano subscribes to the view that an attribute can have attributes, and, as a consequence, that what an adherence adheres to can itself be an adherence.

Ultimately, however, an attribute requires something that is not itself an attribute, but which exists in itself, i.e. a substance. On this account, if there is something real at all, there must also be at least one substance (Bolzano 1827, p. 22, 284). And since mental phenomena are, on Bolzano's account, adherences, there must be something to which they adhere and that is not ultimately itself a mere adherence. In Bolzano's ontology, the simple substance to which our mental phenomena adhere is our "self" (*unser Ich*) or our "mind" for which Bolzano uses different German words: '*Geist*' and '*Gemüt*' and which he in certain contexts agrees to use interchangeable with '*Seele*', i.e. 'soul'[20] (Bolzano 1827, p. 26, 284f.). To be precise, *in reference to humans*, Bolzano identifies both "my soul" (*meine Seele*) and "my self" (*mein Ich*) with "my mind" (*mein Geist*) (Bolzano 1827, p. 26). He does not, however, take the words "soul" and "mind" to be coextensive in all contexts, let alone synonymous. For Bolzano a soul – but not a mind – is always connected to a body (Bolzano 1827, p. 284), and all living beings, including animals but presumably excluding plants,[21] have a soul (Bolzano 1834 I, p. 221). Not all animals have a mind, however. By "mind", Bolzano means specifically something that has a certain degree of self-consciousness (Bolzano 1827, p. 284)

These metaphysical views Bolzano developed in *Athanasia* were ultimately meant to support Bolzano's claim that the soul is immortal.[22] Compared with earlier philosophical attempts, Bolzano's "proof" for the immortality of the soul contained several improvements. But what is relevant to our purpose here is another aspect of Bolzano's theory – a point emphasised by Konzelmann-Ziv (2009, p. 5; see also ibid., p. 10) – namely that Bolzano's account of soul in terms of substance (and his account of mental states in terms of adherences) is consistent with a form of substance monism that understands mental performances in terms of causal powers.

When it comes to understanding the relationship between mind and body, what Bolzano says in *Athanasia* benefits from being read in conjunction with what he has to say in *On the Concept of an Organism*, a later essay on which Bolzano worked in the last decade of his life, and posthumously published in 1851 by Franz Příhonský.[23] Part of what is at stake in *On the Concept of an Organism* is to provide an account of what we usually understand to be "living substances", i.e. organisms. Bolzano's views on organisms and ultimately on the soul are rooted in a theory that is both original and interesting, although they are admittedly also rooted in a conceptual framework that will seem somewhat esoteric to the contemporary reader.[24]

On Bolzano's views, the world is composed of substances, some of them simple and some of them complexe, all of them having attributes. The soul is a "simple substance". Just like all other simple substances, it is a real (*wirklich*) thing that has powers (*Kräfte*), where a power or capacity (*Vermögen*) is understood to consist in those attributes (*Beschaffenheiten*) (i) by virtue of which a given substance can bring about certain effects (*Wirkungen*) and which (ii) ultimately explain change.[25] That substances have powers is a fundamental truth – an axiom - of

Bolzano's ontology; it is by virtue of the powers it has that a substance can bring about the relevant kinds of changes in reality (*Wirklichkeit*):

> Whatever is actual (*wirklich*) must also act and, therefore, have powers to act. A finite substance [. . .] must have mere alteration powers (*Veränderungskräfte*) and the latter can incidentally be either immanent, like the power of sensation (*Kraft des Empfindens*), or transient, like the power of movement (*Bewegkraft*).
> (Bolzano 1851a §51).

According to Bolzano, *all* substances have the same "fundamental powers" (*Grundkräfte*) or capacities. What explains the diversity of substances is the fact that there are different combinations of substances, each having these fundamental powers to different degrees:

> There are metaphysical reasons why we are required to assume that two substances (indeed, things in general) cannot be fully identical to one another, but that the differences [. . .] there are can always in the end be attributed to merely finite scalar differences [*Graduntserschied*] (to a More or Less), so that in all these substances, essentially the same fundamental powers can be encountered, but developed to different degree.
> (Bolzano 1851b, §1)

Some of these capacities are "immanent" in the following sense: their *immediate* effects are to be found *in* the substance itself (Bolzano 1851b, §3). Those powers Bolzano calls "mental powers" (*psychische Kräfte*) or "powers of representation" (*Vorstellungskräfte*) broadly speaking this terminology may seem artificial, but let's bear with Bolzano for now. They include:

(1) The power of representing (Vorstellen)
(2) The power of sensing (Empfinden)
(3) The power of desiring (*Wünschen*) or detesting (*Verabscheuen*)
(4) The power of willing (*Wollen*)

Substances however also have the capacity to act on other substances and in general on things that are external to them. The powers by virtue of which a substance acts on other substances Bolzano calls "transient" powers. Transient capacities – there are three kinds on Bolzano's account : mechanical, chemical and organic – are what explains change *in the world* (i.e. outside the substance). Change is (merely) "dynamic" if it is the outcome of either mechanical or chemical forces. When change in a substance cannot *in principle* be explained mechanically or chemically, then it is said to be "organic".

Noteworthy is the fact that organic change only ever occurs in "complex substances", i.e. entities whose (numerically infinite) parts are ultimately themselves simple substances. If we follow Bolzano, the infinitely many simple substances that form a complex substance, say a plant or an animal, cluster together as a result of their exercising their (immanent and transient) powers in various degrees, at once multidirectionally and reciprocally, on each other – Bolzano, in this context, talks of "powers of attraction". Organic relations among its parts are what *explains* that a plant grows or that the animal moves (intentionally) and engages in various behaviours.

The soul is that aspect of a complex organism that explains, according to Bolzano, how it changes. Specifically, we are entitled to conclude that a complex substance has a soul – and therefore that is a living organism – whenever recourse to mechanical or chemical causes falls short of explaining how the substance changes, for instance how it can grow or reproduce or move. What makes growth and (voluntary) movement "organic" – and not merely mechanical or chemical – is precisely the fact that *explaining them* requires us to evoke (*the action of mental powers* belonging to) a "soul". On Bolzano's account, we ought to conclude that a complex substance has a soul whenever explaining that complex substance's behaviour requires us to evoke its "mental capacities", i.e. the immanent powers (see above) of the simple substance that makes out its soul:

> if the manner in which many bodies can by and by originate from one or other of these bodies, that is, how they reproduce, is incomprehensible on the basis of mere mechanical and chemical powers, we would call them plants. If, in addition, we perceive movements in them for the explanation of we must presuppose powers that act not merely externally, but rather inside a simple substance, i.e. mental powers, for instance the power of sensation, then we would call them living organisms or animals.
> (Bolzano 1851b, §17)[26]

In Bolzano's theory, a "soul" is a simple substance that "rules over" a given complex substance. What it means for a simple substance to "rule over" a complex substance – which may itself be composed of numerous other complex substances – can putatively be explained by the comparatively superior "strength" of its powers.

Bolzano's proposed account of organisms is a fertile ground for his philosophy of mind. For one thing, it commits him to a form of substance monism in the context of which the traditional mind-body problem is fundamentally reformulated. Recall that on Bolzano's account, all substances have the same (immanent and transient powers): what explains that individual substances differ, in addition to the fact that they occupy different spatial points, is the fact that their fundamental powers are not exercised to the same degree and that they thus exercise different combinations of forces on each other (cf. 1851b, §1).[27] As a result, what distinguishes the soul in animals and, in particular, what distinguishes the human soul from the human body is *not* the fact that the latter is "material" while the former isn't. As Bolzano puts it, attacking by the same token one of the tenets of post-Cartesian dualistic metaphysics:

> The first scholastic tenet we must abandon is the doctrine, invented by the Ancient physicists, of the dead or merely inert matter whose simple parts, if it has any, are all identical and eternally unalterable, and are supposed to have no powers except for the so-called power of intertia. Whatever is actual (*wirklich*) must certainly also act (*wirken*), and therefore have powers to act (*Kräfte zu wirken*).
>
> (1851a, §51)

Any question concerning the way in which the soul (the "ruling substance" in a complex substance) and the body (the rest of the complex substance) can interact causally in this context becomes a special case of the general question as to how any set of simple substances can interact causally and, in particular, cluster to form complex substances. The answer to this question, on Bolzano's account, requires nothing that is not already presupposed by Bolzano's metaphysics: an account of substance as having powers exercised multidirectionally and reciprocally, to various degree, which results in various forms of "attraction".

Bolzano's account of organisms as complex substances equipped with mental powers that explain their behavior "organically" is a remarkably propitious framework when it comes to explaining animal and human action. Bolzano's metaphysics of mind is rooted in the view that everything that exists in reality, including minds, is liable to causal explanation – although there is more to causality on his account than the product of mechanistic and chemical causes: there are "organic", i.e. mental causes as well. In particular, in order to explain all aspects of the changes that affect a living organism, one must in many cases also resort to its capacity to represent (*vorstellen*) (and judge), sense (*empfinden*), desire (*begehren*) and will (*wollen*), the latter being in turn understood to be causally potent capacities. Not all organisms exercise all their mental powers to the same degree and this, on Bolzano's account, broadly explains that different animals present different levels of mental organisation. But generally, in order to explain (causally) a given behaviour, one may appeal to what is in the mind: perceivings, believings, desirings and willings or, more generally, "intentions" (*Absichte*).[28] One interesting question as regards Bolzano's theory is thus ultimately the following: how do we come to recognize which mental states are likely to have "caused" particular actions, and more generally, what are the principles that underlie the interpretation of intentional action?

Before we set out to answer this question, let us stress the connection between Bolzano's views on action and practical rationality and the metaphysics that underwrites his account of living, soul-endowed organisms: both are grounded in the same account of agency and cashed out in mental terms. What ultimately explains the changes that agents and organisms, as organisms, bring about in the world, i.e. their actions, are ultimately the cognitive, affective and conative states in which they find themselves.

On Bolzano's account, an action (*Handlung*) is minimally something we bring about (*bewirken*) through our will or volition (*Wollen*):

> By an acting (*Handeln*) I mean the change that we cause by our volition, either in our own mind or in certain substances that are different from us, such as the organs of our body, and through them, in other surrounding objects.
>
> (Bolzano 1837 §143, p. 68)

The assumption that an action is a type of effect is what does the theoretical heavy-lifting when it comes to Bolzano's formulating the principles of a theory of mind. Bolzano does not claim to establish the principle of a theory of mind by virtue of some putative capacity to introspect.[29] "Mental powers" are what *cause* action and, as such, a theory of mind is precisely a theory of what causes intentional action. Bolzano's approach is rooted in substantial views about the kind of abductive reasoning involved, in general, when epistemic agents infer from effects to causes, the rules of which Bolzano presents over more than 20 pages in a section that almost immediately precedes the discussion of intentional action in the *Theory of Science* (1837).[30] Bolzano is also explicit about the connection.

As Bolzano conceived of it, intentional action is causally explained by what Bolzano calls "willing" or "volition".[31] Arguably – however this is not an argument I wish to make here - resorting to mental powers to explain change "causally" is somewhat problematic. Intentions and other types of mental acts - notoriously - are by contrast sometimes understood as "reasons" for action. Arguably, to be a reason to act and to be the cause of an action are two different things, and it's not clear that Bolzano has the conceptual resources to make sense of the distinction systematically. In what follows, I will use sometimes 'cause' and sometimes 'reason' when referring to Bolzano's "*Grund*", as seems appropriate in context.[32] The point to be emphasized here is that theories that resort to mental states and, in particular, to propositional attitudes to explain behaviour normally assume that, whether or not its explanation should resort to causes or reasons (or both), *behaviour is constrained by certain normative principles*, e.g. by some form of rationality. Behaviour can be explained, for instance, by the fact that it is "prudent" or "moral" for agents, given the beliefs and desire that they have, to intend a given action or refrain from acting in certain ways. Bolzano is also committed to some such view.

Key to Bolzano's account of rational agency is the fact that will is not isolated from cognitive and affective powers: the will does not cause the action directly, all by itself. What causes the action, as he puts it, is the fact that we have *an intention (Absicht) that determines (rationally) the will* or volition. As Bolzano puts it:

> But I understand by an intention which a being had in his action (by seiner Tätigkeit) [. . .] a (rightly or mistakenly) expected effect of his

action, which precisely determined the will of this being to this action, or (as one usually says) constitutes the motive (*Beweggrund*) of this action.

(1837, §386, p. 534)

Intentions, as Bolzano conceives of them, are a specific type of judgement or belief (*Urteile*); they are something we hold to be true. On Bolzano's view, agent a's intention when she performs action p is a twofold belief: it is the belief (i) that action p is a reliable way of bringing about the expected effect e and (ii) that e is something that she is "capable of willing". Given what Bolzano says about what agents are capable of willing, (ii) effectively narrows down the range of things that can ultimately explain why the agent acted, i.e. the cause/reason of the action. As Bolzano puts it, an agent is only ever capable of willing either that which is commanded to her by reason, i.e. an "ought" (*Sollen*),[33] or that which she knows would satisfy her particular desires (*Begierde*) or needs (*Bedürfnisse*) and would thus increase her happiness[34] (cf. Bolzano 1837, §386, p. 535). When it comes to explaining why an agent did p, I need to know e, i.e. what she expected to bring about through her action p, and e must also be something consistent with either duty or happiness.

If I want to know why, for instance, Marie gave money to charity, I need to find out – read: 'infer abductively to' – the expected effect she sought to bring about, and this, on Bolzano's model, will be a function of what she can will. This abductive task is relatively more manageable if I know that *as a rule* Marie is constrained normatively and can only will what she believes is her duty to do, or what she believes will make her happy. Bolzano's theory is, in this respect, consistent with many standard theories of practical rationality. If I have sufficient reason to think that Marie, in this case, sought to be good or virtuous and if, in addition, I know that Marie is a Utilitarian, then I can reasonably infer (abductively) that she expected her charitable act to be a reliable way to increase the sum total of happiness.

3. Conclusion

It is hard to overemphasize how remarkably ground-breaking and prophetic Bolzano's views on mind and action were. If Bolzano is right, the mind is not so much what produces consciousness – although it does – as what structures our behaviour in a way that makes sense to those who need to understand our intentions in order to come up with adequate responses. As such, it incorporates views on agency and communication that would not be articulated systematically until well into the twentieth century. What precedes, while it remains superficial, should make clear that more needs to be written on Bolzano, and that what remains to be written would benefit from getting off the beaten path. Bolzano's philosophy of mind deserves a thorough treatment – nothing short of a monograph – and such work, if it does justice to Bolzano's philosophical acumen, will not disappoint.

Notes

* Many thanks to Edgar Morscher who contributed much to this paper and without whose kind hospitality and generous enthusiasm it would have never been written in the first place. I'm also grateful to Mark Johnstone and Lydia Patton for their helpful comments.
1. See Lapointe 2014.
2. See, e.g. Chisholm 1991.
3. See Bolzano 1837, §13. The section is titled: "Whether logic is an independent science"
4. For a more detailed presentation of Brentano's views on mind, see Rollinger *infra*; see also Kriegel (forthcoming).
5. For a discussion of Mach's view on neutral monism, for instance, see Banks, *infra*.
6. Brentano himself devoted Chapters 5–9 of the second book of his *Psychology from an Empirical Standpoint* of 1874 to providing a disjunctive and exhaustive classification of all psychic phenomena that would at the same time be "materially adequate". He took this task to be absolutely crucial and indeed so important that he even planned to republish the five chapters in questions in the form of a self-standing book in 1911. For an excellent discussion of Brentano's theory, see Kriegel (forthcoming).
7. In what follows, I will follow standard translation uses and translation 'Vorstellung' by 'presentation' in reference to Brentano and his school, and 'representation' in reference to Bolzano. Although this is only part of the rationale, this terminological choice serves to emphasize Bolzano's close proximity to Kant and the German rationalist tradition.
8. One interesting exception is Sigmund Freud! See Bergo, *infra*.
9. Whether this content is propositional is a question I will leave open.
10. Twardowski 1894, 4.
11. See Betti 2013.
12. The thesis according to which there are empty or objectless representations played an important role in Bolzano's philosophy (cf. Bolzano 1837 §38, §67, §70, §170, §196), allowing him to argue among other things, against the "picture theory" of representations and to develop, accordingly, a theory of meaning and reference that would be appropriate, for instance, in mathematical contexts, where concepts cannot in any sense be understood to be pictures of the object – the numbers and operation – they represent.
13. Meinongian objects are notoriously problematic. At the very least, it is often difficult to see clearly which semantic role they are meant to fulfil. When it comes to identifying the objective correlate of judgements, for instance, Meinong introduces the notion of an "objective". But he also claim that they correspond to Bolzanian propositions in themselves, which is inconsistent since for Bolzano, objective propositions are not the object, but the content of judgements. Meinong's theory also assumes that emotions and desires have objects of their own, in the form of so-called *dignitatives* and *desideratives* (Meinong 1917, § 11, 102–118; Meinong 1921, 14, 20).
14. Transcriptions of both manuscripts are to be found in (Husserl 1979).
15. The glossary for the terms 'Vorstellung', 'gegenstandlos' and 'wirklich' is deliberately borrowed from Bolzanian literature. It is meant to emphasise the fact that Husserl is here using Bolzanian – as opposed to Brentanian – notions.
16. However, the position according to which desires (*Wunschen, Verlangen, Begehren*) are not representational raises a number of problems. One question, for instance, that needs to be answered is how one's desire for peace and one's desire for honesty differ if not by virtue of their representational content.

17 Within the category of thoughts, Meinong further drew sharp boundaries between judgements and assumptions (*Annahmen*). The latter notion is remarkably interesting. (See Mulligan 2015 and Textor 2015.) What is common to both judgement and assumption is the fact that they are capable of being true or false, the difference – and it is a crucial one – being that while judging that *p* requires one to accept *p* as true, merely assuming *p* does not. One may assume *p* while being convinced that not-*p*, as is the case when one conducts an indirect proof. See Textor 2015 for an excellent discussion of Meinong's views on assumptions. Meinong deals comprehensively with assumption and devotes to this class of psychic phenomena a hefty tome (Meinong 1910). Bolzano also discusses assumption, but he does not take assumptions to constitute a psychic category of its own. An assumption, on Bolzano's account, is a type of representation in which what is represented is a proposition (WL I, pp. 99, 155).

18 Bolzano 1827, pp. 25f., 32f., 36, 44; RW I, pp. 41ff., 191, 217f., 2030; WL II, pp. 67f.

19 Cf. Bolzano 1827, 26, 283. See Schnieder (2002).

20 In reference to humans, Bolzano identifies both "my soul" (*meine Seele*) and "my self" (*mein Ich*) with "my spirit" (*mein Geist*) (Bolzano 1827, p. 26). He does not however take the words 'soul' (*Seele*) and 'spirit' (Geist) to be coextensive. For him a soul – but not a spirit – is always connected to a body (Bolzano 1827, p. 284), and all living beings, including animals, have a soul (Bolzano 1834 I, p. 221). Not all living beings have a spirit, however. By 'spirit' we always mean something that has a certain degree of self-consciousness (Bolzano 1827, p. 284).

21 Whether plants are alive is something Bolzano does not affirm straightforwardly. He discusses the question in (Bolzano 1851b, §29).

22 Bolzano's argument has the following form (Cf. Bolzano 1827, 26–84; see also Bolzano 1834 I, pp. 215–227):

(1) The soul cannot be a mere adherence, but must be a single substance or a collection of substances.
(2) The soul cannot be a collection of substances, but must be a single substance which can be either simple or complex.
(3) The soul cannot be a complex substance. It must be simple.
(4) Since simple substances cannot come into being or cease to exist, therefore, the soul as a simple substance can never cease to exist and is therefore immortal.

23 There are other relevant remarks on the nature of substances and organisms in some passages from the better known *Paradoxes of the Infinite*, also published posthumously.

24 Bolzano's views are reminiscent of Leibniz's theory of "monads", but they also draw on other views. Here the "force-shells" of Boskovich and the young Kant have come to mind. See Konzelmann-Ziv (2010, 22) and Jan Berg (1976, 30). The Kant-Boskovich theory of force-shells is developed to offer a remarkably sophisticated and interesting account of matter and to solve classical problems raised by the mechanistic approach, in particular that of action at a distance. For a discussion of the Kant-Boskovich account of atoms, see Holden (2005, Chapter 6). Bolzano's views nonetheless are quite original. Whether Bolzano was influenced by Kant's early views or by those of Boskovich is a question I leave open.

25 Cf. Bolzano (1837, §270, note 2). See Konzelmann-Ziv (2010, p. 23)

26 On Bolzano's account, the changes that occur in plants and animals cannot all be explained physically or chemically. The difference between them is that the kind of external (or "transient") change we find in animals can only be explained by resorting to the idea that they are equipped with "powers of representation" (*Vorstellungskraft*). Whether this is supposed to mean that plants are not "living" organisms is unclear. He discusses the question in Bolzano (1851b, §29).

27 In this passage, Bolzano does not tell us what explains that some substances manifest a fuller range of these powers than others, but this is a question his theory needs to answer.
28 Of course, not all behaviours in an organism amount to intentional action. In the case of involuntary behaviours, an explanation cannot appeal to intentions – although the principles involved may not be reduced to mechanical or chemical causes either and are still deemed "organic" on Bolzano's account. See Bolzano (1851b, §21).
29 Bolzano does think that we can form representations of at least some of our mental states, but this does not seem to be something Bolzano considers helpful when it comes to formulating an account of what is in our mind.
30 See Bolzano (1837, §379). Equally interesting is the fact that Bolzano also thinks that the principles that underlie the interpretation of intentional action would provide their basis to an account of linguistic understanding (Ibid., §387) and communication (Ibid., §388). Unfortunately, those are two aspects of Bolzano's theory that cannot be discussed in detail here. Gieske (1997) offers some insight into the latter.
31 That willing is causally effective follows from the fact that willing is a mental *power*. Powers, by definition, are causally effective.
32 It is consistent with Bolzano's views on causality and grounding (*Abfolge*) that if p causes q, then the fact that p also grounds the fact that q and p is thus the "reason why" q is the case. But more needs to be said about what is involved in the notion of a reason for action to see if this observation can be put to work in the context of Bolzano's views on mind.
33 Whether these "oughts" are always identified with moral duties is a question I will leave open.
34 Bolzano identifies pleasure and happiness. For a discussion of Bolzano's utilitarianism, see Rosenkoetter (2012).

Bibliography

Berg, Jan (1976) "Bolzanos Metaphysik" in *Ost-West-Begenung in Österreich: Festschrift fürt Eduard Winter zum 80. Geburtstag*, Wien/Köln/Graz, Böhlau, 27–33.

Betti, Arianna (2013) "We Owe It to Sigwart! A New Look at the Content/Object Distinction in Early Phenomenological Theories of Judgment from Brentano to Twardowski" in *Judgement and Truth in Early Analytic Philosophy and Phenomenology*, Mark Textor (ed.), Houndmills, Palgrave Macmillan, 74–96.

Bolzano, Bernard (1827) *Dr. B. Bolzanos Athanasia oder Gründe für die Unsterblichkeit der Seele*, Sulzbach, Seidel (Second Edition, 1838).

Bolzano, Bernard (1834) *Lehrbuch der Religionswissenschaft*, Sulzbach, Seidel. (4 volumes).

Bolzano, Bernard (1837) *Wissenschaftslehre*, Sulzbach, Seidel. (4 volumes) [*Theory of Science*, trans. by Paul Rusnock and Rolf George, Oxford, Oxford University Press, 2014].

Bolzano, Bernard (1851a) *Paradoxien des Unendlichen*, Leipzig, Reclam.

Bolzano, Bernard (1851b) *Über en Begriff des Organismus nebst einigen damit verwandten Begriffen* in Bernard Bolzano Gesamtaugabe, Series II A, vol. 12.3, Stuttgart, Fromann Holzboog, 83–104.

Bolzano, Bernard (1935) *Der Briefwechsel B. Bolzanos mit F. Exner*, Eduard Winter (ed.), Prag, Königliche böhmische Gesellschaft der Wissenschaften [English translation of selections in *On the Mathematical Method and Correspondence with Exner*, trans. by Paul Rusnock and Rolf George, Amsterdam/New York, Rodopi, 2004, 83–174].

Brentano, Franz (1874) *Psychology from an Empirical Standpoint*, 2nd edition, 1995, London, Routledge.
Chisholm, Roderick (1991) "Bolzano's Philosophy of Mind" *Philosophical Topics* 19/2, 205–214.
Gieske, Carsten Uwe (1997) "Bolzano's Notion of Testifying" Bolzano and Analytic Philosophy, *Grazer Philosophische Studien* 53, 249–266.
Höfler, Alois and Alexius Meinong (1885) *Über philosophische Wissenschaft und ihre Propädeutik*, Vienna, Alfred Hölder.
Holden, Thomas (2005) *The Architecture of Matter*, Oxford, Oxford University Press.
Husserl, Edmund (1979) *Aufsätze und Rezensionen 1890–1910*, The Hague, Martinus Nijhoff.Konzelmann-Ziv, Anita (2009) "Naturalized Rationality: A Glance at Bolzano's Philosophy of Mind" in *Baltic International Yearbook for Logic, Cognition and Communication* vol. 4. (http://newprairiepress.org/biyclc/vol4/iss1/15/).
Konzelmann-Ziv, Anita (2010) *Kräfte, Wahrscheinlichkeit Und "Zuversicht": Bernard Bolzanos Erkenntnislehre*, Sankt Augustin, Academia Press.
Krause, Andrej (2004) *Bolzanos Metaphysik*, Freiburg/München, Karl Alber.
Kriegel, Uriah (forthcoming) "Brentano's Concept of Mind" in *Innovations in the History of Analytical Philosophy*, Sandra Lapointe and Chris Pincock (eds.), Houndmills, Palgrave Macmillan.
Künne, Wolfgang (1998) "Substanzen und Adhärenzen: Zur Ontologie in Bolzanos Athanasia" *Logical Analysis and History of Philosophy* I, Paderborn, Mentis, 233–250.
Lapointe, Sandra (2011) *Bolzano's Theoretical Philosophy: An Introduction*, Houndmills, Palgrave Macmillan.
Lapointe, Sandra (2014) "Bolzano and the Analytical Tradition" *Philosophy Compass* 9/2, 96–111.
Meinong, Alexius (1910) *Über Annahmen*, 2nd edition, Leipzig, Barth [*On Assumptions* trans. James Heanue, Berkeley, 1983].
Meinong, Alexius (1917) *On emotional Presentation*, trans. by Marie-Luise Schubert Kalsi, Evanston, Northwestern University Press, 1972.
Meinong, Alexius (1921) "A. Meinong" in *Die deutsche Philosophie der Gegenwart in Selbstdarstellungen*, Raymund Schmidt (ed.), Vol. I, Leipzig, Meiner.Schnieder, Benjamin (2002) *Substanz und Adhärenz: Bolzanos Ontologie des Wirklichen*, Sankt Augustin, Academia Press.
Mulligan, Kevin (2015) "Annehmen, Phantasieren und Entertaining: Husserl und Meinong" in *Themes from Ontology, Mind, and Logic*, Sandra Lapointe (ed.) *Grazer Philosophische Studien* 91, 245–283.
Rosenkoetter, Timothy (2012) "Kant and Bolzano on the Singularity of Intuitions" *Grazer Philosophische Studien* 85, 89–129.
Textor, Mark (2015) "Meaning, Entertaining, and Phantasy Judgement" in *Themes from Ontology, Mind, and Logic, Grazer Philosophische Studien* 91, 285–302.
Twardowski, Kazimierz (1894) *Zur Lehre vom Inhalt und Gegenstand der Vorstellungen. Eine psychologische Untersuchung*, Vienna, Alfred Hölder.

3

JOHANN FRIEDRICH HERBART ON MIND[*]

Christoph Landerer and Wolfgang Huemer

1. The Kantian challenge and the scientific context in Europe in the early 19th century

"He aims at being a Napoleon of the intellectual world":[1] this is how William James described Wilhelm Wundt, who is widely considered to be the founding father of scientific psychology. Wundt's main achievement was the systematic introduction of experiments and laboratory work to the study of the mind. Eight decades earlier, Johann Friedrich Herbart took an even bolder step, arguably aspiring to become the "Newton of the intellect" – something Kant had thought impossible.

To fully appreciate what Herbart achieved for the study of the mind, we need to understand some of the central changes that took place in the wider framework of European science in the so-called "*Sattelzeit*" (saddle period) around 1800. According to Kant, there is a deep and unsurmountable gap between the study of natural and that of mental phenomena.[2] The study of the mind, he suggested, could only be properly called a science if it managed to apply quantitative methods to its subject matter[3] and base itself on the collection of empirical data. Unlike natural phenomena, however, mental phenomena have no spatial dimension, which, in the Kantian perspective, renders a "mathematization" of psychology impossible.

A second problem stems, according to Kant, from the very source of our knowledge about those phenomena. To effectively study the workings of the mind, the agents conducting the study would need to observe its own mental products, and she would need to do so in a "disinterested" manner. It seemed obvious to Kant, however, that this condition could not be met, as both the mental phenomena observed and our knowledge about them are subject to restrictions that lie in the very nature of mental phenomena. In consequence, Kant assumed it would be impossible to achieve for the study of mind what Newton had achieved for the study of phenomena in the natural world, that is, for phenomena that have spatial dimensions and are independent of the observer.

Kant's outlook, however, not only on psychology, but on the sciences in general – and in particular the conditions he set for the possibility of scientific knowledge – were soon to be disputed. Already in the early 1800s – when Herbart started his academic career – the European sciences were about to change dramatically and several of Kant's "Ignorabimus"[4] statements were challenged. These include his claims about biology: In a famous passage of the *Critique of Judgement* Kant suggested that the origins of organic life were beyond the limits of knowledge; the world will never, as he put it, see a "Newton of the grass blade".[5] In 1809, when Herbart became Kant's successor in Königsberg, Jean-Baptiste Lamarck formulated his theory about a "transmutation" of species,[6] which paved the way for theories of evolution that were taken to show that the Kantian approach to limits of scientific knowledge was too narrow. Ernst Haeckel, ironically citing Kant's above-quoted dictum, declared Darwin to be the "Newton of the grass blade".

In the decades around the turn of the century (roughly 1775–1825), a completely new approach to the empirical study of natural phenomena was developed, most notably in the disciplines that we now consider natural sciences. In the eyes of baroque (and still late eighteenth century) science, history could only play a marginal role in our understanding of how natural phenomena are organized. "Natural history", despite the name of the discipline, was not conceived as a study of how species developed over time, but rather as the mere collection of existing species as natural phenomena. Instead of taking a dynamic, historical approach, empirical data were organized only by way of *classification*.[7] According to philosophers of that period, such as Kant and Tetens, the realm of mental phenomena was organized in a similar way. Before Herbart, and in Kant in particular, the mind was usually considered to be a composite of more or less distinct "faculties" (module-like classes of psychic functions) that were to be classified and built into an explanatory model of behaviour. "Faculties" were seen as static and stable, but not much thought was spent on trying to figure out how the mental phenomena were organized, nor on how the structural architecture of "faculties" could be governed by more basic mental units. In *Beyond Good and Evil*, Nietzsche ridiculed what was now considered to be an empty concept of times past:

> There came a time when people scratched their heads: some still scratch them today. There had been dreamers: first and foremost – the old Kant. 'By virtue of a faculty' – he had said, or at least meant. But is that really – an answer? An explanation? Or instead just a repetition of the question? So how does opium cause sleep? 'By virtue of a faculty', namely the *virtus dormitiva* – replies the doctor in Molière.
>
> (Nietzsche 2002: 13)

2. Faculties, presentations and the soul

Herbart criticized the dominant faculty psychology for various reasons. For one, he rejected its methodology by pointing out that the conception of "faculties" as basic psychological concepts has no sound empirical basis. In biology, the notion of classes and species can be abstracted from observable properties of real plants and animals. The mind, on the other hand, does not provide us with basic observable elements and therefore does not provide a basis for systematic abstraction. Moreover, self-observation is prone to many sources of error[8] and its results cannot be trusted to the same degree as the results of the natural sciences can. Herbart's criticism is not primarily directed against the traditional higher-order concepts (emotion, volition, intellect) themselves, but rather at the idea that they are putative "faculties", and have an explanatory role to play when it comes to knowledge. According to him, these and other assumptions cause the study of the mind to degenerate into a "mythology".[9] Here, Herbart proposes an argument that could be regarded as "Ordinary Language Philosophy" *avant la lettre*. Faculty psychology tempts us to conceive of basic psychological concepts as agentive powers which, in some (mysterious) way, drive the actions of an individual. But in reality they merely serve to classify phenomena in a certain way. For Herbart, the traditional conception of faculties "personifies" ("personificirt") such classificatory concepts.[10] The result of this conception is a hypostatization that goes far beyond classification. As Horst Thomé put it: "The 'personified psychological faculties' bring about psychic phenomena in the same way the homeric gods bring about natural events: Sensuality receives impressions, they get stored by memory, and rearranged by imagination".[11]

Herbartian terminology is based on the common-sense notions of psychology. According to him, it is not so much the (mental) concepts themselves that are wrong and misleading as the conception of relations they entertain. Philosophy in general, Herbart claims, can be seen as a special procedure that aims at an "elaboration of concepts" (*Bearbeitung der Begriffe*). Though his solution to the problem of psychological terms was very different from, say, Ryle's, he is in a way sympathetic to the view "that the logical categories in terms of which the concepts of mental powers and operations have been co-ordinated have been wrongly selected" (Ryle 1949: 8). *Elaboration of concepts*, thus, does not aim at constructing an ideal language for our treatment of psychological concepts, but rather accepts existing concepts and tries to clarify them.[12]

Whereas traditional faculty psychology postulates a multitude of module-like capacities with rather unclear relations to one another and is based on dubious principles of classification, Herbart's approach is radically reductionist. According to him, all psychic life is composed of "presentations" (*Vorstellungen*, more on that term later). Even higher order mental concepts are nothing but combinations of presentations. This starting point guarantees the study of the mind a special sphere of theorizing that is detached from biological considerations. Though not fully *cognitivistic* in today's sense of the word, Herbart's theory is in line with later cognitive approaches in that its focus lies entirely on internal processes and an internal mechanism that explains how the mind functions. Herbart can thus rightly be considered the "great-grandfather of contemporary information-processing approaches to the mind" (Leary 1990: 17). In the context of 19th-century psychology, Herbart's insistence on a special sphere of psychological theorizing was as untimely as it is meritorious from the point of view of 20th-century cognitive psychology. After Herbart's death, the neo-Kantian movement has moved beyond Herbart by setting the agenda for a new and exciting way of understanding the mind in terms of its biological organization. With physiology's increasing leadership more and more in the field of the life sciences (including psychology), neo-Kantians such as Helmholtz adopted the old Kantian scepticism about psychology as science and took refuge in what was seen as a "physiology of the mind".[13] Their views of psychology as science were radically different from the study of presentations and their combination that Herbart had in mind, though.

In one central point, however, Herbart's concept was hopelessly dated, compared to the ideas of the neo-Kantians. Whereas neo-Kantian scholars such as Lange advocated a "psychology without soul", Herbart remained a stubborn defendant of a rather traditional concept of the "soul". While some aspects of Herbart's views about the mind were ahead of their time and astonishingly progressive, particularly with regard to late twentieth-century cognitive approaches, his views about a timeless and immortal "soul" manifest his deep indebtedness to traditional eighteenth-century philosophy. Herbart considered the soul a necessary point of reference for all presentations. According to him, presentations were the means of "self-preservation" ("Selbsterhaltung") of a timeless and undividable soul which he conceived as simple substance ("einfache Substanz").

3. Herbart's theory of presentations

The fact that according to Herbart presentations persist even after death gives an idea about the uniqueness of this basic concept of Herbart's psychology. The very term "Vorstellung" is difficult to translate – let alone clear. In our view, translating it with "presentation" (rather than as "representation", "ideation", "idea", or "concept"),[14] best captures the core meaning of the concept. For Herbart, everything *present* in the mind, from basic sensation to abstract concepts, counts as a "Vorstellung". With a key concept so encompassing, it is easy to see why Herbart could get along without higher-order concepts or even any form of inbuilt structures or an implicit architecture of mind.

Herbart's strategy to base his entire theory on the key concept of presentation made it possible to demonstrate how the study of mind can be undertaken along the lines of the study of natural phenomena, i.e., *more mechanico*. Contra Kant, Herbart suggested that presentations have such properties as duration, intensity, and quality that can be made the subject of equations and allow us to apply mathematical methods, at least insofar as their relations to each other is concerned. The study of presentations can thus be seen as a formal-structural endeavour that can employ the same mathematical methods as physics. Key to mathematization is the *relational* nature of presentations. Hence, the study of mind focuses on relational properties: "relation is the object towards which the psychological investigation is to be directed."[15]

Though Herbart's ideas played a central role in what later became psychophysics (most notably in the work of Gustav Fechner), his own mathematical approach remained purely abstract and without any quantitative-empirical component. Nowadays it strikes us as a curious mix of exact method and armchair speculation, of 18th-century metaphysics and 19th-century science. Herbart's approach, however, is unique in that it did not regard quantification (at the basis of psychophysiological measurements, for example) a goal of his theory. Mathematical formula were not meant to lead to actual measurements, they rather serve to demonstrate the "universal laws of psychological phenomena".[16] According to Herbart, there are limits to quantification and measurement as presentations have a non-empirical dimension that only pertain to "abstract forces". As inhabitants of the timeless and unempirical soul, presentations lose their empirical qualities after the individual's death but continue to be effective as force, thus maintaining the existence of the soul.

Of course, the central and most interesting aspect of the theory concerns the actual psychic existence of the individual. How can a mere combination of presentations explain the rich mental life of the agent? Herbart's answer shows his indebtedness to the cognitive models of classical physics. Presentations are either compatible with each other, as is the case with tone and colour, or in opposition to each other, like, for example, sweet and sour. In the latter case, they cannot be present in consciousness at the same time. The number of presentations that can co-occur is limited in principle due to the narrowness of the mind; this creates conflict that turns presentations into forces. Everything that happens in the soul can thus be understood as a constant struggle for the limited space the mind has to offer. Presentations that lose this battle do not get destroyed but "repressed" (*verdrängt*) under the "threshold of consciousness".[17]

Presentations vary in magnitude. If a presentation is inhibiting, it combines with other conflicting presentations, which constitute what Herbart calls an "inhibition sum" (*Hemmungssumme*). This inhibition sum, a core concept of Herbartian psychology, is "the result of all the striving of opposing presentations against each other" (Herbart 1993: 312). In the process of striving against each other, some presentations are driven out of consciousness, which reduces the overall conflicting power and diminishes the inhibition sum. According to Herbart, this process can be expressed in the following formula: $t = \log \frac{S}{S-\sigma}$ with S being the inhibition sum and σ its already sunken part which can be determined as $\sigma = S(1-e^{-t})$. Herbart considers these equations as proof that as far as presentations that are present in consciousness are concerned, inhibition never comes to an end but rather leads to a state of "floating" (*Schweben*).

Herbart's understanding of presentations as forces, the movements of which explain everything that happens in the mind, is central to his mathematical approach and the way he understands it to relate to science (especially the kind of science that Newton had established in physics). He thought that a scientific psychology ought to be based on infinitesimal calculus (in the tradition of Newton and Leibniz), and considered the latter to be the key to our understanding of the mind. Evoking Newton, he described presentations as relating to each other like stars in the sky.[18] At the same time, however, Herbart was reluctant to accept experimental data as the basis of quantification and even rejected psychological experimentation on moral grounds.[19] Instead, he relied on the traditional concept of an undividable soul, a feature of his theory that stresses his indebtness to the more traditional metaphysical approaches of Kant and even Wolff. It is only later in the development of psychology that experimentation and quantification, combined with mathematical methods, developed into a core element of the psychological study of mind. In Herbart's time, the striving for exactness, based on Leibniz' mathematics and Newton's mechanics, was the prevailing paradigm and the most accepted model of scientific rationality. These standards only changed in the course of the 19th century, when biology (based on physiology) replaced physics as the general model for research in the field of psychology.[20]

4. Herbartians and Herbartianism: the reception of Herbart's thought

Herbart formed a powerful school that exerted its influence in a number of disciplines, with pedagogy, psychology, and aesthetics being the most prominent.

After Herbart's death in 1841, Herbartianism proved especially attractive to empiricist philosophers interested in the developing sciences. What caught the attention of young philosophers in post-Hegelian Germany was not his attempt to save metaphysics but, rather, his emphasis on both the formal aspects of science and the empirical roots of knowledge. Herbartianism became a major source of philosophical influence for academics opposed to Hegel and German idealism, and Herbartian psychology came to play a major role in academic debates. Herbart's theory was still perceived as one of the most promising approaches in the early 1850s, i.e. although it seems that, by that time, Herbart's thoughts were seen as directed not primarily against Hegel, but against another anti-Hegelian philosopher – Arthur Schopenhauer.[21] With further developments in science and the introduction of experimental methods in psychology, however, Herbart's decision to apply mathematics in a rather speculative way was soon viewed with scepticism. Friedrich Albert Lange, though acknowledging Herbart's openness for science and mathematics, wrote a fierce attack on Herbartian psychology, arguing that it was a fundamental logical error to combine mathematics and speculation which, in his view, has no place in empirical knowledge. By the time of Lange's death in 1875, his criticism of Herbart was already widely accepted in German psychology.

A rather orthodox version of Herbartian psychology in Germany, however, survived these attacks for another couple of decades. In Austria, after the revolution of 1848, Herbartian psychology continued to be taught in high schools until the late 19th century (and in some cases, even up to the 1920s). Psychology was part of a newly created subject called "philosophical propaedeutic". This introductory course in philosophy was less extensive than its title might suggest for it comprised only empirical psychology and formal logic. Philosophical propaedeutic has a rather peculiar history – it was introduced in Austria as a compulsory subject only one year after a similar subject had disappeared from the Prussian curriculum (in 1849). Before 1848, the year of the revolution, philosophy in Austria was taught in a rather traditional and uninspired way. At the university level, it was kept to a minimum; in high schools it was not taught at all. But the events of 1848 showed that even a marginalization of philosophical thought was no guarantee that it would not spread. Herbartianism, on the other hand, with its political abstinence and its focus on the formal and empirical aspects of knowledge (both thought to be rather apolitical), seemed an ideal antidote to Kant, who continued to be seen as the "philosopher of the revolution", and any philosophy that could lead to political unrest. It is interesting to note that the combination of a logical and an empirical perspective, with an almost total exclusion of metaphysics (which was not even part of the curriculum), was still present in the philosophical programme of the Vienna Circle in the 1930s.

Once a core area of philosophical investigation – and even at the centre of Herbart's own writings – metaphysics lost its prominence in the works of Herbart's followers, especially in Austria, where Herbartians were appointed at the universities, while Hegelians like Hanusch and Smetana were removed from their academic positions.[22] Academic discourse, however, relied on Herbart's aesthetics more than on his psychology; Herbartian aesthetics is even seen as an "Austrian route to modernism".[23] The effects of Herbartian aesthetics were still present in the Vienna school of art history as well as in early Austrian musicology,[24] and even in Austrian economics the work of Herbart had a considerable impact.[25]

In the 1870s and 1880s, however, Herbartianism gradually lost influence and eventually gave way to the new school of Franz Brentano. But still in 1883, when Charles University in Prague was divided between Germans and Czechs, Bohemian Herbartianism was strong enough to dominate in what now became the Czech Department of Philosophy while the German Department was taken over by the school of Brentano. Most of the young Brentanists had links to Herbartianism, if only through Robert Zimmermann, the most powerful member of the Herbartian movement in Austria. Zimmermann's own "Philosophical Propaedeutic", a textbook widely used in high schools all over the Austro-Hungarian Empire, influenced more than a generation of the pre-academic elite in the Hapsburg empire. Kasimir Twardowski, for one, still referred to Zimmermann's textbook, which he had studied in high school, in his influential Habilitation-thesis (Twardowski 1894/1977).

When it comes to the influence of Herbart's philosophy of mind, we should look at the reception of Herbart's ideas outside of the Herbart school, after Herbart's death. In the following, we illustrate how core ideas of Herbart's conception of the mind were integrated, sometimes clandestinely, into philosophical theories that moved far beyond the original framework of Herbartian thought.

5. Conscious and unconscious presentations: Herbart's impact on early scientific psychology and psychoanalysis

Herbart's eminently traditional metaphysical views were, already in his lifetime, considered outdated. By contrast, Herbart's views on the working of the mind, most notably some of the details of his mechanistic approach, remained highly influential well beyond his death,. This is particularly true of Herbart's concept of a "threshold of consciousness" – which became a key concept in later psychophysics (though with an adapted terminology) and in early psychoanalysis.[26] In Herbart, we find the first systematic approach to the theory of the unconscious that attempts to explain, not only how unconscious content can persist over time, but also how to provide an elaborate mechanistic perspective on the laws that govern both the realm of the conscious and that of the unconscious.

According to Herbart, only occurrent mental states are legitimate sources for psychology. They form the basis for all scientific psychology: "The facts of consciousness are without doubt the starting point of all psychological reflections".[27] He uses the term "consciousness" to describe the totality of all presentations occurring in the mind at a given time; a point, in which Herbart's indebtedness to British Empiricism and Locke's idea of a "narrowness of the human mind" becomes apparent.[28] Herbart agrees with Locke that, due to the "narrowness of the human mind", consciousness can only accommodate a relatively small number of presentations at any given time. The ones that are not present in the conscious mind inhabit the realm of the unconscious – either entirely or to a certain degree, depending on the number of their unconscious, "dark", components.[29]

Herbart's terminology for describing the interrelatedness of conscious and unconscious mental phenomena had a strong impact on German academic philosophy and the emerging discipline of psychology. It is no accident that we find the notions of "threshold", "inhibition", and "repression" in Gustav Theodor Fechner's work; unlike Herbart, however, Fechner was an outspoken advocate of experiment. Even more obvious – and highly influential – is Sigmund Freud's adaption of Herbart's idea of a "threshold of consciousness". Contrary to what is often assumed, Freud's theory of "repression" (the idea that psychic content may be "repressed"), however, is not the starting point, but rather the result of continued psychological theorizing that originated with Herbart's *Psychologie als Wissenschaft* (*Psychology as Science*). Although Freud did not explicitly acknowledge a direct influence of Herbart, he was exposed to elements of Herbart's thought – most importantly through Gustav Adolf Lindner's *Lehrbuch der empirischen Psychologie* (*Textbook of Empirical Psychology*),[30] which was used in Freud's high school. There he found not only the notion of "repression" that became so central to his psychoanalysis, but the mechanistic theory of mind in which Herbart's idea of repression was embedded. Freud's own rather mechanistic approach bears astonishing parallels to that of Herbart. What might be even more surprising is that Freud also seems to have borrowed parts of Lindner's – rather exotic – vocabulary. Lindner, who still follows the Herbartian idea of presentations as the basic elements of mind, sees "repression" as the "fate of presentations" (*Vorstellungsschicksal*), whereas Freud conceives repression as the "fate of drives" (*Triebschicksal*). This shift in the focus of analysis – from Herbart's rational-cognitivistic presentations to Freud's highly non-rational, non-cognitivistic drives – illustrates well the main differences between Herbart's and Freud's psychological conceptions. While Herbart was exclusively concerned with the mechanics of a rational mind, it was Freud's aim to find the mechanistic laws that govern the psychological activity behind the facade of reason. In both, however, the general outlook and the basic vocabulary are astonishingly similar.

6. Presentations, sensations, and the I: the case of Ernst Mach

Presentations make up the whole variety of psychic life. They also build the basis for traditional higher-order concepts. Herbart's own – often lengthy – discussions of how the traditional objects of faculty psychology can be understood in terms of presentations and their combinations in *Psychology as Science* did not influence academic psychology to any great extent. Other Herbartian ideas, however, continued to be powerful, and often exerted their influence in disguise. In a somewhat strange but highly influential passage in his *Analysis of Sensations*, for example, Ernst Mach describes how the death of the individual does not essentially change anything to the content of the "I".[31] According to Mach, the "I" is a useful fiction, a product of a principle of economy of thought. All we can find is a relatively stable bundle of sensations which, in the moment we refer to as death, lose some of their connections to the other ones, but just like Herbartian presentations, continue to exist. The "I", Mach concludes in a famous quote, in "unsavable";[32] its unity is an illusion.

Mach's ideas about the "I" were in fact inspired by Herbart. Mach however, following contemporary trends, and focusing his attention on physiology and science, does not talk about purely mental *presentations*. Instead, he focuses on *sensations* ("elements"). The historical connection between Mach's and Herbart's ideas about the "I" is documented in Mach's notebook entries, where he cites Herbart's views on the "I" as "presentations that are more strongly connected with each other".[33] In *Analysis of Sensations*, Mach talks about a "more strongly cohering group of elements" (Mach 1914: 28), or about "a viscous mass, at certain places (as in the ego) more firmly coherent than in others" (Mach 1914: 17). That Mach should have been influenced by Herbart and, in particular, by Herbart's idea that the "I" is no more than a loose connexion of presentations is unsurprising. Though critical of other aspects of Herbartian philosophy and psychology, Mach was impressed by Herbart's mathematical-mechanical approach.[34] In one of the later prefaces of *Analysis of Sensations*, Mach admitted that at the time, when he developed the ideas of the book, his philosophical knowledge was restricted to Kant and Herbart.[35]

Mach's reception of Herbart's ideas, and the way in which these ideas fit into the Machian theoretical frameworks, demonstrates a typical feature of the Herbartian legacy. As part of a philosophical-psychological system, Herbart's ideas about the mind were only of limited importance and impact. Herbart's views, rather, were used as templates and tools, and they only gained significance because his core ideas were assimilated and built into the theories of others. Freud reinterpreted Herbart's idea of "repression" in a way that freed it from its strong rationalist and purely mechanistic bias. Herbart, who tended to speak about the specific strength of presentations, did not postulate an inner "censorship". The idea, however, became central in Freud. Mach, on the other hand, reinterpreted Herbart in a manner that mitigated Herbart's purely cognitivist approach to presentations and linked it, instead, with sensual input. Both "reformulations" show the potential of Herbart's views about the mind – a potential that Herbart himself did not fully develop.

7. Intentionality and the emotions

"'Willing' is not 'desiring', striving, longing for: it is distinguished from these by the affect of commanding. There is no such thing as willing but only a willing something".[36] Nietzsche's remark in one of his late unpublished notes is obviously directed against Schopenhauer's concept of willing as a simple and unanalysable psychological concept. The reasons for Nietzsche's turn against Schopenhauer are manifold. Some of his late remarks, however, rest on a Herbartian argument. Indeed, central aspects of Herbart's psychology became widespread after Herbart's death, and his ideas on the mind were integrated into philosophical frameworks that reached far beyond the Herbartian school. Nietzsche's growing awareness of the complexities of actual willing and the complex interplay of factors in psychological functions that Schopenhauer believed to be basic, simple, and self-explanatory, was inspired by his reading of Johann Baumann, whose theory of willing builds upon Herbart's psychology – although Baumann's version improved on Herbart's views to reflect contemporary physiological findings. Baumann conceives willing as a complex interplay of physiological and cognitive factors that only appears simple because its psychological analysis is too complicated for the individual. The cognitive-physiological theory of willing Baumann sketched led him to the conclusion "that Schopenhauer's conception of the will has to be rejected in its entirety".[37]

Baumann's theory also shows the development of early ideas about intentionality, and the way Herbart's cursory remarks on intentionality were built into philosophical views of the mind. In Baumann (1879), Nietzsche underlined a sentence on p. 1, "The will has to will something, it must have an object that is willed". This view however rests on what Herbart called the "Methode der Beziehungen". The method pertains to Herbart's "elaboration of concepts": philosophical concepts, including concepts we use to explain functions of the mind, require a certain form of critique that aims at uncovering their mutual relations.

In addition, these concepts must be "complemented" in such a way that hidden relations become clear.[38] Particularly relevant to the study of the mind is the way psychic functions interrelate with each other and the way they can be related to (intentional) objects. Baumann's theory of the will reflects what Herbart wrote about "Begehren" (desire): "Desire has an apparent relation to presentation for it has an object to which, as its goal, it is directed".[39] It is not by chance that Baumann's and Herbart's observation bear analogies to Franz Brentano's concept of intentionality: In his *Psychology from an Empirical Standpoint*, Brentano refers to a similar passage from *Pychologie als Wissenschaft*.[40] Herbart's method did not only have an impact on theories of the will, though.

Herbart can also be considered as a forerunner as regards cognitive theories of emotions.[41] On Herbart's view, emotions have to be described exclusively in terms of presentations, though presentations that usually have more "dark" (unconscious) components. As a result, the defining features of emotions are their cognitive and intentional dimensions. Herbart's opposition to Schopenhauer, at the end of his life, led him to develop an account of emotions that focused on cognitive components, and that was further elaborated – and is still discussed today – in the field of aesthetics. The theory that is nowadays widely known as the "cognitive theory of emotions" in the aesthetics of music builds upon arguments that originated in a Herbartian context. Peter Kivy describes the theory as follows:

> For a garden-variety emotion, let us say fear, to be aroused, the following must happen: The person feeling fear must, in the standard case, have some belief, or set of beliefs, appropriate of the experience of that emotion: must, in other words, have a belief or set of beliefs that can reasonably be thought to cause fear in the person. . . . The fear must have an object: that is to say, the person must be afraid *of* something or other. . . . And there usually is also, although not necessarily, a particular feeling, the feeling of fear in one of its many forms – that the fearful person is experiencing."
>
> (Kivy 2002: 25f)

Because the theory is a "cognitive theory", the relation of a certain emotion to an intentional object, embedded in a (belief or) set of beliefs is essential for the theory, and reflects Herbart's "method of relations" –psychic states relate to objects to which they are directed. The cognitive theory of emotions entered the sphere of music aesthetics via Eduard Hanslick's treatise *On the Musically Beautiful* (1854/1986), though Hanslick's analysis did not gain currency until more than 100 years after it was first proposed (see Kivy 2002: 25). Hanslick's theoretic approach is assuredly modern, anticipating arguments that became part of cognitive psychology in the 1950s. But Hanslick's treatise is also known for its strong Herbartian undercurrent.[42] Obviously directed against Schopenhauer's theory of feelings "in abstracto", Hanslick describes feelings/emotions[43] as dependent upon their cognitive and intentional content:

> The feeling of hope cannot be separated from the representation of a future happy state which we compare with the present; melancholy compares past happiness with the present. These are entirely specific representations or concepts. Without them, without this cognitive apparatus, we cannot call the actual feeling 'hope' or 'melancholy', it produces them for this purpose. If we take this away, all that remains is an unspecific stirring, perhaps the awareness of a general state of well-being or distress.
> (Hanslick 1986: 9)

Hanslick's argument is based on Herbart's theory of representations as the sole base of all mental phenomena – a theory that is sharply opposed to Schopenhauerian views of emotion as class of psychic states of its own as well as traditional approaches of feeling as a "faculty".[44] In Herbartian terms, emotions are "nothing beside and apart from representations . . . but varying states of those representations in which they are based."[45]

Hanslick's use of Herbart's argument led to the conclusion that the traditional view of music as the "language of feelings" was no longer tenable. Though Hanslick's treatise, the "inaugural text in the founding of musical formalism as a position in the philosophy of art" (Kivy 2009: 53), is mostly known for its aesthetic theories, it is again Herbart's views of the mind that form the basis for one of Hanslick's most central arguments.[46]

In sum, Herbart's conception of the mind had a strong influence on the philosophical and psychological debate in the 19th and 20th centuries. While in the early days this can be traced to the ascent of the Herbartian school, his views have later on penetrated traditions that were not directly linked to those of his more orthodox followers. Some of his insights are still discussed today, though often in disguise: Herbart is hardly accredited explicitly and his ideas are embedded in theoretical frameworks very diverse and different from his own.

Notes

* We would like to thank Sandra Lapointe for helpful suggestions on an earlier version of the paper.
1 Cited in Boring (1950: 346).
2 Throughout this article, we will use the term "phenomena" in a broad sense in order to cover a variety of meaning in 19th-century philosophy.
3 Cf. Kant (2004: 6): "I assert, however, that in every special doctrine of science there can be only as much *proper* science as there is mathematics therein."
4 In his 1872 lecture *Über die Grenzen unseres Naturerkennens*, the German physicist Emil du Bois-Reymond launched a debate on the limits of knowledge. He postulated several "Ignoramus and Ignorabimus" (things we do not know and will never know).
5 Kant 2009: 228.

6 Cf. (Lamarck 1809).
7 Cf. (Lepenies 1986).
8 "Self-observation mutilates the facts of consciousness even in the act of seizing them; it wrests them from their natural combinations and delivers them over to a restless process of abstraction which finds a point of response only when it has reached the ultimate species – namely conception, feeling, and desire. Under these large classes, by definitions, (a method precisely opposite to that of empirical science), it subsumes the mental facts observed so far as it can be done" (Herbart 1891: 3).
9 Ibid.
10 Herbart uses the expression "*personificirte[s] Seelenvermögen*" in the first edition of his *Lehrbuch der Psychologie* in a passage that is omitted in the second edition (1834) and re-introduced in a footnote to the third edition (Herbart, 1850: 9). Smith's English translation (Herbart 1891) is based on the second German edition.
11 Thomé 2001: 70.
12 In a somewhat peculiar way, Herbart's "elaboration of concepts" resembles the later Wittgenstein's approach to philosophy. According to a famous phrase from Wittgenstein's *Philosophical Investigations*, philosophy "leaves everything as it is" (§ 124), that is, "apart from the adjustment of disorder in the concepts by rearranging them" ("*abgesehen von der Behebung von Unordnung in den Begriffen durch Ordnen derselben*" (Lange 1998: 125). Both Herbart and Wittgenstein focus on a clarification of existing concepts without aiming at creating an "ideal language". For Herbart, creating such an "ideal language" is entirely outside the scope of his "realistic" approach to philosophy: "We are completely locked inside our concepts; and it is precisely for that reason that concepts decide about the real nature of things" (Herbart 1993: 232). As Barry Smith has remarked, there are "no investigations on the possibility of an influence upon Wittgenstein of Herbart's thought" despite Herbart being an "*Urgroßvater*" (Smith 1978: 31f.) (great-grandfather) of Wittgenstein as well as greater parts of Austrian philosophy. Curiously, this situation did not change to this day.
13 "Physiologie des Geistes", Kaiser-El-Safti in her foreword to Herbart (2003: XX).
14 In Herbart (1891), Margaret K. Smith translates "Vorstellung" with "concept" or "conception".
15 "Die Relation ist gerade der Gegenstand, worauf die psychologische Untersuchung zu richten ist" (Herbart 1993: 312).
16 Herbart 1993: 310.
17 This aspect of Herbart's theory influenced Freud. See Bergo, *infra*.
18 Cf. (Herbart 1891: 15): "The conformity to law in the human mind resembles exactly that in the firmament [*Sternenhimmel*]".
19 Cf. (Herbart 1891: 4): "Psychology must not experiment with men, and there is no apparatus for this purpose" [translation slightly altered].
20 From a different perspective and with the eyes of later 19th-century psychology, Brentano gave a very critical account of Herbart's peculiar mixture of traditional metaphysics and modern methodology: "Herbartian psychology contains . . . a lot of which experience shows us nothing: like the soul, for example. However, also according to him, we can only infer to it. It is supposed to be a completely simple essence that does not cause or suffer anything. It is, of course, completely incomprehensible how one could infer to it, if it does not cause anything" (Brentano 1977: 56).
21 According to Klaus Christian Köhnke, Schopenhauer and Herbart were seen as opposing philosophical alternatives in the debates around 1850 (after Herbart's death). Cf. Köhnke (1986: 109–121).
22 The missing success of German Idealism in Austrian universities is, at least in part, due to the strong influence of the Roman Catholic Church as well as the absolutist politics and a *system* of censorship for which "all progressive philosophising was suspect of

revolutionism" (Haller 1991: 48). William Johnston notes that in Austria the authorities were convinced "that Hegel was dangerous to the Catholic faith . . . Compared to such incitements, the humanism of Herbart seemed safe indeed. It reinvigorated the apolitical, nonsectarian classicism of the late Goethe while inculcating a Biedermeier spirit of resignation" (Johnston 1972: 286). Cf. also Haller (1979).

23 Cf. Jäger (1982).
24 For Herbartianism and the Vienna school of art history cf. Schlosser (1934). Eduard Hanslick's links to Herbartianism were intensely discussed around the turn of the century and in later scholarship from the 1990s onwards, cf. Khittl (1992).
25 Cf. Johnston (1972: 86f.)
26 Bergo (infra) also discusses Herbart's influence on Freud.
27 Herbart 1968: 15.
28 Wolfgang Prinz notes that it was Herbart who had introduced this notion of Locke's into German discourse (cf. Prinz 1983: 66).
29 The doctrine of "dark presentations" ("dunkle Vorstellungen") is typical of 18th- and early 19th-century psychology. Contrary to fully conscious presentations, "dark presentations" have a varying degree of unconscious components.
30 As Wilhelm Hemecker has shown, Freud used the edition of 1872; cf. Hemecker (1993).
31 "The primary fact is not the ego but the elements (sensations) . . . . The elements constitute the I. . . . *I* have the sensation green, signifies that the element green occurs in a given complex of other elements (sensations, memories). When *I* cease to have the sensation green, when *I* die, then the elements no longer occur in the ordinary, familiar association. That is all. Only an ideal mental-economical unity, not a real unity, has ceased to exist. The ego is not a definite, unalterable, sharply bounded unity. None of these attributes are important; for all vary even within the sphere of individual life. . . . *Continuity* alone is important. . . . But continuity is only a means of preparing and conserving what is contained in the ego. This content, and not the ego, is the principal thing. This content, however, is not confined to the individual. With the exception of some insignificant and valueless personal memories, it remains preserved in others, even after the death of the individual. The elements that make up the consciousness of a given individual are firmly connected with one another, but with those of another individual, they are only feebly connected, and the connexion is only casually apparent. Contents of consciousness, however, that are of universal significance, break through these limits of the individual, and, attached of course to individuals again, can enjoy a continued existence of an impersonal, superpersonal kind, independently of the personality by means of which they were developed" (Mach 1914: 23f).
32 "Das Ich ist unrettbar". The famous phrase is translated "The ego must be given up" in the Williams translation (Mach 1914: 24).
33 Notebook entry of February 17, 1877. Cf. (Haller and Stadler 1988: 171).
34 Cf. Swoboda (1988).
35 "At that time I was only acquainted with Kant and Herbart" (Mach 1914: XIII).
36 Nietzsche 1980: 54 (11[14], November 1887 – March 1888. The passage is related to what Nietzsche describes as one of the "fundamental truths about human will" in the *Genealogy of Morals*: "*it must have a goal* – and it would even will nothingness rather than *not* will at all" (Nietzsche 1996: 77).
37 Baumann (1879: 16). Baumann's attack is underlined in Nietzsche's copy of the book, as is a longer passage that explains Baumann's theoretical background and closes with the following remark: "As far as I know, it was Herbart who formulated the first thought on that now prevailing view" (Baumann 1879: 6).
38 Cf. (Herbart 1808: 14f.): "In this unity, that is in the forms of the given, as they are initially thought by concepts, there must be contradictions: speculation will get hold of

these contradictions; and resolve them; by complementing the forms, i.e., by adding to formal concepts that are given in experience those concepts, to which they necessarily refer."
39 Herbart 1968: 33 (I § 12).
40 The passage quoted reads: "Thus Herbart asserts quite rightly 'Every time we have a feeling, there will be something or other presented in consciousness, even though it may be something very diversified, confused and varied, so that this particular presentation is included in this particular feeling. Likewise, whenever we desire something . . . we have before our minds that which we desire'" (Brentano 1995: 80f [*omission in the original*]). For a more detailed discussion on Herbart and Brentano, cf. (Huemer and Landerer 2010).
41 For Herbart and modern theories of emotions, see Kaiser-El-Safti foreword to Herbart (2003: LXIff).
42 Hanslick even declared himself a Herbartian in his habilitation theses of 1858. Unfortunately, almost no attention has been given to the Herbartian roots of Hanslick's theory of emotion.
43 The German term "Gefühl" that Hanslick uses can be (and has been) translated as either "feeling" or "emotion". Today, "emotions" are generally more seen as cognition-laden, making "emotion" an apt translation. The Payzant translation (i.e. Hanslick 1986), however, decided to use the term "feeling" and translates "Vorstellung" as "representation".
44 Kivy describes the argument as "remarkable both for its cogency and for its foresight" (Kivy 2002: 25)
45 "Gefühle und Begierden sind nichts neben und außer den Vorstellungen . . . sondern sie sind veränderliche Zustände derjenigen Vorstellungen, in denen sie ihren Sitz haben" (Herbart 1993: 317).
46 For Hanslick's indebtness to Herbart's theory of emotions, see also Landerer (2010).

Bibliography

Baumann, Johann Julius. 1879. *Handbuch der Moral*. Leipzig: Verlag von S. Hirzel.

Boring, Edwin. 1950. *A History of Experimental Psychology*. New York: Appleton-Century-Crofts.

Brentano, Franz. 1995. *Psychology from an Empirical Standpoint*, ed. by Oskar Kraus, trans. by Antos C. Rancurello, D.B. Terrell and Linda L. McAlister, intro. by Peter Simons. London: Routledge.

Brentano, Franz. 1977. *Grundzüge der Ästhetik*, ed. by F. Mayer-Hillebrand. Hamburg: Meiner.

Haller, Rudolf. 1991. "On the Historiography of Austrian Philosophy", in T. E. Uebel (ed.) *Rediscovering the Forgotten Vienna Circle*. Dordrecht: Kluwer, pp. 41–50.

Haller, Rudolf. 1979. "Österreichische Philosophie", in *Studien zur Österreichischen Philosophie*. Amsterdam: Rodopi, pp. 5–22.

Haller, Rudolf and Friedrich Stadler. 1988. *Ernst Mach – Werk und Wirkung*. Vienna: Hölder Pichler Tempsky.

Hanslick, Eduard. 1986. *On the Musically Beautiful*, trans. by Geoffrey Payzant. Indianapolis: Hackett.

Hemecker, Wilhelm. 1993. *Vor Freud. Philosophiegeschichtliche Voraussetzungen der Psychoanalyse*. Vienna/Munich: Philosophia.

Herbart, Johann Friedrich. 1808. *Hauptpuncte der Metaphysik*. Göttingen: Justus Friedrich Dankwert.

Herbart, Johann Friedrich. 1850. *Lehrbuch zur Psychologie*. 3rd edition, ed. by G. Hartenstein. Leipzig: Verlag von Leopold Voss.

Herbart, Johann Friedrich. 1891. *A Text-book in Psychology*, trans. by Margaret K. Smith. New York: Appleton.

Herbart, Johann Friedrich. 1968. *Psychologie als Wissenschaft*. Amsterdam: E. J. Bonset.

Herbart, Johann Friedrich. 1993. *Lehrbuch zur Einleitung in die Philosophie*. Hamburg: Meiner.

Herbart, Johann Friedrich. 2003. *Lehrbuch zur Psychologie*, ed. by Margaret Kaiser-El-Safti. Würzburg: Königshausen und Neumann.

Huemer, Wolfgang and Christoph Landerer. (2010). "Mathematics, Experience and Laboratories: Herbart's and Brentano's Role in the Rise of Scientific Psychology", *History of the Human Sciences* 23 (3): 72–94.

Jäger, Georg (1982). "Die Herbartianische Ästhetik. Ein österreichischer Weg in die Moderne", in Herbert Zeman (ed.) *Die österreichische Literatur: Ihr Profil im 19. Jahrhundert (1830–1880)*. Graz: Akademische Druck- und Verlagsanstalt, pp. 195–219.

Johnston, William. 1972. *The Austrian Mind: An Intellectual and Social History*. Berkeley: University of California Press.

Kant, Immanuel. 2004. *Metaphysical Foundations of Natural Science*, trans. and ed. by Michael Friedmann. Cambridge: Cambridge University Press.

Kant, Immanuel. 2009. *Critique of Pure Judgement*, trans. by James C. Meredith, revised edition and intro. by Nicholas Walker. Oxford: Oxford University Press.

Khittl, Christoph. 1992. "Eduard Hanslicks Verhältnis zur Ästhetik", in: Friedrich C. Heller (ed.) *Biographische Beiträge zum Musikleben Wiens im 19. und frühen 20: Jahrhundert*. Vienna: Verband der wissenschaftlichen Gesellschaften Österreichs, pp. 81–109.

Kivy, Peter. 2002. *Introduction to a Philosophy of Music*. Oxford: Clarendon Press.

Kivy, Peter. 2009. *Antithetical Arts: On the Ancient Quarrel between Literature and Music*. Oxford: Oxford University Press.

Köhnke, Klaus Christian. 1986. *Entstehung und Aufstieg des Neukantianismus*. Frankfurt am Main: Suhrkamp.

Lamarck, Jean-Baptiste. 1809. *Philosophie zoologique, ou, Exposition des considérations relative à l'histoire naturelle des animaux*. Paris: Dentu.

Landerer, Christoph. 2010. "Eduard Hanslick und die österreichische Geistesgeschichte", in Theophil Antonicek, Gernot Gruber, and Christoph Landerer (eds.) *Eduard Hanslick zum Gedenken: Bericht des Symposions zum Anlass seines 100. Todestages*. Tutzing: Hans Schneider, pp. 55–64.

Lange, Ernst Michael. 1998. *Philosophische Untersuchungen – eine kommentierende Einführung*. Paderborn: Schöningh.

Leary, David E. 1990. *Metaphors in the History of Psychology*. Cambridge: Cambridge University Press.

Lepenies, Wolf. 1986. *Das Ende der Naturgeschichte*. Frankfurt am Main: Suhrkamp.

Lindner, Adolf. 1872. *Lehrbuch der empirischen Psychologie als inductiver Wissenschaft*. Wien: Verlag Carl Gerold's Sohn.

Mach, Ernst. 1914. *The Analysis of Sensations and the Relation of the Physical to the Psychical*, trans. C. M. Williams. Chicago/London: Open Court.

Nietzsche, Friedrich. 1980. *Kritische Studienausgabe*, vol. 13, ed. by Giorgio Colli, Mazzino Montinari. Berlin/New York: Deutscher Taschenbuch Verlag/de Gruyter.

Nietzsche, Friedrich. 1996. *On the Genealogy of Morals*, trans. by Douglas Smith. Oxford: Oxford University Press.

Nietzsche, Friedrich. 2002. *Beyond Good and Evil*, ed. by Rolf-Peter Horstmann and Judith Norman. Cambridge: Cambridge University Press.

Prinz, Wolfgang. 1983. *Wahrnehmung und Tätigkeitssteuerung*. Berlin: Springer.

Ryle, Gilbert. 1949. *The Concept of Mind*. London/New York: Hutchinson's University Library.

Schlosser, Julius von. 1934. "Die Wiener Schule der Kunstgeschichte", in *Mitteilungen des Instituts für österreichische Geschichte* 13/2, pp. 141–228.

Smith, Barry. 1978. "Wittgenstein and the Background of Austrian Philosophy", in Elisabeth Leinfellner (ed.) *Wittgenstein and his Impact of Contemporary Thought*. Vienna: Hölder Pichler Tempsky, pp. 31–35.

Swoboda, Wolfgang. 1988. "Physik, Philosophie und Psychophysik – die Wurzeln von Machs Empiriokritizismus", in R. Haller and F. Stadler (eds.), pp. 356–403.

Thomé, Horst. 2001. "Metaphorische Konstrukte der Seele: Zu Herbarts Psychologie und ihrer Nachwirkung", in Andreas Hoeschen and Lothar Schneider (eds.) *Herbarts Kultursystem: Perspektiven der Transdisziplinarität im 19. Jahrhundert*. Würzburg: Königshausen und Neumann.

Twardowski, Kasimir. 1894/1977. *On the Content and Object of Presentations: A Psychological Investigation*, trans. by R. Grossmann. The Hague: Nijhoff.

Wittgenstein, Ludwig. 2009. *Philosophical Investigations*, trans. by G.E.M. Anscombe, P.M.S. Hacker and Joachim Schulte, revised, 4th edition. Oxford: Wiley-Blackwell.

4
ERNST MACH'S CONTRIBUTIONS TO THE PHILOSOPHY OF MIND*

Erik C. Banks

1. Mach's contributions to psychology

1.1 Early influences: Fechner and Herbart

Mach was trained as a physicist in Vienna. He entered psychology in 1860, when the appearance of Fechner's two-volume *Elemente der Psychophysik* had an electrifying effect upon him. The young Mach eagerly corresponded with Fechner and engineered a series of experiments to test Fechner's logarithmic law relating stimulus and sensation intensity. In particular, Mach tested the sensation of time duration and found that it did not agree with Fechner's law but that instead the sensitivity to just noticeable differences of duration actually falls off with time leading to the familiar perspectival phenomenon of the "telescoping" of durations as they fade into memory (see Mach 1865b). Nevertheless, as Michael Heidelberger has shown, Mach was deeply influenced by Fechner's idea of a "functionally connected" whole of appearances, where mental and physical were simply two sides or two orders of functional relations (see Heidelberger 1993; Banks 2003: Chapter 6).

Mach had also made a study of Herbart's mathematical psychology in the *Psychologie als Wissenschaft* of 1824–1825, an approach he thought could also serve to model inner processes as Newtonian forces. During this time, Mach was also influenced by Müller, Lotze, Helmholtz (especially through his professors Ernst Brücke and Carl Ludwig in Vienna), and Wundt's researches in vision, in particular his "complex local sign" theory. All of these figures and their contributions appeared in summary in Mach's "Vorträge über Psychophysik" (1863) a masterful account of the history of psychology in the German-speaking world up to that time.

As regards philosophy, Mach tells us later in the *Analysis of Sensations* (Mach 1959: 30n) that, during the 1860s, he was pulled toward a Herbartian "psychophysical monadology" and toward panpsychist and "idealist" views. A "long struggle" awaited him before he could achieve any unity and stability in his views of both physics and psychology as part of the same neutral domain of inquiry: the mature theory of elements and functions. I have shown (Banks 2003: Chapter 3) that in addition to Fechnerian functionalism, Herbart's "force like" qualities and functional relations that "press and inhibit one another" like forces, were probably the most important model for Mach's later theory of neutral elements, neither exclusively physical nor psychical, as was also true of Herbart's force-qualities according to Mach (Banks 2003: 92).

1.2 Mach Bands and lateral inhibition

Mach's first job was as a professor of mathematics in Graz. Lacking a physical laboratory and funds to do research, he turned to a series of psychological experiments, with himself as subject. In a series of articles in the *Sitzungsberichte der kaiserlichen Akademie der Wissenschaften*, all translated and reprinted by Floyd Ratliff (1965), Mach gave his theory of the familiar Mach Band phenomenon. The effect is best produced by a luminance distribution where solid light and dark regions are separated by a ramp of gradually rising or falling luminance. In these cases a light band appears on the edge of the solid dark region and a dark band appears on the edge of the light region producing a sensation brightness curve that appears "scalloped" in appearance. Ratliff later showed that the steeper the ramp, the more pronounced the effect (Figure 4.1).

Mach's explanation was in terms of what is now called lateral neural inhibition. That is, the cells responsible for registering the light intensity are also laterally connected to each other and "pool" their responses before passing on the results to the optic nerve and brain. Mach theorized that the dark and light bands are due to the flexions in the luminance curve where the point is below or above the average

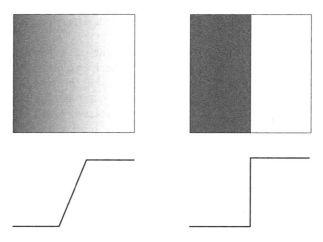

Figure 4.1 Mach Bands (from Banks 2001).

brightness of its neighbors (Figure 4.2) and is thus sensed as especially darker, or especially lighter, than average (see Ratliff 1965 and Banks 2001).

His idea was that sensations are often processed a great deal before they reach consciousness and that it is the differences or contrasts that appear, not the absolute intensity of the sensation, as for example on the Fechnerian conception. In this way, contrasts stand out, and flat, or steadily increasing, sensations are ignored by the visual system. This is why we do not notice the increase or decrease of luminance along the ramp, seeing instead a uniformly lighted surface canted toward or away from us, according to Mach ([1886] 1959: 216–220).

Mach's hypothesis has been challenged, for example by Morrone et al. (1986), who claimed the spectrum of the spatial frequency Fourier components accounted for the phenomenon (explaining, for example, why black and white square waves do not exhibit the effect), but it still survives in some form, even today where the phenomenon is accounted for in terms of on- and off-center surround regions in the retina discovered by Hubel and Wiesel (Palmer 1999: 65). The on- and off-center cells themselves operate by inhibition or by excitation. Interestingly, research in the meantime has shown that the inhibition pattern, or Gabor function, is often more "hat shaped" and exhibits differences in spatial frequency for different regions (see Palmer 1999: 169–170), again feeding into the idea of spatial frequency channels in the visual system. (I myself see no reason why the inhibition theory and the

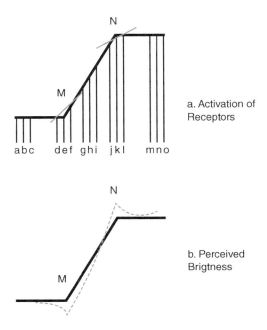

Figure 4.2 Mach Bands Explanation (from Banks 2001).

spatial frequency theory could not both be true, the way that Helmholtz's and Hering's theory of color are both true but at different levels of processing.)

The famous physiologist Georg von Békésy generalized the phenomenon of Mach Bands to the skin and especially to the cochlea, where he claimed it produced a high peaking and sharpening of the stimulus of the hair cells in the ear by traveling waves, thus accounting for the "tuning" of the organ to specific frequencies of sound, by "Mach's law of contrasts" (von Békésy 1960: 418). I do not know if this theory is still upheld in contemporary studies. In previous work, I thought the contrast law might allow for fusion of blurred or double images into a single high peak signaling depth, but I could not find a psychologist who wanted to do the experiments (Banks 2001).

After discovering the Mach Bands, Mach explicitly rejected Fecher's psychophysical law, around 1865 (see Mach [1886] 1959: 81n), declaring instead that the stimulus and sensation are directly proportional and that the Weber-Fechner effect, the fact that small differences are unnoticed compared to large differences, is more likely due to neural inhibition, since a sensation needs to be quite significantly above the intensity of its neighbors to be noticed at all. This (for Mach) is the true mechanism behind the famous Weber fraction of psychophysics. Around 1866, Mach thought of publishing many of his results in book form and wished to dedicate the work to Fechner. Fechner politely refused, and the rejection apparently devastated Mach, who said it "pursued him even in his dreams" even at the age of 73! (Heidelberger 1993: 208). It does not seem to have been Mach's rejection of Fechner's law that was the issue but rather what Fechner perceived as Mach's "divergent" (*abweichend*) philosophical standpoint, perhaps the Herbartian psycho-monadology of the "Vorträge über Psychophysik"?

1.3 Bewegungsempfindungen *and sensations of form and symmetry*

By the 1870s Mach was a professor in Prague and occupied with sensations of space, time and motion, parallel with his critique of these ideas in physics. However, although Mach was a staunch relationist and empiricist in his physics (as announced in his 1868 "Definition of Mass" article and especially his 1872 pamphlet on the "History and Root of the Principle of the Conservation of Energy"), he was an equally staunch *nativist* in psychology, like his colleague in Prague, Ewald Hering, believing that sensations of space, time and motion were innate and favored by evolution. Mach thus made a strong distinction between physical and psychological space and time (for which see his [1905] 1976).

Using a whirling chair, Mach was able to identify sensations of orientation of the head and sensations responding to various motions of the head. Both of these are reflected in involuntary eye motions, such as ocular torsion – as Mach apparently discovered when riding in a railway car rounding a curve – and nystagmus where the eyes carry out rachet-like back and forth movements as the head rotates, or when the eyes follow a moving object like a subway train. (You can simulate the latter effect easily even with your eyes closed by touching your eyelids and spinning yourself on a swivel desk chair.) Although these involuntary motions were known to other researchers, Mach successfully located the sensations to the semicircular canals and otoliths, simultaneously with Crum Browne and Josef Breuer. We thus have an "absolute" psychological sense of acceleration, even though Mach also upheld the equivalence of accelerated reference frames in physics.

Also during this time, in an 1871 article "Über die physikalische Bedeutung der Gesetze der Symmetrie," Mach identified sensations of symmetry and form, which he considered innate to the apparatus of the eye muscles. Since the eye muscles are symmetrical on either side of a plane through the nose, figures symmetrically situated about that plane tended to elicit agreeable "form sensations." Sensations of similar figures were explained in like manner as a repetition of feelings of scanning with the eyes over figures of different sizes but similar form, provided they were oriented to evoke the sensation (mere geometric or intellectual similarity is not enough). See Mach [1886] 1959: 105–109.

Mach also postulated that a special register of time sensations accounted for our sense of rhythm and temporal repetition, independent of the tones, and that a special register of space sensations (like Lotze's local signs) was present on the surface of the body independent of what might be felt as a color or a tactile sensation. As I will explain below, Mach thought that the "simple" sensation of visual location, of a blue dot for example, was actually divisible into the place of the sensed content on the retina and the place in the system of space sensations of the eyes and body, two different and sometimes even separable systems:

> The facts compel us to separate these space-values into two components, one of which depends upon the coordinates of the point of reflection on the retina, and the other on the coordinates of the point of vision, which components undergo mutually compensating alterations corresponding to voluntary alterations of the point of vision.
> (Mach [1886] 1959: 178, see also 127–131)

The idea may have been suggested to Mach by Wilhelm Wundt's complex local sign theory. In Wundt's view, the mosaic of individual retinal sensations of color and light was separated out by motion from the system of eye muscles which served to gauge the distances of retinal points from each other by the amount of muscular effort needed to scan from one to another. As Mach wrote in an 1865 article: "we might say we reach the vision of space by the registering of light-sensations in a schedule of graduated muscle sensations" (Mach 1865a: 5). The same theory held *mutatis mutandis* for time, whereby the inner "register" of time sensations could order sensations of tone in a melody. As Mach wrote in the "Untersuchungen über den Zeitsinn des Ohres" (1865b):

> One can completely liberate the rhythm of a melody from the sensations of tone, like the contour drawing of a painting, in that one can tap out the

melody without tones. This would not be possible if there were not, to
some extent, self-standing series of rhythm sensations.

(Mach 1865b: 146–147, translation mine)

As he said later in the *Analysis of Sensations*, a reordering of the register of time sensations could even change the order in which a series of light or sound sensations are experienced, sometimes the later sensation appearing first, as previous investigations of the personal equation in astronomy had shown, for example, when an observer sees a moon appear from behind a planet *before* the clock ticks off the correct time of the event, simply because he expects it more intensely. In all of these cases, Mach claimed there were special holistic and independent "form sensations" of space, time and form or rhythm, over and above the collection of dots or lines making up the shape, or the sounds making up a melody. These investigations were later cited by Christian von Ehrenfels as the beginnings of Gestalt psychology.[1]

1.4 Monocular depth sensations and the empiricist-nativist controversy

In the third article in his series of Mach Band articles (Ratliff 1966) Mach had discovered that steadily increasing light sensations on a surface like an angled wall were not perceived, but instead a uniformly lighted surface in depth appeared. He hypothesized some sort of innate functional connection: the monocular sensation of depth could be rigidly connected to certain differences in light sensation without conscious, or unconscious, inference or thought (see Banks 2001: 339–340; Ratliff 1965: 289).

He also investigated monocular sensations of depth for line drawings. Here he hypothesized that sensations of monocular depth were subject to mutual inhibition, just like the sensations of light, such that only departures from the mean depth of a figure or surface were sensed (Mach 1959: 225, Banks 2001: 343–345). The figure drawing of a solid in depth is always the minimum solution, or solutions if there is more than one, of distributing the depth sensations along the various lines. All angles tend to become right angles and all lines tend to be inclined at a right angle to the line of sight. This is why he believed we see the drawings as solids in just a few possible and not the infinitely many arrangements of lines in space they could represent.

As I have written elsewhere, Mach believed that monocular depth sensations were somehow primary (Banks 2001: 342) since they usually overrode binocular cues, for example, when viewing landscapes with the pseudoscope (in which the left-right roles of the eyes in stereopsis are switched by mirrors). These monocular cues were developed by simple automatic mechanisms in the sense organs themselves without any higher thought or inference by the brain. Mach rather boldly declared:

I now have grounds to believe that the majority of the phenomena which we have believed to be errors of judgment (essentially due to processes in the central nervous system) actually have their basis in a more autonomous behavior of the sense organs. I will describe a series of observations that led me to the view that is already becoming familiar in comparative anatomy, namely that the sense organs are to be considered as subordinate central organs.

(Ratliff 1966: 308).

This was a direct attack upon Helmholtz's doctrine of "unconscious inference," an important doctrine of the magisterial *Handbuch der Physiologischen Optik* of 1866 (see Patton, infra). According to Helmholtz, for example, two slightly misaligned sensations of blobs of light in two binocular images will produce a sensation of luster because, normally, a lustrous object like a shiny, embossed metal coin would cast such images on the two retinas, and the brain will simply infer that this is another case like one it has seen in the past. Helmholtz also believed that the brain (albeit unconsciously) "calculated" distances from binocular retinal disparities as if it were doing trigonometry and coming to an intellectual "conclusion" of depth rather than a directly experienced depth sensation.

In taking on Helmholtz, Mach was declaring his allegiance to the nativist cyclopean theory of Ewald Hering, which appeared in his *Beiträge zur Physiologie* (Hering 1865) and *Die Lehre vom binocularischen Sehen* (1868). Mach and Hering were also colleagues at Prague. According to Hering, the system of the two eyes innately produces the sensation of depth by means of fusing local "depth" signs on the two retinas, without inference, as the two visual directions through the optical axes of either eye fuse to a single visual direction of the so-called cyclopean eye. Local signs near the nasal side indicate increasing depth while local signs on the temporal side indicate decreasing depth. As Stephen Turner has masterfully related (Turner 1994), Helmholtz responded to Hering's theory and focused his attack on these supposed monocular depth sensations. Did they remain active even when only one eye was used? Why then does a flat wall not seem to be angled toward us when viewed with one eye? As I have written elsewhere (Banks 2001), I believe Mach's experiments on monocular stereoscopy were meant to buttress Hering against this attack, since for Mach, monocular depth sensations for one eye are clearly triggered by different mechanisms than those nasal-to-temporal binocular depth signs active in stereopsis and can even override the weaker binocular mechanism. I speculated perhaps rashly (Banks 2001) that Mach's neural inhibition mechanism could also "level off" weak monocular depth signs of one retina, if they occurred in the case of Helmholtz's flat wall objection, but I now think it is enough that they are simply overridden by the more primitive monocular cues.

In particular, for Mach, there is a strong "automatic" functional connection between light, length, and depth sensations in monocular stereoscopy which is instinctual, not intellectual. Consider the phenomenon of the Mach Card in Figure 4.3 (Mach [1886] 1959: 223), a plain white visiting card bent upward like a roof and illuminated with a desk lamp so that one side is in strong light and the

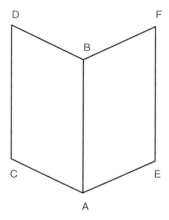

Figure 4.3 The Mach Visiting Card.

other is in shadow. We now monocularly reverse the picture, so that it seems to lie open like a book. Immediately, without thinking, the light sensations change reciprocally. Now what we see is a card in uniform light but with gray "painted on" the side that was in shadow. In addition the central line AB is canted forward in space, and the lines BF and BD appear longer than AC, AE.

(When doing the Mach Card myself, I have even observed a third possibility where the "painted on" effect is lessened and the shapes BADC and BAFE contract into flat trapezoidal sections at uniform depth.) The important fact is that sensations of light, depth, and length all seem rigidly connected like the parts of a machine giving, as a result, different possibilities for a light surface to be perceived as a visual object (see Mach [1886] 1959: 233).

The proponent of unconscious inference would no doubt say that the inference from a light surface to an object is what forces the other sensations to change as it were mechanically, but really as a result of an unconscious intellectual inference. The object is the primary thing and the sensations adjust accordingly. For Mach or Hering it was just the opposite, the native evolved reflexes are what make up "objects" of perception as *innate* functions of the light surfaces, processed by mechanisms in the sense organs themselves, not central inferences. These reflexes are the reason *why* we are preconditioned to perceive objects in a changing mass of sensations, not the other way around. Again, there is no reason why both sorts of explanations might not be correct.

1.5 Sensations of innervation and the debate with William James

As we noted above, for Mach, a visual sensation of place, such as the place of a speck in the visual field, is actually a combined sensation of a speck on the retina with a certain color and shape, and the "space sensation" due to the orientation of the head and the eyes, the position of the body, and so forth. It is important to separate these factors to differentiate between when the body moves, and the images of objects should appear fixed, and when the body is fixed in place and objects are seen moving around it. For example, when the head moves, involuntary movements of the eyes, such as torsion and nystagmus, compensate the motions of the head in order to keep the images of objects fixed. We do not even feel these compensatory sensations as motions. Similarly, when we watch a subway train go by, our eyes track forward and back, forward and back, but the train seems to move steadily and the eye movements do not affect the perception of motion of the train.

Mach also believed that sensations that cause voluntary movements of the head and eyes, called *Innervationsgepfühle* by Wundt, Helmholtz, and others could be used to distinguish voluntary movements of the head and eyes from the motion of objects. In cases where the relative motions do not distinguish them, the sensation of innervation tells me I am moving my head, eyes, or body and things are not instead moving around me. So, for example, if my eyes sweep across the room, the images will sweep over my retinas, occupying different retinal points, but since I *know* I am voluntarily moving my eyes, the motions of my eyes will compensate the motions of the images on my retinas and the entire room will be sensed as fixed. In the 1870s, Mach proposed a crucial experiment (Mach [1886] 1959: 128). He fixed his eye in place with putty and then suddenly tried to "look right" whereupon the objects in the room seemed to suffer a strong displacement to the right. His explanation: normally sending the voluntary sensation would mean the eyes were moving right to compensate an apparent leftward motion of the objects. The leftward moving objects are thus assigned a compensating "rightward" value, which counteracts their leftward drift and they remain fixed. In this case, however, there is no leftward drift and they receive only the rightward component and thus *seem* to move rightward. Remember again the sensation of location in the visual field is, for Mach, a resultant of two components: the position on the retina and other information about the space sensations of the direction the eye is pointing or moving. These are clearly separable.

William James, who knew Mach and even came to visit him in Prague in 1882 (cf. Thiele 1978) disagreed. In *Principles of Psychology* (1890) James repeated the putty experiment and reported a null result. Mach in turn wrote in a later edition of the *Analysis* that he had "often repeated it and found it confirmed." Unfortunately, it was often the case in introspective psychology of the 19th century that two competent experimenters could arrive at different introspective data.

According to James and Hugo Münsterberg, sensations of innervation are unnecessary, since peripheral kinesthetic feelings – the muscular sense of how the body is held for example – always suffice to differentiate the cases of a moving body from moving objects. Mach strongly disagreed, holding that "the will to move the eyes is itself the space sensation" (Mach [1886] 1959: 129) which he had long claimed to exist. I suppose the idea here is that sensations of space must form a manifold which is not directly sensed all the time but which is mostly imagined to exist around the observer. Nevertheless this manifold is innate. Sensations of will to direct the eyes this way or that are, in fact, needed to fill in this imagined manifold even when we do not execute these motions. These include the will to converge the eyes on points with different innately sensed depth values. Mach credited Hering with the discovery of this triple system of space sensations, mirroring the will to move the eyes in three physiologically different ways, left-right, up-down, and convergent-divergent (Mach [1886] 1959: 124–125). I do not know if Hering shared this interpretation.

2. Mach's neutral monism

Many of Mach's discoveries in psychology are reflected in his mature philosophy of mind announced in the opening chapters of the *Analysis of Sensations*. Mach had sought for years to achieve a single metascientific view to unite his interests in physics with those in psychophysics. The biggest problem for him was to figure out what to do with sensations. Physics denied their existence, shunting them into the realm of "mental" secondary qualities, and psychology, by contrast, could not connect its introspective data with a physical foundation and system of objective measurement. Only the physiological correlates and parallel processes in the central nervous system could be measured. Such "psychophysical parallelism" (then as today) was an acceptable compromise for the sake of practice, as Mach duly recognized, and the only pathway for the actual conduct of physiological psychology. But as philosophy, it was dualistic and as such amounted to a simplistic non-answer to the deeper questions. It also made no sense to have psychophysical equations with units of sensation intensity on one side and physical units on the other, which Mach recognized as "purely conventional" fictions.

In later years Mach spoke proudly of the fact that he stood apart from professional philosophy. Yet, Mach ([1886] 1959: 30n) had encountered Kant's philosophy in his youth and developed a Herbartian psycho-monadology in his 1863 "Vorträge über Psychophysik" (see Laass 1991). He also mentions an idealist period ([1886] 1959: 56) during which he attempted to exclude any physical events that were not possible sensations for an ego: "a proposition to which it is difficult to yield serious assent" as he said later (ibid.: 28). There is also some evidence for a panpsychist period in the 1860s in which Mach speculated about sensation being "a general property of matter" (see Haller and Stadler 1988: 173ff), but this too was ultimately rejected, since it seems to require thinking sensations spatially inside matter, a fallacy Mach later criticized as the "error of introjection" (more on this as follows). Like Fechner and Herbart before him, Mach was determined to break through the barriers between the sciences and one-sided philosophies, to an original metascientific philosophical view. He says that this was the only reason he, a scientist, had found it necessary to do philosophy:

> I make no pretention to the title of a philosopher. I only seek to adopt in physics a point of view that need not be changed immediately on

glancing over into the domain of another science, for, ultimately, all must form one whole.

([1886] 1959: 30)

Mach briefly presents his mature "neutral monist" position at the end of the 1872 pamphlet *Geschichte und Wurzel des Prinzips der Erhaltung der Arbeit*. He discussed it more fully in the *Analyse der Empfindungen* of 1886, and again in his *Erkenntnis und Irrtum* of 1905. Mach's solution was to deconstruct both the physical body and the ego into functional complexes of what he called neutral "elements."

These elements are constantly changing individual events in the physical world like the pressure of a force or a collision of two solid objects, but also complex individual events in the human nervous system like the seeing of a color or the hearing of a sound. In themselves, events are neutral: neither exclusively "physical" in the old sense which excludes psychology, nor exclusively "mental" in the old sense which isolates them from events in physics. Sensations of course have qualities, like red or blue, which many scientists and philosophers regard as "secondary qualities" that are not part of the physical world of matter, motion, and other primary qualities described by physics. But the fact that sensations exhibit manifest qualities like red or blue is no argument for Mach against their being considered as real as any event in physics, like the shock of two billiard balls or the expression of a physical force. Indeed, elements only become "sensations" when we investigate their relations to other events in the human nervous system, their connection with images and functions of memory and association. In another direction, the same qualities can be investigated as "physical" events in the brain connected with other physical events. Only the ordering of the neutral element in one set of relations or another makes the inquiry a psychological one as opposed to an investigation in physics, and even these labels are only provisional in nature:

> In what follows wherever the reader finds the terms "sensation," "sensation complex" used alongside of or instead of the expressions "element," and "complex of elements" it must be borne in mind that it is *only* in the connexion and relation in question, *only* in their functional dependence that the elements are sensations. In another functional connection they are at the same time physical objects. We only use the additional term "sensations" to describe the elements, because most people are more familiar with the elements in question as sensations.
>
> (Mach [1886] 1959: 16)

Similar contemporary ideas can be found in the article "On the Nature of Things in Themselves" by Clifford (1878) and in the works of Richard Avenarius such as the *Kritik der reinen Erfahrung* (Avenarius 1878).[2]

Now it is true that Mach sometimes tried to restrict his investigation to sensation/elements exclusively, at least in his psychological works, so he sometimes says that in that domain, every sensation is an element and every element is a sensation.

There are quotes to this effect in nearly all of his works. But it is also clear on a closer look that Mach admitted elements of unknown quality, which are *only* elements and never appear as anyone's sensations, so called mind-independent world elements, as I called them in my 2003 book, like Russell's later 'unsensed sensibilia'. These, he said, "were added in thought" (Mach [1886] 1959: 15) to observed elements, but not just in thought since they were also causally connected continuously with our experience. So long as causal continuity is established, there is no need for every physical element to also be an observable sensation.

The important point for philosophy of mind is that Mach was granting sensations *concrete physical reality*, as real as physical events but investigable through a different set of functional variations in psychophysics. These two sets of variations did not of course indicate separate orders of mental and physical variations or any dualism of properties either, but only provisionally different departments of inquiry. Bertrand Russell, who discovered neutral monism in the work of Mach and James, praised Mach as the "inaugurator of the movement" (Russell 1927: 15) and earlier declared Mach's and James's contributions a "service to philosophy . . . that what is experienced may itself be part of the physical world and often is so" (Russell [1914] 1984: 76–78). The neutral elements, the functional variations, and the deconstruction of the ego and the object which are the distinctive theses of neutral monism in James and Russell (Stubenberg 2010) all stem originally from Mach's *Analysis of Sensations*.

As we saw, Mach's decomposition of the conscious ego, and its mental acts or judgments, into a set of "functional connections" between sensations, images, thoughts, feelings, and so forth, was presaged by his work in psychology and especially his rejection of Helmholtz's unconscious inferences in the theory of binocular vision and in the experiment of the Mach Card.

Mach, along with William James, also strongly rejected the idea, promulgated by his fellow Austrian Franz Brentano, that mental acts had some kind of special, non-physical, relation to their contents, which Brentano called "intentional inexistence." Anton Marty, a pupil of Brentano, tried to convince Mach that he must distinguish between the tone a person hears, as content, and the intentional higher order conscious act of hearing the tone (see Thiele 1978). For Mach, mental acts or judgments are simple functional relations of their contents, where even the functions are physiologically grounded in the brain and sense organs; the act does not precede or envelop the contents in any special intentional relation. For Mach, the content is in no way dependent on being embedded in a higher order conscious act; the tone or color, for example, does not get its quality by being apprehended (see the quote which follows). When considered as a physical event, the same sensation is bound causal-functionally to other physical events and not to an apprehending subject at all. Once the element is freed from any dependence on an ego, or an object, it becomes truly neutral. As Mach wrote in his late masterpiece, the 1905 *Erkenntnis und Irrtum:*

> Consciousness is not a special mental quality or class of qualities different from physical ones; nor is it a special quality that would have to

be added to physical ones in order to make the unconscious conscious. Introspection as well as observation of other living things to which we have to ascribe consciousness similar to our own shows that consciousness has its roots in reproduction and association: their wealth, ease, speed, vivacity and order determine its level. Consciousness consists not in a special quality but in a special connection between qualities . . . A single sensation is neither conscious nor unconscious: it becomes conscious by being ranged among the experiences of the present.

(Mach [1905] 1976: 31–32)

Similarly, in Mach's causal theory of "cognition and error" (which he adopted as the title of *Erkenntnis und Irrtum*) there are no special intentional links between a belief and its fulfillment – besides ordinary causal connections – which would tend to associate a belief that has successful consequences with other events it leads to via a causal chain. The same goes for errors. There is no sense in which a correct cognition internally or intentionally "pictures" or "represents" a state of affairs: the correspondence must be created by linking the two together successfully or unsuccessfully. As Mach wrote:

Cognition and error flow from the same mental sources, only success can tell the one from the other. A clearly recognized error, by way of corrective, can benefit cognition just as a positive cognition can.

(Mach [1905] 1976: 84)

William James would simultaneously articulate Mach's *aperçue* into a full-blown causal theory of knowledge as part of his radical empiricism (Banks 2013b, 2014).

3. Metaphysical errors and pseudoproblems of psychology

Armed with his new view, Mach set to work attacking what he called the "metaphysical pseudoproblems" which plagued psychology and prevented it from becoming a genuine science. In my opinion, this is some of the strongest philosophy Mach ever wrote: fierce and unrelenting.

Mach's chief innovation is what he calls a "causal-functional" presentation of the elements (Mach [1886] 1959: 35). This is a network, or graph, of elements all connected by functional relations and mapped alongside each other, whether they are my sensations, the physical elements of the brain as observed by others or sensations, images, or feelings, or the contents of other minds. He uses A,B,C . . . for physical elements/sensations, K,L,M . . . for elements of the body like the retinal surfaces or the skin and muscles, and α,β,γ . . . for mental images, and K'L'M' for the sensations of my body or brain to another observer with the clear understanding that any of them (even the images) are potentially interpretable as physical elements in other variations. The variety of causal-functional connections between these elements also requires an abstract multidimensional array, not just the three-dimensional psychological space of a single observer, but a system with at least enough dimensions for a three-dimensional observer at every point in it, as Mach points out.

> When I speak of the sensations of another person, those sensations are, of course, not exhibited in my optical or physical space; they are mentally added and I conceive them causally, not spatially, attached to the brain observed, or rather, functionally presented.
> (Mach [1886] 1959: 27, cf. 361)

Mach's justly famous "headless body" picture (Mach [1886] 1959: 19, Figure 4.4) gives us a subset of the overall map of the elements: a spatial projection of all of the elements as they actually appear to a single egocentric observer.

One problem Mach seeks to solve with his causal-functional map is the so-called Problem of Introjection, or of thinking sensations spatially into the observed brain. The problem was so named by his colleague Richard Avenarius. The problem is: I see a green leaf and I know that with this event is exactly

Figure 4.4 Mach's "Headless Body" Picture.

correlated the event of certain electrical (we would say electro-chemical) processes in my brain. Hence, we think, the green must be found somewhere spatially "introjected" into my brain tissue. But in investigating the brain we find only electrical currents, never the color green (Mach [1886] 1959: 62, 43). If, for example we were to regard our own brain in a mirror and conduct an exact investigation, we would indeed find a point in the observed brain that is associated with the green sensation. (Using a thought experiment from my (2014), we can imagine siphoning off the neural energy and making the green disappear while the electrical current is picked up on an external measuring device, then allowing it to reappear when the current is no longer diverted.) We can even map out the complex of cells and chart their firing pattern, but still we never find that green quality of the sensation. The conclusion of the neuroscientist will be that the cluster of cells simply *is* what the person thinks of as his green sensation and the actual quality of sensing green is some kind of mirage. But according to Mach, this is also a mistake, since the green sensation, color and all, is a *real* concrete natural event, as real as any event in physics. The correct solution, he says, is as follows:

> When I see a green leaf (an event which is determined by certain brain processes) the leaf is of course different in its form and color from the forms, colors, etc. which I discover in investigating a brain, although all forms, colors, etc. are of a like nature in themselves, being neither physical nor psychical. The leaf which I see, considered as dependent on the brain process, is something psychical, while this brain process itself represents, in the connection of its elements, something physical.
> (Mach [1886] 1959:61–62)

Hence in this case we have confused the class of elements of the investigated brain in the mirror for the entirely different elements of the green sensation which belong *alongside* them in a different position on the causal graph, not spatially "inside" them. The events are causally associated causally with each other as closely as you wish but they appear in different places and are distinct. The green sensation is something psychical since it interacts causally with the observed elements of brain tissue seen in the mirror, but it is also a physical event when we consider its dependence upon other elements such as the lighting, the physical leaf, and so on. The observed brain tissue is something physical in the sense of its connection with measuring devices, but it is also something psychical in the sense that it is made up of elements of color and form I observe of my brain in a mirror. As Mach says of the headless body picture, the green obviously "shares the same space" with the elements of my observed head or brain in the mirror, so the green does not belong spatially inside the (observed) brain, but rather "alongside" the externally observed brain tissue on the graph.

The second problem of "bilocation" is just the opposite of the first. It was stated well by Arthur Lovejoy in his *Revolt Against Dualism* (Lovejoy 1930: 15–16) which was directed against James and Russell's neutral monism (oddly, Lovejoy seems unaware of Mach). The argument is as follows. We know that sensations are somehow identical with brain processes (not seen in a mirror this time but as they are). How, then, can the same experience of seeing an apple be both five feet in front of me and in a region of my occipital lobe at the back of my skull?

The solution is the same as in the case of introjection. The sensation of the apple is not "inside" my observed head, but rather my sensations of my own head and brain are clearly in a different place from my sensation of the apple. But the presumed location of the sensation process in my actual brain does not appear in the headless body picture. The headless body "loops around" the location in the brain "x" that is presumably responsible for the sensation of the apple. This "x" will of course not actually appear in the brain in the mirror, or in the headless body picture, but you could poke around it and get a good sense of where it might be. So, then, there is nothing to prevent me from assuming that the sensation of the apple *is* actually the same event I am poking around and would find at "x." There is only one event not two, bilocated ones and the objection is met. A more detailed account of these arguments and further applications of the technique to "metaphysical pseudoproblems" in the philosophy of mind can be found in my (2014) treatment.

3.1 Critical reception

Mach's philosophy of mind was enormously influential, especially his rejection of the substantial ego. Nevertheless, Mach's idea of the neutral element, so highly praised by Russell, was often misunderstood by less sophisticated authors. For example, V. I. Lenin's brutal *Empiricism and Empiro-Criticism* (1908) attacked Avenarius and Mach along with other "Machists" such as Josef Petzoldt and Alexander Bogdonov because Lenin sensed a political threat to Marxist materialism, not because he wished to conduct an impartial review of contemporary ideas. To Lenin, Mach's elements were just sensations and Mach was therefore just another idealist like Berkeley (this despite Mach's warnings not to interpret him this way):

> Mach and Avenarius secretly smuggle in materialism by means of the word "element," which supposedly frees their theory of the one-sidedness of subjective idealism, supposedly permits the assumption that the mental is dependent on the retina, nerves and so forth and the assumption that the physical is independent of the human organism. In fact, of course, the trick with the word "element" is a wretched sophistry, for a materialist who reads Mach and Avenarius will immediately ask: what are the "elements"? Either the "element" is a sensation, as all empirio-criticists, Mach, Avenarius, Petzoldt, etc. maintain – in which case your philosophy, gentlemen, is idealism, vainly seeking to hide the nakedness of its

solipsism under the cloak of a more "objective" terminology; or the element is not a sensation – in which case absolutely no thought whatever is attached to the "new" term; it is merely an empty bauble.

(Lenin [1908] 1952: 48–49)

The idea took hold that "neutral monism is not neutral at all": Mach's elements are mental and his world is just a sum of sensations. One reader after another simply falls headlong into the same facile misreading, often without even consulting Mach's original works. Mach's biographer John Blackmore (1972) has been especially dismissive of his philosophical views, dubbing them sensationalist and phenomenalist, but he is hardly alone. Somehow only James and Russell seemed to understand Mach correctly, and they, too, became subject to the same misunderstandings.

The logical positivists of the Vienna Circle adopted Mach as a local hero, but their views owed more to the rise of modern logic, and their second order studies of language and the structure of science had nothing to do with Mach's first-order scientific investigations of the elements of nature (see Banks 2013a and Stadler 1997). For example, Carnap and Ayer use Machian language when they describe sensations as neither mental nor physical, or talk about the elimination of metaphysical pseudoproblems, but these expressions meant something different for them. For Carnap and Ayer it is not the metaphysical neutrality of the elements that is meant, but the possibility of adopting different languages that makes the subject matter neutral. The idea of neutral sensations did survive in James and Russell and their followers and Herbert Feigl and Wilfred Sellars and others who upheld neo-Russellian views. In more recent times, neutral monism has made a comeback, beginning with the work of Grover Maxwell and Michael Lockwood among others. David Chalmers and Daniel Stoljar have identified neutral monism as a viable option in the contemporary philosophy of mind while not endorsing it. Stubenberg's excellent (2010) review article identifies these many strands in the neutral monist movement, while correctly tracing its roots back to Mach.

Notes

* I would like to acknowledge the helpful comments and suggestions of Profs. Sandra LaPointe and Lydia Patton.
1 On Ehrenfels, see Ierna, *infra*.
2 For more on this, see Stubenberg (2010); Banks (2014).

Bibliography

Avenarius, R. 1878. *Kritik der reinen Erfahrung*. Leipzig: O. Reisland.
Banks, E.C. 2001. "Ernst Mach and the Episode of the Monocular Depth Sensations". *Journal of the History of the Behavioral Sciences* **37**(4): 327–348.
———. 2003. *Ernst Mach's World Elements: A Study in Natural Philosophy*. Dordrecht: Kluwer.

———. 2010. "Neutral Monism Reconsidered". *Philosophical Psychology* **23**(2): 173–187.
———. 2013a. "Metaphysics for Positivists: Mach Versus the Vienna Circle". *Discipline Filosofiche* **23**(1): 1–20.
———. 2013b. "William James's Direct Realism: A Reconstruction". *History of Philosophy Quarterly* **30**(3): 271–291.
———. 2014. *The Realistic Empiricism of Mach, James, and Russell*. Cambridge: Cambridge University Press.
Blackmore, J. 1972. *Ernst Mach: His Life, Work, and Influence*. Berkeley: University of California Press.
Clifford, W.K. 1878. "On the Nature of Things in Themselves". *Mind* **3**(1878): 57–67.
Feyerabend, P.F. 1984. "Mach's Theory of Research and Its Relation to Einstein". *Studies in History and Philosophy of Science* **15**(1): 1–22.
Haller, R. and Stadler, F. (eds.). 1988. *Ernst Mach: Werk und Wirkung*. Vienna: Hölder, Pitchler Tempsky.
Heidelberger, M. 1993. *Die Innere Seite der Natur: G.T. Fechners wissenschaftliche-philosophiche Weltauffassung*. Frankfurt am Main: Vittorio Klostermann.
Hering, E. 1865. *Beiträge zur Physiologie*. Leipzig: Wilhelm Engelmann.
James, W. [1890] 1952. *The Principles of Psychology*. Chicago: Encyclopedia Britannica.
———. 1977. *The Writings of William James*. J.J. McDermott (trans.). Chicago: University of Chicago Press.
Lenin, V.I. [1908] 1952. *Empiricism and Empirio-Criticism*. Moscow: World Publishing House.
Lovejoy, A.O. 1930. *The Revolt Against Dualism*. New York: Open Court.
Laass, Andreas. 1991. "Vom Sinne des Machschen Philosophierens" in Hoffmann D. and Laitko H. (eds.) *Ernst Mach: Studien und Dokumente zu Leben und Werk*. Berlin: Deutscher Verlag der Wissenschaften.
Mach, E. 1863. "Vorträge über Psychophysik". *Österreiche Zeitschrift für praktische Heilkunde* **9**.
———. 1865a. "Bemerkungen über die Entwicklung der Raumlichen Sehen". *Fichtes Zeitschrift für Philosophie und philosophische Kritik* **46**: 1–5.
———. 1865b. "Untersuchungen über den Zeitsinn des Ohres". *Sitzungsbereichte der kaiserlichen Akademie der Wissenschaften: mathematische- naturwissenschaftliche Klasse* **51**: 133–150.
———. 1866. "Bemerkungen über die Entwicklung der Raumvorstellungen". *Fichtes Zeitschrift für Philosophie und philosophische Kritik* **49**: 227–232.
———. 1871. "Über die physikalische Bedeutung der Gesetze der Symmetrie". *Lotos* **21**: 139–147.
———. 1875. *Grundlinien der Lehre von den Bewegungsempfindungen*. Leipzig: Wilhelm Engelmann.
———. [1872] 1910. *History and Root of the Principle of the Conservation of Energy*. P.E.B. Jourdain (trans.). Chicago: Open Court.
———. [1886] 1959. *The Analysis of Sensations*. C.M. Williams and Sydney Waterlow (trans.). New York: Dover.
———. [1883] 1960. *The Science of Mechanics*. Thomas McCormack (trans.). Chicago: Open Court.
———. [1905] 1976. *Knowledge and Error*. Thomas McCormack and Paul Foulkes (trans.). Dordrecht: D. Reidel.

Morrone, M.C., Ross, J., Burr, D. and Owens, R. 1986. "Mach Bands Are Phase Dependent". *Nature* **324**(20): 250–253.
Palmer, S.E. 1999. *Vision Science: From Photons to Phenomenology*. Cambridge, MA: MIT Press.
Patton, Lydia. 2018. "Helmholtz's Physiological Psychology". *Philosophy of Mind in the Nineteenth Century*. Abingdon: Routledge.
Ratliff F. 1965. *Mach Bands: Quantitative Studies on Neural Networks in the Retina*. San Francisco: Holden-Day.
Russell, B. 1927. *The Analysis of Matter*. London: George Allen and Unwin.
———. 1963. *Mysticism and Logic*. London: George Allen and Unwin.
———. [1914] 1984. *Collected Papers of Bertrand Russell*. Vol 7. London: George Allen and Unwin.
Stadler, F. 1997. *Studien zum Wiener Kreis*. Frankfurt am Main: Suhrkamp.
Stubenberg, L. 2010. "Neutral Monism". *The Stanford Encyclopedia of Philosophy* http://plato.stanford.edu/archives/win2013/entries/neutral-monism (accessed March 2014).
Thiele, J. 1978. *Wissenschaftliche Kommunikation: Die Korrespondenz Ernst Machs*. Kastellaun: A. Henn.
Turner, S. 1994. *In the Mind's Eye: Vision and the Helmholtz-Hering Controversy*. Princeton: Princeton University Press.
Von Békésy, G. 1960. *Experiments in Hearing*. New York: McGraw Hill.

5

HELMHOLTZ'S PHYSIOLOGICAL PSYCHOLOGY[1]

Lydia Patton

Hermann von Helmholtz (1821–1894) contributed two major works to the theory of sensation and perception in the nineteenth century. The first edition of *The Doctrine of the Sensations of Tone* was published in 1863, and the first edition of the *Handbook of Physiological Optics* was published in toto in 1867. These works established results both controversial and enduring: Helmholtz's analysis of mixed colors and of combination tones, his arguments against nativism, and his commitment to analyzing sensation and perception using the techniques of natural science, especially physiology and physics.

This study will focus on the *Physiological Optics* (hereafter *PO*), and on Helmholtz's account of sensation, perception, and representation via "physiological psychology". Helmholtz emphasized that external stimuli of sensations are causes, and sensations are their effects, and he had a practical and naturalist orientation toward the analysis of phenomenal experience.

Helmholtz's epistemological methodology and his sign theory were part of his response to nineteenth-century nativism and direct realism. On his view, sensation must be interpreted to yield representation, and representation is geared toward objective representation (the central thesis of contemporary intentionalism). The interpretation of sensation is based on "facts" revealed in experiment, but extends to the analysis of the quantitative, causal relationships between stimuli and responses. A key question for Helmholtz's theory is the extent to which mental operations are to be ascribed a role in interpreting sensation and in the occurrence and quality of phenomenal experience.

1. Naturalizing the mind

Gary Hatfield distinguishes between "normative" accounts of the mental, on which reasoning, judging, perceiving, and the like are "subject to appraisal as true or false, right or wrong," and "natural" accounts, according to which mental activity should be investigated using the techniques of natural science, without normative presuppositions (1990, 1). Kant's a priori justification of the categories as objectively valid concepts, and of space and time as formal principles of intuition, is characteristic of the normative approach. In contrast, Helmholtz "naturalizes" Kant by using the methods of natural science to investigate mental activity. Helmholtz considers perceiving and representing, and the conscious and unconscious inferences employed in these, to be psychological and physiological operations amenable to empirical treatment.

Helmholtz uses several terms for what we would call the "mind" in the *Physiological Optics*: *Psyche* (or *psychisch*), *Seele*, and *Geist*. These terms sometimes are translated "soul" or "spirit", and for many German-speaking philosophers responding to the Aristotelian tradition and to natural philosophy, they denoted functions associated with the body (sensing, feeling, desiring) as well as those associated with the mind (judgment, reasoning).[2] Some in these traditions used the terms, and their equivalents in other languages (*âme* in French, *psyche* in Greek), to represent the animating principle of the material human body.

In his *Handbook of Human Physiology*, Helmholtz's mentor Johannes Müller defends the vitalist position: that the body must have an organizing force beyond the mechanical forces at work in processes like metabolism. Müller draws his inspiration from Kant, but marshals evidence from Ernst Stahl's and Georges Cuvier's naturalist studies.[3] On Müller's reading of Stahl, the "Seele" is a "rational creative force," "the force of organization itself, expressing itself according to rational laws" (1844, 22). Müller distinguishes the *Seele* from the "unconsciously effective purposeful operation" of material forces and instinct (ibid., 23). The *Seele* is expressed in physical processes, but it is the source of the organization of physical processes toward a rational purpose.

Hermann Lotze's 1852 *Medical Psychology, or Physiology of the Mind*[4] locates the study of psychology in the examination of the *Seele*, which is the seat of psychological activity. However, Lotze argues that psychology has made the unscientific presupposition that there is a single, substantial "subject" that underlies all operations ascribed to the *Seele*, including observation, perception, feeling, and desire. But there is no introspective evidence for such a unified subject, Lotze urges, nor is there any scientific way as yet to prove its existence from empirical evidence.

Helmholtz calls the third part of his *Physiological Optics* the "psychological" part, but Helmholtz, in tune with Lotze and others, distinguished physiological psychology from pure or abstract psychology. Lotze's *Medical Psychology* is subtitled "physiology of the mind", and Wundt's *Outline of Physiological Psychology* (1874) connects the physiological to the psychological. Helmholtz engages in a "physiological psychology" in the "psychological" part of the *Physiological Optics*, and rules out more abstract psychological speculations:

> our purpose is only to investigate the matter of sensation, which occasions the formation of representations, in those connections which are important for the perceptions derived therefrom. This business can be carried out entirely according to the methods of natural science. In the process, we cannot avoid speaking of mental operations and their laws, insofar as they come into the consideration of sensible perception, but we will not

regard the investigation and description of these mental operations as a significant part of our work at hand, because in doing so we will hardly be able to remain on the ground of secure facts and a method grounded in general, recognized, and clear principles. So I believe it to be necessary, at least provisionally, to distinguish the domain of the psychological part of the physiology of sense from pure psychology, whose principal task is to establish the laws and nature of the operations of the mind.[5]

Helmholtz takes the study of psychological phenomena to be divided between the physiological study of the "mental operations" that act to bring about perception and the formation of representations and "pure psychology," the study of the "laws and nature" of the mind as it acts independently of perception and representation, sometimes resting on what Helmholtz sees as the scientifically immature analysis of introspective evidence.[6]

Helmholtz separates Lotze's question of whether there is a single, unified mind or *Seele*, along the lines of Kant's transcendental unity of apperception or Müller's rational organizing force, from the question of whether perception, representation, and intuition can be given an empirical treatment by investigating the "psychological part of the physiology of sense".[7]

2. Sensation, perception, and representation

In the third, "psychological" part of the *Physiological Optics*, Helmholtz "attempted to provide explanations of a variety of the phenomena of spatial perception by bringing them under universal psychological laws; he also sought to extend his naturalistic account of the mind to the domain of 'higher' cognition" (Hatfield 1990, 167). Helmholtz "characterized the psychological processes underlying perception as unconscious inferences, and he emphasized the role of active experience in the formation and testing of such inferences" (ibid.) As de Kock puts it, "Helmholtz's empirical approach starts out with the basic assumption that the perceptual process is crucially mediated by psychological activity" (de Kock 2014, 106).

The naturalist approach Helmholtz takes raises the question: what, on his view, is the difference between perception, a mental operation, and sensation, a physical response? Helmholtz's approach begins with the observation that sensation presents us with indeterminate information. Bare or uninterpreted sensation consists of a set of electrical impulses sent along nerve fibers, which do not in themselves constitute determinate perceptions or representations. Sensation alone, as response to a stimulus, never adds up to perception or representation of an object. Sensation presents us with:

1 A stimulation of a nerve, which is like an "insulated telegraph wire."[8] Nerve fibers, for Helmholtz, carry signals independently of any other nerves, and carry those signals to the brain if they are associated with sensory nerves. Thus, importantly, each nerve or nerve fiber carries only information about

the degree of stimulation of *that* nerve, and no information about other responses to stimuli in the nervous system.
2. A set of "accessory impressions". "For Lotze, and for Helmholtz, each sensory impression of color on the retina – red, for example – produces the same sensation [associated with] redness on all parts of the retina **a, b, c**, ... But in addition to this impression at the parts **a, b, c**, ... the light source also makes an accessory impression, ... **α, β, γ**, independent of the color seen and dependent entirely on the place excited" (Lenoir 1993, 122).

Visual representations, perceptions, and intuitions are "derived from", "associated with", or "tied to" sensation. Helmholtz remarks,

> If we restrict the name of *representation* [*Vorstellung*] to the remembered image of visual objects that is not derived from any present sensations, that of *intuition* [*Anschauung*] to the perception$_W$ [*Wahrnehmung*] derived from the respective sensations, that of *perception$_p$* [*Perception*] to such an intuition in which nothing is contained that does not arise from the immediate present sensations, thus an intuition as it can be formed even without all memory of earlier experiences, then it is clear, first, that one and the same intuition can be derived in very different ways from the corresponding sensations, and that, therefore, representation and *perception$_p$* can be associated with intuition through quite diverse relationships.
> (*PO* 26:435)[9]

An initial taxonomy, based on this passage:

Representation [*Vorstellung*]: "the remembered image of visual objects that is not derived from any present sensations".
Intuition [*Anschauung*]: "the perception$_W$ derived from the respective sensations".
Perception$_W$ [*Wahrnehmung*]: a kind of intuition (and representation, see the following) derived from sensation.
Perception$_p$ [*Perception*]: "an intuition in which nothing is contained that does not arise from the immediate present sensations".

Helmholtz uses the Latin term 'Perception' and the German term 'Wahrnehmung', both usually translated by "perception". I distinguish between them with subscripts. Intuitions are perceptions$_W$, while perceptions$_p$ are special cases of intuitions and of perceptions$_W$. Perception$_W$ is the most general type of mental activity Helmholtz describes. In turn, perception$_W$ is a form of representation, insofar as it is perception of an external object:

> We use the sensations that light stimulates in our apparatus of sensory nerves, to form for ourselves representations from [the sensations]

concerning the existence, the form, and the location of external objects. We call such representations *visual perceptions [Gesichtswahrnehmungen]*. [. . .] Since perceptions$_W$ of external objects thus belong to the representations, and representations always are acts of our mental operation,[10] perceptions$_W$ can come about only in virtue of mental operation, and thus the doctrine of perceptions$_W$ in fact already belongs to the domain of psychology.

(*PO* 26:427)

All of the terms in the above taxonomy refer to mental activity. Perceptions$_W$ are already a form of representation, and this requires mental activity. In the remarks at the beginning of the "psychological" section 26, Helmholtz says:

Thus, in the forthcoming section we have to investigate to which characteristics of retinal images, of muscular feelings, and so forth are tied the perception$_W$ of a specific position of the object seen with respect to direction and distance, on which particular features of the images depends the perception$_W$ of a corporeal form of an object extended in three directions, under which circumstances it [*the object*] appears single or double when seen with both eyes, and so forth. Thus, essentially, our purpose is only to investigate the matter of sensation,[11] which occasions the formation of representations, in those connections which are important for the perceptions$_W$ derived therefrom. This business can be carried out entirely according to the methods of natural science.

(*PO* 26:427)

Determining the distance of an object from the subject, the position of the object, and so on requires inference from the signs[12] on the retina, and that inference requires experience and memory. Even the initial perception$_p$ of external objects must incorporate inferences from experience if the objects are to be perceived in their proper spatial relationships to the subject.

3. The physiology of sensation

Helmholtz adapted his characteristic physiological stance on sensation from Johannes Müller. Müller objected to the "copy" theory of sensation, which has it that sensations are copies or direct impressions of their objects. In the work of Johann Georg Steinbuch and Caspar Theobald Tourtual, the copy theory was allied with an epistemological position, spatial realism, according to which sensations and perceptions of objects are immediate evidence for the properties of those objects.[13] Mid-nineteenth century debates over stereoscopic vision and binocular rivalry inform Müller's and Helmholtz's accounts on this score. Müller and Helmholtz cite results found using the novel stereoscopes created by Charles Wheatstone, David Brewster, and James Elliot[14] (Figures 5.1 and 5.2).

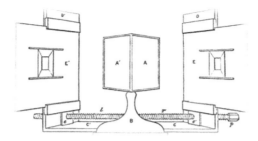

Figure 5.1 Wheatstone's stereoscope.

Figure 5.2 Brewster's stereoscope.

A stereoscope separates the visual field of each eye, and presents each eye with a separate picture, which the brain then fuses into a single image only if the pictures are kept at the right distance and angle of sight. If not, the viewer comes to be aware that each eye is presented with a separate image. As Helmholtz observes,

> Very frequently, people who first are made aware of binocular double vision are amazed, usually because they would not have noticed otherwise even though at each moment, as their lives go on, they have seen singly only a small number of objects that lie more or less the same distance from the eye at about the same focal point, and [they have seen] the larger majority, namely the group of farther and nearer objects, double.
> (*PO* 26:432)

Wheatstone investigated cases in which the visual appearance of depth (of three-dimensional figures) was apparent when two separate pictures were synthesized by the brain into a single visual image. But when a viewer looking through the stereoscope shuts one eye, the visual appearance of depth vanishes. Moreover, as Helmholtz observes, the apparent position of objects in the picture can change depending on which eye one is viewing the picture with, and on the angle of the line of sight: this is known as stereoscopic parallax (*PO* 30:637–638). The stereoscope also made easier the investigation of the phenomenon of binocular rivalry, in which, when the two eyes are presented with distinct images, the two do not fuse into a single image, rather, they are perceived alternately.

The opthalmoscope allowed for the inspection of retinal images. It had been known at least since Descartes's dissection of a bull's eye in the *Optics* that images on the retina are upside down, even though we perceive them as upright. Helmholtz himself constructed opthalmoscopes in the 1850s, and could verify this for human eyes.

For Helmholtz, the facts demonstrated using these novel instruments are evidence against the projection or copy theory of perception.[15] Visual images are not copies of the stable properties of the external objects that are their stimuli. Rather, sensations, as reactions of sense organs to stimuli, are *effects*, and the stimuli should be regarded as *causes*.[16] Physiological sensations are not transparent to the properties of external objects; they must be interpreted to give evidence of objective properties.[17]

On Helmholtz's account of the physiology of sensation and perception, the physiological process of sensation alters or transforms the stimulus, so that we cannot make a direct inference from properties of the effect (the sensation) to properties of the cause (the external stimulus). For Lotze, a principal source of this argument, sensation is

> a complicated chain of events consisting of several stages: external stimulus [. . .]; the effect of the stimulus on the nerves; the transmission of the nerve signals to the brain; the transmission of signals from the brain to the soul [*Seele*]; and finally the sensation as an object of self-awareness [. . .] the quality of the stimulus is transformed throughout this process, so that in the end there is no similarity between cause and effect. We therefore cannot conceive of sensations as a kind of copy or image of the objects that cause them.
>
> (Beiser 2013, 225)

Helmholtz concurs:

> Our intuitions and representations are effects, which the intuited and represented objects have brought about on our nervous system and on our consciousness. [. . .] To demand a representation that copied the nature of the represented, thus was true in an absolute sense, would be to demand an effect that was entirely independent of the nature of that object on which the effect was brought about, which would be a palpable contradiction. Thus all our human representations [. . .] are depictions[18] of objects whose kind essentially co-depends on the nature of the representing consciousness and is co-determined by its characteristics.
>
> (*PO* 26, 442–443)

Intuitions and representations are brought about in a necessarily two-sided relationship between the causes (the intuited and represented objects) and the effects (the intuitions and representations). To understand intuition and representation requires investigating the "nature of that object on which the effect was brought about," that is, the nature and characteristics of the sensorium and the "representing consciousness."

Müller had argued that the possibility of giving a scientific account of physiological sensation required distinguishing the sensations specific to each type of sensory nerve: haptic, visual (optic), auditory, gustatory, and olfactory. He associated each kind of nerve with a distinctive type of response to stimuli, a principle called the "Law of specific nerve energies" (LoSNE) or "Müller's law".[19] In the *Physiological Optics*, Helmholtz restates Müller's law of specific nerve energies:

> Physiological experience has found, as far as testing is possible, that *through stimulation of each single sensory nerve fiber only those sensations can arise that belong to the quality sphere*[20] *of each single specific sense, and that each stimulus that is capable in general of stimulating these nerve fibers generates only sensations in these specific spheres.*
> (*PO* 17:193)

Helmholtz's reading of Müller's law leads to the following claim:

> the quality of sensible experience depends primarily on the specific constitution of the nerve apparatus, only secondarily on the constitution of the perceived object. Which sense's quality sphere an occurrent sensation belongs to does not depend on external objects, but exclusively on the type of nerve struck. Which particular sensation from the encountered quality sphere will be generated, this, above all, depends on the nature of the external object that stimulates the sensation.
> (*PO* 17:194)

For Helmholtz, it is possible to identify which features of a sensation are objective by inquiring into the specific observed quality of the sensation.[21] The ability to identify a particular sensed quality as occupying a specific, limited position within the quality sphere of a nerve requires a causal inference. Such inferences take the following form:

1 The nerve at issue has a quality sphere, the range of which can be investigated.
2 Nerves are not stimulated for no reason; the properties of external objects or events are, *ceteris paribus*, the sources of our sensations.[22]
3 A specific observed quality of a sensation is thus a *limitation* of the quality sphere of possible sensations of a particular nerve.
4 Any such qualitative limitation must have a ground or cause.
5 The cause of the qualitative limitation is a particular external object or event.

Thus, the specific qualities of our sensations can serve as evidence for the properties of the causes of those sensations, the external objects or events.

The particular qualities of sensations are the basis for a set of abductive inferences to the properties of external objects and events. While Helmholtz agrees with the Kantian distinction between the phenomenal and the real, he also argues that there are well-grounded inferences from sensations to their external sources.[23] Helmholtz has a long-standing commitment to the view that any perception of an external object requires representation, which at the least requires positing an object as the cause of the perception.[24]

For Helmholtz, the law of causality is an a priori, transcendental presupposition necessary to natural science in general and to the assertion that our sensations are effects of objective causes in particular.[25] We cannot prove any correspondence between our sensations and their stimuli, with one exception: "The only respect in which an actual agreement[26] can obtain between our perceptions and actuality is the temporal sequence of events" (*PO* 26:445). Any causal connection in nature will be reflected by a regular sequence of sensations, as signs that indicate the regularities in the phenomena:

> Each law of nature states that on preconditions that are similar in certain respects consequences that are similar in certain other respects always occur. Since similars in our sensible world are indicated by similar signs, the nomological sequence of similar effects following similar causes corresponds to an equally regular sequence in the realm of our sensations.
> (Helmholtz 1878, 13)

Sensations, as signs of their stimuli, may have no "agreement" with those stimuli other than the time sequences of their occurrence.[27] The regularities in what Helmholtz calls the "sign system" of perceptions of, and inferences from, those sensations are indications of causal regularities. Mental activity is necessary to transform sensations into objective representations of the regularities among the sensations.

4. Unconscious inference and objectivity

Helmholtz argues that inferences from sensation to objective representation, in many cases, are inductive "unconscious inferences".[28] Descartes treated the body as a mechanism operating separately from the mind. But Leibniz left room for "petites perceptions," minute perceptions of which the primary monad need not be aware. Acknowledging that sensation, and features of perception and representation, take place physically means acknowledging the possibility that elements of these occur outside consciousness.

In the first half of the nineteenth century, physiologists had begun to argue that even representations and ideas could be unconscious. Herbart argued that some representations could be "suppressed" from consciousness by other representations.[29]

In an early essay, Lotze argued that the "perceptions of the [Leibnizian primary] monad [. . .] constitute the 'essence' or 'meaning' of the body, because they realize its implicit, inchoate and subconscious forces" (Beiser 2013, 146). In *Medical Psychology*, Lotze argues that even conscious thoughts, including voluntary acts of will, incorporate the physical actions of a substance that take place outside the arena of consciousness (§109, 125–126). On Helmholtz's account,

> The mental operations through which we come to the judgment that a particular object in a particular state in a particular place outside us is present, are in general not conscious operations, but unconscious. In their results, they are similar to an *inference*, insofar as we achieve from the observed effect on our senses the representation of a cause of this effect, whereas, in fact, we can only perceive directly the nerve stimulations, that is, the effects, never the external objects.
>
> (*PO* 26:430)

Unconscious inferences are judgments that external objects bearing certain properties are present and are the causes of our sensations. I will elaborate on Helmholtz's own example of cast shadows. From the perspective of an observer on the Earth's surface, the shadows cast by tall buildings grow longer as the sun sets. The general relationships established by inductive inferences from observation are the major premises for an inference: an oblong, long shadow on the sidewalk at dusk probably is cast by a tall building, for instance. If I see an oblong, long shadow on the sidewalk at dusk (the minor premise), I infer that the object casting the shadow is a building (the conclusion).

That "conclusion" is not a conscious inference, but a feature of the formation of my image that takes place in response to longtime habit. I interpret the glimpse of the shadow-casting object in my perception of a building, and my perceptual image of the building includes inferential information that may depend on my experience and on my practice interpreting sensations. I may perceive an outcropping on the shadow as a window, because I have interpreted, tacitly, the shadow's source as a building. When the outcropping moves, I may perceive this as the window opening, because of another unconscious inference.

All these interpretations could be false, and my reading of the sensory indications – which affects the formation of the image – depends on contextual clues. Maybe I am walking along a sidewalk at dusk in a new city, and I don't realize that on the other side of the sidewalk is a river with a line of ships at harbor, not a line of buildings. The "building" casting the shadow could be a ship, and the moving "window" a sail. If I look closely at the "building" and realize that it is a ship, the sensory material of my perception rearranges itself into a distinct "intuitive image." As Helmholtz puts it,

> the remembered images from earlier experiences work together with present sensations to bring forth an intuitive image, which intrudes upon

our power of perception with compelling force, without what is given through memory and what is given through present perception being separated in consciousness. The influence of understanding on sensations is even more striking in individual cases, in particular when with imperfect lighting a visual image is initially unintelligible, because we do not know how to give it the correct depth dimensions, when we, for instance, take some distant light as close, or a close one for distant. Suddenly it occurs to us what it is, and simultaneously under the influence of the correct understanding the correct intuitive image is developed as well in its full power, and we are not in a position to turn back from this one to the earlier incomplete intuition. This occurs quite often with complex stereoscopic drawings of crystal forms and others, which are intuited in complete sensible clarity as soon as one successfully achieves correct understanding.

(*PO* 26:436–437)

Helmholtz observes that is difficult to distinguish which contents of our images are contributed by experience and practice, and which by sensations. This problem is just as pressing for perception as it is for representation. While it is true that perception allows access to the sensory material available from present stimuli, sensory material is never given passively, for Helmholtz. Observation is active, selective, and directed:

We do not merely abandon ourselves passively to the impressions impinging on us, rather we *observe*, which means we bring our organs into those conditions under which they can distinguish the impressions most exactly. For instance, in the observation of a complex object we direct our two eyes toward each other, accommodated as well as possible so that both continually are fixed on that point to which our awareness already has guided itself, that is on the position of clearest sight, and allow the eyes to wander together over all the points of the object worth noticing.

(*PO* 26:438)

Helmholtz argues that our perception and observation are so geared toward perceiving distinct objects and their properties that practiced observers become unable to bring more purely subjective sensations, without objective import, to conscious awareness. For Helmholtz, this practical fact is a "general characteristic of our sensations":

we attend to our sensations easily and exactly only insofar as they can be used for knowledge of external objects, but [. . .] *we are used to abstracting away from all those parts of sensations that have no significance for external objects*, so that most of the time special encouragement and practice is necessary for the observation of these latter subjective sensations.

(*PO* 26:431)

The blind spot is a classic example of a subjective sensation that is unnoticed in normal perception. Helmholtz also explains binocular rivalry, the phenomenon in which each eye is presented with distinct images but the brain does not fuse the two into a single image, by appeal to selective attention: the brain attends to one image, then the other, not both at once. Objective perception, for Helmholtz, is tied up with selective and guided attention.

On Helmholtz's view, our mental activity in experience is "directed" at representing objects. His theory could be seen as an early version of the "intentionality" thesis defended by Brentano – and later by Crane – according to which the mind's direction (*Richtung*) toward its own activity or toward objects is the distinguishing characteristic of mental activity, the "mark" of the mental.[30] Helmholtz's argument for intentionality extends to the claim that our selective awareness is directed unconsciously toward objective representation, and away from subjective sensations that are not employed in objective representation.

5. Phenomenal experience: plasticity and cognitive penetrability

Helmholtz saw establishing the mathematical, lawlike relationships that describe the interaction between external stimulus and subjective perceiver as fundamental to his account of experience. Establishing these relationships required commitment to the plasticity of perceptual experience: the subject can engage in voluntary motions, for instance, that test the boundaries of the self against those of the object, and can bring novel sensations and perceptions into view.[31] These cannot be anticipated a priori. The "perceived sphere of presentabilia cannot be posited through a *conscious* act of our representation or will" (Helmholtz 1878, 38). We interact with "actual" *(wirkliche)* objects; they work *(wirken)* on us to produce sensory experience and perception.

Helmholtz's account, according to which sensations are effects of external causes, and perception and concepts of external objects involve "practical" knowledge of the possible effects objects may have on us and their modal physical properties generally, may appear to have much in common with recent "sensorimotor" or embodied approaches to consciousness and to phenomenal experience (O'Regan and Noë 2001a, 2001b). On the sensorimotor view,

> seeing is a way of acting. It is a particular way of exploring the environment. Activity in internal representations does not generate the experience of seeing. The outside world serves as its own, external, representation. The experience of seeing occurs when the organism masters what we call the governing laws of sensorimotor contingency. The advantage of this

approach is that it provides a natural and principled way of accounting for visual consciousness, and for the differences in the perceived quality of sensory experience in the different sensory modalities.

(O'Regan and Noë 2001b, 939)

Prinz (2008) criticizes the sensorimotor approach for its "radicalism," arguing that, on this view, visual experience and consciousness depend on the location of the subject in a particular environment, the subject's "situatedness". On a strong reading of the sensorimotor view, consciousness isn't in the head.[32]

Helmholtz captures one of the attractive elements of the sensorimotor view, that our experience depends on causal relationships, interactions between features of the environment and the subject. But Helmholtz falls into another camp, one in which, as Prinz observes, Dretske, Tye, and Lycan fall as well: the combination of externalism with representationalism, including intentionalism about representation. On this view, the character of consciousness, including visual experience, can depend on causal interactions. But these interactions are described in nomological terms, as lawlike relationships necessary to determine objective representations, not as particular instances of situated consciousness being caused by particular external features of the environment.

There is a simpler, illuminating difference between Helmholtz's approach and sensorimotor theory. Helmholtz's theory of representation is *epistemological*. His main question of interest, as he puts it in "The Facts in Perception," is "What is truth in our representations?"[33] His analysis of phenomenal experience is aimed at finding the truth, not "accounting for visual consciousness". Accounting for visual consciousness is important to him, but the goal of doing so is to find the causal relationships and facts revealed in experience. These can be found only by reading sensory "signs" or indications, and interpreting the signs requires mental representation. By the time a sensation makes it to the subject, it is no longer really "external", because the process of sensing and perceiving fundamentally alters properties of the stimulus. To O'Regan and Noë, "The outside world serves as its own, external, representation". This would be anathema to Helmholtz: for him, any representation requires inference and interpretation.

The "truth" in our perception and experience is a practical truth, on Helmholtz's account (*PO* 26:443). Concepts of external objects are constructed using our knowledge of their effects on us as perceiving subjects. Knowledge of their properties is limited to the relational properties revealed by these interactions. We learn to read the signs revealed in these interactions, and we test our understanding by engaging in experiments that vary the conditions under which the interactions take place. Although the truth in perception is practical, it is not for that reason infinitely mutable. Stable regularities are revealed in these experiments, which cannot be overridden in experience. For instance, if I try to hear the note produced by a tuning fork tuned to C as an F, in normal conditions, I cannot. If I wish to see sunlight as a spectrum of color, I can cast the light through a prism, but I cannot vary the colors I see at will.[34]

On the basis of his account of the stable, nomological properties of interactions between subject and object, Helmholtz defends what now is called an "adverbial" theory of the qualities of perception.[35]

> To ask whether vermilion is actually red, as we see it, or whether this is a sensory illusion, is therefore senseless. The sensation of red is the normal reaction of normally formed eyes to the light reflected by vermilion. A colorblind person would see vermilion as black or dark grey-yellow; this too is the correct reaction for a different eye. [. . .] In itself the one sensation is not more correct or more false than the other.
>
> (*PO* 26:445)

On the ground level of Helmholtz's multi-level account of sensation and perception, there are law-governed regularities between the external object, as cause, and the subject's nervous system, as effect. Vermilion has a certain wavelength; light reflected from it is taken up by the cells in the retina and sensed as red. This is the usual effect of that cause. Someone with a sensory mechanism configured in a certain way *must* see vermilion as red, and so it is "senseless" to ask whether vermilion is "seen as" red by that person.

On another level, the perceived *shade* of a vermilion object varies with its distance from the subject. The farther away it becomes, the hazier or lighter its color will appear (*PO* 26:433). Many perceived qualities that depend on spatial conditions, including distance and depth, can be "overridden" in experience by changing the conditions or interpretation of that experience. They are not ground-level sensory facts. They are stable, but malleable perceptual regularities.

Helmholtz's experimental techniques in physiological acoustics and optics make concrete Müller's notion of specific nerve energies, explaining the characteristics of each type of sense nerve stimulation. Helmholtz isolated a number of simple sensory responses, and showed how some complex perceptions arise from the composition of such simple sensations. He defends a general principle for differentiating pure sensation from what is constituted by mental activity:

> *nothing in our sense perceptions can be recognized as sensation that, through moments demonstrably given in experience, can be overridden in the intuitive image and transformed into its opposite.* Thus, we must regard whatever can be overridden through moments of experience as itself a product of experience and practice. It will be shown that if we follow this rule, only the qualities of sensation are to be regarded as actually pure sensation, but most spatial intuitions by far as a product of experience and practice.
>
> (*PO* 26:438)

On the basis of facts[36] revealed in experiment, Helmholtz crafts a multilevel account of perceptual experience. On one level, there are sensory responses to stimuli, the effects of objective causes. These are stimulations of nerves in response to present stimuli. On another level, there are "representations" or "intuitions", which are constructed by the mind, and can be "overridden" in experience. Helmholtz argues that any non-sensory element of experience can be changed by training the observer. If you put the observer back in the initial situation after that training, the observer will no longer see things in the same way.

Helmholtz's view might be seen as an early version of Susanna Siegel's thesis of cognitive penetrability, according to which:

> If visual experience is cognitively penetrable, then it is nomologically possible for two subjects (or for one subject in different counterfactual circumstances, or at different times) to have visual experiences with different contents while seeing *and attending to* the same distal stimuli under the same external conditions, as a result of differences in other cognitive (including affective) states.[37]

Helmholtz's remark that a visual representation takes on a certain determinate form only once the observer has "understood" what is being represented supports such a reading, as does his position that features of complex sensations are the result of mental activity. His statement that "one and the same intuition can be derived in very different ways from the corresponding sensations, and that, therefore, representation and perception can be associated with intuition through quite diverse relationships", allows for the possibility of cognitive penetrability as Siegel describes it.[38] Finally, Helmholtz points out that subjects can be trained to "see" the same scene in a different way, or to "hear" the same chord differently, to the point that the subject can no longer perceive the scene or the chord as before.

Helmholtz's account allows for at least two ways phenomenal experience can be changed. One is through training, by manipulating the causal relationships between sensing subject and external object, so that "normal" perceptual relationships are disrupted and novel perceptual regularities emerge. It might be objected that this is not cognitive penetrability, because the same subject is being placed in different contexts, not seeing the same scene differently. But Helmholtz's point is that, after such training, subjects placed back in their original context may have a distinct perception of the same external stimuli. The relevant question is whether this penetration is cognitive, since it results from training, which may involve learning but also may involve behavioral conditioning.

Phenomenal experience also can be changed in cases in which, when the subject reaches the correct understanding, a scene snaps into focus and can be interpreted correctly. This is also cognitive penetrability, because interpretation is required for perception. A difference in cognitive states allows for distinct interpretations, and distinct perceptions, of the same scene.

Helmholtz argues that there are limits to the extent to which our understanding or interpretation can influence the content of perceptual experience. These limits are given by the stable regularities, grounded by causal relationships, revealed in the subject's experience: regularities describing the stable relationships between cause (stimulus) and effect (sensation).

Still, Helmholtz argues that phenomenal experience has remarkable plasticity. The nomological regularities of the stimulus-response curve, or of the relationship between the wavelength of light and the stimulation of retinal cells, do not exhaust the content of sensory representation and experience. In support of his hypothesis of the plasticity of experience, Helmholtz argues against the nativist view held by Ewald Hering and Peter Ludwig Panum, according to which spatial perception is underwritten by innate mechanisms or perceptions:[39]

> it can be quite difficult to judge what, in our intuitions achieved through the visual sense, is determined immediately through sensation, and what on the contrary is determined through experience and practice. The primary, fundamental dispute that exists between different researchers in this area is connected to this difficulty. Some tend to allow the influence of experience the widest latitude possible, and in particular to derive all spatial intuition from it; we can describe this view as the *empirist theories*. Others indeed must allow the influence of experience for a certain class of perceptions, but believe they must presuppose for certain elementary intuitions that occur uniformly for all observers a system of innate intuitions not grounded on experience, namely spatial relationships. We may describe this latter view in contrast to the first as the *nativist theory* of sense perceptions.
>
> (*PO* 26:435)

For Hering, our awareness and perception of spatial relationships is not inferred by the mind, but rather is a product of our binocular or "cyclopean" sensory mechanism.[40] Nativists employ innate mechanisms to explain the same phenomena Helmholtz explains through unconscious inference. Helmholtz remarks that

> the combination of sensations is maintained with the representation of their objects to seem so fixed and compulsive, to many physiologists and psychologists, that they are so little inclined to recognize that this combination rests on acquired experience and thus on mental operation, at least in large part, that they seek on the contrary a mechanical way that it takes place through pre-formed organic structures.
>
> (*PO* 26:431)

For Hering, there are innate relationships between cells on the retina, and between the retinas and nerves of the two eyes, that determine how spatial relationships are perceived. Elements of spatial relationships may be learned, as are particular spatial judgments, but our perception of spatial relationships is based on the innate constitution and mechanisms of our sensory apparatus.

In objecting to Hering's view, Helmholtz cites experimental facts according to which perceived spatial relationships can be changed in experience and through practice. But the most significant argument is against the notion that the retina and the visual apparatus limit the determination of spatial relationships in sensation: "for the empirist theory [Helmholtz's theory] it is entirely unimportant how the retina is configured" (*PO* 33:801). Helmholtz does investigate, and in detail, the properties of the retina. His point is that, for him, the retina is a sensory instrument to be employed by the mind in constructing complex representations, not an organ that independently fuses sensations into complex images or representations. The empirist, unlike the nativist, need not assume any configuration or innate function of the retina itself, only a set of lawlike relationships between retinal points and their projections into space.

To Helmholtz, Hering and Panum do not allow for the plasticity of spatial construction in experience in response to sensory cues, which hampers their ability to investigate thoroughly the law-governed relationships between subjects and objects as revealed in experience. For him, nativists are required to assume a pre-established harmony between mind and nature, in which spatial representations that arise through an innate mechanism are supposed to correspond to actual phenomena (*PO* 26: 442).

Helmholtz's arguments for the plasticity of experience accompany a nomothetic methodology. Nativism, on Helmholtz's view, is a bar to investigating the full range of possible spatial relationships that can be revealed in experience. This hinders the thorough investigation of the lawlike relationships between, for instance, the voluntary movements of a perceiving subject and the spatial properties of external objects that can be revealed through those movements. On Helmholtz's view, sensations are effects on the subject caused by external objects. All spatial, quantitative features of our sensations are determinable in a two-sided causal relationship, governed by physical and physiological laws.

Helmholtz pioneered an approach to perceptual experience according to which experience is geared toward representing external objects and the environment, representation is interpretive and intentional, and sensory signs must be interpreted to achieve representation. The occurrence and variance of a particular sign or class of signs can be shown to be governed by physical laws that describe the interaction between subjective sensation (effect) and external stimulus (cause). The account of these laws and these relationships is anchored by perceptual facts, revealed through practical investigation and experiment.

Helmholtz's approach is an early version of the influential blend of externalism and representationalism advocated by Dretske, Tye, and Lycan. His defense of an epistemological theory of perceptual experience gives support to a response to sensorimotor theories proposed by O'Regan and Noë. On Helmholtz's epistemological account, for visual experience to represent external objects requires inference and interpretation, which appears to rule out the sensorimotor theory. Helmholtz argues for an early, though limited, thesis of cognitive penetrability, defended recently by Siegel, and for an adverbial theory of color and of sensory qualities, related to a recent account by Chirimuuta. Helmholtz's view is a synthesis of naturalism and of nomothetic apriorism in the philosophy of mind, the former informed by his early engagement with the physiological tradition, and the latter influenced by Kant and Fichte.

Helmholtz's scientific results in his texts on sound and color have influenced present scientific and philosophical approaches to sensation and to sensory qualities. Helmholtz's view was intended, not solely as a philosophical position, but as a scientific approach to perceptual experience and its epistemological significance, and both aspects of his theory have had a deep influence.

Notes

1 Above all, I would like to thank Sandra Lapointe for her insight into the configuration and promise of this project, for conceiving of this volume, and for astute and perceptive responses to earlier versions, which shaped the project as it stands now. Clinton Tolley read the penultimate version of the paper and contributed invaluable suggestions, including preventing me from making a most consequential error of translation, for which I am grateful. Erik Banks's encouragement and suggestions made a real difference. Gary Hatfield published *The Natural and the Normative* twenty-five years ago, which introduced me to Helmholtz, to the significance of his work, and to the possibilities it contains.
2 For a discussion of "*Seele*" and "*Geist*" in the context of "faculty psychology," see Beiser (2014, 136–138 and 156–157).
3 1844, *Prolegomena* §2.
4 *Medicinische Psychologie oder Physiologie der Seele.*
5 "Seelenthätigkeiten". Helmholtz 1867, hereafter *PO,* 26:427. Citations of *PO* give the section, then page, number.
6 One might associate the German word "Geist" with "pure psychology" or with idealism, and "psychisch" and "Seele" with the physiological, naturalist approach. But Helmholtz, Wundt, and others seem to use the word "geistig" as a synonym for "psychisch," which undermines the basis for a principled distinction. Helmholtz does employ "Geist" more often when discussing idealist philosophers (*PO*, "Geist" and variants: Plato (17:207), Kant, Fichte and Schelling (26:456)), and "psychisch" and "Seele" more often when discussing physiological theories (*PO*, "psychisch" and variants: 32:772–774, §33, throughout; "Seele": §26, throughout; 29:620; §33, throughout). See Wundt (1874), "Psychologische Vorbegriffe: Die Begriffe Seele und Geist. Die Lehre von den Seelenvermögen," pp. 8–20. For more on the "Seele" in German idealism, see the concluding sections of Clinton Tolley's essay in this volume.
7 Helmholtz's theory of perception and sensation is born from his acquaintance with Müller, Lotze, Johann Friedrich Herbart, Gustav Fechner, and Ernst Weber, and from his early work with the Berlin Physical Society, with Emil du Bois-Reymond, Sigmund Freud, and others. For the former, see Hatfield 1990, Ch. 5; for the latter, see Sulloway 1992, 13ff. and 65ff.
8 Hatfield 1990, 172; see *PO* 17, 191–192.
9 I would like to thank Clinton Tolley on bended knee for saving me (and the reader) from a mis-translation of this passage, and from a terminological and interpretive confusion.
10 "psychischen Thätigkeit". On *PO* 17:207, Helmholtz uses "Thätigkeit" for Empedocles's "energeia".
11 *Empfindungsmaterial.*

12 See the section following for a discussion of "signs" in Helmholtz.
13 See Hatfield (1990, Chapter 4: "Spatial Realism and Idealism") for a detailed account.
14 Brewster 1856 provides a one-sided but entertaining history.
15 See Lenoir 2006, 143–144.
16 *PO* 26:456. In the case of illusion, there may be no external stimulus, or we may form a mistaken judgment about the nature of the stimulus, but there was still *some* cause for the sensation, on this account.
17 For more on the sign theory, see Patton (2009 and 2014), including the citations to further work.
18 "Bilder".
19 The shorthand LoSNE appears to be due to Liesbet de Kock. She discusses Müller's law in De Kock (2014 and 2015).
20 "Qualitätenkreise". The term comes from Fichte (Helmholtz 1878, 9).
21 Hyder (2009) analyzes Helmholtz's related notion of determinacy.
22 Helmholtz does allow for illusory sensations, but he observes that even they have some source, though it may be internal to the subject.
23 See, for instance, *PO* 26, 427.
24 *PO* 26, 427, see Hatfield (2011, §5). As Hatfield notes, in 1855 Helmholtz argues that representation of objects in space requires "our positing objects as the causes of our sensations, and we make such posits in accordance with the proposition, 'no effect without a cause'" (Helmholtz 1855; Hatfield 2011, §5, 329).
25 "Every alteration in nature *must* have a sufficient cause" (Helmholtz 1847, 4). "The causal law is actually a given a priori, transcendental law. A proof of it from experience is not possible" (Helmholtz 1878, 41).
26 "Uebereinstimmung".
27 My hearing a thunderclap will take place at approximately the same time as the thunderclap itself. Though, as Helmholtz observes, we see the light from the stars many years after it is emitted, we can determine the temporal relationship between the star shining and my seeing the light.
28 "unbewusste Schlüsse". De Kock (2014, §3, 725–728) analyzes Mill's influence on Helmholtz's view of inductive inference.
29 Herbart (1816, 106–107): "one of the older representations can be suppressed entirely from consciousness for a while by a new one that is much weaker. However, its striving is not to be regarded as ineffective [. . .] rather, it works with its whole might against the representations found in consciousness".
30 See Robin Rollinger's and Peter Simons's contributions to this volume for discussion of nineteenth-century theories of intentionality, including Brentano's. Brentano objected to Helmholtz's theory of unconscious inference. Crane (2003) is a contemporary explanation and defense of intentionality.
31 Fichte's "nicht-Ich", in the "Facts in Perception" lecture (Helmholtz 1878, 35–38).
32 Prinz cites empirical evidence against these claims, but my focus here is on the philosophical account.
33 Helmholtz (1878, 42).
34 Studies of Helmholtz on compound colors and tones include Hatfield (2011), Heller (2012), Hui (2013), Hyder (2009), Kremer (1993), Sherman (1981), and Turner (1996). Helmholtz's papers on color mixing are collected in Helmholtz (1882).
35 Chirimuuta (2015) is a recent defense of the adverbial theory.
36 "Fact" ("Thatsache") is a technical term for Helmholtz, referring to a regularity demonstrated in experience, ideally in experiment. For instance, Helmholtz (1878) is entitled "The Facts in Perception."
37 Siegel (2012, §1); thanks to Preston Lennon for mentioning this work.
38 *PO* 26, 435.

39 *PO* 26: 431, 456, and passim; §33, throughout. See §I.4 of Erik Banks's article in this volume for a discussion of the nativism controversy.
40 Hering (1861, 330ff.); see Banks, this volume, §I.4.

Bibliography

Unless cited in another work, translations from German texts are by Lydia Patton.

Beiser, Frederick. 2013. *Late German Idealism*. Oxford: Oxford University Press.
———. 2014. *The Genesis of Neo-Kantianism*. Oxford: Oxford University Press.
Brewster, David. 1856. *The Stereoscope*. London: John Murray.
Cahan, David. (ed.). 1993. *Hermann von Helmholtz and the Foundations of Nineteenth-Century Science*. Berkeley: University of California Press.
Chirimuuta, Mazviita. 2015. *Outside Color*. Cambridge, MA: MIT Press.
Crane, Tim. 2003. *The Mechanical Mind*. London: Routledge.
De Kock, Liesbet. 2014. "Voluntarism in Early Psychology," *History of Psychology* 17 (2): 105–128.
———. 2015. "Hermann von Helmholtz's empirico-transcendentalism Reconsidered," *Science in Context* 27 (4): 709–744.
Hatfield, Gary. 1990. *The Natural and the Normative*. Cambridge, MA: MIT Press.
———. 2011. "Kant and Helmholtz on Primary and Secondary Qualities," in Lawrence Nolan, ed. *Primary and Secondary Qualities*. Oxford: Oxford University Press.
Heller, Eric. 2012. *Why You Hear What You Hear*. Princeton: Princeton University Press.
Helmholtz, Hermann. 1855. *Über das Sehen des Menschen*. Leipzig: Leopold Voss.
———. 1867. *Handbuch der physiologischen Optik*. Leipzig: Leopold Voss. Published in parts from 1856 to 1866, then published in toto in 1867 as Volume Nine of the *Allgemeinen Encyclopädie der Physik*, ed. Gustav Karsten.
———. 1870. *Die Lehre von den Tonempfindungen als physiologische Grundlage für die Theorie der Musik*, third rev. ed. Braunschweig: Vieweg.
———. 1879/1878. *Die Thatsachen in der Wahrnehmung*. Berlin: Hirschwald.
———. 1882/1847. *Ueber die Erhaltung der Kraft*, repr. *Wissenschaftliche Abhandlungen*, zweiter Band, erste Abtheilung. Leipzig: Johann Ambrosius Barth.
Herbart, Johann. 1816. *Lehrbuch zur Psychologie*. Königsberg und Leipzig: August Wilhelm Unzer.
Hering, Ewald. 1861. *Beiträge zur Physiologie*. Leipzig: Engelmann.
Hui, Alexandra. 2013. *The Psychophysical Ear*. Cambridge, MA: MIT Press.
Hyder, David. 2009. *The Determinate World*. Berlin: Walter de Gruyter.
Kremer, Richard. 1993. "Innovation Through Synthesis," pp. 205–258 in Cahan 1993.
Lenoir, Timothy. 1993. "The Eye as Mathematician," in Cahan 1993.
———. 2006. "Operationalizing Kant," in Michael Friedman and Alfred Nordmann, eds. *The Kantian Legacy in Nineteenth-Century Science*. Cambridge, MA: MIT Press.
Lotze, Hermann. 1852. *Medicinische Psychologie oder Physiologie der Seele*. Leipzig: Wiedmann'sche Buchhandlung.
Müller, Johannes. 1844. *Handbuch der Physiologie des Menschen*, fourth rev. ed. Coblenz: J. Hölscher.
O'Regan, Kevin and Noë, Alva. 2001a. "What It Is like to See: A Sensorimotor Theory of Perceptual Experience," *Synthese* 129 (1): 79–103.

———. 2001b. "A Sensorimotor Account of Vision and Visual Consciousness," *Behavioral and Brain Sciences* 24: 939–1031.Patton, Lydia. 2009. "Signs, Toy Models, and the A Priori," *Studies in the History and Philosophy of Science* 40 (3): 281–289.

———. 2014. "Hermann von Helmholtz," *The Stanford Encyclopedia of Philosophy*, Edward N. Zalta (ed.), URL = <http://plato.stanford.edu/archives/fall2014/entries/hermann-helmholtz/>.

Prinz, Jesse. 2008. "Is Consciousness Embodied?" in P. Robbins and M. Aydede, eds. *Cambridge Handbook of Situated Cognition*. Cambridge: Cambridge University Press.

Sherman, Paul. 1981. *Color Vision in the Nineteenth Century*. Philadelphia: Heyden.

Siegel, Susanna. 2012. "Cognitive Penetrability and Perceptual Justification," *Noûs* 46 (2): 201–222.

Sulloway, Frank. 1992. *Freud*. Cambridge, MA: Harvard University Press.

Turner, R. 1996. "The Origins of Colorimetry," in G. Schubring, ed. *Hermann Günther Graßmann*. Dordrecht: Kluwer.

Wundt, Wilhelm. 1874. *Grundzüge der physiologischen Psychologie*. Leipzig: Wilhelm Engelmann.

6

NIETZSCHE'S PHILOSOPHY OF MIND

Mattia Riccardi

1. Introduction[1]

1.1 Nietzsche, a philosopher of mind?

Nietzsche's name is usually associated with a vitriolic criticism of morality and Christianity, as well as with the somewhat fanciful notions of "eternal recurrence" and "will to power" that figure in his metaphysics. Most are likely to assume that the problems typically discussed in the philosophy of mind seem to lie, at the very best, at the periphery of his own interests. However widespread this impression might be, it is doubtless mistaken. First, Nietzsche's criticism of the Judeo-Christian tradition is intimately connected with his own moral psychology, which in turn presupposes a peculiar – and often insightful – take on a range of central issues in the philosophy of mind that include, among others, consciousness and its place in nature, the relation between mind and language, the working of the affects, the nature of the unconscious and the role it plays in the production of our beliefs and actions. Second, that our mental life represents for Nietzsche a vital concern is something he explicitly declares. In a famous passage from *Beyond Good and Evil*, he emphatically insists that psychology, due to its constituting "the path to the fundamental problems", should "again be recognized as queen of the sciences" (Nietzsche 1886, 24). Moreover, his praise – e.g. of Dostoevsky and of the French moralists – or blame – e.g. of Kant and of the English positivists – of other writers often depends on his assessment of their psychological views. Finally, the centrality of psychological issues to Nietzsche's project is further evidenced by the fact that he is generally recognized as having anticipated significant aspects of Freudian psychoanalysis – so significant indeed that the possible influence of Nietzsche's ideas on Freud's theories has been heatedly debated ever since.[2]

This chapter aims at illustrating the centrality of Nietzsche's reflection on the nature and functioning of the mind within his overall philosophical project. I will start with some introductory remarks on Nietzsche's naturalistic approach to the investigation of human nature in general and then examine in some detail his views on conscious and unconscious mind (part 2 and 3, respectively). Finally, and as a way of conclusion, I shall briefly consider how, on his conception, conscious mental life might be taken to relate to the unconscious (part 4).

1.2 The background: Nietzsche's naturalism

It is now widely recognized that Nietzsche was committed to (some version of) naturalism, a position he vigorously recommends in the following passage:

> To translate humanity back into nature; to gain control of the many vain and fanciful interpretations and incidental meanings that have been scribbled and drawn over that eternal basic text of *homo natura* so far; to make sure that, from now on, the human being will stand before the human being, just as he already stands before the *rest* of nature today, hardened by the discipline of science, – with courageous Oedipus eyes and sealed up Odysseus ears, deaf to the lures of the old metaphysical bird catchers who have been whistling to him for far too long: "You are more! You are higher! You have a different origin!"
> (Nietzsche 1886, 123)

The idea seems clear enough: there is no reason for us humans to feel entitled to consider our nature to be, in some sense, superior or even just essentially different from that of all other natural beings. Many interpreters take this programmatic statement to imply that all aspects of human existence, including those pertaining to the domain of psychology, are amenable of the same kind of empirical explanation typically employed in the natural science (see, most notably, Leiter 2015). Others take Nietzsche to maintain that genuine thought and agency cannot be made sense of in purely causal terms, as they are irreducibly normative (see, in particular, Clark and Dudrick 2012). Thus, the precise scope of Nietzsche's naturalism remains a disputed issue. For the present purpose, what matters is only the way in which his naturalistic approach bears on his view of the mind.

What's clear is that the kind of naturalism put forward in the passage just quoted rules out dualism with regard to the mind-body problem. Indeed, Nietzsche is known for holding that the mental is essentially part of the natural world: as he puts it in *Thus Spoke Zarathustra*, "soul is just a word for something in the body" (Nietzsche 1883/1885, 23, translation changed).[3] However, the version of naturalism Nietzsche embraces does not entail a commitment to reductive physicalism, i.e. to the view that all mental and psychological phenomena are reducible to facts describable in physical or biological terms. In particular, he takes consciousness to emerge from our linguistic and communicative practices and thus to depend, in part, on essentially social facts. Thus, Nietzsche's project is best understood as a form of non-reductive naturalism.[4]

2. The conscious mind

2.1 Which consciousness?

Nietzsche talks about consciousness in a number of passages scattered throughout his work, both published and unpublished. Aphorism 354 from *Gay Science* however stands out, as it highlights all the crucial features Nietzsche takes consciousness to have. (i) Consciousness is neither a condition for mentality, nor for agency. As Nietzsche puts it, "we could think, feel, will, remember, and also 'act' in every sense of the term, and yet none of all this would have to 'enter our consciousness'" (this and the following quotations are all from aphorism 354, Nietzsche 1882/1887, 211–214). In this sense, consciousness is somewhat superfluous. (ii) Nietzsche's characterization seems to imply that consciousness involves some kind of reflexivity, i.e. a certain cognitive relation to oneself. On the one hand, Nietzsche formulates the problem of consciousness as that of one's "becoming conscious of oneself (*Sich-Bewusst-Werdens*)" (translation changed). On the other hand, that consciousness implies reflexivity is also suggested by the mirror metaphor he employs: for an organism to become conscious is like "seeing itself in the mirror". (iii) Nietzsche seems to assume a tight connection between consciousness and language: he claims that "*consciousness in general has developed only under the pressure of the need to communicate*". (iv) He also claims – a point closely related to the previous one – that (all and only) conscious thinking "*takes place in words, that is, in communication symbols*". In other words, Nietzsche claims that (all and only) the content of conscious mental states is articulated propositionally (see Katsafanas 2005).

(i)-(iv) offer a characterization of consciousness that does not seem to fit paradigmatic cases of conscious states as pains or perceptual experience, for such states are not usually taken to depend on linguistic and communicative capacities (iii). Nietzsche goes as far as claiming that "the solitary and predatory person" would not have needed consciousness. This seems very puzzling indeed: should we conclude that a non-social person or animal is just a zombie-like creature lacking consciousness altogether? To avoid this unwelcomed conclusion, it is important to clarify what kind of consciousness Nietzsche is talking about. According to the proposal I would like to defend, the relevant notion is that of self-consciousness. To prevent confusion, it will be helpful to specify what I mean by self-consciousness in the present context. The basic idea is that, for a certain mental state M to be conscious in the relevant sense, it is required that M be ascribed to a self. This is the sense in which Nietzsche usually uses the term.[5]

Leaving aside for the moment the issue of superfluousness, i.e. (i), my proposal has the virtue of making sense of the other features Nietzsche discusses in aphorism 354. Self-consciousness arguably entails reflexivity, i.e. (ii) and, in turn, reflexivity involves some kind of self-referential capacity. Moreover, it is at least plausible to hold that the capacity to self-refer depends on linguistic abilities such as the mastery of the first-personal pronoun, i.e. (iii) and that such abilities are acquired through communicative interaction with the members of one's linguistic community, i.e. (iv).

I now turn to a further feature of Nietzsche's notion of consciousness. As many scholars have recently argued, the account of consciousness he puts forward is strikingly similar to contemporary higher-order thought (HOT) theories of consciousness.[6] According to HOT-theories, a mental state M is conscious iff it is targeted by a (proper) higher order thought. This view can be seen as the conjunction of two claims. First, for any mental state M, M may or may not be conscious (at time *t*). Second, what makes M conscious (at time *t*) is its being targeted – or accompanied – by a (proper) higher order thought. Nietzsche comes close to holding the first claim when he endorses the thesis – entailed by HOT-theories – that mental states need not be conscious. For instance, he sympathetically presents Leibniz's "incomparable insight" to the effect that "consciousness is merely an *accidens* of representation and *not* its necessary and essential attribute; so that what we call consciousness constitutes only one state of our mental and psychic world . . . and *by no means the whole of it*" (GS 357, translation changed).

Moreover, there are good reasons to think that Nietzsche also endorses the further claim that a mental state turns conscious when targeted by a higher order thought. This view is at least entertained in an unpublished note suggesting that a conscious representation is a "represented representation" (Nietzsche 1980, xi, 161). More relevantly, it nicely fits with the description – again offered in aphorism 354 from *Gay Science* – of consciousness in terms of the ability "to 'know' what distressed him, to 'know' how he felt, to 'know' what he thought" (Nietzsche 1882/1887, 213). On this account, I could not be conscious that I desire to eat an ice-cream without being in a position to "know" that I desire to eat an ice-cream; and being in a position to "know" that I desire to eat an ice-cream is just to have a proper higher order thought – something like a Kantian "I think", for instance – accompanying my first-order desire to eat an ice-cream.

By the usual standards of Nietzsche scholarship, the agreement on his being a HOT-theorist of consciousness is unusually widespread. Importantly, it nicely fits with the reading proposed here. Although HOT-theories are not typically presented as theories of self-consciousness, they nonetheless usually entail that consciousness involves a similar pattern of self-attribution. For instance, David Rosenthal – one of the most famous contemporary advocates of HOT-theories – argues that the higher order thought targeting a mental state M necessarily entails a reference to the self who is in M in virtue of its being a first-person thought (see Rosenthal 2005, 343). Thus, the now popular HOT readings of Nietzsche lend support to the claim that the kind of consciousness he talks about is actually self-consciousness in the sense specified earlier.

2.2 Consciousness and the falsification claim

In *Gay Science* 354 Nietzsche describes a last feature of consciousness that appears especially hard to make sense of: "all becoming conscious – he writes – involves a vast and thorough corruption, falsification, superficialization, and generalization" (Nietzsche 1882/1887, 213–214). To have a handy label, I shall refer to this thesis as the Falsification Claim (FC). How are we to make sense of this apparently bizarre claim?

To start with, it is important to note that the intended target of (FC) is consciousness as a reliable tool for self-knowledge. Intuitively, we assume conscious episodes to reveal how things actually are with ourselves. If I consciously desire to eat another slice of cake, I usually take such an episode to indicate that I actually have that very desire. In other words, I would typically self-ascribe the desire to eat another slice of cake without further inquiry. The reliability of this process of conscious introspection is precisely what (FC) claim aims at undermining. As Nietzsche puts it, "each of us, even with the best will in the world to *understand* ourselves as individually as possible, to 'know ourselves', will always bring to consciousness precisely that in ourselves which is 'non-individual'" (213).[7] In other words, by introspecting we inescapably miss what is genuinely "individual" about us. But what does it mean exactly that consciousness only reveals those features of ourselves which are not genuinely individual? And why should one find this claim at all plausible?

The story Nietzsche tells in support of (FC) is complicated and needs to be pieced together from claims that are spread throughout his work.[8] However, the main motivation behind it is the view that consciousness is intimately related to language. Since Nietzsche takes the content of conscious states to be linguistic, there are limits on what we can be conscious of. Indeed, he argues that "[l]anguage and the prejudices upon which language is based are a manifold hindrance to us when we want to explain inner processes and drives"(Nietzsche 1881, 71). Why is this so? On the one hand, Nietzsche argues, "words really exist only for *superlative* degrees of these processes and drives" (71). To put it differently, whereas our psychological states and their underlying processes are extremely varied and complex, our repertoire of psychological concepts is typically very meagre and thus far too coarse-grained. This means that when we apply such concepts to our inner life, we tend to lump together mental states of quite different nature. On the other hand, psychological concepts are social, as they are typically shared by all the members of a given community (see *Beyond Good and Evil* 268). For instance, we all apply concepts like "desire", "belief", "fear", "anger", etc., when we describe or simply reflect on our own inner life. This means that, however different and even unique the experiences each of us might have, we will all tend to conceive of them in a very similar way. This is, roughly, what Nietzsche has in mind when he says that only the "non-individual" can be brought to consciousness.

To summarize, (FC) is actually a claim about the unreliability of self-consciousness as a source for genuine self-knowledge. In other words, we should not take conscious introspection to reveal what is really going on in us, at least not as offhandedly as we usually do.

2.3 Sensory states and the scope of Nietzsche's notion

If we accept Nietzsche's treatment of consciousness as it emerges from *Gay Science* 354, what shall we say of sensory states like perceptions and sensations? For such states to be conscious in Nietzsche's sense, they would need to be linguistically articulated. It therefore seems that he has to accept either that sensory states have language-dependent content, or that they are unconscious. Unfortunately, none of these two options seems particularly attractive.

Some passages may seem to suggest that Nietzsche is indeed committed to the view that sensory states are propositionally articulated, as argued for by Katsafanas (2005). For one thing, given that Nietzsche's motivation for (FC) is, at least in part, the claim that consciousness' nature is linguistic, the fact that he sometimes argues that perceptual experience *also* involves falsification could be seen as suggesting that its content, too, is language-dependent. For instance, Nietzsche writes that the "habits of our senses have woven us into lies and deception of sensation" (Nietzsche 1881, 73). In the case of vision, "our eyes find it more convenient to reproduce an image that they have often produced before than to register what is different and new about an impression" (Nietzsche 1886, 81). Thus, our visual perception of a tree is far from accurate, for instead of actually seeing it "precisely and completely, with respect to leaves, branches, colors, and shape", it is for us "so much easier to imagine an approximate tree instead" (82).

According to Katsafanas, this characterization of perception shows that for Nietzsche sensory consciousness has full-blown propositional, language-dependent content. This reading is problematic, as it entails the counter-intuitive view that non-linguistic beings lack conscious sensory states altogether.[9] In my view, it is more plausible to assume that for Nietzsche the content of perceptual states is not language-dependent. As a matter of fact, his texts seem to offer some evidence in support of this interpretation.

First, note that Nietzsche's characterisation of perceptual experience in *Beyond Good and Evil* 192 does not explicitly mention linguistic abilities. Rather, as illustrated by the tree example, vision is described as involving the re-activation of a stored "image". This suggests that Nietzsche takes the content of perceptual states to be imagistic or pictorial. As – contrary to propositional content – pictorial content is arguably language-*in*dependent, states having it can be easily ascribed also to non-linguistic creatures.

Of course, this reading immediately raises a serious worry. For if Nietzsche does not take the content of sensory states to be language-dependent, such states do not qualify as conscious in his sense. This claim, however, is extremely implausible, as it would amount to an outright denial of sensory consciousness as such. So how can we avoid this unfortunate conclusion? One possibility we haven't explored so far is that Nietzsche admits of different kinds of consciousness.[10] In *Gay Science* 354 and related passages, Nietzsche is talking about self-consciousness, not consciousness *tout court*. On this interpretation – to borrow from the terminology proposed by Block (2011) – Nietzsche is best seen as a modest HOT-theorist whose account does not aim at explaining the basic kind of qualitative consciousness typically exhibited by sensory states, but rather deals with a more circumscribed cluster of reflexive capacities possessed by cognitively sophisticated beings like humans and, to a lesser extent, other species of social animals.

As a matter of fact, the view that qualitative consciousness consists in a fundamental kind of consciousness independent from other cognitive and linguistic abilities is suggested in some unpublished notes, where Nietzsche writes that "every being different from us senses different qualities and consequently lives in another world from the one we live in" (Nietzsche 2003, 125, translation changed). This seems to indicate that sentience constitutes a basic form of world-awareness consisting in the capacity to "sense mere quantitative differences as something fundamentally different from quantity, namely as qualities, no longer reducible to one another" (125, translation changed).

3. The unconscious mind

3.1 Drives: what are they?

Though Nietzsche does offer a partial picture of the conscious mind, this endeavor is essentially a negative one. On his own account, its primary aim is to demonstrate the "ridiculous overestimation and misapprehension of consciousness" (Nietzsche 1882/1887, 37) that is not only typically displayed by philosophical theories, but also deeply entrenched in our ordinary self-conception. Contrary to the view that considers it as the "*kernel* of man" (37), Nietzsche stresses that, at best, consciousness plays but a marginal role in the production of our actions and, generally, in our mental life. Moreover, far from constituting our most individual self, consciousness works as the paramount tool by which society assimilates each of us to the "herd" (see, again, *Gay Science* 354). Therefore, it should be no surprise that he does not resort to this notion when it comes to articulating a positive theory of mind and action. The notion he frequently appeals to instead is that of drive. As Richardson (2004, 5; see also Katsafanas 2014) notes, drives are the "principal explanatory tokens" figuring in Nietzsche's treatment of a wide range of psychological and social phenomena. In particular, they prove central to his treatment of traditional philosophical questions concerning the nature of thought, will and self, which he all conceives as depending on, or being constituted by, the relation obtaining between one's drives (from *Beyond Good and Evil*, see aphorism 36 for thought, aphorism 12 for the self, aphorism 19 for the will).

Nietzsche's usage of the term "drive" is somewhat loose (see Katsafanas 2014). For one thing, he does not seem to differentiate between "drive" (*Trieb*) and "instinct" (*Instinkt*), as the two terms are often used interchangeably. On some occasions, the term "will" (*Wille*) also seems to bear a similar meaning. What's more, the list of different items which, at some point or other in Nietzsche's writings, are referred to as drives is rather long and varied. Some correspond to basic biological functions, as the "sex drive" (Nietzsche 1888b, 215). Others involve sophisticated cognitive skills, such as, for instance, the "drive to truth" (Nietzsche 1882/1887, 112). This equivocation notwithstanding, it seems possible to work out some of the general features at the core of Nietzsche's conception.[11]

First, it seems clear that Nietzsche conceives of drives as constituting inclinations, or dispositions, to act in specific ways. (Richardson 2004, Ch. 1; Janaway 2012; Katsafanas 2014; Welshon 2014, Ch. 4). For instance, the sex drive induces the individual to search for mating partners. Similarly, the drive toward cruelty predisposes the individual to inflict pain. Second, such inclinations are not inert. In other words, a drive does not merely wait about for a suitable stimulus in order to get activated, but actively seeks for discharge. Drives, therefore, manifest themselves as urging forces. Third, drives induce an "affective orientation" (Katsafanas 2014, 740): they predispose the agent to certain patterns of emotive reaction. Accordingly, a drive is individuated not only by the "actions" it inclines us to perform, but also by a set of characteristic "sensations" and "feelings" (Nietzsche 1980, x, 304). Finally, although Nietzsche situates the drives largely at the unconscious level, he thinks they shape our conscious experience of the world. Typically, a drive "turns the spotlight of one's cognitive capacities on those features of reality focus on which will increase the drive's chances of attaining its end" (Clark and Dudrick 2012, 145; see also Katsafanas 2014).

A more problematic feature of Nietzschean drives emerges from passages where they are described as embodying a specific point of view. As he puts it, a drive always possesses its own "perspective" (Nietzsche 2003, 139) and "evaluation" (Nietzsche 1980, xi, 167); it is always a "drive toward 'something good', as seen from a certain standpoint" (167). A drive's point of view is partial, each of them being "a one-sided view" (Nietzsche 1882/1887, 185) of the relevant thing or event and tending to exclude those expressed by other, competing drives. As Nietzsche remarks elsewhere, "every drive craves mastery" (Nietzsche 1886, 9).

By characterizing the drives in this way, Nietzsche may be taken to commit a version of the homuncular fallacy, as he seems to ascribe to the drives the same kind of psychological properties they are supposed to explain (see Poellner 1995, Ch. 5.2). For instance, our commitment to certain values is typically explained by him as resulting from the specific, mutual arrangement of our drives. However, if drives themselves are taken to possess an evaluative viewpoint, it is hard to see how the alleged explanation could possibly work. Recent discussion has produced three main attempts to solve this problem:

(1) *Non-Mentalism*: Richardson (2004) argues that although Nietzsche sometimes reverts to mentalistic descriptions of the drives, one should nonetheless consider them as strictly non-mental posita. More specifically, Richardson contends that drives are biological dispositions resulting from natural selection. The main motivation behind Richardson's appeal to natural selection resides in its allowing to make sense of the apparent intentionality of the drives in terms of their essential, adaptive goal-directedness by, at the same time, avoiding the kind of problematic mentalistic talk highlighted above.

(2) *Qualified Homuncularism*: By appealing to Daniel Dennett's early distinction between personal and subpersonal levels of explanation, Clark and Dudrick (2012, 195–200) argue that homuncularism would prove explanatorily idle only if the behavior of which the postulated microagents are supposed to be capable were to display the same kind of complexity found at the personal level. If, however, the patterns of behavior ascribed to the subpersonal posita are sufficiently simple, they can qualify as genuinely explanatory. According to their proposal, this is precisely the case for Nietzsche's conception of the drives.

(3) *Non-Homuncularism*: A third strategy is put forward by Katsafanas (2014). like Richardson, Katsafanas rejects a homuncularist construal of the drives, but – like Clark and Dudrick – he accepts that they are, in some sense, mental. Katsafanas argues that it is wrong to conceive of the drives as intentional in themselves. Rather, a drive embodies a certain perspective *only if considered as part of an agent*. Thus, the sex drive does not represent a given individual as an appropriate mating partner, but I myself represent her, or him, in this way as long as I have the corresponding drive.

What can we say about these three options? Though (1) surely counts as one of the most insightful treatment of Nietzsche's view, it comes at the cost of screening off the kind of intentional characterization of the drives that proves so pervasive in Nietzsche's works and unpublished notes. That drives have a genuinely mental aspect is however recognized by both (2) and (3). Nor need any substantial disagreement actually exist between these two options, for nothing prevents a defender of (2) from accepting that drives can be ascribed mental properties only in virtue of their being embodied in an agent, as suggested by Katsafanas. Therefore, though proponents of (2) still have to make sure that the features assigned to the postulated microagents are genuinely explanatory, the two approaches seem to converge toward roughly the same picture.

3.2 The working of the drives

Nietzsche often claims that most of our conscious life depends on the way in which the drives interact with each other. The following unpublished note offers a particularly clear formulation of this view:

> *Each thought*, each feeling, each willing (*Wille*) is *not* born out of one determinate drive, but is rather a *total state* (*Gesamtzustand*), the overall surface of the whole consciousness, and results from the momentary power-arrangement (*Macht-Feststellung*) of *all* the drives constituting ourselves – just of the dominant drive and of those obeying and disputing it alike.
> (Nietzsche 1980, xii, 26)

Here, Nietzsche claims that mental states result from some kind of antagonistic interplay among the drives. It should be no surprise that their interaction is in some sense adversarial, for as long as a drive directs the organism toward a certain course of action, it naturally conflicts with different drives orienting it otherwise. The problem is rather to understand how Nietzsche exactly conceives of such a tense interaction.

To start with, it is important to stress that Nietzsche does not think that the conscious self is responsible for negotiating the drives' clashing goals:

> *that* one *desires* to combat the vehemence of a drive at all, however, does not stand within our own power; nor does the choice of any particular method; nor does the success or failure of this method. What is clearly the case is that in this entire procedure our intellect is only the blind instrument of *another drive*, which is a *rival* of the drive whose vehemence is tormenting us. . . . While "we" believe we are complaining about the vehemence of a drive, at bottom it is one drive *which is complaining about another*; that is to say: for us to become aware that we are suffering from the *vehemence* of a drive presupposes the existence of another equally vehement or even more vehement drive, and that a *struggle* is in prospect in which our intellect is going to have to take sides.
>
> (D 109; see also *Daybreak* 129)

This aphorism makes two things clear. First, drives typically operate at the unconscious level. Second, transactions between different drives are not mediated by some higher-order, external power.

As regard the second point, Nietzsche often describes the relation obtaining between the drives as a matter of rank (*Rangordnung*) (see Nietzsche 1886, 8; Nietzsche 1980, xi, 119; Nietzsche 2003, 8). A drive may become "dominant", so that the other drives end up "obeying" or "disputing" it (see Nietzsche 1980, xii, 26, quoted above). According to another note, they "either attack or submit to each other" (Nietzsche 2003, 130). Similarly, an episode of willing is said to consist in a drive commanding other drives to execute the relevant action (see Nietzsche 1886, 18–20, 19).

Taken at face value, Nietzsche's pervasive talk of rank and dominance relations seem to warrant the conclusion that we are not dealing with a *merely causal* interplay, but rather with *normative* transactions. Wotling (2011), for instance, argues that the arrangement obtaining between one's drives cannot be captured in causal terms, as it involves a specific form of communication and interpretation: a subordinate drive, for instance, needs to "understand" the command it receives from the dominant one. Similarly, Clark and Dudrick (2012, 199) deny that the hierarchy of the drives is merely causal. Rather, they propose to see the drives as genuine "political agents" engaged in transactions based on authority. As they maintain that the most basic posita of Nietzsche's philosophical psychology are irreducibly non-causal, proposals of this kind challenge a fully naturalistic interpretation of his project.

A problem with such accounts is that they are liable to the homuncular fallacy already discussed in the previous section. Wotling (2011, 76), for instance, admits that drives have "interpretative perceptions". Clark and Dudrick (2012, 194), in turn, allow that the subordinate drives "recognize the authority" of the dominant ones. However, it is hard to make sense of the idea of such capacities being realized at the subpersonal level. Moreover, even if we were to accept this possibility, the resulting view would likely suffer from explanatory sterility.

In light of such difficulties, a deflationary account of the (hierarchical) relation obtaining between the drives seems preferable. For instance, one could take it to result from the drives' unequal efficacy in securing the resources provided by the organism (see Gemes 2009). Such a deflationary account would arguably offer a causal description of how the arrangement among one's drives emerges, thus undermining the motivation for more demanding normative interpretations.

So far we have been considering Nietzsche's general claim that drives stand in relations of rank to one another. It is, however, still unclear what it means for a drive to be subordinated to another, higher-ranked drive. Though it seems fair to say that Nietzsche allows for different varieties of the dominance-obedience relation, it nonetheless tends to take one of two fundamental forms: subordinate drives either "obey" or "dispute" the dominant drive (see Nietzsche 1980, xi, 26, quoted above). In the first case, the dominant drive imposes its own goal on the subordinate one. Drives, as we saw, are dispositions to engage in typical patterns of behavior. Of course, the subordinate drive is in no position to direct the agent toward its own goal. Rather, it either contributes to the realization of goals set by the dominating drive – the "obedience" case – or unsuccessfully opposes such realization – the "dispute" case. In situations of the latter kind, it is unclear what the fate of the suppressed drive might be. It may continue to act as a recalcitrant force the dominant drive fails to recruit. Alternatively, it may become inert and virtually disappear. This seems to be, for instance, the case of asceticism (see 331 *Daybreak* 331).[12]

It is important to note that Nietzsche does not take one's drives to be necessarily arranged in a somewhat stable configuration. There are cases where no clearly dominant drive manages to emerge, or where, for some reason, the rank structure among one's drives simply begins to crumble, resulting in what Nietzsche usually calls the "anarchy" among one's "instincts" (Nietzsche 1886, 152; see also Nietzsche 1888b, 216). These seem to be cases in which the second, merely disruptive kind of subordination prevails, thus preventing the achievement of goals shared by sets of hierarchically structured drives.

4. Relating conscious and unconscious mind

4.1 The puzzle of superfluousness

In section 2.1, we saw that according to Nietzsche one of the key feature of consciousness is that it is, in some sense, "superfluous": mental life and agency do not seem to depend on it in any substantial way. On Nietzsche's account, what is supposed to do the real work are one's unconsciously operating drives. This view does not imply that human beings are zombie-like entities. As I argued in section 2.3, there is no need to read Nietzsche as denying either the existence or the efficacy of phenomenal consciousness. What Nietzsche believes to be superfluous is, rather, the cluster of cognitive capacities constituting linguistic-mediated, reflective self-consciousness.

The claim that reflective self-consciousness is superfluous is likely to strike many philosophers as extremely unpalatable. So how can we make sense of Nietzsche's view? A first option would be to interpret him as endorsing the view that while many, perhaps even most, of our actions and mental states are produced *without consciousness playing any causal role*, certain instances of thought and agency, however rare, do constitutively depend on it (Katsafanas 2005, 2014; Constâncio 2011). Another alternative is to hold that Nietzsche's conception of causality is compatible with the kind of downward causation needed to vindicate consciousness' efficacy (Doyle 2011). These readings, however, seem at odds with those passages where Nietzsche either denies that consciousness possesses any causal power whatsoever or suggests that what is really efficacious are just the unconscious drives. For instance, in *Twilight of the Idols* he writes that "the conception of a consciousness ('mind') as cause, and then that of the I (the 'subject') as cause are just latecomers that appeared once causality of the will was established as given, as *empirical*. . . . Meanwhile, we have thought better of all this" (Nietzsche 1888b, 178). According to an unpublished note, "what becomes conscious is subject to causal relations entirely concealed from us", such that "the succession of thoughts, feelings, ideas in consciousness tells us nothing about whether this succession is a causal one" (Nietzsche 2003, 228). Similarly, in another unpublished passage Nietzsche summarizes his position as follows: "everything which becomes conscious is a final phenomenon, a conclusion – and it causes nothing" (Nietzsche 1980, xiii, 335).

Alternatively, Nietzsche has been interpreted as defending some version of epiphenomenalism about consciousness (see, for instance, Welshon 2014; Leiter 2015; Riccardi forthcominga). Unsurprisingly, this reading too raises serious worries. First, it seems to conflict with claims Nietzsche makes elsewhere about the tremendous effects that consciously entertained beliefs may have on someone. An example is the nearly convertive impact the thought that everything eternally recurs is supposed to have, according to him, on certain individuals.[13] Or, to take a more mundane case, consider how the reflectively formed belief that one is guilty of or blamable for something typically influences both our mental life and the course of our action.[14] In general, as Richardson (2008, 139) puts it, the fact that, rather than being "neutral servants of the drives, consciousness and language compete with them on behalf of . . . social interests", seems to militate heavily "against the idea of consciousness as a mere epiphenomenon". After all, how could something lacking any kind of causal efficacy contribute to make us a herd animal, as Nietzsche argues in *Gay Science* 354?

Proponents of the epiphenomenalist reading try to counter worries of this kind. A first move consists in arguing that epiphenomenalism about consciousness does not entail that conscious states are causally inert. Rather, it simply denies that a mental state has the causal powers it has *in virtue of* its being conscious. According to Welshon (2014, 162), for instance, the claim is that consciousness does not lend any extra efficacy to a certain mental state, and not that a conscious state lacks any causal power whatsoever. Thus, an epiphenomenalist needs not deny that consciously believing in the eternal recurrence may have a profound impact on one's life. The relevant claim is that the impact such belief happens to have does not depend on its being conscious, but on some other of its mental properties.[15]

A second strategy is to narrow the scope of Nietzsche's superfluousness claim. I have argued elsewhere (see Riccardi forthcominga) that although reflexive self-consciousness does not play any causal role in the *production* of token actions, it does play a role in the *acquisition* of beliefs that can subsequently become involved in the issuing of such actions. Let me illustrate this view with an example. A smoker often acquires the belief that smoking is dangerous through linguistic interaction. Since for Nietzsche the propositional attitudes someone is in when engaged in communicative practices are conscious in the reflexive sense, this kind of consciousness plays a role in the smoker's acquisition of the relevant belief. Once acquired, then, this belief may or not contribute to her behavior. Many smokers, after having acquired the belief that smoking is dangerous, keep on smoking for decades. In certain cases, however, smokers do quit smoking (in part) because they believe it is dangerous. What distinguishes cases of this kind? My proposal is that a belief can become behaviorally efficacious only if properly *internalized*, i.e. integrated in whatever psychological mechanism is responsible for producing our actions. According to Nietzsche, the basic psychological items involved in such mechanism are the drives. If, for instance, the smoker's drive toward self-preservation occupies a dominant position in her psychological economy, the belief that smoking is dangerous is likely to become behaviorally efficacious. The important point is that, at this stage, consciousness no longer plays any direct causal role, for, according to Nietzsche, the working of the drives occur at the unconscious level.

Ascribing to Nietzsche this qualified version of epiphenomenalism has two additional benefits. First, it helps make sense of his recurring claim according to which consciousness is a "tool" of the drives. As we saw in section 3.1, the drives typically recruit our cognitive resources in order to direct our behavior toward their own satisfaction. This is also the case for those language-related capacities involved in reflexive self-consciousness. Second, and more importantly, my interpretation allows consciousness to contribute to the practices of social assimilation chastised by Nietzsche in *Gay Science* 354 and elsewhere, for some of the beliefs we acquire through language-mediated engagement with the members of our community and subsequently interiorize are precisely the moral norms to which we usually conform in ordinary life.

4.2 Conclusions

As Nietzsche puts it in *Ecce Homo*, "consciousness *is* a surface" (Nietzsche 1888a, 97). The superficiality of (what I have argued should be identified with) reflexive self-consciousness derives from two of its main features. On the one hand, it turns out to be superfluous. One's psychological life and agency does not seem to depend on it, but rather on the specific arrangement obtaining among one's drives. On the other hand, the conscious experience we have of ourselves does not constitute a reliable source for genuine self-knowledge, but, quite to the contrary, supplies a profoundly distorted picture of what is really going on in us. The general outlook of Nietzsche's view of the mind thus seems to point toward some version of epiphenomenalism about consciousness.[16] This picture raises a pressing question about the emergence of consciousness: if it doesn't add anything to the causal powers the unconscious mind already possesses, why are we at all equipped with it? Nietzsche's answer to this question is strikingly similar to one the psychologist Chris Frith has tentatively articulated in recent years. As Frith (2012, 524) argues, "consciousness is a critical component of our ability to share experiences with each other and create a cooperative, communicative society". Of course, whereas consciousness' involvement "in the mechanisms that generate cooperation and altruism" (521) makes it enormously valuable to Frith's eyes, Nietzsche's judgment is way more pessimistic. For him, the fact that it depends on social and communicative interactions means that consciousness, far from serving the interests of the individual, "is finely developed only in relation to its usefulness to community or herd" (Nietzsche 1882/1887, 213). Here, however, Nietzsche touches on problems a treatment of which transcends the scope of this chapter.[17]

Notes

1 When no English translation is available, references to Nietzsche's unpublished notes are to the *Kritische Studienausgabe*. In such cases, translations are mine.
2 For some recent contributions to this debate, see Gemes (2009) and Gödde (2011).
3 For a recent investigation of Nietzsche's claims about the mind's embodied and embedded nature, see Welshon (2014), in particular Ch. 2.
4 See Leiter (2015), Ch. 1. This seems also to be the claim defended by Abel (2001), who labels Nietzsche's position a version of "adualism".
5 For a similar reading see Welshon (2014, Ch. 5.1), who talks of "reflective consciousness".
6 Proponents of this view include Doyle (2011), Katsafanas (2014), Welshon (2014), Ch. 5, Riccardi (forthcominga); for an older suggestion in the same direction, see also Abel (2001).
7 Compare also, in the same aphorism: "At bottom, all our actions are incomparably and utterly personal, unique, and boundlessly individual, there is no doubt; but as soon as we translate them into consciousness, they no longer seem to be" (Nietzsche 1882/1887, 213).
8 In the benefit of space, I shall try to convey what I take to be the gist of Nietzsche's argument. For a more detailed treatment, see Riccardi (2015 and forthcominga).
9 For more on this issue see Katsafanas (2015) and Riccardi (forthcominga).

10 This conclusion is also endorsed by Constâncio (2012, 214) and Welshon (2014, Ch. 5.1). For a more detailed discussion, see Riccardi (forthcoming-b).
11 See, however, Stern (2015), who is sceptical about the prospect of construing any coherent theory of the drives out of Nietzsche's scattered remarks.
12 Gemes (2009) offers an insightful parallel between these two modalities of drive subordination and Freud's notion of sublimation and repression.
13 The *locus classicus* for Nietzsche's thought of eternal recurrence is *Gay Science* 341.
14 Both examples are taken from Katsafanas (2005), who sees them as posing an insuperable challenge to any epiphenomenal reading.
15 Importantly, the view that a mental state's role depends on its relation to other mental states and that such relations do not in turn depend on its being conscious is typically associated with the kind of HOT-theory also held by Nietzsche. See, for instance, Rosenthal (2005, 362).
16 Importantly, even if one were to resist this suggestion and privilege a deflationary reading of his superfluousness claim, the weakest position that could be sensibly ascribed to Nietzsche would still be that consciousness' role is minimal and reduced to an extremely limited number of cases.
17 I would like to thank Sandra Lapointe for her detailed comments and insightful suggestions on an earlier version of this chapter, to the improvement of which they greatly contributed.

Bibliography

Abel, G. (2001): Bewusstsein – Sprache – Natur. Nietzsches Philosophie des Geistes. *Nietzsche-Studien* 30: 1–43.

Block, N. (2011): The Higher Order Approach to Consciousness Is Defunct. *Analysis* 71.3: 419–431.

Clark, M. and Dudrick, D. (2012): *The Soul of Nietzsche's Beyond Good and Evil*. Cambridge: Cambridge University Press.

Constâncio, J. (2011): On Consciousness: Nietzsche's Departure from Schopenhauer. *Nietzsche-Studien* 40: 1–42.

Constâncio, J. (2012): Consciousness, Communication, and Self-Expression: Towards an Interpretation of Aphorism 354 of Nietzsche's Gay Science. In J. Constâncio and M. J. Mayer Branco (eds.), *As the Spider Spins: Essays on Nietzsche's Critique and Use of Language*. Berlin, Boston: De Gruyter: 197–232.

Doyle, T. (2011): Nietzsche, Consciousness and Human Agency. *Idealistic Studies* 41.1–2: 11–30.

Frith C. (2012): What Is Consciousness for? *Pragmatics and Cognition* 18.3: 497–551.

Gemes, K. (2009). Freud and Nietzsche on Sublimation. *Journal of Nietzsche Studies* 38.1: 38–59.

Gödde, G. (2011): Perspektiven des Unbewussten im Rahmen des Freud-Nietzsche-Diskurses. In J. Georg and K. Zittel (eds.), *Nietzsches Philosophie des Unbewussten*. Berlin, Boston: De Gruyter: 49–70.

Janaway, C. (2012): Nietzsche on Morality, Drives and Human Greatness. In C. Janaway and S. Robertson (eds.), *Nietzsche, Naturalism and Normativity*. Oxford, New York: Oxford University Press: 183–201.

Katsafanas, P. (2005): Nietzsche's Theory of Mind: Consciousness and Conceptualization. *European Journal of Philosophy* 13.1: 1–31.

Katsafanas, P. (2014): Nietzsche's Philosophical Psychology. In J. Richardson and K. Gemes (eds.), *The Oxford Handbook of Nietzsche*. Oxford, New York: Oxford University Press: 727–755.

Katsafanas, P. (2015): Nietzsche on the Nature of the Unconscious. *Inquiry* 58.3 (*Special Issue: Nietzsche's Moral Psychology*, ed. by B. Leiter): 327–352.

Leiter, B. (2015): *Nietzsche on Morality*, 2nd ed. London: Routledge.

Nietzsche, F. (1881): *Daybreak. Thoughts on the Prejudices of Morality*. Ed. by M. Clark and B. Leiter, trans. by R. J. Hollingdale. Cambridge: Cambridge University Press, 1997.

Nietzsche, F. (1882/1887): *The Gay Science*. Ed. by B. Williams, trans. by J. Nauckhoff and A. Del Caro. Cambridge: Cambridge University Press, 2001.

Nietzsche, F. (1883/1885): *Thus Spoke Zarathustra*. Ed. by A. Del Caro and R. Pippin, trans. by A. Del Caro. Cambridge: Cambridge University Press, 2006.

Nietzsche, F. (1886): *Beyond Good and Evil: Prelude to a Philosophy of the Future*. Ed. by R-P. Horstmann and J. Norman, trans. by J. Norman. Cambridge: Cambridge University Press, 2002.

Nietzsche, F. (1888a): Ecce Homo. In *The Anti-Christ, Ecce Homo, Twilight of the Idols and Other Writings*. Ed. by A. Ridley and J. Norman, trans. by J. Norman. Cambridge: Cambridge University Press, 2005.

Nietzsche, F. (1888b): Twilight of the Idols. In *The Anti-Christ, Ecce Homo, Twilight of the Idols and Other Writings*. Ed. by A. Ridley and J. Norman, trans. by J. Norman. Cambridge: Cambridge University Press, 2005.

Nietzsche, F. (1980): *Kritische Studienausgabe in 15 Bände*. Ed. by G. Colli and M. Montinari. Berlin, New York: De Gruyter.

Nietzsche, F. (2003): *Writings from the Late Notebooks*. Ed. by R. Bittner, trans. by K. Sturge. Cambridge: Cambridge University Press.

Poellner, P. (1995): *Nietzsche and Metaphysics*. Oxford: Clarendon Press.

Riccardi, M. (2015): Inner Opacity: Nietzsche on Introspection and Agency. *Inquiry* 58.3 (*Special Issue on Nietzsche's Moral Psychology*, ed. by B. Leiter): 221–243.

Riccardi, M. (forthcominga): Nietzsche on the Superficiality of Consciousness. In M. Dries (ed.), *Nietzsche on Consciousness and the Embodied Mind*. Berlin, Boston: De Gruyter.

Riccardi, M. (forthcomingb): Nietzsche's Pluralism about Consciousness. *British Journal for the History of Philosophy*.

Richardson, J. (2004): *Nietzsche's New Darwinism*. Oxford, New York: Oxford University Press.

Richardson, J. (2008): Nietzsche's Freedoms. In K. Gemes and S. May (eds.), *Nietzsche on Freedom and Autonomy*. Oxford, New York: Oxford University Press: 124–149.

Rosenthal, D. (2005): *Consciousness and Mind*. Oxford: Clarendon Press.

Stern, T. (2015): Against Nietzsche's "Theory" of the Drives. *Journal of the American Philosophical Association* 1.1: 121–140.

Welshon, R. (2014): *Nietzsche's Dynamic Metapsychology: This Uncanny Animal*. Basingstoke: Palgrave MacMillan.

Wotling, P. (2011): What Language Do Drives Speak? In J. Constâncio and M. J. Mayer Branco (eds.), *Nietzsche on Instinct and Language*. Berlin, Boston: De Gruyter: 63–79.

7

WILLIAM JAMES'S NATURALISTIC ACCOUNT OF CONCEPTS AND HIS 'REJECTION OF LOGIC'[1]

Henry Jackman

1. Introduction

William James was one of the most controversial philosophers of the early part of the twentieth century, and his apparent skepticism about logic and any robust conception of truth was often simply attributed to his endorsing mysticism and irrationality out of an overwhelming desire to make room for religion in his world-view. However, it will be argued here that James's pessimism about logic and even truth (or at least 'absolute' truth), while most prominent in his later views, stem from the naturalistic conception of concepts developed much earlier in *The Principles of Psychology* (1890), and it is his commitment to naturalism about our conceptual powers, rather than to any sort of mysticism or irrationalism, that motivates his skepticism about the scope and power of logic, and ultimately about the objectivity of truth itself.

2. Concepts from *the principles of psychology* to *some problems in philosophy*

James's naturalistic understanding of concepts is most explicit in his *The Principles of Psychology* (1890), though it can be found in earlier papers such as "The Sentiment of Rationality" (1879) and "The Function of Cognition" (1885) that fed in to that work. James's view has always been, as he puts it in these early works, that a concept is a "teleological instrument" with which partial aspects of a thing (which "for our purpose" we regard as the "essential" aspects) are used to represent the whole.[2] James takes such conceptualizations to be indispensable because they allow us to make sense of experience by breaking it up into kinds about which general inferences can be made.

As James puts it: "A conceptual scheme is a sort of sieve in which we try to gather up the world's contents,"[3] and concepts allow one to formulate the general claims that make the 'web of belief' a *web* (rather than the mere "big blooming buzzing confusion" (James 1890, p. 462, James 1911, p. 32)). Such general claims rely on our dividing experiences into *kinds*, and there are, of course, many ways to do this. James recognized this, and it should be stressed that he viewed the 'essential' properties that our concepts pick out as having as much to do with our interests as with the world itself:

> There is no property ABSOLUTELY essential to any one thing. The same property which figures as the essence of a thing on one occasion becomes a very inessential feature upon another. . . . But as I am always classifying it under one aspect or another, I am always unjust, always partial, always exclusive. My excuse is necessity – the necessity which my finite and practical nature lays upon me. My thinking is first and last for the sake of my doing, and I can only do one thing at a time. . . *the only meaning of essences is teleological, and that classification and conceptions are purely teleological weapons of the mind*. The essence of a thing is that one of its properties which is so *important for my interests* that in comparison with it I may neglect the rest.
>
> (James 1890, pp. 959–961)

Concepts are thus not heavenly forms that we somehow grasp or intuit. Nor are they forced upon us by a 'ready made' world that has essential properties of its own. Rather, they are natural simplifications/adaptations that *we* develop in order to make sense of our experience, and thus cope with our current environment. As James puts it, the concepts under which we characterize a given object "characterize *us* more than they characterize the thing" (James 1890, p. 961).

In later works, particularly *A Pluralistic Universe* (1909) and *Some Problems of Philosophy* (1911), James stresses that our concepts are themselves independent objects of experience. Concepts "are realities of a new order", and the relations between them "are just as much directly perceived, when we compare our various concepts, as the distance between two sense-objects is perceived when we look at it" (James 1909, p. 122).[4]

James further expands on how our concepts can collectively make up self-standing *models* (or "maps" (James 1911, p. 43)) which we can inspect, and in terms of which perceptual experience can be understood. Concepts help make up a kind of 'notional world' in terms of which the world we perceive is understood. We map perceived objects onto their notional counterparts and predict their behavior based on what their notional counterparts would do.

> The 'rationalization' of any mass of perceptual fact consists in first assimilating its concrete terms, one by one, to so many terms of the conceptual series, and then in assuming that the relations intuitively found among the latter are what connect the former too . . . To 'explain' means

to co-ordinate, one to one, the *thises* of the perceptual flow with the *whats* of the ideal manifold, whichever it be.

(James 1911, pp. 41–42, see also p. 33.)

As James later puts it, in order to be successful, the models of reality constructed with our concepts need only do justice to those aspects of reality that they are used to cope with.[5] Our concepts have been developed and selected through our history for their usefulness, not necessarily their complete fidelity to all aspects of what is conceptualized (though the two will not be entirely unrelated), so the types of inferences that our concepts license may not be true of everything (or always true of anything) that they are applied to.

Concepts as more traditionally conceived by philosophers should automatically match (perhaps even determine) reality's structure, but there is no guarantee that concepts as James understands them will do so. Especially since James doesn't try to account for our concepts being *about* external realities in terms of their *resembling* them (James 1890, pp. 437, 455).[6] Roughly put, a concept is about an external reality if it allows us to *handle* that reality, and so while some sort of structural isomorphism between concepts and their objects is always nice, there is no reason to think that it must always be present.

A simple model that allows one to act successfully most of the time is often more useful than a more 'truthful' model that is too complex to be used effectively in actual practice. For instance, the primitive 'model' of the world deployed by frogs treats all small flying objects as things to be eaten, and while the actions endorsed by this model are not always optimal (the frogs will occasionally eat fly-sized bits of non-organic material that is shot past them, etc.), it works often enough for frogs to survive in their environment. A more complex model, by contrast, while it might produce fewer misidentifications, might also be slower to implement, resulting in many flies that would have been captured with the simpler model getting away.

Indeed, James argues that we frequently use *different* models to cope with different aspects of reality, and while this practice is useful, it would inevitably lead to contradictions if the models were all viewed as true theoretical descriptions of reality. This is one of the sources of James's 'instrumentalism.' Our models are useful instruments to cope with experience but their theoretical incompatibility prevents them from being viewed as absolutely true descriptions of reality. As James famously put it "Common sense is better for one sphere of life, science for another, philosophic criticism for a third; but whether either is truer absolutely, Heaven only knows" (James 1907, p. 93). James's 'instrumentalism' does not stem from any sort of prudishness about 'unobservables' (as if we had a single coherent theory of the world, but refused to commit ourselves to the existence of the theoretical entities postulated in it). Rather, it derives from the recognition that we have a number of indispensable yet incompatible models of the world, no single one of which is adequate for all of our purposes, and no two of which could be 'absolutely true' together.

Furthermore, James is very sensitive to the analogical nature of many of our conceptual models. We often understand novel ranges of experience by analogy with other experiences that we are more familiar with. This 'metaphorical' form of understanding is a very powerful tool for comprehending not only novel experiences, but also things as familiar as our own minds. Indeed, James was very aware of our tendency to understand 'abstract' phenomena such as the mind in terms of 'concrete' metaphors relating to our practical interactions with the physical world. As he puts it "To deal with moral facts conceptually, we have first to transform them, substitute brain-diagrams or physical metaphors, treat ideas as atoms, interests as mechanical forces, our conscious 'selves' as 'streams' and the like."[7] These 'concrete' metaphors are, according to James, essential to our understanding precisely because human cognition evolved not in the context of having to solve theoretical problems about comparatively abstract objects, but rather in the context of practically coping with our concrete environment. Concrete objects and "things of the sort we literally *handle*, are what our intellects cope with the most successfully," and this suggests that "the original and still surviving function of our intellectual life is to guide us in the practical adaptation of our expectancies and activities" (James 1909, p. 111). The notional model we build up to understand the world we perceive will often thus be metaphorical through and through.

However, while importing the inferential structure of one domain into another is often a successful way of coping with experience, it can occasionally misdirect our thinking. If an analogy that is successful for certain practical purposes is treated as a literal reflection of reality, then *all* of the inferential transitions licensed in the primary domain would be licensed in the analogical one. Losing sight of the (often very real) *differences* between the two domains can lead reasoning astray, and while James follows Bain in characterizing genius as "a native talent for seeing analogies,"[8] he warns that not making sufficient allowances for the differences between the two domains is "the common fallacy in analogical reasoning" (James 1909, p. 71). If we were to uncritically tease out all of the 'logical consequences' of our analogically structured concepts (and uncritically take our model to reflect reality perfectly), we would frequently be led into error.[9] Consequently, while analogical concepts are useful, indeed indispensable, they should be used with caution outside of the 'everyday' practical use for which they originally evolved.

Concepts are, then, for James, simply tools with which we practically cope with our environment, and they come to be about objects in the environment because they lead us to literally handle them, not necessarily because they 'mirror' any part of their essential structure. This conception of concepts (and their resulting limitations) is radically at odds with that of most philosophers in James's day, and it ultimately led to his endorsing radical views on the authority of logic and the possibility of our reaching any sort of 'objective' truth.

3. James's 'rejection of logic'

A general willingness to either accept the logical consequences of one's beliefs, or to revise those beliefs, is viewed by many philosophers as inseparable from rationality, so it is not surprising that James's 'rejection of logic' in *A Pluralistic Universe* (1909) was viewed as perhaps the most flagrantly 'irrational' strand in his philosophy,[10] with passages like the following being met with incomprehension and disappointment by many of James's contemporaries.[11]

> I have finally found myself compelled to *give up the logic* [of identity], fairly, squarely, and irrevocably. It has an imperishable use in human life, but that use is not to make us theoretically acquainted with the essential nature of reality. . . . Reality, life, expedience, concreteness, immediacy, use what words you will, exceeds our logic, overflows and surrounds it. If you like to employ words eulogistically, and so encourage confusion, you may say that reality obeys a higher logic, or enjoys a higher rationality.
> (James 1909, pp. 96–97).

However, James's 'anti-logical' writings, while perhaps not as happily put as they could be, pick out something very deep and important that runs throughout his philosophy. In particular, James's target is not so much *logic*, as it is a certain attitude towards our *concepts*. If (formal) logic (particularly the logic of identity) occasionally fails to apply to reality, the problem may not be with logic itself but rather with our attitudes towards the *conceptualizations* of reality upon which our logic is applied. Logical inferences are only applicable to conceptualizations of reality, and our conceptualizations may not (for certain theoretical purposes) adequately reflect reality's actual structure. As James also puts it:

> logic, giving primarily the relations between concepts as such, and the relations between natural facts only secondarily or so far as the facts have been already identified with concepts and defined by them, must of course stand or fall with the conceptual method. *But the conceptual method is a transformation which the flux of life undergoes at our hands in the interests of practice essentially and only subordinately in the interests of theory.*
> (James 1909, p. 109, italics mine.)

James's claim is that logic can take concepts that have evolved to cope with reality on a *practical* level, and derive a *theoretical* picture that grotesquely distorts reality. In such cases the rational thing to do is to "subordinate logic. . . [and] throw it out of the deeper regions of philosophy to take its rightful and respectable place in the world of simple human practice" (James 1909, p. 97). The claim that logic will not always lead us to the truth is not the same as the claim that its laws are not themselves true. James defends the former claim, but he is not committed to the latter.

James views in this area become clearer when we recognize that he works with a picture of our belief and belief revision that he describes as follows:

> The individual has a stock of old opinions already, but he meets a new experience that puts them to a strain. Somebody contradicts them; or

in a reflective moment he discovers that they contradict each other; or he hears facts with which they are incompatible; or desires arise in him which they cease to satisfy. The result is an inward trouble to which his mind till then had been a stranger, and from which he seeks to escape by modifying his previous mass of opinions. He saves as much as he can, for in this matter of belief we are all extreme conservatives. So he tries to change first this opinion, and then that (for they resist change very variously), until at last some new idea comes up which he can graft upon the ancient stock with a minimum of disturbance to the latter.

(James 1907, pp. 35–36)

Such a view fits into the now familiar "web of belief" approach to belief and belief revision,[12] and the similarities with the following passage from Quine should be familiar:

The totality of our so-called knowledge or beliefs . . . is a man-made fabric which impinges on experience only along the edges. Or, to change the figure, the total science is like a field of force whose boundary conditions are experience. A conflict with experience at the periphery occasions readjustments in the interior of the field. Truth values have to be redistributed over some of our statements. Reëvaluation of some statements entails reevaluation of others, because of their logical interconnections – the logical laws being in turn simply certain further statements of the system, certain further elements of the field.

(Quine 1951, p. 42)

It should be noted that for Quine, the logical laws are themselves items in the web,[13] and James shares much the same view here. There is a common view that we are *rationally required* to keep our web of belief consistent,[14] but for James such consistency is just one more factor that can be traded off case by case, and while one would hope that all such strains are removed in the long run, they need not be immediately resolved. Giving up any single belief of an inconsistent set may produce more strain than the inconsistency itself. James's position can be understood as suggesting that while keeping the more 'abstract' beliefs at the center of the web consistent with the rest has considerable value, we should not always do so at the expense of rejecting the more 'perceptual' beliefs that make up the periphery.[15] Indeed, he often suggests that we not only *needn't* revise such peripheral beliefs, but also that we *can't* give them up simply because some argument shows them to be incompatible with other beliefs that we hold.[16] James is effectively arguing that the periphery can (and typically does) hold, in spite of its apparent inconsistency with the center. He is not, *pace* his critics, arguing that the logical beliefs at the center must go. We can recognize that there is something inadequate about the way that our total belief set is structured in these cases, but also recognize that no available candidates for change make things any better.

Ideally, perhaps at some 'end of inquiry' the web will be completely consistent,[17] but we need not toss the whole thing just because it fails to be so now.

To understand how James's account of concepts is tied to his views on logic, we should remember that the main target of the 'anti-logical' lectures in *A Pluralistic Universe* is not just the sort of metaphysical monism associated with the Absolute Idealists (such as Bradley and Royce) who he criticized in those lectures, but a broader tendency towards *Intellectualism* in philosophy, a tendency characteristic not only of the Absolute Idealists, but also of more empiricist and 'scientific' philosophers such as Bertrand Russell.

According to James, intellectualism has as its source "the faculty which gives us our chief superiority to the brutes," namely, our power "of translating the crude flux of our merely feeling-experience into a conceptual order" (James 1909, p. 98). James claims that whenever we conceive a thing, we attempt to *define* it,[18] and intellectualism involves taking concepts to capture reality so well that the inferential patterns flowing from our definitions become the measure of reality itself. James traces this tradition of 'abusing' our concepts back to Socrates and Plato:

> Intellectualism in the vicious sense began when Socrates and Plato taught that what a thing really is, is told us by its *definition*. Ever since Socrates, we have been taught that reality consists of essences, not of appearances, and that the essences of a thing are known whenever we know their definitions. So first we identify the thing with a concept and then we identify the concept with a definition, and only then, inasmuch as the thing *is* whatever the definition expresses, are we sure of apprehending the real essence of it or the full truth about it.[19]

If the inferential consequences that flow from our concepts' definitions reflect the 'essence' of reality, then logic (by being able to tease out these inferential consequences) would be "an adequate measure of what can and cannot be."[20] Logic is able to determine the structure of, and relations between, the models we construct to understand the world, and if we can assume that the structure of these mental models is isomorphic to the structure of the world, then such logical investigations would reveal the structure of the world as well.

This assumption that our concepts match reality, coupled with the use of logic to determine just what does, and does not, fall under our concepts, leads the intellectualist to deny the reality of seemingly obvious features of experience. Consequences that can be teased out of the conceptual beliefs at the center of our web of belief are endorsed at the expense of the psychologically more robust beliefs found at the periphery. Such priorities are characteristic of the 'verbal' nature of Lotze's, Royce's and Bradley's idealistic arguments which James claims all rely on the properties of words rather than things (James 1909, pp. 31–33). Such arguments, James would insist, properly draw conclusions about the nature of our conceptual models of the world, not about the nature of the reality conceived. In such cases, concepts, "first employed to make things intelligible, are clung to even when they make them unintelligible."[21]

James claims that ordinary logic "substitutes concepts for real things" (James 1909, p. 67), and this raises for him the question of the extent to which inferences relying on such substitutions are legitimate. If (as the intellectualist supposes) the structure of our concepts 'mirrors' the structure of reality, then conclusions logically derived from the structure of our concepts should also be true of the reality conceived. On the other hand, if the conceptual order does not mirror the order of reality, no such conclusions follow. Of course, from James's naturalistic picture of concepts outlined above, there is little, if any, reason to think that such a mirroring relationship must exist. If concepts are effective but imperfect instruments we developed to cope with reality, there is no *a priori* reason to think that the structure of these tools must be *completely* isomorphic to the structure of what they work on. Some fit is to be expected, but it will often be limited to the area of everyday practice.

James's reservations about the unbridled use of conceptual logic can thus be understood as tied to his denial of the existence such 'analytic' conceptual inferences about the world, and such a rejection is characteristic of those who endorse more naturalistic accounts of concepts. Since concepts do not pick out objects in the world in virtue of their 'logical' structure, there is no reason to think that inferences based on this logical structure must be truth-preserving.

It is this potential gap between concepts and what they represent that lets James see a distinction (invisible to most of his contemporaries, yet essential to his own position) between logic and rationality. James is not here making the now familiar claim that logic is concerned simply with truth, while rationality is concerned with a wider range of human concerns (not the least of which is utility). This familiar distinction between truth and utility is associated with a popular reading of James's philosophy, particularly his *Pragmatism* (1907) and *The Will to Believe* (1897),[22] and might also seem supported by James's claim that "rationality has at least four dimensions, intellectual, aesthetical, moral, and practical" (James 1909, pp. 54–55). However, James's claim that there are at least four dimensions of rationality does not in itself suggest that there are forms of rationality that are not truth-sensitive. Indeed, such a reading of James would suggest that truth was the exclusive concern of intellectual rationality, and thus that the aesthetical, moral and practical dimensions of rationality have no business with truth. This would be a very un-Jamesian concession to his rationalist opponents. In any case, James is clearly talking about rationality in *all* its dimensions when he claims right before the passage quoted above that any hypothesis that makes the world appear more rational "will always be accepted as more probably true than an hypothesis that makes the world appear irrational" (James 1909, p. 54). Consequently, such passages give us no compelling reason to think that James's distinction between logic and rationality should be understood as mirroring the distinction between truth and utility.[23]

Rather than relying on a division between truth and utility, James's distinction between logic and rationality is best seen as drawing on the potential differences between the conceptual order and the reality that it is supposed to represent. Rationality is concerned with optimizing the relation between our beliefs and reality, while logic is concerned more narrowly with the inferential relations between our concepts. If (as the intellectualist assumes) our concepts capture the structure of reality, then there will be no room for a conflict between logic and rationality. However, if (like James) one feels that our concepts are a practically adequate, but nevertheless imperfect reflection of reality, then there will be space for a conflict between logic and rationality. James sees his intellectualist opponents' uncritical use of conceptual logic as leading them to conclusions that are radically out of touch with any robust sense of the reality of the world we experience. Such philosophers, in virtue of being "loyal to the logical kind of rationality" end up being "disloyal to every other kind" (James 1909, p. 94). The contradictions which can follow from the unrestricted use of conceptual logic point to a dilemma that James takes his opponents to simply ignore.[24] Namely, in some cases we must either "give up the logic of identity" or "believe human experience to be fundamentally irrational", and while "neither is easy", "we must do one or the other."[25] When he faces up to the dilemma, James has no doubt about which horn to grab.

> That secret of a continuous life which the universe knows by heart and acts on every instant cannot be a contradiction incarnate. If logic says that it is one, so much the worse for logic. Logic being the lesser thing, the static incomplete abstraction, must succumb to reality, not reality to logic. Our intelligence cannot wall itself up alive, like a pupa in its chrysalis. It must at any cost keep on speaking terms with the universe that engendered it.
> (James 1909, p. 94)

What James chooses to preserve, it should be noted, is not only the legitimacy of naïve perceptual experience, but also the assumption that the world we experience is fundamentally *rational*. If a conceptual treatment of perceptual reality ("when radically and consistently carried out," (James 1911, p. 46)) leads to the conclusion that perceptual reality is not real at all, this simply illustrates our concepts' inability to adequately capture (for the purposes of theory) the reality perceived. In such cases, James suggests, we should "turn a deaf ear" to the apparent contradictions that logic reveals.

> [T]he immediate facts don't sound at all, but simply *are*, until we conceptualize and name them vocally, the *contradiction results only from the conceptual or discursive form being substituted for the real form*. But if . . . that form is superimposed for practical ends only, in order to let us jump about over life instead of wading through it; and if it cannot even pretend to reveal anything of what life's inner nature is or ought to be; why then we can turn a deaf ear to its accusations.
> (James 1909, p. 121, italics mine.)[26]

A proper 'sense of reality' is crucial when making inferences with our concepts. If they seem to be leading us astray, that may be a good indication that they in fact are.

Nevertheless, the use of concepts is essential to coping with reality, and James is certainly not suggesting that we try to get by without them. If concepts had a purely *theoretical* function, then their leading to contradictions might suggest that they should be given up. On the other hand, if (as James insists) they have primarily a *practical* function, and their use leads to no practical problems, then the fact that they can lead philosophers to certain theoretical difficulties gives us no reason not to keep using them. James thus advocates a 'pragmatic' approach to the use of our concepts. Use them when they help us understand and cope with reality (as they typically do) but discard them whenever they seem to lead us to contradiction and confusion.[27] This paradigmatically pragmatic attitude towards our concepts is firmly grounded not in a lack of concern with truth or rationality, but rather in a naturalistic attitude towards concepts and their limitations.[28]

James's rejection of conceptual logic is thus deeply connected not (or at least not only) to his sympathy with mysticism,[29] but rather to the understanding of concepts coming out of his work in psychology, and his resulting views on the limitations of human conceptualization. There is no reason to think that an intellect "built up of practical interests" (James 1890, p. 941) need develop concepts that are perfectly isomorphic to the structure of reality. Our concepts may be flawed from the point of view of pure theory, but in absence of a more adequate set (and in face of the fact that they work fine for practical purposes), giving them up is neither a realistic nor a *rational* option. The concepts are not only practically useful, but may serve as a starting point that may ultimately help us find a more theoretically adequate set. James's rejection of logic can thus be understood as reflecting a type of *anti-rationalism*, in that it undermines the 'rationalist' program that extends from Plato right though to twentieth-century 'conceptual analysis.'[30] Nevertheless, it is not a form of *irrationalism*. That is to say, it is not committed to the claim that life or the world is fundamentally irrational. James's position is, then, not so much that we should give up logic, but rather that we should give up the assumption that we are rationally obligated to endorse all of the apparent logical consequences of all the claims that we accept.

4. Conclusion: conceptual pessimism and pessimism about 'Absolute' truth[31]

This picture of how our concepts relate to reality also explains James's notorious caginess about 'objective' truth, even when the latter is understood merely in the Peircian sense of the "opinion which is fated to be ultimately agreed to by all who investigate" (Peirce 1877, p. 139). James has something like Peircian truth in his system, namely, "absolute" truth, but he presents it as something that we may never attain.

> The 'absolutely' true, meaning what no farther experience will ever alter, is that ideal vanishing-point towards which we imagine that all our

temporary truths will some day converge. It runs on all fours with the perfectly wise man, and with the absolutely complete experience; and, if these ideals are ever realized, they will all be realized together.

(James 1907, pp. 106–107)

'Absolute' truth requires there to be beliefs that we *would* converge on were we to investigate long enough, and James's picture of concepts leaves it a real possibility that prolonged inquiry might simply result in our oscillating between claims and their denials.

This shouldn't be surprising, if concepts emerged to serve our *practical* ends, and our most fundamental concepts evolved to serve the most basic of these ends, then our conceptual system may not be well suited to provide the kind of consistent *theoretical* account of reality that Absolute Truth requires.[32] What we have instead are sets of concepts that work piecemeal in particular contexts (most famously, the contexts of 'common sense', "science" and "philosophic criticism" (James 1907, pp. 92–93)), but none of which work in every context. Inquiry into a question will never produce a stable answer, since there is not a stable framework for inquiry, and when we adopt, say, a scientific framework, many claims that were previously endorsed in, say, the common sense framework will be denied because their ontological presuppositions will be rejected.[33]

Like James's views on Logic, this view of truth is undoubtedly pessimistic, but it is ultimately motivated not in terms of any commitment to the irrational, but rather from his fundamentally naturalistic approach to the mind and its powers.

Notes

1 I'd like to thank Jim Campbell, Richard Gale, Sandra Lapointe and audience members at the Eugene Oregon meeting of the Society for the Advancement of American Philosophy for comments on an earlier version of this paper.
2 James (1890, pp. 961–962). Furthermore, these 'partial' aspects, while they are important to us, need not even be shared by all the elements in the relevant class. (For a more extended discussion of this last point, see Jackman, forthcoming).
3 James (1890, p. 455). See also James (1909, pp. 98, 105).
4 See also, James (1902, p. 54).
5 If one is driving from New York to Boston, one doesn't want a map that shows *every* road, alley and cow path between those two cities, nor does one typically want one that shows every little bend and curve in each road. Still less do we usually need information about the terrain, vegetation and population. A map that had every such detail would typically be *less* effective in guiding one between the two cities than the less 'cluttered' maps we typically use.
6 For a fuller discussion of this, see Jackman (1998).
7 James (1909, p. 111). In this respect, James anticipates some of the claims about the 'metaphorical' character of cognition worked out in more detail in Lakoff and Johnson (1980, 1999).
8 James (1907, p. 500), see also James (1890, pp. 972, 984) and James (1909, p. 71).
9 Treating ideas as objects is a notorious case of this, and the fact that we typically conceptualize experience in terms of concrete bounded objects is part of the reason

why James thinks that it will be so difficult (if not impossible) for us to come up with adequate conceptualizations for phenomena which are not 'static' (James 1911, pp. 51, 54–55).
10 Other candidates include, of course, *Pragmatism*'s (1907) purported equation truth with what is expedient to believe, and his purported claim in *The Will to Believe* (1897) that we are rationally entitled to form any belief that makes us happy. I argue in Jackman (1998, 1999) that such attributions of defenses of irrationality to James are not, ultimately, justified.
11 Peirce was happy to group James's "intense hatred for logic" with his "almost unexampled incapacity for mathematical thought" (Peirce 1911, p. 182), and for more of the negative reaction of James's contemporaries to his rejection of logic, see Perry (1935, v. II pp. 594–597). For a contemporary manifestation of such disappointment, see Gale (1999 p. 298).
12 See Quine (1951) and Quine and Ullian (1970). Though one could argue that for James what needs to be held together is more than just a set of beliefs, but rather a general web of mental states such as beliefs, fears, hopes and desires. (For a discussion of this, see Putnam 1995, p. 26; Gale 1999, p. 126).
13 Quine's commitment to this consequence seems to be qualified seriously in Quine (1970).
14 This assumption is something like what Wilson has referred to as the "the moral imperative of first-order logic" (Wilson 1994, p. 527.) For a recent attack on the principle that we can, or even should, keep our beliefs consistent, see Sorensen (2001).
15 And of course, our 'mystical experience' was for James, more like perception in this respect than conception (see James 1902, pp. 319–320).
16 For a discussion of the ineffectiveness of argument against intuition, see James (1902, p. 67).
17 Though, as we will see soon, James has a good deal of skepticism about this possibility.
18 James (1911, p. 47). This might seem like a stretch to some, but it is entirely natural if viewed as a consequence of the then prevalent idea that all categorization is in terms of sets of necessary and sufficient conditions. If categories did really work this way, then all concepts would at least involve 'implicit' definitions in terms of the necessary and sufficient conditions that they embody. For a discussion of the popularity of this conception of concepts and categorization, and a criticism of its empirical accuracy, see Lackoff (1987).
19 James (1909, p. 99).
20 James (1909, p. 101).
21 James (1909, p. 99). Once again, idealists such as Bradley are the immediate target, but the larger one is the 'intellectualism' such idealists share with a much broader philosophical community.
22 This popular reading remains, nevertheless, a mistaken one. In particular, James's 'pragmatism' about truth is best understood as stemming from his naturalistic and pragmatic explanation of how our representations get their content. For a discussion of this, see Jackman (1998, 1999).
23 Which is not to say that one couldn't draw a distinction between logic and rationality in this way. Prudential and truth-directed rationality need not always give the same advice about, say, what to believe, and James was certainly aware of this (see Jackman 1999). Furthermore, it bears repeating at this point that while there is still a widespread view that James's "pragmatic theory of truth" collapsed truth and utility, a closer reading of his texts provides fairly compelling grounds for thinking that he kept the two quite separate (see Jackman 1998).
24 "Few philosophers have had the frankness fairly to admit the necessity of choosing between the 'horns' offered. Reality must be rational, they have said, and since the

ordinary intellectualistic logic is the only usual test for reality, reality and logic must agree 'somehow'" (James 1909, p. 96).
25 James (1909, p. 96). James further claims, "I must squarely confess that the solution to the problem impossible, and then either give up my intellectualistic logic, the logic of identity, and adopt some higher (or lower) form of rationality, or, finally, face the fact that life is logically irrational" (James 1909, p. 95); see also James (1909, pp. 108–109).
26 See also James (1902, p. 67) for the claim that we often can't help doing so.
27 James (1911, p. 53).
28 James can thus be understood as making a type of 'Wittgensteinian' point (of course, one courts trouble whenever one characterizes any position as 'Wittgensteinian', and those who do not find the analogy suggestive should feel free to ignore it). Our concepts are fine for their 'everyday' use, but if the inferential moves they license are applied indiscriminately, they can lead us to the sorts of contradictions and paradoxes characteristic of philosophy. A similar stance is taken in his *Pragmatism*, where he argues that "the moment you pass beyond the practical use of these categories . . . to a merely curious or speculative way of thinking, you find it impossible to say within just what limits of fact any one of them apply" (James 1907, p. 90).
29 See James (1902, Lectures XVI and XVII).
30 For a discussion of this program and its ambitions, see the fourth chapter of Rorty (1979).
31 The material in this section is covered in considerably more detail in Jackman (2015).
32 James seems to suspect that it will be a problem with *any* conceptual system, since *conceptualization itself* misrepresents the 'continuous' nature of reality. Concepts require sharp boundaries, and while the imposition of models of the world where things are sharply defined has tremendous practical value, it inevitably misrepresent the richness of reality, and thus are unable to get to a point of Absolute Truth. For instance, James is pessimistic about our ever finding a set of concepts that would capture aspects of reality such as time and change (see James 1911, pp. 51, 54–55). For a discussion of this, see Gale (1999). While they are at the forefront of these later works, remarks about the difficulty about capturing experience with 'static' concepts go all the way back to *The Principles of Psychology* (e.g. James 1890, p. 442).
33 Of course, one might think that this is only a *temporary* state, and that we should expect, eventually that we should be able to find a single stable system that will explain everything. However, James seems pessimistic about the *status quo* changing, and the conception of concepts outlined above is, once again, the source of his doubts.

Bibliography

Campbell, J. 1992. *The Community Reconstructs*, Chicago: University of Illinois Press.
Gale, R. 1999. *The Divided Self of William James*, New York: Cambridge University Press.
Jackman, H. 1998. "James's Pragmatic Account of Intentionality and Truth" *Transaction of the Charles S. Pierce Society*, Winter 1998, Vol. XXXIV, No. 1.
Jackman, H. 1999. "Prudential Arguments, Naturalized Epistemology, and the Will to Believe" *Transaction of the Charles S. Pierce Society*, Winter 1999, Vol. XXXV, No. 1.
Jackman, H. forthcoming. "James, Intentionality and Analysis" in Klein (ed.) *The Oxford Handbook of William James*, Oxford University Press.
Jackman, H. 2015. "James's Pessimism about 'Absolute' Truth". Presentation given at the William James Center, Potsdam, June 2015.
James, W. 1879. "The Sentiment of Rationality", reprinted in James 1897.

James, W. 1885. "The Function of Cognition", reprinted in James 1912.

James, W. 1890, 1981. *The Principles of Psychology*, Cambridge, MA: Harvard University Press.

James, W. 1897, 1979. *The Will to Believe and Other Essays in Popular Philosophy*, Cambridge, MA: Harvard University Press.

James, W. 1902, 1985. *The Varieties of Religious Experience*, Cambridge, MA: Harvard University Press.

James, W. 1907, 1975. *Pragmatism*, Cambridge, MA: Harvard University Press.

James, W. 1909, 1977. *A Pluralistic Universe*, Cambridge, MA: Harvard University Press.

James, W. 1911, 1979. *Some Problems of Philosophy*, Cambridge, MA: Harvard University Press.

James, W. 1912, 1976. *Essays in Radical Empiricism*, Cambridge, MA: Harvard University Press.

Lakoff, G. 1987. *Women, Fire and Dangerous Things*, Chicago: University of Chicago Press.

Lakoff, G. & Johnson, M. 1980. *Metaphors We Live By*, Chicago: University of Chicago Press.

Lakoff, G. & Johnson, M. 1999. *Philosophy in the Flesh*, New York: Basic Books.

Lamberth, D. 1999. *William James and the Metaphysics of Experience*, New York: Cambridge University Press.

Peirce, C. S. 1877. "The Fixation of Belief" Reprinted in Peirce. C. S. 1992. *The Essential Peirce, Volume 1*, Bloomington and Indianapolis: Indiana University Press.

Peirce, C. S. 1911. "A Sketch of Logical Critic" Reprinted in *The Collected Papers of Charles Sanders Peirce*, Vol. 6, Cambridge, MA: Harvard University Press, 1934, 1935, pp. 122–131.

Perry, R. B. 1935. *The Thought and Character of William James*, 2 Vols. Boston: Atlantic – Little, Brown.

Putnam, H. 1995. *Pragmatism: An Open Question*. Cambridge: Wiley-Blackwell.

Quine, W.V.O. 1951. "To Dogmas of Empiricism" in his *From a Logical Point of View*, Cambridge, MA: Harvard University Press, 1953.

Quine, W.V.O. 1970, 1986. *Philosophy of Logic*, Second Edition, Cambridge, MA: Harvard University Press.

Quine, W.V.O. & Ullian, J.S. 1970. *The Web of Belief*, New York: Random House.

Rorty, R. 1979. *Philosophy and the Mirror of Nature*, Princeton: Princeton University Press.

Sorensen, R. 2001. *Vagueness and Contradiction*, New York: Oxford University Press.

Wilson, M. 1994. "Can We Trust Logical Form?" *The Journal of Philosophy*, 1994, Vol. XCI, No. 10.

8

SIGMUND FREUD ON BRAIN AND MIND

Bettina Bergo

1. Introductory remarks

This essay explores the neurological roots of Freud's views on mind, showing the innovations he contributed in brain science and language pathology.[1] Freud's work merits philosophical attention for a number of reasons – some better known than others – notably in its beginnings when it was tied to neurology, materialism, mechanism, as well as to Franz Brentano's act psychology.[2] Early on, Freud sought to develop a systematic account of embodied mind, including explanations of interactions between 'representations' (ideas, memories) and affects. Today, he is increasingly recognized as a naturalist whose psychoanalysis combines self-analysis with a dynamic, functionalist neurology. His contributions to the comparative anatomy of the nervous system, begun in Ernst Brücke's laboratory and influenced by Hermann von Helmholtz, were carried out in the hope that discoveries concerning neural synapses, energy, and its transmission might eventually clarify nervous system function in humans (Gamwell and Solms 2006, 15–17). Moreover, while the philosophy of mind (as act psychology) he discovered with Franz Brentano long remained with him (Brook 1998, 73–77; Pribram and Gill 1976, 17–18), had he obtained the university post he sought in Vienna, and had his 1895 physiology of brain function (posthumously entitled the *Project for a Scientific Psychology*) been published instead of that of his rival, Sigmund Exner, Freud might well have stayed in neurology and psychiatry.[3]

Freud's work in the natural sciences began with anatomy and histology in Brücke's laboratory; it passed thereafter into neurological investigations of the brain and central nervous system under Theodor Meynert. Freud produced over 200 articles in neurophysiology.[4] It should not be supposed that neurology did not confront philosophical questions, such as those relating to the all-important relationship between brain and mind and, in particular, what precisely is meant by "psycho-physical parallelism". With this in mind, this chapter will first consider an encyclopedia entry Freud wrote entitled "*Das Gehirn*" ("The Brain") and which appeared in 1888. After reviewing Freud's innovations in brain physiology and the persistence of his debt to Brentano's act psychology, I will turn to his monograph *Zur Auffassung der Aphasien* (*On Aphasia*). This work is unique because, against the dominant localizationism of brain science in the 19th century, Freud argued for a whole-brain theory in which language perception, comprehension, and production resulted from the dynamic organization of "fields" in the brain. This challenged the doctrine of "comprehension centers" in the brain, as well as Meynert's idea that discrete brain "centers" (not fields) were connected by neural conductions pathways across empty, that is to say functionless, brain "space." Freud believed that any aphasia diagnosis had to take into account not only lesions of varying kinds, but also socialization and the way the brain was configured in the process of language acquisition. This "psycho-social" dimension, which was neglected in Freud's time, went hand in hand with his research on and treatment of hysterias, dating from 1882.[5] Together, the article and monograph testify to the originality of Freud's views, among other things, on mind-brain parallelism, the scope of functionalism,[6] the concern with the dynamics of brain fields, and the nature of sub-cortical interactions between the nervous system, the midbrain, and the brainstem. Freud also challenged the "cortico-centrism" of his time, with its theory of the "homunculus" in the cortex, equivalent to a "little man" guiding all our actions, both reflex and willed. Even before the reductionist project he undertook in his 1895 *Project for a Scientific Psychology*, Freud was working toward a science of mind and brain that could be both materialist *yet* non-reductionist, functionalist *and* dynamicist, social *and* biological. Behind this science lay important philosophical questions concerning the activity of the cortex and the meaning of free will.

In *Mal d'archive* (1995b) Jacques Derrida observed that all of Freud's concepts are "divided," meaning among others things that Freud consistently sought to think mental activities in light of corporeal (neurological and functional) dynamics – and vice versa.[7] This approach was the result of what would prove to be a short-lived period in the history of 19th-century philosophy, when the scientific psychology of Helmholtz and Wundt was investigating perception and sensation, and when philosophers like Brentano were concerned that philosophy of mind should integrate the rigorous empirical investigations of psychology, or "naturalism." By the time he entered Carl Claus's Institute of Zoology and Comparative Anatomy in 1875, Freud had oriented his studies in the direction of Darwinian biology (Ritvo 1990, 113–149). Everything he would do in Brücke's and Meynert's institutes (the first, of physiology; the second of cerebral anatomy), would be part of *Naturwissenschaft* (natural science). Even when Freud admitted that working with hysterics involved interpretation (the "Dora" case in 1905), he still had *Naturwissenschaft* in mind (Freud 1971, 134–135); namely, questions concerning the interaction between neural networks, "synaptic" inscriptions, memory, and the emergence of consciousness and cognition in light of defense mechanisms both normal and abnormal. Although a casual reading of Freud's psychoanalytic case studies may not reveal much of this naturalistic concern, this is largely because, after 1896, he was forced to distance himself from neurophysiology, which lacked the chemical and energetic tools[8] with which to study the interaction between consciousness, neural dynamics, and pathology. But we should not lose sight of the fact that the work he was doing in the 1880s and 1890s involved a great deal of science, for this casts light on the development of psychoanalysis, which is being rediscovered in some cognitive science circles today.[9]

For a brief time at the end of the 19th century, a plethora of psychologists debated and discussed each other's findings, contesting and contributing to philosophy of mind. Frege's attack on Edmund Husserl's psychologism, and Husserl's own criticisms of psychology in the *Prolegomena* to the *Logical Investigations* (1900), contributed to segregating the scientific psychology of Wundt and Helmholtz from other philosophical attempts at developing a comprehensive approach to consciousness (like that of William James). By 1913, when Husserl marked his own decisive "transcendental turn," away from empiricism, an important episode in the philosophical backlash against naturalism in psychology had come to a close. Between 1910 and 1920, fewer chairs in experimental psychology would open – and collaborations between philosophers and psychologists on questions relating to mind largely ceased.[10] Indeed, by 1920, Freud's own insistence on seeing psychoanalysis as a natural science had become less urgent: confronting the phenomenon of war trauma, he seems to have thrown up his hands at the explanatory impotence of both experimental psychology and even philosophy. (See Freud 1955, Vol. XVIII, 7.) Despite this, he never abandoned his scientific heritage consisting of systematic observation, classification of pathologies, and clinical therapeutics in his case analyses. Their roots lay in his approach to neurology and in the physiology of the nervous system he learned with Brücke, Meynert, and Charcot.[11]

2. "*Das Gehirn*" ("The Brain" 1888): Freud against metaphysics in neurophysiology

Freud contributed two articles to Albert Villaret's *Handwörterbuch der gesamten Medizin* (Comprehensive Dictionary of Medicine) in 1888, one of which was entitled "The Brain."[12] In that year, Freud stood astride his neurological career, carried out principally in Theodor Meynert's university clinic, and his work on hysteria, a significant impetus for which he found in 1885–1886, studying at Jean-Martin Charcot's Paris Salpêtrière clinic. His interest in brain anatomy, here as well as in his *On Aphasia*, was characterized by two innovative intuitions. First, the brain-mind relationship should never imply material (physical) reductionism *tout court*. Second, and against Meynert's distinction between specific neural pathways (into and out of the cortex) for voluntary movement, and his postulation of utterly different pathways for reflex movements, Freud argued that there is likely no physical, *neuro-cerebral* difference between conscious voluntary movement and unconscious, involuntary movements or reflexes. Freud could make this claim because his approach was, early on, more dynamic and relational than many neurological models of his time, which tended to be topological and static. I will return to this important distinction shortly. Like Meynert, he made theoretical hypotheses, even engaged in speculation, as it was no more possible to measure interactions between brain centers than it was to study the movement of energy through neural bundles. But hypothetical or not, Freud's "The Brain" argued for a new approach to brain dissection and a radical re-evaluation of the contributions of largely neglected areas of the brain to movement, consciousness, and sensation (notably the medulla oblongata and the cerebellum for movement).

Important in this entry was Freud's attack on both psychical and physical reductionisms, like that of Meynert (1833–1892) who sought to determine the cortical grounds of the activity of the mind and of reflexes by ascribing to each its respective neural bundles leading into and out of the cortex. It is important to note the metaphysical or metaphoric debt of cortico-centrism. Meynert's neurological topography had all movement arise from the interaction of neurons in the spine and the cortex, which implied speculation about specific nerve bundles for freely willed movement, not to mention hypotheses about the direction of neural charges. The cortex thus became the physical locus of rational deliberation, while sub-cortical brain regions, the cerebellum, and the spine were conceived according to the dualism of conscious-unconscious action, or the reflex arc (bodily movement) versus freely chosen activity (intentional movement).

In 19th-century cerebral anatomy and physiology, the paradigm was localizationist and parallelist, ironically reflecting Gall's 1835 intuition of brain sites corresponding to types of cognition and affects (part of which led to the expansion of phrenology) (Keegan 2003, 59).[13] Against the influential physiologist Johannes Müller (1801–1858), Marshall Hall (1790–1857) defined the reflex arc in sharp distinction to "voluntary" movements. His 1833 paper, "The Reflex Function of the Medulla Oblongata" (Hall 1833), set forth four types of movements: voluntary and commanded directly by the cortex; involuntary respiratory movements from the medulla oblongata; involuntary movements caused by irritations from stimulating a neuro-muscular fiber, and movements caused by stimuli at the periphery of the organism (reflex mechanisms). Hall's theory was abundantly debated, in part for the philosophical reason that Hall and others were arguing for grounds of movement independent of the will or any higher cerebral function.

While Hall's thesis was not new, it came to be incorporated into a conception of the brain as a curious "federation" of discrete regions in which each had its specific function. Meynert integrated it into his conception of the brain-mind relationship with its two types of neural bundles for reflexes and for voluntary action. On Meynert's view, the cerebral cortex receives "all excitations and . . . dispatches all motor impulses" ("The Brain" 1990, 56). Certain excitations, however, require association with other, soon to be related ones (vision, hearing, speech), while others give rise directly to bodily actions. Meynert thus organized the fibers of the cortex into "association systems" and "projection systems". However, he insisted that a (voluntary) projection system could never be merely reflexive. On his model, the (metaphysical) distinction between voluntary and reflex movement was epitomised at the level of the brain itself. In other words, conscious processes are separate from (remaining in a sense superior to) unconscious muscular movements. It was this conception that Freud would discreetly but systematically dismantle.

How did Meynert establish the existence of these two "pathways"? The standard technique was to study brain lesions that occasioned various types of cerebral and behavioral degeneration. Freud did not reject this methodology; he refined staining techniques allowing him to study fetal neural networks and trace these back to mature specimens. He also resorted to Hartnack's multi-layered refraction microscope, which produced very clear enlargements of neurons (Gamwell and Solms, 15). This allowed him to counter Meynert's claim that the brain stem carries separate reflex and free will pathways. By showing that the size of the physical pathways of Meynert's projection system (reflex) decreased once leaving the cortex, Freud began to throw into question the viability of the two separate "pathways" thesis ("The Brain" 1990, 57).

Let me sketch Freud's argument. First, using the work of Meynert's rival, the Leipzig neurologist Paul Flechsig (1847–1929), Freud showed that the "interruptions" by grey masses in Meynert's projection system implied that their passage from the cortex and cerebral ganglia, into the spinal cord and peripheral nerves, *missed* important parts of the brain associated with involuntary movement, including the pons and the cerebellum, whereupon it diminished continually in breadth (Solms and Saling 1990, 57). In addition to pointing out that the projection system did not pass through the part of the brain that Meynert himself identified as directly involved in motor control and motor learning (the cerebellum), Freud mobilized Flechsig's research to correct Meynert, arguing that this pathway "only takes up a third of the transverse section of the cerebral peduncle . . . thus prov[ing] to be the unreduced continuation of the pyramidal bundle from the cerebral cortex and to be *exclusively motor* [i.e., not voluntary]" ("The Brain" 1990, 57, emphasis added).

Freud used similar data to argue that the voluntary pathway ultimately proved indistinguishable from the association pathway, and that Meynert's explanation of the distinction between voluntary movement and reflex movement was again untenable. On Freud's view, *there is therefore no neurophysiological distinction between conscious and unconscious motor processes*. Meynert's conception of a dual system – the one conscious and indebted to cortical activity, the other motor but similarly commanded by the cortex (though without the complex association paths) – was thus implausible. Indeed, reflex movement did not require "regulation" by the cortex at all. And since many motor processes were neither needed to reach the supposed adjudication site that was the cortex, nor even passed beyond the pons, tegmentum, or cerebral peduncle, Freud ironized that Meynert's "conception of the construction of the brain" was a "*grossartige Komposition*" (grandiose composition).

Following his critical analysis of Meynert's cortico-centric doctrine, Freud turned to the physiology of the brain, pursuing an idea that was already becoming quite clear in his anatomy: while there is no question that the brain is complexly active in conscious thought, the nature of the relationship between "mind" and "brain" could not yet be clearly established. The nature and topology, mapping and interaction, of mind-brain parallelism remained obscure. Nevertheless, breaking with neurological orthodoxy (Solms and Saling 1990, 100), Freud opened the physiology section with the argument:

> The b[rain] is that organ which converts centripetal excitations, supplied by the sensory pathways of the spinal cord and through the gateway of the higher senses, into purposive and coordinated centrifugal movement impulses. This part of brain functioning can be traced back, according to the general schema of the reflexes, to the simple causal nexus of a mechanical event.
> ("The Brain" 1990, 62)

Cerebral anatomy, when properly carried out, provides insight into reflex movements. But anatomy cannot explain mental states like the unfolding of ideas or having ideas accompanied by affects.[14] For this, Freud appears to resort to what he had learned from Franz Brentano's "act psychology":

> there exists the fact, inaccessible through mechanical understanding, that simultaneously to the mechanically definable excited state of specific brain elements, specific states of consciousness, *only accessible through introspection*, may occur.
> ("The Brain" 1990, 62, emphasis added)[15]

Of the connection between the brain's converting centripetal excitations into coordinated centrifugal movement impulses, one could employ techniques of fiber staining and dissection of paths whose degeneration showed their specific brain routes. While both of these techniques were static rather than dynamic, Freud nevertheless observed that "the actual fact of the connection of changes in the material state of the brain with changes in the state of consciousness, even though mechanically incomprehensible, makes the brain the organ of mental activity" ("The Brain" 1990, 62). Of the precise connection between this coordinating activity and consciousness, Freud would admit that, although incomprehensible, it "is itself not lawless" ("The Brain" 1990, 62). Such laws could be learned through a combination of "experiences of the external senses on the one hand and introspection on the other hand" ("The Brain" 1990, 62).

To oppose Meynert, Freud resorted to resources like introspection from Brentano's act psychology and the theoretical armature of neurologist John Hughlings Jackson, whom Freud likely discovered thanks to Jean-Martin Charcot in 1885–1886.[16] Jackson flatly disavowed concern with parallelisms like Meynert's distinction between voluntary and reflex movement by refusing to investigate the simultaneity of neural processes and mental states. (See Hughlings Jackson 1958, 52.) Having insisted on the value of introspection for understanding mental states, a claim that Brentano also made, Freud followed his Jackson-Charcot connection toward an anatomy that held mental states and neural activity in the cerebrum apart from ideation, even as he argued against Meynert's distinct fibers and isolated centers for mental states. For Freud, Meynert's materialist reductionism committed the error of preserving, at the cerebral level, an ethico-metaphysical distinction between willing and non-willing, consciousness and non-consciousness. Like others of his generation, Meynert emphasized a cortico-centrism that set all executive functions exclusively in the neocortex, much the way in which the homunculus theory of mind attributed "agency" to it (or even *an* agent, a "little man," observing mental images in the so-called "Cartesian theater"). Meynert's reductionism dressed a crypto-metaphysical conception of mind in the garb of a materialism that asserted its independence from non-physical conceptions. Hughlings Jackson, already in 1875, and Freud after him, in 1888, rejected both. Freud understood that "to give a materialist explanation" did not solve the problem of parallelism, and was likely, as a result, to contain errors of anatomy. Moreover, for Meynert, high level functions like speech and understanding resulted from connections between cortical centers provided by fibers running across unused brain regions; this, even though it was impossible to determine the *direction* of electrochemical impulses in the fibers, and there were no distinctive characteristics to identify voluntary versus involuntary fiber bundles! Of course, Freud also insisted that topographical relations be understood dynamically and "economically" (as energy exchanges) even as he attacked Meynert's metaphoric highway system. In 1888, he urged that anatomy describe the connections between the areas of purely grey matter (presence of nerve cells and vascularization), between grey and white matters (glial cells, axons and low vascularization), and between grey areas and the spinal cord. Anatomy had to address adequately the question of the complex organization of brain fibers. Moreover, as Hughlings Jackson would argue,

> Betwixt our morphology of the nervous system and our psychology there must be an anatomy and a physiology. Morphology has to do with cells and fibres or with masses of them. Anatomy has to do with sensorimotor *processes*.
> Hughlings Jackson 1958, 52, emphasis added)

Over a decade before the young Freud wrote his "Brain" entry, Hughlings Jackson and others in the British school (including Herbert Spencer) had embraced a conception of consciousness, the brain, and the nervous system as consisting of levels, higher and lower, requiring correlated but irreducible methods of inquiry. The reason for this was thought to be that passive sensation engendered reflex action, whereas stimuli reaching higher mental operations produced conscious motions, open to psychological examination. But Jackson's lack of interest in consciousness was due to his conviction about the irreducibility of these levels and his sustained argument, to which Freud subscribed, that the cortex was *not* the command center for both voluntary and reflex movement.

On the other hand, if Meynert was right, and if reflex actions evinced activity in "higher" *and* "lower" brain centers, then while bodily events proved to be processes spread throughout the brain, they did not ascend to the cortex only to be sent back to the midbrain or the cerebellum in the form of "cortical commands". This was part of the reason why, for Freud, neurological processes could *never* correspond to a mere conscious-unconscious distinction. There was Brentano's argument for the irreducibility of consciousness to its physiological "substrata," and there remained the duality of what we might call, following Henri Bergson, the musical score versus the concert recital, or what Freud called states "inaccessible to mechanical understanding."

> If a specific change in the material state of a specific brain element connects with a change in the state of our consciousness, then the latter is entirely specific as well; however, *it is not dependent on the change in the material state alone* whether or not this connection occurs. If the same brain element undergoes the same change in state at different times, then the corresponding mental process can be linked with it on one occasion... (at) another time *not*.
> ("The Brain" 1990, 62, emphasis added)

For Freud, the question as to whether and when mental processes correspond to specific "brain states" had as much to do with neurology as it did with conscious and unconscious "representations" (*Vorstellungen*) clustering around and vying for passage across the "threshold of consciousness" (*Schwelle des Bewusstseins*), a notion Freud adapted from the rationalist psychology of Friedrich Herbart. Becoming conscious of very simple cognitions, like "the sensation of prevailing needs... or sensory perceptions" ("The Brain" 1990, 63) entailed elements whose neuro-cerebral "parallels" could only be studied causally. Freud's example was the perception of a grape and the subsequent eating of it. The movement of the hand and arm toward it, that of the head and the eyes are "certainly in a mechanical causal nexus with the material excitation process in the *nervus opticus* which preceded it, and several segments of the entire chain of material events surely lie in the brain" ("The Brain" 1990, 63). But this causal nexus has limits: we cannot say that the perception of "the (colour) blue, in a specific form, excites the ideas of the other attributes of the grape as well." Freud then added that such "psychical processes may link with the seriate excitation of the [brain]," but they also might not! It all depends on how many of the "segments of the [perceptual] chain cross the threshold of consciousness" ("The Brain" 1990, 63). On this account, perceptual chains are rarely integrally conscious and consequently Freud could not argue that they mapped clearly and directly onto neuronal events and concatenations. A comparable argument arises in the *Project for a Scientific Psychology* (1895) in Freud's discussion of dreams and memory chains in which only two of four events are conscious or dream-associated. In conscious recollection, a peer or a physician can bring missing elements in the associative chain back to awareness, even if we cannot do so by ourselves. In the "talking cure," Freud always began by urging that the patient relate everything that came to mind, precisely in the hope of unraveling the chain of associations and reactivating latent ideas and affects.

Freud thus argued, contra Meynert, that the "quality" of a perceptual chain (notably, whether it is conscious or not) made no difference to the neurological processes accompanying it. He held that the degree to which a perceptual chain could in fact become conscious was clearly determined by a phenomenon first discussed by Herbart, which would play a significant role in Freud's psychoanalysis: repression (*Verdrängung*). Freud's characterisation of repression was initially ambiguous. "[The psychical process] may, on the other hand, become complicated by considerations of ethical and other nature," what we might call social inputs ("The Brain" 1990, 63). On Freud's view, under the influence of these presumably affective forces (the psychological 'force' experienced in states of profound shame, for example), aspects of a perceptual or evaluative process might remain "under the threshold of consciousness, whereby nothing needs to be changed in the form of external effects" ("The Brain" 1990, 64). Hence, in addition to acknowledging the emerging possibility of unconscious forces of an "ethical" nature and interpersonal etiology, Freud was setting the stage for an en masse rejection of Meynert's *neurological* distinction between conscious and unconscious processes, between (free) willing and reflex movements. Freud's argument to this effect is of a Brentanian *and* Jacksonian character:

> So the essential criterion for voluntary movement is entirely immaterial and only accessible through internal introspection. The material process with voluntary movement is not essentially different to that of reflex movement; the former is only differentiated from the latter in that with it such material segments in the excitation process become drawn in, with (the excitation of) which changes in consciousness can co-exist, and also that certain of these changes in consciousness really do take place.
> ("The Brain" 1990, 64, modern translation)[17]

Freud could make this claim because of the way he approached the distinction between quality (consciousness) versus quantity (brain physiology) in brain science. Nerve fiber excitations, brain regions, and neural pathways are amenable only to variations in quantity ("The Brain" 1990, 65). Each complex perception requires the coordination, or "association," of different sensory elements in the cortex. However, such coordination had also to be the result of one's perceptual history: "if different cortical sensory elements are repeatedly excited simultaneously with the peripheral sensory elements belonging to them – which happens whenever the same thing . . . works repeatedly on our senses – then excitation-conducting pathways *appear to develop* between these cortical elements" ("The Brain" 1990, 65, emphasis added). The process of repetition also conditions our anticipations of perception. But the idea that something within the quantitative frequencies of excitations, or accompanying their passage along nerve fibers, might account for their breaking into consciousness would have to wait for Freud's theorization of "periodicity" of charge, in his 1895 *Project for a Scientific Psychology* (Section 7: "The Problem of Quality").

It is important to note, here, that Freud was already paying considerable attention to repetition, and thus to *the history of the body* in its environment(s). On Freud's evolutionary account, neural pathways "develop" ("The Brain" 1990, 65), and they do so long past infancy. There is nothing fixed about them – contrary to what Meynert assumed. ("The Brain" 1990, 56, 62–65). Freud thus remapped the general functions of the brain mantle (cortex), brainstem, and the spinal cord ("The Brain" 1990, 67), arguing that, for reflex actions, it was the brainstem and *not* the cortex whose task it was to integrate efferent excitations "always and entirely . . . below the threshold of consciousness" ("The Brain" 1990, 67–68). He provided extensive evidence for this from pathology and living encephalectomized animals.

Following a minutious examination of each region of the brain, Freud was explicit about the two assumptions he would criticize: 1) the principle of the "continuity of the nervous system," or the argument in favor of "an uninterrupted network" that carried excitations "constantly . . . along a nerve-fibre," and 2) the "principle of isolated conduction," which claimed that "only nerve fibers that were contiguous" could carry excitations or information between the nervous system and the parts of the brain.[18] "If [either or both of] these two physiological premises are incorrect, then all conclusions upon which brain research presently builds would collapse," he added ("The Brain" 1990, 52). Though he could not prove its impossibility, Freud argued convincingly that the continuity of the nervous system was untenable as such, thereby dismantling Meynert's theory. Together with his rejection of physical determinism for psychical processes and his embrace of the physiological interaction between voluntary and reflex processes (Solms and Saling 1990, 16), it seems clear that Freud was following two sets of unorthodox viewpoints on the brain: an interactionism not compatible with passive associationism understood as mere neural continuity, and a sustained concern with Brentano's conception of intentionality and act psychology (see Solms and Saling 1990, 17; Silverstein 1985). Freud's last published essays in neurology thus carried with them a proto-phenomenological quality that he would progressively expand in connection with his clinical observations of dreams, his own and that of his patients, and his unique "talking cure" (Van de Vijver and Geerardyn 2002, 27).

3. *On Aphasia* 1891 (*Zur Auffassung der Aphasien*)

When the work *On Aphasia* appeared, Freud found himself definitively barred from Meynert's clinic. Reduced to practicing privately, he mostly collaborated with his benefactor, Josef Breuer. Unlike the dictionary entry on the brain, *On Aphasia* (Freud 1953) was a large-scale study of multiple kinds of aphasias and their etiology. Freud dedicated it to Breuer who, reportedly, was unimpressed by what he deemed to be casuistic arguments (rather like Brentano's), rather than clinical investigation.[19] Yet, this essay is important for a number of reasons. The most salient is that, mobilizing a reinterpretation of the findings of Meynert's students Wernicke and Lichtheim, Freud attacked the respected Meynertian-Lichtheimian thesis of "conduction aphasias." This was a theory based on a strict form of localizationism. It hypostatized brain centers as static functions, connected over empty brain space by neural association bundles. In this, again, 19th-century psychology showed its debt to Gall's phrenology, to neural continuism, and to the metaphysics of the centrality of the cortex. Wernicke, for one, proceeded on the principle that words (whether heard or read) provided incoming "information" that entered the brain through what Wernicke conceived as the "sensory center" (left side generally), and then passed through other, as yet unknown parts of the cortex, before they could be processed as words spoken, repeated, or written (thanks to Broca's "motor center"). The hypothesis of "conduction aphasias" rested notably on the phenomenon of paraphasias (nonsense syllables inserted in words, eruptions of foreign words in sentences), which suggested to Wernicke that the comprehension of words heard, or the conduction from the sensory center to a comprehension center, and finally to the speech center was hindered in one of several ways.

Wernicke's theory was important because it proceeded on the assumption that "meaning," and by extension, "comprehension" of meaning, required the cooperation of multiple brain localizations, which were static. This so called Meynert-Wernicke thesis was interesting as well, because it denied that hearing and speaking might develop and be produced simultaneously. Now, it suggested, fairly, that much of the cortex was active in the processes of listening, speaking, reading, and writing. On this account, aphasia had to be considered as a multiform disorder, with conduction aphasias appearing where paths of conduction (via white brain fibers) were impeded between the sensory and the motor centers, *or* between one of these and the various centers responsible for cognitively "mediating" inputs of hearing or seeing.

Freud did not doubt the plausibility of generalized activity in the cortex in high-level activities such as cognition. However, as we will see, Freud urged that both Wernicke's localization and his brain activity be integrated into a larger, developmental picture. Lichtheim had schematized the association process in what is known as his "house diagram". It carried such explanatory power that Freud confronted the question of how to propose a better model for the multiple types of aphasia without postulating discreet conduction centers running across unused brain space via neural bundles (in which the very direction of energy transmission could not be determined). Now, Freud's own explanation should be considered in light of his ongoing psychological discoveries around hysteria (Keegan 2003, 57; Porath 2009, 56; Brook 1998, 67–70). In some ways the tasks were similar: 1) to avoid surreptitiously introducing metaphysical explanations like the hypothesis of indemonstrable "comprehension centers"; 2) to avoid introducing neural bundles operating like highways between centers; 3) and above all, to integrate psychological and developmental considerations into the study of aphasia, notably how the child learns to speak, to read, and to write. The latter task was similar to that of understanding the array of physical and psychical symptoms, from paralysis to language loss, in hysteria. It concerned the relationship between the brain and the "mind," and the mind and the outside environment. Let us examine Lichtheim's "house" (Figure 8.1).

In Lichtheim's diagram, represented above, the lateral strokes from 1 to 7 indicate lesions. Only strokes 1 and 2 are squarely *in* the motor (Broca) or sensory (Wernicke) centers themselves. Points M and A correspond to localizable centers in the cortex. Point B represents a speculative, as-yet undiscovered "comprehension center." The strokes 5, 4, 6, 3, and 7 correspond to interruptions of conduction potential, due to lesions in neural bundles. Thus, the line from α to A represents the disruption (stroke 7) of neurological conductions leading to the sensory center, presumably through a disruption in the hearing of words. In the case of A to B, it is the *understanding* of words heard that is disrupted (stroke 6). Stroke 4 on the line from B to M represents a conduction disruption impeding the *understanding* of words to be said in response. Stroke 5, finally, represents a motor disruption; i.e., a disruption in the production of speech out of Broca's center.

Lichtheim's scheme predicted the possibility of seven types of aphasia, five of which were conduction aphasias (not counting lesions to the centers themselves, strokes 1 and 2). Most significant in this scheme is that the architecture of the centers, including Lichtheim's speculative "comprehension center," required neural highways across empty cerebral space whose disruption would impede motor or sensory functions. As a result, there was no room for function to be loosened from its static "centers". We will see how Freud introduced dynamics into function by moving away from the static centers with their neural bundle pathways. As indicated, Freud pointed to a significant problem in Lichtheim's model, similar to Meynert's neural pathways into and out of the cortex: neither neurologist could demonstrate the *direction* of the movements of energetic charges between the centers. Moreover, their "vacant brain space" theory seemed to be influenced by

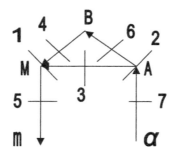

Figure 8.1 W. Lichtheim's diagram for aphasia types (in *Über Aphasie* (1884), cited by Freud in *On Aphasia* (1891).

a metaphor of roadways into and out of cities, not by the neurological data. They never imagined that different parts of the brain might actually perform the task of *aggregating* functions. But this is precisely what Freud would argue.

Freud's aim in *On Aphasia* is to gradually but decisively dismantle Lichtheim's metaphysics of the mind, i.e., the hypothesis of comprehension centers in the cortical and subcortical areas. He modestly noted a number of "difficulties" in Lichtheim's argument. The first was that Lichtheim's claims were anchored in the idea that the destruction of one language "center" might contribute to numerous types of aphasia. It had been established beyond a doubt that damage to a part of the frontal gyrus in the left hemisphere, known as Broca's center, contributed to motor difficulties in speech. It was also known that lesions in Wernicke's center, covering parts of the temporal and parietal lobes of the left hemisphere of the cortex, contributed to difficulties in speech comprehension. But difficulties in speech comprehension or speaking as a motor activity did not mean integral linguistic incapacitation. Some patients who seemed not to understand what was said to them could, according to Lichtheim, repeat words spoken (Freud 1953, 26). Others understood but could utter only simple words like "yes" and "no" (Freud 1953, 27).[20] Indeed, even Lichtheim and others in Meynert's school found that the idea of the well-separated centers (A and M, and M and B in Lichtheim's house) was insufficient to explain the array of paraphasias observed. Hence, they hypothesized that there must be other areas in the brain contributing to the understanding of words spoken or read. The underlying difficulty with their theory was their own conception of the function and definition of brain centers, again based on a rigid localizationism that assumed that movement, sounds, and images formed cortical or subcortical "representations" (cf. the homunculus theory), situated in the nerve cells of the discrete centers. Fibers between centers, cortically or subcortically, ferried information about these images between centers. Consequently, when a sound entered the brain, it had to be carried to comprehension center(s) that would "interpret" it. Before a word could be uttered, its "interpretation" had to pass from the comprehension center to the motor center.

Freud began by questioning the necessity of "comprehension centers". The very idea of conduction paths was misguided. Freud acknowledged that damages to Wernicke or Broca's centers did not necessarily lead to complete motor or sensory incapacitation. But he contested that clinical evidence could be adduced for patients who were able to repeat words said to them but not to speak spontaneously. This suggested that there might be no need for a "comprehension center" in an adult speaker, whatever her lesion. Following Watteville, Freud pointed out that "the destruction of a so-called center comes about only through simultaneous interruption of *several* fiber tracts." Thus, precise localization was not decisive. Without denying the reality of Broca and Wernicke's centers, Freud contested the way they communicated and the nature of the cortical space across which, precisely, communication occurred. "[A]ny assumption of a centre lesion can be replaced by one of a lesion of several tracts, without abandonment of the theory of localization of psychic functions in the areas of the centres. Such a hypothesis can be replaced by that of the lesion in several conducting paths" (Freud 1953, 17). In short, the correct theory had to be more complex than the one proposed by Meynert-Lichtheim. Centers (above all the "comprehension centers") and single conducting paths across unused space were insufficient to explain aphasias.

Frege had many reason to think that the Meynert-Lichtheim picture of incapacitation was incomplete. First, our understanding of conducting paths, in their multiplicity, should not be guided by metaphors of "representation" highways or telegraph systems (Porath 2009, 60), as Meynert and Lichtheim's appeared to be. Freud argued that speech, like all communication activities, mobilized *spontaneous* connections within vast regions of the cortex. Meynert and Lichtheim were convinced that the brain areas around the centers were essentially unused space, awaiting the eventual expansion of a given center through learning or use. Freud's point was that regions should not be reduced to mere brain centers individuated by their functions, because brain regions were *dynamic and spontaneously interactive*. Second, while Freud thought that it is correct to identify some brain centers, a radical localizationism, with ultra-specialized centers fixed in unmodifiable parts of the brain, had to be abandoned. This cast doubt on the understanding of centers, as well as the nerve cells in the centers supposedly carrying "representations," but without integrally jettisoning localization theory.[21] Again, this hypothesis came from John Hughlings Jackson's evolutionary approach to aphasia. It was Jackson who first urged that localization of functions be understood as *trans-cortical*, and sometimes subcortical. It was Jackson's trans-cortical emphasis that Freud took up against Meynert-Lichtheim.

> We have rejected the assumptions that the speech apparatus consists of distinct centres separated by functionless areas, and that representations (memory images) [*Vorstellungen (Erinnerungsbilder)*] serving language are stored in determined sites of the cortex called centres, while their association is provided exclusively by subcortical white fibres.
> (Freud 1953, 62, modern translation)

Against Meynert-Lichtheim, Freud recurred to a whole-brain theory. Jackson maintained that the right side of the brain contained an acquired, immanent or "subjective" language center, while the left side held the centers required for the production of "objective" speech and writing: "the Subject-proposition followed by the Object-proposition [was the prerequisite for producing] speech" (Hughlings Jackson 1958, 187). The right side was responsible for passive ideation, the left for mechanical iteration; their spontaneous communication allowed "the survival of the fittest image at the termination of a struggle which the presented [object] has roused in us" (Hughlings Jackson 1958, 187).

Discarding Herbert Spencer's notion of survival of the fittest representation in the brain, as well as a Darwinism of mental capacities, Freud used Jackson's examples taken from paraphasic patients with extensive damage to the left hemisphere to argue, first, that the *entire* cortex, and parts beneath it, was active in reading, listening, speaking, and writing. This required that Freud elaborate his own alternative to Meynert-Wernicke's localizationism. Rather than centers, Freud spoke of brain "fields" (*Felder*), spontaneously configuring and reconfiguring according to the circumstances of language acquisition and production. Freud then turned the Meynert-Wernicke hypothesis about the form of the cortex against them: rather than being shaped like an umbrella to "receive" neural inputs, the cortex was hemispheric because, among other things, "the language area is a *continuous cortical region* within which the associations and transmissions underlying the language functions are taking place; they are of a complexity beyond comprehension" (Freud 1953, 62, emphasis added, modern translation). Consequently, no area in the brain could be considered a vacant space without function; areas between language centers were not "filled in" as language education progressed. Instead, Freud argued that each so-called center was *super-associated*, with new knowledge expanding or dynamizing the *fields* (*Felder*), all composed of multiple centers. It was trans-cortical fields, then, that formed and reformed, allowing associations to occur. Fields schematized and coordinated inputs of sensory and motor qualities. Because they amounted to the intersection of a host of different centers, from the visual to the auditory to the motor centers, the need for some vague "comprehension center," as postulated by Wernicke, was abrogated. Freud's super-associated fields – forming functionally according to activities and need – reduced Wernicke's seven forms of aphasia to approximately three because, in the absence of comprehension centers, no interruptions of pathways into or out of them existed.

Against Hughlings Jackson this time, Freud argued that the bi-hemispheric organization of the brain meant that "all the cortical areas are bilateral, *while* [only] that of language *association* is organized in one hemisphere" (Freud 1953, 65, emphasis added, modern translation). Damage to visual or auditory centers on one side of the brain did not by itself produce aphasia, as the other hemisphere took on those bi-hemispheric tasks lost in the damaged one. Pathology had shown that in some patients the integral loss of vision made writing difficult, although motor sensitivity in the hand could take the place of lost visualization. Nevertheless, language was indeed left hemispheric and its elements, such as writing, were acquired in a learning series passing from the initial acquisition of language sounds, to word formation, to sentence formation, early writing, spelling, and written sentence construction. Instead of proceeding from hypothetical comprehension centers, Freud proposed a theory of infantile stages of speech-, reading-, and writing-learning, all of which required *only* the initial mimetic capacity to repeat, memorize, and associate. This incidentally implied that family relationships and tribulations could contribute to the evolution of certain aphasias (something Charcot taught). Freud's collaboration with Breuer on hysterical patients suffering from aphasia in 1895 provided evidence for this. In 1891, however, he showed his abiding allegiance to Brentano's psychology, which had argued for the autonomy of psychological processes relative to motor ones, by emphasizing the distinction between the motor processes in speech acquisition and the psychological significance of certain words for hysterics suffering from temporary aphasias (Freud 1953, 74–75). Over a decade later, Freud retained the lessons of his philosophical mentor Brentano, who insisted that cooperation between empirical and intentionalist psychology could produce a synthetic conception of mind.[22]

Interesting for the philosophical reader is the way, unique in its time, in which Freud worked with psycho-physical parallelism.[23] There is not enough space here to examine Freud's much discussed *Project for a Scientific Psychology* (1895). The work, which surfaced after his physician friend, Wilhelm Fliess's death in 1928,[24] though it retained the dynamics and interactionism already found in "The Brain" and *On Aphasia*, was Freud's most comprehensively reductionist effort, possibly in response to Sigmund Exner's 1894 publication *Entwurf zu einer physiologischen Erklärung der psychischen Erscheinungen* [*Project for a physiological explanation of psychic phenomena*]. In his own *Project*, Freud undertook the reduction of consciousness and all cognitive processes to the interaction between neural networks, notably around the synapses. He even attempted to explain the possibility of conscious sensations – of *qualia* – on the basis of variations in the periodicity in neural firing across "contact barriers" (synapses).[25] In many ways an astounding and prescient venture (Solms, in Van de Vijver and Geerardyn 2002, 34), Freud nevertheless abandoned it and urged, decades later, that the copy found in Fliess's posthumous papers be destroyed. Much ink has flowed over the reasons for Freud's dislike of the work, from arguments tying it to the demise of his friendship with Fliess (Tabin 2006, 391–394), to those based on failure to provide a neurological explanation for the distinction between normal and pathological defense mechanisms.[26] Assuredly, the neurology of the time was not advanced enough to explain chemical activity at the synapses, much less the different types of chemicals found there (today's neuro-transmitters). But the relevance of the *Project* has been acknowledged at least since the mid 1970s.[27]

While "The Brain" is a relatively insignificant encyclopedia entry (Freud complained to Fliess that it had been heavily edited), *On Aphasia* is no minor work. I have focused on these two documents from the "archive" because they aptly document Freud's unique contribution to 19th-century philosophy (and science) of mind. From Franz Brentano he learned the relative autonomy of psychological states, when approached from the clinical side, relative to neuro-cerebral processes. He re-defined brain activity in terms of whole-brain interactive fields, configuring sensory, motor, and memory activities across the entire cortex. He criticized cortico-centrism for picturing the cerebrum in the likeness of a sovereign executive Reason. In so doing, he also destroyed residues of the homunculus conception of his time. He rejected Meynert's special neural bundles for freely willed activity, as well as Wernicke and Lichtheim's "comprehension centers." Freud's insistence on interactive fields, his attention to the role of development and socialization in aphasics, and his concern with trauma as physiological *and* intersubjective events, account for the contemporaneousness of his early thought. The complexity of the causes and conditions he adumbrated explains Derrida's observation, cited earlier, that Freud's concepts are dual, "cleaved". They had to be; he was simultaneously pondering the neuro-physiological grounds of aphasia (and hysteria) and the developmental and social factors contributing to pathologies. What Derrida calls "cleaved" reflects Freud's long-standing resolve to think mind, body, and environment, in their interaction.

Notes

1 My heartfelt thanks to Sandra Lapointe for her questions and massively pertinent suggestions, which have vastly improved this essay.
2 Franz Brentano (1838–1917) may be best remembered for his *Psychologie vom empirischen Standpunkt* [Psychology from an Empirical Standpoint] (Leipzig, 1874). He was Freud's teacher at the University of Vienna from 1873 to 1875. To his friend, Eduard Silverstein, Freud praised Brentano for attempting to hold Darwinism and "teleology" together (letter of 7 March 1875): "under Brentano's fruitful influence, I have arrived at the decision to take my Ph.D. in philosophy and zoology" (Boehlich and Pomerans 1990, 95). See the chapter on Brentano, *infra*.
3 See Gamwell and Solms (2006, 14) Also see Solms in Van de Vijver and Geerardyn (2002), 17ff.
4 Solms in Van de Vijver and Geerardyn, 17.
5 See (Keegan 2003). Freud was deeply influenced by Paul Flechsig, whose neuroanatomy of the brain was "evolutionary" – it was developed through research on fetal brain development – and "functional" insofar as certain mental illnesses or speech impediments could be occasioned by "a disturbance of nervous activity without any accompanying anatomical lesion." Flechsig was Theodor Meynert's Leipzig rival and the first to speak of cortical *fields* rather than centers (p. 56). Like Freud, he was interested, in the 1870s and 1880s, in the development of neuronal networks and in pathoanatomical psychiatry – although he would concentrate increasingly on brain anatomy.
6 See (Gamwell and Solms 2006, 15) for a hypothesis as to why the best neuroanatomists and physiologists of the brain were obliged to engage in rational speculation about brain function.
7 See (Derrida 1995b, 56). It is not only the concept of the archive that is divided in Freud.
8 Notably but not exclusively, Otto Loewi's 1921 discovery of acetylcholine, confirming the "contiguist" hypothesis that neurons were separated from each other, but "communicated" by releasing chemicals, today called neurotransmitters, something Freud, and others like Sigmund Exner, suspected but could not investigate.
9 Interest in the early Freud arguably began with Karl Pribram and Merton Gill, *Freud's "Project" Re-assessed* (New York: Basic Books, 1976). Also see the collection *Neuroscience of the Mind: On the Centennial of Freud's Project for a Scientific Psychology*, eds. Robert Bilder and F. Frank LeFever (New York: Annals of the New York Academy of Science, 1998).
10 See, e.g., Kusch 1995, 181–211.
11 On the dialectical relationship between Freud's neurological naturalism and his psychoanalytic 'hermeneutics', see Paul Ricœur (1970), especially Book II, Part I, and Book III, sections 1 and 4.
12 The text was long the object of debates about authorship, since none of the *Handwörterbuch* entries were signed by their authors, whose names were only assembled at the beginning of the dictionary. In spite of some epistolary evidence (see Freud 1985, 59; Solms and Saling 1990, 8), the principal reason for doubting Freud's authorship of "*Das Gehirn*" lies in the truncated character of the entry; a problem due no doubt to the limited dimensions of the *Handwörterbuch* itself (Solms and Saling 1990, 14–16).

13 Franz Joseph Gall (1758–1828), working from the hypothesis that the brain was the *organ* of the mind (his *Schädellehre*), was the first physiologist to ascribe cerebral functions to specific localities. From this, alas, he inferred that skull shape might provide insight into personality and intellect.
14 By 1900, however, Freud's *The Interpretation of Dreams* would claim that "The reflex act remains the type of every psychic activity as well" (Chapter VII, "Repression"), in line with Paul Flechsig's arguments.
15 In 1888, the influence of Brentano on Freud leads the latter to oppose Meynert's style of reductionism, in which any form of action had its neuro-cerebral corollary, *albeit* with the additional, "metaphysical" distinction between neural fibers for voluntary activity and other distinct fibers for involuntary activity.
16 See (Goetz et al. 1995, 127).
17 Freud repeats this claim in Chapter 7 of *The Interpretation of Dreams* (1900). The innovation he brings there to this claim is that between the reception of perceptual data and our motor response, memory traces are inscribe in the body, unconsciously and they have an impact on the motor response in some cases. See Keegan (2003) for Flechsig's influence on Freud's research.
18 This was the continuist-contiguist debate, concerning whether or not there was a gap (synapse) between neurons, and with the gap, resistance or facilitation of energetic transmission from neuron to neuron. The implications were enormous: if nerves did not communicate across synaptic breaks, than it would be much easier to measure the rate of electrical transmission from perception to motility (absent potential resistance at the synapses). Porath (2009, 58–60) reminds us that this model was influenced by the invention of the telegraph.
19 See (Jones 1953, Vol. I, 213).
20 In both of these cases, recorded by William A. Hammond (*A Treatise on the Diseases of the Nervous System*, 1882), Freud followed the clinical outcome and concluded: "in these cases Lichtheim's transcortical motor aphasia had been caused by lesions which had nothing whatever to do with interruption of a tract B-M [from a 'comprehension center' to the motor center]" (Freud 1953, 27).
21 The term "representation" (*Vorstellung*) can be long found in German thought on the mind. Already in the *Critique of Pure Reason*, Kant referred to the schematization of intuition and concept as producing a representation. Friedrich Herbart, his successor at Königsberg, used the term as well. It should be confused with "idea," which was also current in Kant and Herbart's German. Freud uses *Vorstellung*, but he often prefers "*Bild*" (image). It is another, philosophical, question to know what an image, stored in a nerve cell, means.
22 See (Porath 2009, 60).
23 Solms and Saling (1990) present various interpretations of Freud's approach to the mind-body relationship (92–94). Peter Amacher (1965) argued, with others, that Freud was a phenomenalist; i.e., that mental events "are mere shadows of physical events". Solms appears to follow Silverstein (1985), arguing that Freud was an interactionist.
24 Wilhelm Fliess, an ear, nose and throat doctor, and Sigmund Freud were close friends who read and criticized each other's work between 1887 and 1904, when their friendship ultimately broke off following a bitter dispute about the true authorship of the theory of fundamental bisexuation of living beings. See Sulloway (1992, esp. 113–131). Also see Bilder and LeFever (1998); Van de Vijver and Geerardyn (2002, 155–205).
25 "Contact barriers" [*Kontaktschranken*] was Freud's term for the synapse, a term introduced by Charles Sherrington in 1897. With the idea of periodicity in neural firing, an approach to the possibility of consciousness, emerging from a highly specific type of neuronal activity, was proposed. Periodicity depended on neural firing *across* synapses, which also meant that in the brain neurons were discontinuous but contiguous.

The resolution of the continuist-contiguist debate allowed Freud to propose a radical theory of the emergence of consciousness in his materialist neurology of 1895.

26 See Sulloway (1992, 124–126) on Freud's abandonment of the *Project*.
27 Pribram and Gill (1976). In 1995, on the occasion of the centenary of Freud's *Project*, the New York Academy of Sciences organized a conference, attempting to assess the relevance of Freud's neurology and psychoanalysis for contemporary neuroscience. The connections between the *Project*, neurology, and cognitive science have also been discussed in Mark Solms's work, among others. See, for example, Mark Solms and Oliver Turnbull (2002). Also see Solms (2014).

Bibliography

Amacher, Peter. (1965). "Freud's Neurological Education and its Influence on Psychoanalytic Theory," in *Psychological Issues*, Vol. 4 (Monograph 16).

Bilder, Robert and F. Frank LeFever, Eds. (1998). *Neuroscience of the Mind on the Centennial of Freud's Project for a Scientific Psychology*. New York: New York Academy of Sciences, Vol. 843.

Boehlich, Walter and Arnold J. Pomerans, Trans. (1990). *The Letters of Sigmund Freud to Eduard Silverstein, 1871–1881*. Cambridge, MA: Harvard University Press.

Breuer, J. and S. Freud. (2000). *Studies on Hysteria*. Trans. James Strachey and Anna Freud. New York: Basic Books.

Brook, Andrew. (1998). "Neuroscience Versus Psychology in Freud," in *Neuroscience of the Mind on the Centennial of Freud's Project for a Scientific Psychology*. New York: New York Academy of Sciences, Vol. 843: 66–79.

Carhart-Harris, R. L. and K. Friston. (2010). "The Default-Mode, Ego Functions, and Free-Energy: A Neurobiological Account of Freudian Ideas," in *Brain*, Vol. 133: 1265–1283.

Centonze, Diego, Alberto Siracusano, Paolo Calabresi and Giorgio Bernardi. (2004). "*The Project for a Scientific Psychology* (1895): A Freudian Anticipation of LTP-Memory Connection Theory," in *Brain Research Reviews*, Vol. 46: 310–314.

Clark, Andy. (2013). "Whatever Next? Predictive Brains, Situated Agents, and the Future of Cognitive Science," in *Behavioral and Brain Sciences*, Vol. 36: 181–253.

Derrida, Jacques. (1995a). "Archive Fever: A Freudiens Impression," Trans. Eric Prenowitz, in *Diacritics*, Vol. 25: 2.

———. (1995b). *Mal d'archive, une impression freudienne*. Paris: Galilée.

Exner, Sigmund. (1894). *Entwurf zu einer physiologischen Erklärung der psychischen Erscheinungen* (Outline toward a Physiological Explanation of Mental Phenomena). Vienna and Leipzig: F. Deuticke.

Flechsig, Paul. (1896). *Gehirn und Seele: Rede, gehalten am 31 October 1894 in der Universitätskirche zu Leipzig*. Leipzig: Von Veit & Companie.

Freud, Sigmund. (2009). *Contribution à la conception des Aphasies*. Paris: Presses universitaires de France, Bibliothèque de Psychanalyse. (1990).

Freud, Sigmund. (1953). *On Aphasia: A Critical Study*. New York: International Universities Press.

———. (1955). *The Standard Edition of the Complete Psychoanalytic Works*, Vol. XVIII. Eds. James Strachey and Anna Freud. London: Hogarth Press.

———. (1971). *Dora: An Analysis of a Case of Hysteria*. Trans. James Strachey and Anna Freud. New York: Collier Books.

———. (1985). *The Complete Letters of Sigmund Freud to Wilhelm Fliess, 1887–1904*. Ed. Jeffrey Moussaieff Masson. Cambridge, MA: Harvard University Press.

———. (1990). "The Brain," in Mark Solms and Michael Saling, Eds. *A Moment of Transition: Two Neuroscientific Articles by Sigmund Freud*. London: Karnac Books: 39–86.

Friston, Karl. (2010). "The Free Energy Principle: A Unified Brain Theory," in *Nature Reviews Neuroscience*, 13 January. doi:10.1038/nrn2787.

Gallese, Vittorio. (2008). "Mirror Neurons and the Social Nature of Language: The Neural Exploitation Hypothesis," in *Social Neuroscience*, Vol. 3: 317–333.

Gamwell, Lynn and Mark Solms. (2006). *From Neurology to Psychoanalysis: Sigmund Freud's Neurological Drawings and Diagrams of the Mind*. New York: Binghamton University Art Museum and State University of New York.

Goetz, Christopher G., Michel Bonduelle and Toby Gelfand. (1995). *Charcot: Constructing Neurology*. Oxford and New York: Oxford University Press.

Hall, Marshall. (1833). "On the Reflex Function of the Medulla Oblongata and Medulla Spinalis," *Philosophical Transactions of the Royal Society of London (1776-1886)*. Vol. 123: 635–665.

Hammond, William A. (1882, first published 1871). *A Treatise on the Diseases of the Nervous System*. New York: D. Appleton and Company.

Hughlings Jackson, John. (1958). *Selected Writings of John Hughlings Jackson, Vol. II* "Evolution and Dissolution of the Nervous System, Speech, Various Papers, Addresses and Lectures." Ed. James Taylor. New York: Basic Books.

Jones, Ernest. (1953). *The Life and Work of Sigmund Freud (1856–1900): The Formative Years and the Great Discoveries, Vol. I*. New York: Basic Books.

Keegan, Eduardo. (2003). "Flechsig and Freud: Late 19th-Century Neurology and the Emergence of Psychoanalysis," in *History of Psychology*, Vol. 6, no. 1: 52–69.

Kusch, Martin. (1995). *Psychologism: A Case Study in the Sociology of Philosophical Knowledge*. London: Routledge.

Modell, Arnold H. (2013). "Some Comments on the Freudian Unconscious," in *Psychoanalytic Review*, Vol. 100, no. 4: 535–541.

Porath, Erik. (2009). "Vom Reflexbogen zum psychischen Apparat: Neurologie und Psychoanalyse um 1900," in *Berichte zur Wissenschaftsgeschichte*, Vol. 32: 53–69.

Pribram, Karl H. and Merton Gill. (1976). *Freud's 'Project' Re-assessed*. New York: Basic Books.

Ricœur, Paul. (1970). *Freud and Philosophy: An Essay on Interpretation*. Trans. Denis Savage. New Haven: Yale University Press.

Ritvo, Lucille. (1990). *Darwin's Influence on Freud: A Tale of Two Sciences*. New Haven: Yale University Press.

Schott, Geoffrey. (2011). "Freud's *Project* and its Diagram: Anticipating the Hebbian Synapse," in *Journal of Neurosurgery and Psychiatry*, Vol. 82, no. 2: 122–125.

Silverstein, B. (1985). "Freud's Psychology and Its Organic Foundation: Sexuality and Mind-Body Interactionism," in *Psychoanalytic Review*, Vol. 72: 203–228.

Solms, Mark. (2014). "The Conscious Id," in *Neuropsychoanalysis: An Interdisciplinary Journal for Psychoanalysis and the Neurosciences*, Vol. 15, no. 1: 5–19. doi:10.1080/15294145.2013.10773711.

Solms, Mark and Michael Saling, Trans and Eds. (1990). *A Moment of Transition: Two Neuroscientific Articles by Sigmund Freud*. London: Karnac Books.

Solms, Mark and Oliver Turnbull. (2002). *The Brain and the Inner World: An Introduction to the Neuroscience of Subjective Experience*. New York: Other Press.

Sulloway, Frank J. (1992). *Freud: Biologist of the Mind: Beyond the Psychoanalytic Legend*. Cambridge, MA: Harvard University Press.

Tabin, Johanna Krout. (2006). "What Freud Called 'The Psychology for Neurologists' and the Many Questions It Raises," *Psychoanalytic Psychology*, Vol. 23, no. 2: 383–407.

Van de Vijver, Gertrudis and Filip Geerardyn. (2002). *The Pre-Psychoanalytic Writings of Sigmund Freud*. London: Karnac Books.

9

BRENTANO'S EARLY PHILOSOPHY OF MIND[1]

Robin D. Rollinger

> To attain assured knowledge of the soul is one of the most difficult things in the world.
> – Aristotle, *De Anima*, 402 a 10.

1. Introduction

While some philosophers deal with mind as a peripheral topic, this is not at all the case regarding Franz Brentano. His chief contribution to philosophy is indeed to be found in his philosophy of mind, especially in his momentous introduction of the concept of intentionality into modern philosophy. But there are still other important aspects of his approach to mind that are yet to be made known to the wider philosophical public.[2] Here I shall discuss these aspects as well as the more familiar ones. This will be done in four steps. I shall begin by explaining how philosophy as understood by Brentano involves the primacy of mind in all of its investigations. Secondly, the method that Brentano prescribes for investigating mind will be discussed. Thirdly, his philosophy of mind pertaining specifically to mental acts will receive attention. Fourthly, his views on the nature of the bearers of mental acts will be briefly brought into focus. Brentano's philosophy went through different phases of development. In what follows, I will be first and foremost concerned with his early philosophy of mind, i.e. the views he defended before the beginning of the twentieth century[3] (that is to say, before he developed his "reism"; see Chrudzimski 2004; Chrudzimski and Smith 2004).

2. Philosophy

In his lectures on immortality, held in the winter semester 1875/76, Brentano states his conception of philosophy as follows:

> Philosophy includes that part of our general knowledge based on experience which – to use a popular expression – concerns what is "inward",

whereas natural science is directed at what is outward. While the natural scientist determines the laws of the physical, the philosopher establishes the laws of the mental and goes beyond this only if the laws themselves exceed this and have validity as facts that are more general pertaining to both domains, physical and mental.

(LS 22: 29515.)[4]

While contemporary philosophers will hardly have trouble with the characterization of philosophy as general (in contrast with disciplines such as history, in which particulars are investigated), Brentano's claim that it is "based on experience" or that it is "empirical" might appear rather perplexing. Such perplexity is unlikely to diminish in view of the fact that he thought of philosophy as a discipline that encompasses a special subject matter, namely the mental or, as we may also say, the mind. While some philosophers might be more inclined to say that philosophy differs from other disciplines in its method, Brentano thinks that its method is essentially the same as that of the natural sciences (Brentano 1929: 136 f.) and, as indicated previously, that philosophy differs from them with respect to the objects that it investigates. The concern for mind in philosophy, as far as Brentano is concerned, entails that the philosophical endeavour must be "empirical", for he conceives of mind as something that we actually "experience". Just as Locke had identified experience as the source of all knowledge and divided it into sensation and reflection, the likewise empirically inclined Brentano divides experience into "outer" and "inner". Philosophy for him occupies itself with what is *inwardly* experienced. (There will more about inner experience below.)

There are, according to Brentano, five branches of philosophy: two theoretical and three practical. Whether a discipline is theoretical or practical depends on what "unifies" all the items of knowledge in this discipline. This can be explained as follows. The expert in a given discipline knows many different things (here we could say "truths"), all of which together make up the discipline. If we ask what makes these items of knowledge one single discipline, the answer will differ, depending on whether the discipline is practical or theoretical. According to the lectures on ethics Brentano held in the winter semester 1884/85 in Vienna, "In the case of the theoretical ones the affinity of the items of knowledge as such is decisive, whereas in the case of practical ones [it is] a goal that lies outside the items of knowledge" (Brentano, Y 4: 2). All of the truths that the physicist knows, for instance, are truths about the physical. They are intrinsically related to each other, regardless of any external goal. The same goes for psychology. Everything known in this discipline is concerned with the mental. Moreover, all the truths in metaphysics are concerned with being *qua* being. What makes psychology and metaphysics theoretical disciplines is the fact that their truths pertain to a single object-domain, the mind in the former case, being in the latter.

In the case of logic, however, not all of its truths are intrinsically related in that way, by virtue of concerning themselves with a single domain of objects. Brentano defines logic as the "art of correct judging" (Brentano 1956: 1 ff.). This entails that the logician knows about judging, which is for Brentano a mental act (more on this as follows) and pertains to the domain of objects that defines psychology. However, in the treatment of induction, the logician must know about the laws of probability which pertain to the domain of objects associated with mathematics. Likewise, the logician also has to give some attention to how judgements and perhaps other acts of the mind are expressed in language. Therefore, he must draw on yet another discipline, namely linguistics. If the logician merely gathered random truths from psychology, mathematics, and linguistics, logic would hardly be more than a hodge-podge. What unifies these truths is not the fact that they share an object-domain, but the fact that they share a goal: correct judging. These truths are brought together to form an "art" – as opposed to a science – that aims at that goal. This view of logic, to be sure, differs considerably from more contemporary conceptions of this discipline, but it was of great importance to Brentano. His claim that aesthetics and especially ethics are practical disciplines would no doubt be less controversial.

Interestingly, Brentano's psychology directly informs his conception of the division between practical philosophical disciplines. Indeed, as he sees it, logic, aesthetics, and ethics in each case describe norms associated with each class of the three classes of mental phenomena: presentations, judgements, and love and hate. Let's start with judgements. We've already seen that logic is the practical discipline that tells us how we are to judge correctly and avoid judging incorrectly. But logic also tells us how we are to judge with "evidence", for this is also part of its goal. The normative role played by evidence in this context is peculiar to Brentano's epistemology. On Brentano's account, many of our judgements are made blindly due to instinct, habit, wishful thinking, reliance on authority, and perhaps other causes. But when we judge with evidence, we have "knowledge" and we thus achieve our purpose as cognitive agents.

As Brentano sees it, presentations (*Vorstellungen*) make up the fundamental class of mental phenomena insofar as mental phenomena of other classes, e.g. judgements, are based on presentations (Brentano 1874: 104 ff.; Brentano 1995a: 61 ff.). The German term 'Vorstellung' was standardly used as a translation of 'idea' in the works of modern philosophers such as Descartes and Locke. For them, our sensations are presentations, but other examples of ideas can be found in imagination and abstract thinking. On Brentano's account, aesthetics is the discipline that is based on the psychological elaboration of presentations. This discipline is practical because it draws on the truths that pertain to various object-domains to reach a goal: presentations of the *beautiful* (Brentano 1959).

The third class of mental phenomena, love and hate (*Liebe und Hass*), consists not only emotions and feelings, but also of volitions (Brentano 1874: 346 ff.; Brentano 1995b: 183 ff.). Ethics is the practical discipline that tells us what is worthy of love and what is worthy of hate (Brentano 1889, 1952). Brentano thinks that truth and falsehood, on the one hand, and evidence and blindness, on the other, are uniquely applicable to judgements. But he also thinks that love and hate have analogues of truth and evidence – this constituting the basis for Brentano's argument against relativism in ethics. Our love of knowledge, for instance, is characterized as correct (i.e. as analogous to true and evident in the domain of judgement). Hence, ethics instructs us to prefer knowledge over ignorance. Its goal in general is the good.

In sum, the goals of the practical philosophical disciplines (logic, aesthetics, and ethics respectively) are the true, the beautiful, and the good corresponding respectively to the mental acts: judging, presenting, and loving and hating.

There are, as we have seen above, two theoretical philosophical disciplines on Brentano's account: metaphysics and psychology. Brentanian metaphysics includes transcendental philosophy (epistemology), ontology, theology, and cosmology. Metaphysics for Brentano concerns being *qua* being and, as such, it involves generalisations that pertain to both the mental and the physical. Consideration of the mental comes into play in metaphysics to the extent that transcendental philosophy must offer a defence against various types of epistemological scepticism. Brentano's argument here rests on the following idea: Not only is our knowledge of mind known more certainly than the external world is known, but our acts of knowing are themselves in all cases mental phenomena, and thus themselves accessible with maximal certainty.[5]

Psychology, for its part, is the discipline that deals with the mind as such. Interestingly, psychology had traditionally been understood to be the discipline that is concerned with the "soul". By the end of the nineteenth century, however, the possibility of a "psychology without a soul" (Lange 1866: 465) no longer seemed to be absurd. One of the reasons for this was the rejection of the idea that occurrences such as perceiving, imagining, thinking, willing, and feeling require the positing of a substance or substratum (i.e. the soul) underlying them. What the mind is, from this standpoint, is what remains of conscious life once the presumption of a substantial is eliminated – i.e. mental phenomena or acts – and this is what psychology investigates. These phenomena obviously appear to us. Yet, according to certain prominent thinkers such as John Stuart Mill, it is doubtful whether we ever come across a soul in our inner perception or observation. In Brentano's *Psychology from an Empirical Standpoint* the possibility of a psychology without a soul is taken as a starting point (Brentano 1874: 10–24; Brentano 1995a: 14–20). However, he was not ultimately satisfied with the definition of psychology as the science of mental phenomena. This definition he considered to be acceptable only provisionally. Since the soul was viewed by many as a "metaphysical" topic, it was best left aside until generalizations about mental phenomena could be established. The resulting generalizations will be considered below, after we consider the method that Brentano used in his early philosophy of mind.

3. Method

In the 1880s Brentano proposed an important distinction that had not yet been emphasized in *Psychology from an Empirical Standpoint* (1874): the distinction between descriptive and genetic psychology (Brentano 1982: 1 ff.; Brentano

1995b: 3 ff.). On his account, an important difference between these two branches lies in their respective conception of the degree to which the study of physiology should be required in psychological investigations. Descriptive psychology does not involve physiology to a significant degree and is, in this respect, "pure psychology". Genetic psychology, by contrast, includes physiological considerations quite extensively. Another difference is that descriptive psychology contains truths that are in no way qualified, whereas the truths of genetic psychology are only *for the most part* true.

Brentano did not remain content with the term 'descriptive psychology' in reference to the pure and exact description of the elements of consciousness and their modes of connection. In lectures he held in Vienna in the winter semester 1887/88, he says that this branch of psychology is in fact distinguished "from that which is usually called descriptive psychology", i.e. a "special depiction of characters, temperaments, etc.", which is indeed "more appropriate for genetic psychology" (Ps 76/58007). The desire to mark the distinction between the two kinds of investigation, descriptive and genetic, might have played a role in Brentano's introducing other terms, such as "phenomenology" (Ps 77) and finally the uncustomary term "psychognosy" (*Psychognosie*) in order to designate the discipline he took to be concerned with the fundamental investigations of mind or, as he conceives of it, the analysis of consciousness. In what follows, I will give preference to 'psychognosy' for designating this analysis.

The value of psychognostic analysis, as Brentano argues in the 1887/88 lectures on descriptive psychology, lies in a number of features. Firstly, it surveys and elucidates the experiential basis for all science and thereby has consequences for the limits of science. This might at first seem to be an odd claim, but we mustn't forget that sensations, on which natural science relies for its results, are to be investigated in pyschognosy insofar as they are indeed mental phenomena. Secondly, he also believed that the analysis of consciousness has the advantage of the "authenticity of presentations" (*Eigentlichkeit der Vorstellungen*) and contrasts it with natural science and especially physics, which he believes inauthentically presents a merely hypothetical external world (Ps 76/58007). Thirdly, Brentano thought that in addition to its relevance for questions of aesthetics, logic and ethics, psychology would be helpful in the treatment of the "question of immortality" (Ps 76: 58008). Finally, Brentano assumed psychognosy to be the theoretical foundation for genetic psychology.

Brentano's contemporaries, at least in the German-speaking world which indeed came to have a tremendous impact on psychology elsewhere, tended to proceed very differently, notably by giving priority to questions of "psycho-physics" (Fechner 1860) or "physiological psychology" (Wundt 1874), and with few exceptions had little, if any, place for the equivalent of his psychognostic method in their program. He very much doubted the fruitfulness of an approach that excludes psychognosy. Thus, he spoke of the "sad labyrinthine paths of some psycho-physicists" (Ps 76: 58009), i.e. presumably referring here to the paths taken by investigators whom he considered to be ill prepared to meet the challenges of providing an adequate foundation for their psychological theories. Brentano was aware of the fact that disagreements among psychologists and philosophers, when it comes to these foundational questions in psychology, were unlikely to be easily resolved and that the challenges psychognosy faced in this context would thus be extremely difficult (Brentano 1982: 28, 1995b: 31).

As Brentano conceived of it, the method that underlies the psychognostic investigation involves the following conditions to be met by the investigator:

1 He has to experience [*erleben*],
2 he has to notice [*bemerken*],
3 he has to fix [*fixieren*] what he notices, in order to collect it,
4 he has to generalize inductively;
5 where the necessity or impossibility of a unification of certain elements becomes clear from the concepts themselves, he must intuitively grasp these general laws;
6 finally, we can add that he has to make deductive use of what he gained, in one way or another, from general laws. By doing this, he will be able to solve many questions concerning the elements which otherwise he would scarcely have been able to answer.

(Brentano 1982: 28, 1995b: 31 f.)

Each of these requirements must be considered in turn.

When Brentano says that the psychognostic investigator must "experience", he means that he must "inwardly perceive" mental phenomena. By this Brentano does not mean introspection in the sense of turning one's attention to one's mental acts. According to Brentano, we are aware of these acts simply by having them. But this awareness does not require attentiveness. If I am angry, for example, I experience my anger, but as soon as I attempt to focus my attention on my anger it vanishes (Brentano 1874: 35 ff., 1995a: 22 ff.).

Be this as it may, relying on inner perception alone does not suffice for psychognosy. Those who wish to make progress in this discipline must also "notice" what they inwardly perceive. Our consciousness often involves a complexity of elements, sensory and intellectual as well as emotional and volitional, which we only perceive implicitly. Perceiving them explicitly or *noticing* them, according to Brentano, is (like perceiving them) not subject to error, though the range of phenomena considered is bound to be very limited. What is past, for instance, can no longer be noticed. Interestingly, on Brentano's account, the specification of conditions for noticing is not itself a matter for psychognosy, but a psychogenetic matter (Brentano 1982: 33, 1995b: 36). This is not to say that psychognosy cannot advance without knowing these conditions. Brentano obviously thinks that it can.

"Fixing", on Brentano's account, consists in relating what is noticed to other items of knowledge (Brentano 1982: 65, 1995b: 67). If, for instance, one notices some feature of one's experience and finds it to be similar to what had been experienced previously, one is fixing that experience in a way that makes it amenable to be "collected". In this way the psychognostic investigator goes beyond the limitations of merely experiencing and noticing. Once the phenomena are fixed, inductive generalizations can be made. Brentano advises proceeding with caution when it comes to drawing general conclusions from items of knowledge that have been fixed. Nonetheless he thinks that there are cases in which the results are maximally reliable or "certain":

> In many cases, we will be justified in making a claim with certainty: (for example, that there is no third quality apart from affirmation and negation. That there is no [pure] colour except red, yellow, blue, for instance, green, white, black and their mixtures).
> But due care [is] advised.
> And if there is any chance left that there might be things which we or others have not noticed, then the more correct thing to say is: 'as far as one is, or has been able to notice', nothing else exists.
> (Brentano 1982: 71 f., 1995b: 74.)

The examples Brentano gives in the above passage are said to involve "intuitive grasping". The division of judgements into affirmations and negations, for instance, is guaranteed by the very concept of a judgement (which is of course obtained from inner experience). This is precisely the kind of "ideal intuition" Brentano has mind in the Preface to *Psychology from an empirical Standpoint* (Brentano 1874: v; Brentano 1995a: xxv).

Finally, according to Brentano, the psychognostic investigator "has to make deductive use of what he gained in one way or another (inductively or intuitively) from the general laws" (Brentano 1982: 74, 1995b: 76). Brentano is here subscribing to a conception of the correct scientific method that is not only associated with Aristotle, but with many other classical thinkers.

The picture of psychognosy that emerges here is that of a vast and complex discipline that appeals to laws that can be grasped through ideal intuition (akin to what we find in the "pure phenomenology" of Edmund Husserl, one of Brentano's students), as well as a reliance on induction and deductive inference. In view of such vastness and complexity, it is no surprise that Brentano never – not even in his lectures or elsewhere – managed to provide an exhaustive account of this discipline that would go beyond a mere introduction. Nevertheless, he was confident in a number of results which we shall now consider.

4. Psychognosy without a soul

Even if we restrict ourselves to Brentano's early psychology, we are faced with the difficulty of dealing with a variety of sources. They include both the published and the unpublished parts of *Psychology from an Empirical Standpoint* (1874). They also include Brentano's various lectures on psychology. These lectures are important when it comes to giving a faithful picture of Brentano's early psychognostic theory of mental acts. (Concerning his views on genetic psychology, see Rollinger 2014.)

The main results of *Psychology from an Empirical Standpoint* are summed up at the beginning of the unpublished part of the work:

1. All mental phenomena are presentations or have presentations as foundations.
2. Every mental phenomenon is consciousness; that is to say, it has a relation to a content.
3. Every mental phenomenon is a presenting, a judging, or a loving or a hating. (There are three fundamentally different modes of consciousness.)
4. All mental phenomena are conscious. The consciousness of each mental phenomenon, however, is threefold; and in this regard, considered more closely, the three following laws are results:
5. Every mental phenomenon is presented with an intensity that is equal to its own [intensity] (or to the intensity of the presentation that underlies it).
6. Every mental phenomenon is accepted [i.e. taken as something that really exists] with complete certainty and evidence.
7. Every mental phenomenon is loved or hated; more precisely, it is the object of a feeling of pleasure or displeasure whose quality and quantity do not immediately reveal a uniform regularity because they are determined by the influence of different factors.
8. No mental phenomenon is spatially extended. (In all cases which were believed to be in contradiction with this law, it became clear that a mental phenomenon was confused with its content or the content of sensations connected with it.)
9. All mental phenomena of which someone simultaneously has inner consciousness are partial phenomena of a real-unitary phenomenon. In other words, they belong as *divisiva* to one reality.[6]

(Ps 53: 53122–53123)

These results are repeatedly stated in various lectures and other manuscripts and can be regarded as prime candidates for laws belonging to psychognosy – i.e. the pure and exact psychology – as Brentano conceives of it.

For one thing, (1) and (2) both contribute to throw light on Brentano's important distinction between "mental" and "physical" phenomena, fulfilling the role of criteria for identifying the mental. This distinction is important because it allows us to isolate those phenomena which belong to the subject matter of psychology. In Book Two, Chapter 1, § 3 of *Psychology from an Empirical Standpoint*, Brentano argues that while a mental phenomenon is always either a presentation or has a presentation as its foundation, this is never true of a physical phenomenon such as "colour, a figure, a landscape which I see, a chord which I hear, warmth, cold, odour which I sense; as well as similar images which appear in the imagination" (Brentano 1874: 102, 1995a: 61). While he regards such a criterion for distinguishing mental acts from physical phenomena to be sufficient, he nonetheless adds that it "is not completely unified because it separates mental phenomena into two groups" (Brentano 1874: 111, 1995a: 65). That is to say, a disjunctive criterion does not prove to be satisfactory, whereas (2) – the celebrated "intentionality thesis" – offers a way to sustain the distinction between mental and physical phenomena without dividing the mental ones into groups (presentations and other mental phenomena that are founded on presentations).

In Book Two, Chapter 1, § 5 of *Psychology from an Empirical Standpoint*, Brentano elaborates on the intentionality thesis:

> Every mental phenomenon is characterized by what the Scholastics of the Middle Ages called the intentional (or mental) inexistence of an object, and what we might call, though not wholly unambiguously, reference to a content, direction toward an object (which is not to be understood here as meaning a thing), or immanent objectivity. Every mental phenomenon includes something as object within itself, although they do not all do so in the same way. In presentation something is presented, in judgement something is affirmed or denied, in love loved, in hate hated, in desire desired and so on.
>
> (Brentano 1874: 115, 1995a: 68)

This thesis is again and again repeated in Brentano's lectures on psychology. The following passage is from his lectures entitled "Psychognosy":

> the peculiarity which, above all, is generally characteristic of consciousness, is that it shows always and everywhere, i.e. in each of its separable parts, a certain kind of relation, relating a subject to an object. This relation is also referred to as 'intentional relation'. To every consciousness belongs essentially a relation...
>
> Explanation of the term object: some internal object-like thing [*ein innerlich Gegenständliches*] is meant. It need not correspond to anything outside.
>
> To avoid misunderstandings, one may call it 'in-dwelling' [*inwohnendes*] or 'immanent' object.
>
> This is something (a) generally and (b) exclusively characteristic of consciousness. If, as we commonly believe, there is an unconscious world of bodies with sensible qualities (or, instead, with a mass of [qualities] of whatever nature non-intuitive to us, which fill certain spaces), then it will certainly partake in many other kinds of relations, like that of part and whole, agreement and difference, cause and effect, and so forth.
>
> But it absolutely does not take part in this intentional relation. Hence [we call it a] 'psychical relation'.
>
> (Brentano 1982: 21 f., 1995b: 23 f.)

What distinguishes mental phenomena from physical phenomena is said to be its intentional character, its being related to an object. Yet, on this point, Brentano was not consistent in his formulations. In the second edition of *Psychology from an Empirical Standpoint* (1911), Brentano not only omitted the whole discussion of how mental phenomena are to be distinguished from physical ones, but he also included an appendix in which intentionality is described differently, namely as something "relation-like" (*Relativliches*) (Brentano 1911: 122–126, 1995a: 211–214). Although not all commentators agree,[7] there is arguably an important difference between this later characterization of intentionality and Brentano's initial proposal in terms of "mental inexistence". In the latter case, the idea seems to be that whenever there is consciousness of an object there is something that *exists*, namely the object, albeit *in* consciousness. The characterization of intentionality as something "relation-like", by contrast, allows for the possibility of there being a mental act without any corresponding object at all, as in cases when we are thinking of a unicorn. When we say that there is a presentation of a unicorn, there is not really a relation between the act of presenting and the unicorn because there is simply no unicorn. Whether Brentano really did change his conception of intentionality or not, here we are dealing with intentionality as inexistence since our focus is his early philosophy of mind.

Generalization (3) also plays a crucial role in Brentano's account of the mind in its various manifestations. On Brentano's account, mental phenomena (viz. mental acts) are to be divided in three classes. He puts this view forward in Book Two, Chapter 6, § 3 of *Psychology from an Empirical Standpoint*, and it is elaborated on in the next two chapters. His classification of mental acts in terms of presentations, judgements, and acts of love or hate was opposed to the traditional classification in terms of thinking (*Denken*), feeling (*Fühlen*), and willing (*Wollen*). His theory involves two important criticisms of the traditional classification. Firstly, Brentano regards "thinking" as equivocal insofar as it can refer to presenting or judging: two distinct ways of intentionally relating to an object. Secondly, he considers the phenomena of feeling and willing as belonging together in a single class.

Let us look at Brentano's three classes of mental phenomena in somewhat more detail.

4.1 Presentations

Brentano's account of presentations contains a thorough-going consideration of sensations (in Brentano 1982, as well as his other lectures on descriptive psychology, Ps 76 and Ps 77). On his account, sensations are one type of presentation, namely the presentations that we ordinarily regard as corresponding to our perception of outer objects. We cannot perceive anything in the external world unless we have sensations. Brentano considers at length the content of sensations. He maintains that these contents have at least three features, namely quality, intensity, and location. If, for instance, I have an auditory sensation, its content can be specified, for instance, as the tone c. This is what Brentano understands to be the quality of the tone. The tone can of course be louder or softer. This feature is the intensity of the tone. Finally, the tone can be heard to my left or to my right, that is, at a certain location. While the location of a sensory content is for the most part clear in the case of visual, auditory, and tactile sensations, it is more difficult to determine in the cases of taste and odour. What intensity amounts to is also not without difficulties. Though one is tempted to think that the brightness of a colour is analogous to the loudness of a tone and is therefore an example of intensity, Brentano insists that this is not the case. It is possible for black, for instance, to be a very intense content of visual sensation, and yet black cannot be bright.

Brentano considered allowing for a fourth feature of a sensory content, namely its temporality. He insists, however, that this feature is not intrinsic to the sensation, but added via the imagination. When we hear a succession of tones in a melody, only the present one is the content of a sensation. The past tones are "associated" with the present tone, and given their place in the past by virtue of this association. This aspect of conscious life is what Brentano calls "original association" (Brentano 1982: 19; Brentano 1995b: 21), a form of association which cannot be reduced to the kind of association of ideas that we acquire through habit, as this was understood in the empiricist tradition and associationist psychology.

Because Brentano excludes temporality from sensory contents, he is forced to allow for presentations that are not sensations. He calls the latter "fantasy presentations" (*Phantasievorstellungen*). Following Hume, Brentano characterizes presentations of this kind as fainter or weaker than sensations. As Brentano understands it, the content of a fantasy presentation is less intense than the content of the corresponding sensation. However vividly I imagine the explosion I heard yesterday, it cannot be as intense as the sensation I had when I perceived the explosion. But fantasy presentations differ from sensations in at least one other important respect: sensations are a type of "authentic" presentations. Fantasy presentations are by contrast inauthentic or improper ones (*uneigentliche Vorstellungen*). The presentation of God or of a billion are of the latter kind, though these are inauthentic to such an extreme that the objects in questions cannot even be imagined. The inauthenticity of fantasy presentations together with the low intensity of their content is what distinguishes them from corresponding sensations. (See Rollinger 2008: 29–49.)

Brentano also considers "abstract" or "conceptual" presentations. In a manuscript from the 1870s he says:

> A human being has, besides concrete-sensible, animal presentations, abstract ones that we call intelligible, specifically human.
>
> Such abstract ones are: a quality without determinate magnitude, pure quantity, shape, etc. without quality, genus without difference..., thing without properties, number.
>
> (LS 1: 29002)

The process by which we arrive at such presentations – abstraction – is no less puzzling for Brentano than it was for the British Empiricists. He in fact formulated more than one theory to account for it. What remains constant in his philosophy of mind is nonetheless the conviction that a position must be taken between two extremes: nominalism (the view that there are in fact no abstract presentations) and Platonism (the view that such presentations are related to a special class of objects distinct from what we inwardly and outwardly perceive). While the former extreme prevailed among many of his contemporaries, especially those inspired by British empiricism, the latter became increasingly prevalent among his own students, especially for those among them who, like Husserl, came under the influence of Bernard Bolzano. It may be noted that, although Brentano allows for abstract presentations, he rejects innate ideas, i.e. presentations that have no origin in sensations or in the presentations that underlie inner perception (or, it must be added, in original association). This is a constant in Brentano's philosophy of mind and it is the reason why he rejected a good deal of the rationalist tradition, including of course the Kantian theory of categories.

4.2 Judgements

Judgments are mental acts which, unlike presentations, "accept" or "reject" an object. If someone judges that God exists, this object is accepted. The same object is rejected whenever one judges that He does not exist. Brentano's theory of judgment is peculiar insofar as it involves the claim that all judgements are in fact judgements of existence and, as far as the linguistic expression of a judgement is concerned, they can always be reduced to a sentence in which we say of an object that it does or does not exist (Brentano 1874: 279–289; Brentano 1995b: 163–172). Particular judgements, e.g. "Some human beings are mortal", can be expressed by affirmative existential statements, e.g. "There is a human being that is mortal", while universal judgments, "All human beings are mortal", can be expressed as negative existential statements, e.g. "There is no human being that is not mortal". This conception of judgements has great consequences in logic, according to Brentano (Brentano 1874: 302 ff.; Brentano 1995a: 179 ff.).[8] Finally, a judgement for Brentano is either evident or blind. Inner perception is in fact exemplary of an evident judgement. Analytic statements, e.g. the law of non-contradiction, also express judgments that are evident in Brentano's sense (Brentano 1956: 162 ff.). Besides the immediate evidence of inner perception and analytic judgements, judgements can on his view also have a mediated evidence when they are validly inferred from immediately evident ones.

4.3 Love and hate

In addition to presentation and judgements, Brentano's theory recognizes a third class of mental acts to which he often refers as 'love and hate'. As we have already noted, love and hate can, in some cases, have the analogue of evidence and are thereby of importance for ethics. The love of knowledge, for instance, is not just any arbitrary love or merely a matter of taste, but it is "characterised as correct" (*als richtig characterisiert*). Brentano's claim that the class of love and hate include both emotional and volitional acts, however, stands in need of some elucidation. Brentano thinks that this claim is evident, i.e. clearly confirmed by the data of inner perception. He nonetheless puts forward an argument for it. According to this argument, the distinction between emotion and volition is merely a matter of degree, not a matter of them belonging to separate classes. The continuity in the series of mental acts that lead from emotion to action in general is highlighted, for instance, in the following example: "sadness – yearning for the absent good – hope that it will be ours – the desire to bring it about – the courage to make the attempt – the decision to act" (Brentano 1874: 308; Brentano 1995a: 184). As Brentano understands it, the transition in this series from emotion to volition is gradual and all the acts within the series belong to one and the same class.

4.4 Inner consciousness

The psychognostic generalizations (4)-(7) epitomize first and foremost Brentano's views on inner perception, i.e. the perception of one's present mental acts, but his concept of inner consciousness (*inneres Bewusstsein*) is extended to any kind of mental act that is inwardly directed. In this context he of course puts forward the controversial thesis that we perceive all of our acts of consciousness while they occur (Brentano 1874: 187–201; Brentano 1995a: 110–118). There is, on his view, no such thing as an "unconscious consciousness" (*unbewusstes Bewusstsein*). We have already noted that inner perception for Brentano is not introspection or, in his terms, inner observation. That is to say, on his view our perception of our current acts of consciousness cannot be attentive, although he concedes that we can attend to the immediately past acts (as these are given in original association) and other remembered acts. Brentano devotes two whole chapters of *Psychology from an Empirical Standpoint* to demonstrating that the hypothesis of an unconscious mind fails to explain anything at all about mental life (Book Two, Chapters 2 and 3). He also maintains that there is an inner consciousness both in terms of the presentation and acceptance (or affirmative judgement) of one's current acts of consciousness, though he finds it more difficult to defend the thesis that there is in all cases a loving or hating of these acts. In spite of this difficulty, however, he is still willing to uphold this thesis.

5. Psychognosy with a soul

At the time Brentano was writing *Psychology from an Empirical Standpoint* and apparently for some time after that, he was, as we have seen, willing to characterize psychology as the science of mental phenomena. While this characterization was meant as a preliminary one (either as a convenient starting point or an attempt to accommodate certain contemporary tendencies), he eventually arrived at the view that the soul is to be the subject matter of psychology (including psychognosy) from the very outset. "Psychology is the study of the soul" (Ps 66/55087), he states plainly in a manuscript that was apparently written late in the nineteenth century.

"What we understand by 'human soul'", says Brentano in his Würzburg lectures on immortality from 1869, "is a *substance* that is in us the bearer of thinking, willing, sensing, in short of *all inwardly conscious acts*" (LS 23/29676). He was already concerned with this topic in his Würzburg period and certainly did not abandon it after he moved to Vienna and indeed even after he retired.

Considerations about the soul are more likely to be regarded as belonging to metaphysics than empirical psychology. Brentano does indeed see the relevance of such reflections to metaphysics, including of course theology, because they are involved in one of the proofs for the existence of God (LS 23/28670). His concern with the soul, however, is most emphatically *not* metaphysical in character if the subject matter of metaphysics is taken to be "things in themselves", altogether beyond experience. His very concept of philosophy will not allow for metaphysics in this sense. "It is not, as one has often asserted, the opposite of empirical researches," he says of philosophy as such and continues quite sharply: "It is itself based on experience" (LS 22/29511 f.). Accordingly Brentano's philosophy of mind allows for the soul only if the concept of the soul has a basis in experience.

Prior to Brentano, there had been philosophers, especially in the empiricist tradition, who doubted that a substantial bearer of mental acts would be accessible to experience. In this regard we may of course be reminded of David Hume's pronouncement that he could not find a "self" in his experience. If we take "self" as a substitute for "soul", as indeed Brentano often does in his manuscripts, we can understand Hume and his empiricist followers to be saying that the soul is not an object of experience. John Stuart Mill was, in the second half of the nineteenth century, the most outspoken supporter of Hume's refusal to allow for a substantial bearer of mental acts. However, contrary to Hume, Mill, and other representatives of the same view, Brentano maintains:

> Experience offers the concept of the soul everywhere. In every one of our perceptions it is co-grasped. As in the presentation of colour that of extension [is co-grasped], so in both [the presentations of colour and of extension] the thing in the proper sense, i.e. the substance [is co-grasped].... Hence [it is] evident: no extension without something extended, no motion without something moved. Thus the same [holds] in the perception of one's own thinking. Descartes could rightly say, "I think, therefore I am". The perception of one's own thinking is the perception of something that thinks (thing), which we call "I" [or "myself"].
> (LS 23: 29679)

On this basis, Brentano concluded that dismissing psychology as the science of the soul because it is "metaphysical" only served to express "one's incompetence to do justice analytically to actual experience" (Brentano 1982: 147, 1995b: 156). On his account, the soul is the concern of empirical psychology and not that of an inherently non-empirical and therefore unacceptable metaphysics.

This being said, we must not overlook the fact that he thinks that the "experiential" character of the soul has to be upheld above all against the *materialists*. While sceptical and phenomenalist theories such as those of Hume and Mill were only to be found among philosophers, materialism had gained much greater popular appeal, as indeed it has continued to enjoy ever since. In the nineteenth century this view was given a decisive impetus by Erasmus Darwin (1731–1802) (the grandfather of the celebrated Charles Darwin) and carried further by German thinkers who, while they are long forgotten, were part of the context in which Brentano's theories evolved (see Reed 1997). Brentano makes his case against the materialists by emphasizing the unity of consciousness:

> The evidence of inner perception would not be possible if perceiver and perceived [were] not a real unity. Consequently that which inwardly perceives is a real unity with that which is perceived in this way, hence [a real unity] with the bearers of the different mental functions. Thus these are also one *thing*, one *substance*. This is the unity of consciousness which is immediately evident to anyone who reflects upon it and becomes even clearer by concentrated thought [*Nachdenken*] (whenever possible). This is, however, the point against which the materialists most often come up against. It is seen how a one-sided development of the intellectual powers for certain special considerations [i.e. strictly from the standpoint of natural science] has, often in the case of not untalented men, the consequence of an obvious inability to grasp truths of another domain that are easy to understand. Many and important materialists show that they do not even understand the meaning of the objection, resting on the testimony of consciousness, against their doctrine.
>
> (LS 23: 29685 f.)

Brentano's view on the soul, as stated above, is subject to more than one interpretation, especially when we raise a number of questions about it. One might want to know, for instance, how the soul is related to the body. Brentano is plainly putting forth some sort of dualism, which is by no means unproblematic. One might also wonder whether the soul is best understood from an Aristotelian standpoint or a Cartesian one, or perhaps from some other standpoint. Though Brentano's views are to a large extent inspired by Aristotle's, he also owes much to Descartes in some other respects, e.g. as regards his concept of inner perception. Nor should we forget that Brentano was very much concerned with the question of the immortality of the soul. His views on the nature of the soul are by and large developed in the context of dealing with that great enigma.

Brentano grappled with these and many other difficulties concerning the soul and continued to elaborate on the phenomena relevant to psychology, but his thoughts on such matters are unfortunately often to be found in unpublished manuscripts. It is not possible to engage with them in greater detail in the present study. The above will nonetheless suffice as a sketch of Brentano's early philosophy of mind regarding a number of issues, many of which are still with us today.[9]

Notes

1 This chapter is an outcome of the project "From Logical Objectivism to Reism: Bolzano and the School of Brentano" P401 15–18149S (Czech Science Foundation), realized at the Institute of Philosophy of the Czech Academy of Sciences.
2 Some of the recent literature, such as the work of various distinguished scholars published in Jacquette 2004; Tănăsescu 2012; Fisette & Fréchette 2013; Kriegel 2017, has begun to rectify this situation. See also monographs: Textor 2017 and Kriegel 2018.
3 This is the period (consisting itself of various phases) during which he taught Carl Stumpf and Anton Marty in Würzburg (1867–1872) and a host of outstanding students in Vienna (1874–1895). Among the latter students were Alexius Meinong, Christian von Ehrenfels, Alois Höfler, Kasimir Twardowski, and Edmund Husserl. Not all of them were orthodox followers of Brentano, but each of them took a path of inquiry that was in one way or another profoundly marked by Brentano's philosophical orientation in the nineteenth century. (See Smith 1994; Albertazzi et al. 1996; Rollinger 1999.)
4 Quotations from manuscripts will be cited by archival signature number, as indicated in the bibliography. English translations from these manuscripts are my own.
5 Mind also comes into consideration in Brentano's proofs of the existence of God, for God is conceived of by analogy to the human mind. This aspect of his views is not well known. While some of his manuscripts on metaphysics, particularly ontology, have been posthumously published (Brentano 1933, 1966a), most of his views in this area that he held during the nineteenth century are still unknown.
6 Due to restrictions of space, the final two generalizations will not be elucidated in the following. The last one, which might seem especially obscure, was treated in *Psychology from an Empirical Standpoint*, Book Two, Chapter 4 (Brentano 1874: 204–222; 1995a: 120–136) without any reference to the soul, although Brentano was ultimately convinced (even in his early philosophy of mind) that the soul was necessary for uniting the mental phenomena into a real unity. At the end of the present study we shall consider Brentano's concept of the soul, albeit only briefly.
7 Most take this to be a substantive shift in position on Brentano's part (see Chrudzimski 2001). But some have argued that Brentano's conception of intentionality remains constant, and only the formulation has changed. See Antonelli (2012), where the latter interpretation is advocated and various defenders of the opposing one are named. See also Baumgartner and Fréchette (2015) for various views on this issue.
8 The inevitable question is of course: How does Brentano understand truth, which he ascribes to some judgements and denies of others? This is a topic that cannot be discussed at length in the context of the present study. Suffice it to say that in his early work he was thinking of truth under the presupposition that it is the correspondence between "intellect" (or judgement) and reality, the celebrated *adaequatio rei et intellectus*, according the traditional formula. Yet, Brentano also found difficulties with this definition of truth (see the lecture from 1889 in Brentano 1930: 3–29, 1966b, 2–17) which ultimately motived him to define it in other ways in his later philosophy.
9 I thank Sandra Lapointe for her incisive comments and criticisms which have prompted me to improve this overview of Brentano's early philosophy of mind substantially.

Bibliography

Published works

Albertazzi, L., L. Massimo, and R. Poli. (eds.). 1996. *The School of Brentano*. Dordrecht/Boston/London: Kluwer.
Antonelli, M. 2012. "Franz Brentano's Intentionality Thesis", in *Intentionality: Historical and Systematic Perspectives*, A. Salice (ed.): 109–144. Munich: Philosophia.
Baumgartner, W. and G. Fréchette. 2015. *Brentano's Concept of Intentionality: New Assessments (Brentano Studien 13)*. Dettelbach: Röll.
Brentano, F. 1874. *Psychologie vom empirischen Standpunkte*. Vol. I. Leipzig: Duncker & Humblot.
———. 1889. *Vom Ursprung sittlicher Erkenntnis*. Leipzig: Duncker & Humblot.
———. 1911. *Von der Klassifikation der psychischen Phänomene*. Leipzig: Duncker & Humblot.
———. 1929. *Über die Zukunft der Philosophie*, O. Kraus (ed.). Leipzig: Felix Meiner.
———. 1930. *Wahrheit und Evidenz*, O. Kraus (ed.). Leipzig: Felix Meiner.
———. 1933. *Kategorienlehre*, A. Kastil (ed.). Leipzig: Felix Meiner.
———. 1952. *Grundlegung und Aufbau der Ethik*, F. Mayer-Hillebrand (ed.). Bern: Francke.
———. 1956. *Die Lehre vom richtigen Urteil*, F. Mayer-Hillebrand (ed.). Bern: Francke.
———. 1959. *Grundzüge der Ästhetik*, F. Mayer Hillebrand (ed.). Bern: Francke.
———. 1966a. *Die Abkehr vom Nichtrealen*, F. Mayer-Hillebrand (ed.). Hamburg: Felix Meiner.
———. 1966b. *The True and the Evident*, R. M. Chisholm *et al.* (eds.). London: Routledge and Kegan Paul.
———. 1982. *Deskriptive Psychologie*, W. Baumgartner and R. M. Chisholm (eds.). Hamburg: Felix Meiner.
———. 1995a. *Psychology from an Empirical Standpoint*, L. McAlister and Rancurello (trans.). London: Routledge.
———. 1995b. *Descriptive Psychology*, B. Müller and B. Miller. London: Routledge.
Chrudzimski, A. 2001. *Die Intentionalität beim frühen Brentano*. Dordrecht/Boston/London: Kluwer.
———. 2004. *Die Ontologie Franz Brentanos*. Dordrecht/Boston/London: Kluwer.
Chrudzimski, A. and Smith, B. 2004. "Brentano's Ontology: From Conceptualism to Reism", in Jacquette 2004: 197–219.
Fechner, G. 1860. *Elemente der Psychophysik*, vols. I-II. Leipzig: Breitkopf and Härtel.
Fisette, D. and G. Fréchette. (eds.). 2013. *Themes from Brentano*. Amsterdam/New York: Rodopi.
Jacquette, D. (ed.). 2004. *The Cambridge Companion to Brentano*. Cambridge: Cambridge University Press.
Kriegel, U. (ed.) 2017. *The Routledge Handbook of Franz Brentano and the Brentano School*. New York / London: Routledge.
Kriegel, U. 2018. *Brentano's Philosophical System: Mind, Being, Value*. Oxford: Oxford University Press.
Lange, Friedrich Albert. 1866. *Geschichte des Materialismus*. Iserlohn: J. Baedeker.
Niveleau Charles-Édouard. (ed.). 2014. *Vers une philosophie scientific: le programme de Brentano*. Paris: Demopolis.

Reed, E. S. 1997. *From Soul to Mind: The Emergence of Psychology from Erasmus Darwin to William James*. New Haven/London: Yale University Press.

Rollinger, R. D. 1999. *Husserl's Position in the School of Brentano*. Dordrecht/Boston/London: Kluwer.

———. 2008. *Austrian Phenomenology: Brentano, Husserl, Meinong, and Others on Mind and Object*. Frankfurt am Main: Ontos.

———. 2012. "Brentano's *Psychology from an Empirical Standpoint*: Its Background and Conception", in Tănăsescu 2012: 261–310.

———. 2014. "Le psychologie genetique: la conception Brentanienne de la explication de l'esprit dans les cours d'Anton Marty (Prague 1889)", in Niveleau 2014: 153–186.

Smith, Barry 1994. *Austrian Philosophy: The Legacy of Franz Brentano*. LaSalle, IL: Open Court.

Tănăsescu, Ion. (ed.). 2012. *Franz Brentano's Metaphysics and Psychology*. Bucharest: Zeta.

Textor, M. 2017: *Brentano's Mind*. Oxford: Oxford University Press.

Wundt, Wilhelm. 1874. *Grundzüge der physiologischen Psychologie*. Engelmann: Leipzig.

Unpublished manuscripts

Brentano (Ps 53). *Fortsetzung der Psychologie vom empirischen Standpunkte* (c. 1875). Cambridge: Houghton Library.

——— (Ps 66). *Pläne für Psychognosie* (c. 1865–c. 1899). Cambridge: Houghton Library.

——— (Ps 76). *Deskriptive Psychologie* (1887/88). Cambridge: Houghton Library.

——— (Ps 77). *Deskriptive Psychologie oder beschreibende Phänomenologie* (1888/89). Cambridge: Houghton Library.

——— (LS 1). *Unsterblichkeit der menschlichen Seele* (c. 1869). Cambridge: Houghton Library.

——— (LS 22). *Unsterblichkeit* (1875). Cambridge: Houghton Library.

——— (LS 23). *Über die Unsterblichkeit der Seele* (1869–1873). Cambridge: Houghton Library.

——— (Y 4–5). *Praktische Philosophie* (1884/85). Notes by E. Leisching. Leuven: Husserl Archives.

10

MEINONG AND MIND

Peter Simons

To the memory of Rudolf Haller, 1929–2014

1. Introduction

When considering Meinong's treatment of the mind and associated issues, we confront an oddity. There is a sense in which Meinong does not have a philosophy of mind as such at all; but there is another sense in which his account of mind pervades and structures his whole philosophy.

The sense in which he does not have a philosophy of mind as such is that he is singularly unconcerned with otherwise standard categories such as *Geist* or *Psyche*, which words hardly occur at all in his philosophical vocabulary. Nor do many traditional matters of the philosophy of mind occupy space in his writings. He never talks about souls, or whether they might survive death. He is likewise untroubled by the traditional mind – body problem. There are no grand pronouncements on dualism or monism, despite his deep interest in matters of psychophysics and psychophysical measurement.

The obverse of this lack of ontological or methodological *Angst* about mind is that Meinong takes it for granted that we are consciously related to a world beyond our own experiences, a world of material and ideal, and even non-existent things. He bears no sceptical scruples about such access in general, though he is of course keen to argue for those unusual objects, the non-existent, the incomplete, and the inconsistent, that others found (and still find) incredible.

In another way however, Meinong's whole philosophy turns on his view of the mental: his theory of the various kinds of object and their metaphysics, of value and ethics, of knowledge, of meaning all revolve about the conception of mental intentionality that he took and adapted from his teacher Brentano. While his views became ever more objectivistic and his interests shifted from the mental to its objects, Meinong never abandoned the conviction that psychology was central to philosophical thinking. This applied to both the descriptive, *a priori* variety that properly belonged within philosophy, and which would nowadays be considered philosophy of mind, and to the empirical, experimental variety he helped to pioneer in Austria.

In this attitude towards the mental as central to philosophy he remained throughout his life true to the conception of the British empiricists who formed the first object of his philosophical interest. He (unsuccessfully) resisted moves by philosophical contemporaries in Germany to divorce psychology as a university subject from philosophy, at a time when some philosophy chairs were being taken over by psychologists.[1] A more successful enterprise was his campaign to retain psychology alongside logic as a subject in Austrian secondary schools under the title 'Philosophical Propadeutic'. This had been taught in Austrian schools since the education reforms of 1850. In 1884 the Austrian Ministry for Culture and Education proposed reforms cutting down the hours assigned to the subject, which in Meinong's view would be detrimental. In a carefully worded 1885 monograph *Über philosophische Wissenschaft und ihre Propadeutik*, directed at the Ministry, Meinong wrote,

> Philosophy is not psychology, for its name denotes, on closer examination, not a science but a whole group of sciences: but what holds these together is their belonging in common to the domain of mental phenomena.
>
> *(psychische Erscheinungen)*

While the binding cement of Meinong's philosophy later shifted from psychology to object theory, we shall see that the latter originated and remained in the shadow of Meinong's account of the mind.

2. Early studies

Meinong came to philosophy from history, having been inspired – like many others – by the teaching and missionary zeal of Franz Brentano. Brentano's *opus magnum*, his *Psychologie vom empirischen Standpunkt*, was published in 1874, the year he took up his chair in Vienna, and also the year in which Meinong obtained his doctorate in history with Brentano as an examiner in the *philosophicum*. This was an obligatory oral examination in philosophy required by all Doctors of *Philosophy*, whatever their subject.[2] Following this first encounter, Meinong studied with Brentano for four semesters.

For Meinong's *Habilitation*, the qualification entitling him as *Privatdocent* to lecture at the university, and a *conditio sine qua non* for a professorship, Brentano set him the task of using his historical training to give a contemporary – that is, Brentanist – account of British empiricism. Meinong did indeed set about this task. His first published work, *Hume Studien* Volume I (1877), obtained for him the *venia docendi* at the University of Vienna in 1878. But it immediately transpired that Meinong was far more interested in the problems discussed by Locke and Hume than in carefully tracing their writings in historical context. The first volume of *Hume Studien* dealt with a metaphysical problem, that of universals, and was Meinong's first discussion of the existence or otherwise of putative entities, in this case universals or, as Locke and Hume called them, abstract ideas. At this stage Meinong was positively inclined towards moderate (conceptualist) nominalism, and this meant that he needed to focus in some detail on the manner whereby, according to Locke, abstract ideas come before the mind, namely the process of abstraction. Volume II of the *Hume-Studien* followed in 1882 and dealt with the theory of relations in Hume. This in fact marked the inchoate beginnings of what was to turn into Meinong's famous theory of objects (*Gegenstandstheorie*).

It was a conviction drilled into his students by Brentano that the most characteristic distinguishing feature of the mental is what he called mental or intentional inexistence. This was the single most famous and salient thesis of the *Psychologie*, and it was the hottest philosophy in town during Meinong's formative years. Influenced by Aristotle, Augustine, and Aquinas, Brentano contended that mental phenomena, unlike physical phenomena, contain an object or content within themselves, that they can be said to be *about*. Ideas present objects, judgements pronounce on whether things presented exist or not, while attitudes of love or hate take an evaluative stance to objects, particularly those judged to exist. In his early years, influenced by Cartesian and empiricist doubt about a supposed external world providing causes of ideas, Brentano was cautious to sceptical about whether or not such objects correspond in any way to external things. This cautious methodological phenomenalism fully suited Meinong's examination of Locke and especially Hume, who differed from Brentano not in his scepticism about an external world, but in failing to note the intentional existence characteristic of mental phenomena, treating ideas as atoms of experience with no intrinsic structure.

Progress in Meinong's philosophy of mind was not to come before the exclusively inward-looking account of intentionality he inherited from Brentano was overcome. This took a while. Having been called to Graz as an Associate ("Extraordinary") Professor in 1882, Meinong soon found himself at the centre of a political–pedagogical controversy. Instructions from the Austrian ministry of education proposed reducing or eliminating from secondary schools the subject known as Philosophical Propadeutics, a combination of philosophy, psychology, and logic that had been taught in Austrian schools since the mid-nineteenth century. Meinong strongly disapproved of this proposal and wrote his first book *On Philosophical Science and its Propadeutics* (1885) in defence of the subject, not least the inclusion of psychology, and he advocated basic psychological demonstrations in school teaching. As pointed out by Johannes Marek,[3] despite the book's political–pedagogical purpose, it is a wide-ranging statement of method, philosophical and psychological. This included a role for demonstrations and simple experiments in psychology. When the continuation of school propadeutics was guaranteed, Meinong's former Vienna student and colleague Alois Höfler embarked on writing the new textbook of logic, and solicited Meinong's help. The book appeared in 1890 and contained the first published demurral against

Brentano's inexistence theory by any of his former students. On page 6, Höfler and Meinong distinguish between two senses of 'object': an immanent object like Brentano's, part of the mental act, and an external object. When I have a veridical experience of seeing a tree, the immanent object is that part of the mental act that gives it its subjective flavour or quality of tree-presenting, but the external tree is a physical thing that corresponds via similarity and/or causation to the immanent object. This move to a clear form of realism was thenceforth never reversed by Meinong, though it took time for its ramifications to work themselves through in his philosophy.

3. Twardowski and non-existent objects

In 1894, a younger Brentano student Kazimierz Twardowski published his *Habilitationsschrift* with the title *Zur Lehre vom Inhalt und Gegenstand der Vorstellungen* (*On the Content and Object of Presentations*). In it, Twardowski anchored the distinction Höfler and Meinong had made, terminologically and by argument. The content (*Inhalt*) of a presentation is what gives it its subjective flavour: it belongs to the person who has it. The object (*Gegenstand*) is what the act presents that is beyond itself. My seeing of a tree has a visual arboreal content; its object is the tree itself. Different contents may correspond to the same object, as *the city on the site of Roman Juvavum* and *the birthplace of Mozart* both have Salzburg as object. Twardowski's distinction transposes into a psychological key the linguistic distinction made a little earlier by Gottlob Frege between the sense (*Sinn*) and denotation (*Bedeutung*) of an expression. Unlike Frege however, for whom some expressions, such as those found in mythology, false science, and works of fiction, lack a denotation, for Twardowski every presentation has an object. Arguing against Bernard Bolzano's contention that some presentations are objectless, Twardowski insists that rather than a presentation of, say, Zeus, lacking an object, it has an object, but one that fails to exist.

Meinong read Twardowski's treatise and agreed with its fundamental point. He accepted that all presentations have objects, sometimes non-existent ones. Meinong insisted more firmly than Twardowski that the content of a presentation is real, in time, and mental. Twardowski's account of contents is ambiguous, because he is combining influences from Brentano, for whom the content is mental, and Bolzano, for whom content is something abstract, an idea in itself. Twardowski sometimes, especially in connection with language, treats contents as abstract and shareable rather than real, mental and private. Meinong's reception of Twardowski's work was published in his 1899 essay 'On Objects of Higher Order and their relation to Inner Perception'. In this work Meinong distinguished between basic objects on the one hand and complex ones on the other, the latter presupposing more basic ones as their foundations or grounds. He then set about applying Twardowski's content/object distinction to the whole range of mental phenomena.

4. Cognitions and objectives

Like other philosophers, including Brentano and Twardowski, Meinong distinguished between presentation and judgement. Presentation simply puts an object before the mind, whereas in judgement we take up a cognitive stance to something. Brentano had argued that we accept or reject the objects that are presented, so for example in perceiving a tree I not only have a presentation of a tree, I also accept it, but when I judge that unicorns do not exist, I reject unicorns. Meinong came to disagree with this view. In considering the difference between serious judging and more playful make-believe type acts, Meinong was led to distinguish between judgements and assumptions. When making believe there is a troll at the bottom of my garden I do not judge there is, but entertain the idea with an act that is like judging but deprived of its commitment or conviction. Meinong calls such an act an assumption (*Annahme*). He would later extend the distinction between serious and unserious or phantasy character to all kinds of mental acts.

It was while working out the implications of the theory of assumptions, in what was to become his most important work to date, *Über Annahmen* (*On Assumptions*) that it occurred to Meinong that an assumption, like a judgement, must have an object, but it could not consist, as for Brentano, in the acceptance or rejection of the object of a presentation, both kinds of judgement being serious and therefore different from assumptions. I shall call the class consisting of judgements and assumptions taken together *cognitions*. Objects of cognitions are predicative in nature, and are linguistically expressed by whole sentences or clauses, not by names or phrases like presentations. Carl Stumpf had already discussed these peculiar objects and called them *Sachverhalte* (states of affairs). Meinong considered that this term connoted actuality or truth, and so preferred the more neutral latinate term *Objektiv* (objective). He thought the idea of a non-obtaining state of affairs was at least terminologically infelicitous. Subsequent usage of the term *Sachverhalt* by Husserl, Wittgenstein and others has shown Meinong's scruple to have been unfounded.

Objectives quickly came to play a central part in Meinong's developing theory of objects. The objects of presentations, items without predicative structure, he called *Objekte*. We shall call them 'things'. He used the overarching term *Gegenstand* for *Objekte* and *Objektive* together. In the programmatic essay 'Über Gegenstandstheorie', 'On the Theory of Objects', written for a volume published in 1904 commemorating the tenth anniversary of the opening of the Graz Psychology Laboratory, Meinong made out a case for treating object theory as a distinctive, separate and autonomous science, a part of philosophy distinct from psychology, logic, epistemology, and metaphysics, and treating all objects, whether they exist in time, are ideal or subsistent, or neither. In particular, he no longer considered psychology to hold philosophy together as a group of sub-disciplines.

As we shall see, the distinction between things and objectives was not to exhaust Meinong's taxonomy of objects, and in the ensuing addition of further categories of object, his classification of the mental was to play a determining role.

5. The science of psychology

While psychology, the science of the mental, thus came for Meinong to be displaced from its central role in philosophy, the importance of psychology was never doubted by him, and he devoted to it a substantial part of his own efforts. His early writings include several psychological studies: the psychology of abstraction, memory, colour, and Gestalt perception, sensory fatigue, eye-movement, the feelings accompanying judgement, mental analysis, and phantasy. Typically for both Meinong and their epoch, they are not exactly snappy, running to between thirty and eighty pages in his generally clear but belaboured, often tortured prose.

Meinong had at his own expense given rudimentary psychological demonstrations in Vienna and later in Graz, and when the University of Graz built a new main building, he managed to acquire a small amount of room and cupboard space for instruments and experimentation, and eventually, after much patient beseeching of the bureaucracy, obtained permission from the Ministry to found the first specifically funded and recognised psychology laboratory in Austria-Hungary, in 1894. His painstaking struggles to obtain even pitiful financial support and the bureaucratic hurdles with which he had to contend at ministry and university level are catalogued in loving detail in Evelyn Dölling's biography.[4] They include polite requests for soap, towels, pens, scissors, brushes, chalk, and similarly trivial but practically essential items. Meinong's modest success stimulated colleagues elsewhere in the empire to ask his advice and emulate him in setting up similar institutions.

The actual experimenting was conducted by Meinong in conjunction with assistants, as his extreme visual impairment made it hard for him to be in full control. It soon transpired that some of his assistants were extremely talented philosophers and psychologists in their own right. Stephan Witasek, who worked in the laboratory for many years on a pittance, took over its direction from Meinong in late 1914, but Witasek, Meinong's favourite student, died at a tragically early age just months later. Another genial experimenter, Vittorio Benussi, the founder of Graz Gestalt theory, left Graz as a result of the hostilities with Italy and went on to become one of the founding fathers of Italian psychology. Meinong had to reassume the task of running the laboratory, which in wartime and with his visual handicap was no small imposition. It is ironic that a functionally blind director should be running a laboratory in which visual perception was one of the chief areas of research.

Meinong's psychological studies were generally carried out in areas which would nowadays be called cognitive psychology, as he was always interested in the psychological processes behind the acquisition of knowledge. They thus tend to be rather theoretical from a modern perspective. Among his more interesting studies was one ('On the Meaning of Weber's Law', 1896) on the concept of indirect measurement in psychology, a topic which had come up in the 19th century in the discussion of the law linking quantitative variations in physical stimuli with quantitative variations in the sensations prompted by these stimuli. This law, first formulated by Ernst Heinrich Weber (1795–1878) and carried forward by Gustav Theodor Fechner (1801–1887), formed the basis of the discipline of psychophysics. Meinong was interested in Weber's Law not just because of its psychological content but because of what it said about methods of indirect measurement in the sphere of the mental. Rather than directly measuring a quantity associated with a sensation, Weber's insight was that we can work with what he called a "just noticeable difference" (j.n.d.), nowadays called a *discrimination threshold*, between two sensations. Experimenting with the sensation of supported weights, he discovered that we just notice a difference when a weight is varied by an amount proportional to the original weight. Weber's Law then states that the felt difference in sensation intensity ΔI for a given kind of sensation is proportional to the sensation's intensity I: $\Delta I/I$ = constant. Meinong's discussion of the methods of indirect measurement attracted the interest and admiration of the young Bertrand Russell, who reviewed the work for *Mind* in 1899 and in his early masterpiece *The Principles of Mathematics* (1903) refers several times approvingly to Meinong's analysis. This was the beginning of interaction between the two men, which while it brought Meinong international recognition, ironically did more than anything to subvert his work and reputation in the eyes of successive generations.

Although after 1900 object-theoretic work took over the central role in Meinong's work, he remained warmly attached to psychology. While generally welcoming Husserl's critique of psychologism in logic, in his 1912 essay 'For Psychology and Against Psychologism in General Value Theory' he warned against regarding the investigation of the mental as completely irrelevant to matters of value theory, while now upholding the view that not all value is subjective.

6. Values and norms

Meinong's first major publication was his 1894 treatise *Psychological-Ethical Investigations in Value Theory*. Based on lectures given in Vienna and Graz, and incorporating influences from Carl Menger's early lectures on economics in Vienna, it made a case for values being the objects (*Gegenstände*) of feelings (*Gefühle*). Our apprehension of value is therefore non-cognitive in nature. This was a view on which Meinong was never to change his mind. If I perceive a man beating a horse, and judge him to be so doing, that is a purely cognitive matter. But the disclosure of this beating as something bad or outrageous is given by my feelings of anger and disapproval. In the terminology of Brentano, I hate or dislike what I judge to be the case.

Now Brentano, following Descartes, had lumped all non-cognitive mental attitudes together into a single class. Descartes called them *voluntates sive affectiones*; Brentano variously called them 'phenomena of love and hate', 'interests', or 'affects' (*Gemütsbewegungen*). I shall call them 'attitudes'. Brentano's reasons for so doing were that all non-cognitive attitudes form a continuum with no sharp boundaries: from my dislike and disapproval of the man's beating the horse through my desire to stop him to my forming the intention to intervene, there is a single continuous development. Most of Brentano's students however disagreed with him, and preferred to retain as fundamental the more commonly accepted distinction between emotions or feelings on the one hand and desires or acts of will on the other. Certainly this was Meinong's view, and that of his friend and erstwhile student Christian von Ehrenfels. The latter, who had heard Meinong's lectures on value theory in Vienna, published his own book on value theory, somewhat earlier than Meinong's. In it, Ehrenfels upheld a subjectivistic theory of value in which the primary mode of apprehension of value is desire, not, as in Meinong, feeling. Ehrenfels thought we value what we desire, or disvalue that of which what we desire to be rid. Meinong responded to Ehrenfels's criticism by conceding such cases as secondary, but pointed out that when we can value something we already have, such as a nice house or a happy marriage, we cannot desire it, since we already have it, so the mode must be via liking. Ehrenfels likewise conceded this was a secondary way of valuing, but neither succeeded in convincing the other about the primary act of valuing.

While Meinong was occupied in his object-theoretic investigations, he left value theory on one side, but from 1915 he returned to ethics and value theory, intending at first to update his earlier lectures. In fact he produced a complete rewrite, which was finished bar indexing when he died in 1920. Before then however, he produced what he considered to be his finest work, *On Emotional Presentation* (1917). In this, he gave the psychological basis for the apprehension of values, as before, through feelings or emotions. The objects of such emotions are now called *dignitatives*, rather than 'values', and are regarded as distinct in kind from either things or objectives. A valid or 'correct' dignitative is a *dignity*. Desires however now also come to acquire their own kind of object, which Meinong calls *desideratives*. They are what we would less elaborately call *norms*, since they correspond not to what is or is not the case but to what should or should not be the case. A valid or 'correct' desiderative is a *desideratum*. Meinong now has four fundamental classes of object: two cognitive, namely things and objectives, and two evaluative, namely dignitatives and desideratives. In their forms of linguistic expression, dignitatives, like things, correspond to nouns: I see the horse, and I like its beauty. Desideratives on the other hand, like objectives, correspond to sentences or clauses: I judge *that* iron is heavier than water, I desire *that* the speed limit be observed. If the objective that the speed limit is observed obtains (subsists), then my desire is fulfilled, and if not, it is not, but the desiderative, that the speed limit ought to be observed, is unaffected either way.

With this final version of the theory of objects, Meinong completes not only his account of the kinds of object: he also perfects the symmetry between the fundamental kinds of mental act and their corresponding kinds of object. Distinguishing now between the specific role of ideas in giving something (*vorstellen*) and the general role of mental acts in presenting something (*präsentieren*), Meinong can now say: ideas present things, cognitions present objectives, feelings present dignitatives (values), and desires present desideratives (norms). Each kind of mental act comes in a 'serious' and a 'phantasy' or unserious mode, so there can be make-believe or phantasy feelings and desires as well as ideas and assumptions.

From around 1912 Meinong subscribed to value-objectivism: certain dignitatives (not all) are right or good in themselves, or wrong and bad in themselves, and certain desideratives are desirable or undesirable in themselves, irrespective of whether anyone so feels or desires. These Meinong calls *impersonal* (*unpersönliche*) values, preferring this dull adjective to the more dramatic 'absolute' or 'objective', and contrasting them with the personal or subjective values of Ehrenfels's and his own former theory. During this period of the Great War and thereafter, Meinong's printed statements about the righteousness of the cause of the Central Powers in their fight to uphold German culture in the face of a perceived threat of annihilation by the Allies not only represent Meinong's account of impersonal values in application, they also reveal his German-nationalistic political views at their most distasteful.

7. Perfect symmetry

Having rounded out his theory of objects with values and norms, Meinong turns once again to ethics, this time with impersonal values and norms writ large. But if we pause and consider the objects of feeling and desire, we cannot but be struck by the neatness of the correlation between feelings and dignitatives on the one hand and desires and desideratives on the other. It is quite clear that Meinong was not compelled along this route. He could as easily have taken the view of his early hero Hume, whose view is so beautifully expressed in the famous passage when he discusses the comparison between reason and taste, claiming the latter 'has a productive faculty, and gilding or staining all natural objects with the colours, borrowed from internal sentiment, raises in a manner a new creation'.[5]

This would have detracted not one iota from the phenomenology of feeling and desire that Meinong explores at much greater length and with much greater care than the dashing Hume. Even the analogy with colour as a supposed secondary quality is one of which Meinong is well aware, but here too he distinguished between the subjective laws of colour-perception and the objective, *a priori* laws of the colour-solid, a matter of object theory, not of psychology.

When we attempt to find an independent or argued justification in Meinong's late writings for the introduction of dignitatives and desideratives, we look in vain. Meinong simply takes it for granted that distinctive fundamental kinds of mental act will have distinctive fundamental kinds of object. Consider then this (valid) argument:

1 Intentionality

   All mental acts have objects.

2 Correlation

   Distinct basic kinds of mental acts have distinct basic kinds of objects.

3   Mental Classification

   Ideas, cognitions, feelings and desires are all the distinct basic kinds of mental acts.
   therefore

4   Object Classification

   Things, objectives, dignitatives and desideratives are all the distinct basic kinds of objects. (From 1, 2 and 3 with terminological stipulations.)

In this argument, while none of the premises is beyond discussion, the principal questionable premise is obviously the second, CORRELATION.

The late postulation of dignitatives and desideratives follows the pattern of the introduction of objectives a good decade earlier. Meinong was busy with the phenomenology of the relevant mental activities, in this case assumptions, and then noticed that by intentionality, they should have objects. Then the surely implicit premise CORRELATION kicked in, and we get objectives. Meinong had long worked on the psychology of feelings and desires, and only later did it occur to him that they should have their own distinct objects, too, so we get dignitatives and desideratives. A more parsimonious theory respecting the grammar of the relevant expressions would have been to correlate feelings with things and desires with objectives, but that would have ruined the symmetry.

Thus, we see that Meinong's classification of objects is driven by his account of the classification of the mental. Even when discussing the theory of objects and other matters, it is notable throughout how much loving care Meinong continues to devote to discussions of the minutiae of the mental. While honestly professing a robust realism, Meinong is concerned to maintain the symmetric correlation between the mental and the objectual. This is then the sense in which Meinong's account of the mind pervades his whole philosophy, even after psychology, the science of the mind, was displaced from its central, foundational role.

Notes

1 Dölling (1999, 130 f.).
2 This was an institution which persisted in Austria until relatively recently, having been confirmed post-war by a law of 1945. The author examined many *philosophica* before 1995.
3 Marek (2008, Section 1.2).
4 Dölling (1999, pp. 104 ff.).
5 Hume (1751, Appendix 1).

Bibliography

Works by Meinong

1877. Hume Studien I. Zur Geschichte und Kritik des modernen Nominalismus. [Hume Studies I. On the History and Criticism of Modern Nominalism] in *Sitzungsberichte der philosophisch-historischen Klasse der Kaiserlichen Akademie der Wissenschaften in Wien*, **87**, Vienna, 185–260. Separate Edition: Vienna: Gerold, 1877. Reprinted in Meinong 1968–1978, Vol. I: 1–76. Translated in Barber 1966, 98–193.

1882. Hume Studien II. Zur Relationstheorie [Hume Studies II. The Theory of Relations] in *Sitzungsberichte der philosophisch-historischen Klasse der Kaiserlichen Akademie der Wissenschaften in Wien*, **101**, Vienna, 573–752. Separate Edition: Vienna: Gerold, 1882. Reprinted in Meinong 1968–1978, Vol. II: 1–183. Partly translated in Barber 1966, 194–232.

1885. *Über philosophische Wissenschaft und ihre Propädeutik* [*On Philosophical Science and its Propaedeutics*], Vienna: Hölder. Reprinted in Meinong 1968–1978, Vol. V: 1–196.

1894. *Psychologisch-ethische Untersuchungen zur Werth-Theorie* [*Psychological-Ethical Investigations in Value Theory*], Graz: Leuschner & Lubensky. Reprinted in Meinong 1968–1978, Vol. III: 1–244.

1896. Über die Bedeutung des Weber'schen Gesetzes. Beiträge zur Psychologie des Vergleichens und Messens [On the Meaning of Weber's Law. Contributions to the Psychology of Comparing and Measuring] in *Zeitschrift für Psychologie und Physiologie der Sinnesorgane*, **XI**, 81–133, 230–285, 353–404. Separate edition, Hamburg and Leipzig: L. Voss, 1896. Reprinted in Meinong 1968–1978, Vol. II: 215–376.

1902. *Über Annahmen*, Leipzig: Barth. 2nd, rev. ed. 1910, Leipzig: Barth. Reprinted as Vol. IV of Meinong 1968–1978. Translated by J. Heanue as *On Assumptions*, Los Angeles: University of California Press, 1983.

1904. Über Gegenstandstheorie, in A. Meinong, ed., *Untersuchungen zur Gegenstandstheorie und Psychologie* [*Investigations in Theory of Objects and Psychology*], Leipzig: Barth 1904, 1–51. Reprinted in Meinong 1968–1978, Vol. II: 481–535. Translation: The Theory of Objects, in R. M. Chisholm (ed.), *Realism and the Background of Phenomenology*, Glencoe, IL: Free Press, 1960; reprint: Atascadero, CA: Ridgeview, 1981, 76–117.

1912. Für die Psychologie und gegen den Psychologismus in der allgemeinen Werttheorie [For Psychology and Against Psychologism in General Value Theory] in *Logos* **3**. Reprinted in Meinong 1968–1978, Vol. III: 269–282.

1917. Über emotionale Präsentation in *Sitzungsberichte der Kaiserlichen Akademie der Wissenschaften in Wien. Philosophisch-historische Klasse*, **183**, Abhandlung 2, Vienna. Separate Edition: Vienna: Hölder, 1917. Reprinted in Meinong 1968, 283–467. Translated with an introduction by M-L. Schubert Kalsi as *On Emotional Presentation*, Evanston: Northwestern University Press, 1972.

1968–1978. *Alexius Meinong Gesamtausgabe* [*Complete Edition*], ed. by R. Haller, R. Kindinger in collaboration with R. M. Chisholm, 7 vols., Graz: Akademische Druck- u. Verlagsanstalt.

Other works

Barber, K. F. 1966. *Meinong's Hume Studies: Translation and Commentary*, Ann Arbor, Michigan: University Microfilms. (Cf. Meinong 1877 and Meinong 1882).

Brentano, Franz. 1874. *Psychologie vom empirischen Standpunkt*, Leipzig: Duncker & Humblot. Translated by A. C. Rancurello, D. B. Terrell and L. L. McAlister as *Psychology from an Empirical Standpoint*, London: Routledge, 1973 (2nd ed. 1995).

Dölling, E. 1999. *"Wahrheit suchen und Wahrheit bekennen." Alexius Meinong: Skizze seines Lebens*, Amsterdam: Rodopi.

Höfler, A. (unter Mitwirkung von Alexius Meinong). 1890. *Philosophische Propädeutik. I. Theil: Logik*, Vienna: Tempsky.

Hume, D. 1751. *Enquiry Concerning the Principles of Morals*, London: Routledge.

Marek, J. C. 2008. "Alexius Meinong", in E. Zalta, ed., *Stanford Encyclopedia of Philosophy*. URL: http://plato.stanford.edu/entries/meinong/

Russell, B. 1899. "*Ueber die Bedeutung des Weberschen Gesetzes: Beiträge zur Psychologie des Vergleichens und Messens*. Von A. Meinong", *Mind* (n.s.), **8**: 251–256. (Critical Notice of Meinong 1896).

———. 1903. *The Principles of Mathematics*, Cambridge: Cambridge University Press. Reprinted with an introduction by J. G. Slater, London: Routledge, 1992.

Twardowski, K. 1894. *Zur Lehre vom Inhalt und Gegenstand der Vorstellungen: Eine psychologische Untersuchung*, Vienna: Hölder. Reprinted with an introduction by R. Haller, Munich: Philosophia, 1982. Translated with an introduction by R. Grossmann: *On the Content and Object of Presentations: A Psychological Investigation*, The Hague: Nijhoff, 1977.

11
'APPREHENDING A MULTITUDE AS A UNITY'
Stumpf on perceiving space and hearing chords

Mark Textor

1. Introduction

In this paper I will introduce the reader to Carl Stumpf's philosophy through a discussion of a problem about simultaneous perception of several objects. This problem is at the heart of several of his works and therefore well suited for my purpose.

Stumpf (1848–1936) is a philosopher who needs an introduction. Who was Stumpf?[1] He is mainly known as one of the founding fathers of *Gestaltpsychologie*. Stumpf was a student of Franz Brentano and Herman Lotze. Stumpf's own work often combined influences of both of his teachers in a fruitful way. (We will see an example of this in section 2.) Among Stumpf's own students were the founder of phenomenology, Edmund Husserl, and the *Gestaltpsychologists* Kurt Koffka and Wolfgang Köhler. He was also an important influence on William James.[2] Stumpf's main works are *On the Psychological Origin of the Idea of Space* (*Über den psychologischen Ursprung der Raumvorstellung*) (1873), (*Tonpsychologie*, Volume I (1883) and Volume II (1890)), *Gefühl und Gefühlsempfindung* (1928) and a posthumously published book on epistemology and metaphysics, *Erkenntnislehre* (1939–1940).

Stumpf's books *On the Psychological Origin of the Idea of Space* and *Tonpsychologie* are obviously on different topics, yet in both one and the same problem is central. Let us expound it with an example related to Stumpf's book on space. When we see a yellow patch we see spatial extension and colour together, they, as Stumpf said, appear to us as one unity. Is this so because there is one unity that we perceive? If so, how and why can we say that we perceive two things, colour as well as spatial extension? If, in contrast, we indeed perceive simultaneously colour as well extension, *two* qualities, how come that they appear to us as *one* unity? A structurally similar problem arises for hearing. In Stumpf's own words:

> When simultaneously several simple waves act on one, does one experience several tones or ONE tone? How, in the first case, is the apprehension

of the multitude as a unity to be explained? How, in the second case, is the apprehension of the unity as a multitude to be explained?

(Stumpf 1890, 12)[3]

This problem generalises to other sense modalities, but here I will focus on the cases Stumpf discussed. I will retrace the main steps of Stumpf's treatment of this problem and suggest a solution that differs from Stumpf's own. In doing so I will touch on foundational issues in the philosophy of mind that connect distinct topics in Stumpf's work and relate his views to those of other 19th-century philosophers such as his teachers Lotze and Brentano, his student Husserl, and William James.

The plan of the paper is as follows: In the next section I will outline Stumpf's view that spatial properties can be perceived, but only together with non-spatial properties. Against this background I will reconstruct in section 3 Stumpf's answer to the problem that arises if we assume that what we perceive is one thing: we perceive one unity and 'project' on it a multiplicity of parts. For good reasons Stumpf however later rejected this answer and the assumption on which it rests. In *Tonpsychologie* he assumed that when we hear a chord we hear several tones together. On his later view, the multiplicity appears to us as a unity if, and only if, the tones form a 'sensory whole'. I will discuss Stumpf's proposal in section 4 and argue that it is unsatisfactory as an explanation of how one apprehends a multitude of tones as a unity. In the concluding section 5 I will give an alternative answer to this question that is based on defining sensory whole in terms of the collective appearance of some things.

2. Stumpf's 'Nativism' about space

Space is something in which objects are located, they occupy volumes of it, and are related by relations like in front/behind, left-right, on top of etc. How are we aware of these spatial qualities? Sensory qualities are perceived via the relevant sensory modes. *Prima facie*, our five senses reveal to us distinct kinds of properties. But there is apparently no dedicated sense for the perception of spatial properties. How, then, are spatial properties (e.g. extension) given to us?

Stumpf (1873, 7) listed four possible answers that exhaust the space of possible positions:

Either
(I) there are in fact no distinct spatial properties. When we talk about space we refer to combinations of properties that are perceived by the five senses,
or
(II) there are spatial properties and there is a special sense that perceives them,
or
There are spatial properties, but no special sense that perceives them, because either

(III) spatial properties are not perceived at all,

or

(IV) space 'forms together with a sensory quality [such as colour] that is spatially presented one inseparable content[4] of which both are only partial contents'

(ibid.)

The two main answers correspond to empiricism (III) and what Stumpf somewhat misleadingly called 'nativism' (IV).[5] In his lectures on psychology he explained that by 'nativism' 'one ought not to think of inborn ideas. Nativism merely claims that just as colour, space is given through the senses' (Stumpf 1906/7, 143). Nativists answer the question 'How are spatial extension, depth and location given to us?' by saying that they are objects of perception in the same sense as colours, sounds etc.

In contrast, Empiricists take our awareness of these qualities to be non-perceptual. For example, Stumpf's teacher Lotze wrote:

[T]he sum of my thinking is that every spatial arrangement of objects in the soul has to be replaced by a qualitative order of non-spatial impressions and reconstructed in intuition from it.

(Lotze 1873, 322–323)

If we don't perceive spatial properties, how are we aware of them? Empiricists gave different answers to this question. For instance: we associate presentations of spatial properties with perceptions of colours; or our presentation of space is 'produced out of the inward resource of the mind, to envelop sensations, which as given originally, are not spatial, but which, on being cast into spatial form, become united and orderly' (James 1891, 272).

Stumpf 1873 defended nativism by pointing out that while one cannot perceive location and spatial extension 'on their own', one can and does perceive them *together* with colour etc. In retrospect he described his main idea as follows:

The basic thought, the inseparable connection of extension and colour in seeing, has certainly come to me in discussion with Fr. Brentano. His idea can be traced back to Aristotle's doctrine of 'common sensibles'.

(Stumpf 1924, 24 Fn.)[6]

Let us have a brief look at Stumpf's Aristotelian inspiration. Aristotle held that there are distinctive objects for each sense. Colour is the distinctive object of sight, sound the distinctive object of hearing etc. In addition, there are objects that can be perceived by different senses. He listed motion, rest, figure, number and size.[7] Imagine you see a falling star. You see colour and movement; you see both in one perceiving.

Stumpf applied Aristotle's idea that there are common sensibles to the debate between empiricism and nativism. Empiricists had set aside the possibility that one can perceive spatial and qualitative properties like colour *together*. For example, Herbart wrote:

> The resting eye sees no space. [. . .] The apprehension of space does not lie in the very first, immediate perception, it cannot lie in it because it is obvious that the complete intensity of presenting, as long as the presentations are fused into one mass, and as long as each has for all only one nisus of reproduction, all spatiality is nullified.
> (Herbart 1825 II, 127)

Let's focus on Herbart's opening move: *the resting eye sees no space.* Is that right? NO, if you stare at a part of a coloured surface without moving your eyes, you cannot fail to perceive the extension filled by the colour. Referring to colour as 'quality', Stumpf described this in a suggestive way:

> We present quality in extension, extension in quality, they interpenetrate each other.
> (Stumpf 1873, 114)

Imagine further that you see a red apple and that the apple shrinks in size. When the extension shrinks, the colour of the apple is also affected: As Stumpf sees it, there is less red.

Stumpf moved from the observation that one cannot change the apple's volume without changing its colour to a claim about the essence of colour and extension:

> From this it follows that both [colour and extension] are essentially inseparable, that they form in a way one content of which they are only parts.
> (Stumpf 1873, 113)

If colour and extension were distinct, they could be separated. But they cannot be separated. Hence, colour and extension are not distinct; they are 'one inseparable content':

> They are partial contents [Teilinhalte], that is, *they cannot exist separately in a presentation because of their nature, they cannot be presented separately*. From this follows immediately or it is already said by this that *space is just as originally and directly perceived as the quality*, since they form ONE inseparable content. Not only are both contents perceived and presented together now, but already in the first moments of consciousness the one is given with the other [. . .].
> (Stumpf 1873, 114–115)

We perceive movement, namely together and inseparable with colour. Similarly, we perceive spatial extension, namely together with colour.

To sum up: When I see a yellow patch, I see spatial extension and colour together, but not in isolation. Empiricism was mistaken in looking for perception of spatial properties *in isolation* or for a sense whose distinctive object is space. There is no such perception and no such sense. Spatial properties are common sensibles. Perceiving spatial extension together with colour is still *perceiving* spatial extension. Hence, nativism is vindicated. Let us now explore the details of Stumpf's proposal.

3. Apprehending a unity as a multitude

When we see a particular colour and a particular extension together, there is one object that we see; the content they form together. This content is what we see directly:

> In a sense the sensation of location is not primitive, but neither is the sensation of quality. The only original and truly perceived things are those uniform and unnameable contents.
>
> (Stumpf 1873, 136)

How should one conceive of these contents? When he talks about them as 'partial' contents, Stumpf seems to suggest that the content is a complex composed of a particular colour and a particular extension. This impression is however mistaken. According to Stumpf, the parts of a complex can be thought of independently of each other, but colour and extension cannot. When we see a yellow patch, the colour and the spatial extension can not even be separated in thought. The fact that colour and extension cannot be separately perceived or presented is striking and in need of an explanation. Stumpf's explanation is that one can only perceive them together because they are not distinct.

Stumpf could have found the model for this explanation in Hume. Hume wrote in the *Treatise*:

> [W]hen a globe of white marble is presented, we receive only the impression of a white colour disposed in a certain form, nor are we able to separate or distinguish the colour from the form. But observing afterwards a globe of black marble and a cube of white, and comparing them with our former object, we find two separate resemblances, in what former seemed, and really is, perfectly inseparable. After a while we begin to distinguish the figure from the colour by a distinction of reason; that is, we consider the figure and the colour together, since they are in effect the same and indistinguishable; but still view them in different aspects, according to the resemblances, of which they are susceptible.
>
> (Hume 1739–1740, 30)

Figure and colour are inseparable in perception and thought because they are the same. When we distinguish between them, we make a 'distinction of reason', but we don't find out that the figure and colour of the globe of marble are two different particular qualities.

Stumpf applied the Humean model to spatial extension and colour. What is originally perceived is one simple content that is both extension and colour. In order to make this plausible Stumpf spelled out in detail what Hume called 'a distinction of reason'. The simple content does not have colour and extension as components, but we 'project' these onto it. We, as Stumpf (1873, 136) put it, *imagine-in (hinein-phantasieren)* or *think-in* (*hineindenken*) the perceived content the partial contents colour and extension. We have seen other colour-spatial extension contents and can remember them. We can also imagine other such contents and associate them with words of our language. When we perceive an extension-colour content, we automatically episodically remember and or imagine other contents which are like it in colour and differ from it in extension (and *vice versa*). When we see a colour-extension content as similar to another one in one respect (colour), but not another (extension), we make a distinction in what is in fact one thing. We imagine or think one content as belonging to one group of contents, but not another and thereby conceive of one thing differently. Stumpf summed this up as follows:

> The plurality in the unity depends on thinking-in [*hineindenken*]. Every content as we perceive it by sight is, as regards these distinctions, completely unitary, but for us it is immediately connected to a number of relations, as they are fixed in the expression of our language. The content is consequently only seemingly decomposed. But the division is nonetheless, not arbitrary, but necessary. For every similarity and every distinction is forced upon us by the content. We make, to use a scholastic term, a *distinctio cum fundamento in re*.
>
> (Stumpf 1873, 139)

Stumpf used a phrase that we will encounter again: 'thinking of a unity as a plurality'. We think of the one content as a plurality when we *imagine* a plurality of parts *in* it.

Stumpf's view of simple contents of perception is problematic. On the on hand, he holds (plausibly) that the distinction between spatial extension and colour that is thought-in the content has a fundament in it; it is a *distinctio cum fundamento in re*. The reason for this assumption is that he needs to have room for distinguishing between right and wrong imaginings-in. When I imagine blue in a content I imagine-in wrongly if the content is a red-square content. Hence, one can only correctly imagine or think-in a determinate shade of blue in a content if the content itself is related to this very shade of blue. There is something about the content that makes it correct to project the distinction between this shade of blue and that spatial extension onto it. But, on the other hand, if the content is simple, the nature of the fundament for the distinction remains mysterious. By contrast, if the content were a 'complex' of a colour and a spatial extension, the fundament of the distinction would lie in the constituents of the content. One can distinguish the shade of blue in the content because the content *contains* it. But this is against the spirit of Stumpf's view in 1873.

Later, Stumpf himself would argued against his 1873 view as follows:

> A tone as content of an appearance (I don't talk about the tone stimulus) has certainly always a particular pitch and strength whether or not consciousness distinguishes both sides. It does not acquire [particular strength and pitch] in virtue of the act of perception. A long time ago, I tried to locate the origin of such distinctions in experience in a multiple alterability of otherwise uniform sensations [. . .]. But this *hypothesis* [I explicitly stress that his has hypothetical character] at best shows how we come to form the concepts of pitch, strength, etc. that we then use to describe the particular appearances. It does not show how the tone acquires pitch etc.
> (Stumpf 1907, 21–22)

Thinking-in helps us to form a presentation of a particular colour, but it does not allow us to project the colour presented in a content if it was not already presented in it. Otherwise the 'analysis' of what one sees or hears would amount to the 'transubstantiation' of something simple into a complex.[8]

4. Apprehending a multitude as a unity

In *Tonpsychologie* Stumpf continued to investigate the question wherein the joint perception of some things consists. We have seen that this question came to the fore in answering arguments for empiricism about space. Colour and spatial extension are inseparable and hence are supposed to be abstractions from one simple content.

In *Tonpsychologie* (Vol. I 1883, Vol. II 1890) Stumpf gave up the notion of a simple content. When we hear a chord, we hear indeed several tones. For example, when you hear the Tristan chord, *F, B, D♯* and *G♯*, you hear *F, B, D♯* and *G♯ together*. These tones can be heard separately and therefore the Humean argument (from section 3 above) is insufficient to establish them as one simple content. Yet, we hear them *together* and *together* they appear to us as one unity. So while in 1873 Stumpf faced the problem to explain how we discern different qualities in one simple content, in 1890 he came to have the converse problem. When we hear the notes that make up a chord together, we hear indeed several notes. But one seems to hear *one* harmonious sound and not several notes; the experience seems to be that of one thing. Why don't we have the impression that we hear several notes if we indeed hear them?

Stumpf's answer is partly motivated by the observation that simultaneously sounding notes are more difficult to distinguish than successive ones:[9]

> The main reason for the fact that simultaneous sensations are harder to distinguish than immediately successive ones is lies in a more general

fact. All sensory qualities [*Empfindungsqualitäten*] enter, when they change from successive to simultaneous qualities, not only into the relation of simultaneity, but also into a further relation, as a consequence of which they appear as parts of a sensory whole [*Empfindungsganzen*]. Successive sensations form as sensations mere sum, simultaneous ones form as sensations already a whole. The qualities are not changed [. . .], let alone turned into a new quality, but a new relation obtains between them, that produces a unity that is closer between the members of a mere sum whose unity often consists in nothing more than the members are added together [*zusammengerechnet*] (one can sum the most heterogeneous and utterly unconnected things, even an affect and an apple). As a result of this new relation the impression of simultaneous sensations is more like the impression of one sensation than the impression of a series of sensations.

(Stumpf 1890, 64; my emphasis)

In this quote Stumpf stresses that in a sensory whole '[t]he qualities are not changed [. . .], let alone turned into a new quality, but a new relation obtains between them' (1890, 64). When hearing a chord, we hear a sensory whole whose parts are the *same notes* that we sometimes hear in isolation. On this, James will disagree:

The sour and sweet in lemonade are extremely unlike the sour and sweet of lemon juice and sugar, singly taken, yet like enough for us to 'recognize' these 'objects' in the compound taste. The several objective 'notes' recognized in the chord sound differently and peculiarly there.

(James 1895, 123)

The qualities, claims James, such as the sour taste or the perceived objects such as the tone F are changed if they occur together with other qualities or objects. The unity of a chord, for example, consists in the fact that the objects perceived together cannot be perceived in isolation. The chord is therefore distinct from a succession of tones where each of them is heard 'on its own'. However, this description of the unity of the chords has the *prima facie* strange consequence that one does *not* hear the note F when 'one hears F' in a chord. One only hears a note that is very similar to F and confuses it with F.

Now it is difficult to decide, on a mere phenomenological basis, whether one hears the same note in the examples under consideration or only a note that is similar. But Stumpf's description of what he takes to be a 'joint perception' has the advantage over James's that it makes common sense come out right: hearing the Tristan Chord is, among other things, hearing F. And there seems to be no compelling reason to go with James against common sense. The trained musician hears F and not another tone similar to F in the chord.

In *Tonpsychologie* the crucial question is: How is the apprehension of the multitude as a unity to be explained? In this special case the question is: How is the apprehension of some notes as one chord to be explained? Stumpf's answer is: We apprehend a multitude of sensory qualities as a unity if, and only if, they are parts of a 'sensory whole'. Chords are one kind of sensory wholes. When some objects are parts of a sensory whole, they stand in the relation Stumpf called 'fusion' (*Verschmelzung*).

This answer is as good as our grip on the notion of a sensory whole. We know that such a whole is not a mere sum. Stumpf used 'sum' in the everyday sense of the result of adding things together. For example, one may ask: 'What is the sum of two Bananas and three apples?' and receive the answer: 'Their sum is 5'. Anything can be added together to for a sum, but a sensory whole is something different.

Which wholes are sensory wholes? Stumpf gave the following answer:

> What is really involved in the fact that some sensations form a whole and approach more or less the impression of ONE sensation can, in the final instance, only be learned from and through examples.
> (Stumpf 1890, 128)

The notion of a sensory whole is non-analysable. It can be used to analyse what fusion is, namely fusion is the relation that obtains between some qualities if, and only if, they form a sensory whole. But the notion of a sensory whole is supposed to be basic; it can only be learned from examples.

Stumpf pointed out that different sensory qualities become parts of sensory whole when they occur simultaneously. Can one use simultaneity to explain what a sensory whole is? No, several tones may sound simultaneously but because they are dissonant, they are not apprehended as a unity.

If the notion of a sensory whole can only be grasped by perceiving such wholes, Stumpf's answer seems unsatisfactory. For if we acquire the notion of a sensory whole by considering examples such as chords or flocks of birds, it is too close to the datum to be explained in terms of it. How is the apprehension of some things as a unity to be explained? The answer he proposed was, in effect: By saying that these things form a sensory whole, that is, a unity such as a chord etc. This is not an answer, but rather the denial that an explanation can be had. If someone is puzzled by how a multitude can appear as a unity, Stumpf has not resolved the puzzlement by pointing out that some things indeed appear as unities. For instance, Sully writes in his review of Stumpf's book:

> In spite of his prolonged effort, the writer does not, to my mind, make his idea of Verschmelzung quite clear. The several constituent sensations of the tone-complex are, it must be remembered, all present as individual sensations, and yet they tend to merge into a unity, which if it means anything should mean that they lose their individual distinctness.
> (Sully 1891, 276–277).

We need to explain how a sensory unity can be perceived as one thing and yet be composed of several things that are all perceived. Stumpf did not give such an explanation.

5. Perceiving some things together as one

In 1895 James wrote a seminal paper with the self-explanatory title 'The Knowing of Things Together'. In this paper he worked over the same ground as Stumpf before him. James made clear that the phenomenon Stumpf discussed is ubiquitous:

> Most of these experiences are of objects perceived to be simultaneous and not to be immediately successive as in the heretofore considered case. The field of view, the chord of music, the glass of lemonade are examples. But the gist of the matter is the same – it is always knowing-together.
> (James 1895, 113)

James's terms 'knowing things together' or 'perceiving things together' is illuminating: when we hear a chord we hear some things together. Hearing a chord is one perception directed on several objects. James recommended to take the plural in 'things together' seriously:

> To formulate the phenomenon of knowing things together thus as a combining of ideas, is already to foist in a theory about the phenomenon simply. Not so should a question be approached. The phenomenon offers itself, in the first instance, *as that of knowing things together; and it is in those terms that its solution must, in the first instance at least, be sought.*
> (1895, 106; my emphasis)

In this section I will follow James's advice and argue for an answer to Stumpf's question that does explain what a sensory whole is by making use of the notion of perceiving some things together.[10]

My starting point is the distinction between distributive and collective properties. A property *P* is *distributive* if, and only if, the fact that some things have it implies that each of them has it; otherwise it is *collective*.[11] For example, if John, Bill, and Tom surround the building, it is not the case that John surrounds the building, Bill surrounds the building, and Tom surrounds the building. They can only surround the building *together*; in this case *surrounding the building* is a *collective* property. Some properties are neither distributive nor collective. Perhaps surrounding the building is such a property. A very big, yet flexible, animal might surround the building on its own.

Just as some things can have a property together without each of them having the property on its own, some things may look together a particular way, although none of them looks that way on its own. One can point at a picture of Elisabeth Anscombe and Peter Geach and say truly:

Elisabeth Anscombe and Peter Geach look like a happy couple.

This look is a look Peter Geach and Elisabeth Anscombe can only have together. They look together like a happy couple, neither Peter Geach looks like a happy couple nor Elisabeth Anscombe looks like a happy couple. We have a good intuitive grip on the idea that some things look together a particular way, while none of them looks that way on its own. Consider another example. The geese of a gaggle have a distinctive 'joint look' that distinguishes *them*, for example, from the crows in a murder. The birds that fly together have the look together, not each of them.[12]

When it comes to articulating what it is to see (perceive) some things together, Dretske's notion of 'non-epistemic object seeing' is an essential starting point. When do you see an object, in contrast to seeing that it is thus-and-so? When the object looks to you different from its environment. For example, you don't see the well-camouflaged chameleon because it does not look different to its environment to you. You can only see the chameleon if, to you, the chameleon looks different from its environment.[13] Dretske captured our intuitive conception of seeing an object as follows:

Non-epistemic (singular) seeing: S sees D iff D looks some way to S and this way of looking differentiates D from its immediate environment.
(Dretske 1969, 20)

Now let us build on Dretske's idea. Imagine you see a flock of birds. You may be seeing each or at least some of the birds, in which case what we have is what we may call 'distributive *non-epistemic plural seeing*': S sees D_1 to D_N because each of D_1 to D_N looks some way to S and this way of looking differentiates each of them from their immediate environment. But the birds may also have a collective look for you: Together they look different from their environment. Whenever that is the case, what you have is a *collective non-epistemic plural seeing*: S sees D_1 to D_N because *they* look *together* some way to S and this way of looking differentiates *them* from their immediate environment.

In the limiting case, the birds may *only* look together different from their environment. In such case none of the individual birds is on its own visually differentiated from their immediate environment for you. Consider the case in which some geese come gradually together to fly in formation. *At first*, many of the birds, individually, may have looked to you different from their environment, but they may also have had a collective look. *After a while*, the birds, as one might put it, merged into one unity: Now none of the birds looks distinct from its surroundings to you, only the birds together do. They look together, for example, like one big dark triangle in the sky.

Examples like these help one the grasp the notion Stumpf (and Husserl) have in mind.[14] They give talk of 'fusion' intuitive content. With the notion of a collective look we can analyse the examples further. The birds look to you like one unity if they look together some way to you and *only* their joint look distinguishes them from their environment and, we need to add, this is the look one thing may have. For example, a big triangle in sky would look on its own like the birds look together.

In the light of this example we can define the notion of a sensory whole Stumpf had in mind as follows:

> (SW) Some things form a sensory whole for S at a time if, and only if, at that time they only appear *together* distinct from their surroundings for S and the way they appear distinct from their surroundings is a way one object alone can appear to S.

The geese look together like one thing and this look distinguishes them together from their surroundings.

With (SW) in mind, Stumpf's question: 'How is the apprehension of a multitude as a unity to be explained?' can now be answered. S sees some objects as one unity because they look together some way to S and this look differentiates them together from their environment and it is a look one object can have. In this case your perception presents some objects, a multitude, as one object.

This answer is explanatory: We see a particular case of perception in light of a general principle about object perception. This principle is needed in the theory of perception for independent reasons and its extension to the plural case is independently plausible.

This answer disarms Sully's criticism of Stumpf's own 'fusion' metaphor. When some things make up a sensory whole, they stand in the fusion relation. But this does not mean that these things 'lose their individual distinctness' (Sully 1891, 277). They have not become one thing. Just as the fact that some things can have a property together does not imply that these things have become one thing, the fact that many things can look together a particular way to you does not imply that there is now only one thing – their fusion – that looks this way. We also don't need to assume, as Stumpf 1873 did, simple contents to give an account of apprehending a multitude as a unity. Acknowledging that things can look together a particular way is sufficient. There might be further fusion phenomena that will make revisions of (SW) necessary. But the appeal to ways things look together provides a general strategy to describe the phenomena Stumpf had in mind that avoids the problem to find a single object that is truly perceived in simultaneous perception of several objects.

(SW) captures central aspects of what Stumpf and others meant by 'fusion'. According to Stumpf, 'the impression of simultaneous sensations is more like the impression of one sensation than the impression of a series of sensations' (see Stumpf 1890, 64; see also Husserl 1891, 231). In perception some things can seem to us more or less like one thing. Later Brentano explicitly mentioned 'degrees of fusion' in his discussion with Stumpf:

> Fusion has several degrees decreasing to the case where the fusion is zero for the plurality is obvious to everyone although one may not be able to distinguish the individual components and to describe their difference in pitch.
>
> (Brentano 1907, 218)[15]

If you see a number of birds and some of them look different from their surroundings to you, the birds are not fused to the highest degree for you; the sensory whole is not perfect. If none of the birds looks different from its surroundings to you and the birds look *only together* different from their surrounding and this is the look of one thing, the degree of fusion is maximal.

The degree of fusion need not be maximal for one to see some birds as a complex whole. When the birds together look some way to you such that this way of looking differentiates them from their surroundings, some birds, a multitude, is still perceived as one whole. In this case your perception presents them as one complex object: a flock. This is different from cases in which no elements in the multitude stand out.

This brings us back to Stumpf's example of the chord. Hearing a chord is different from hearing a succession of notes that make it up. Yet, when one hears the chord one hears several notes; the same notes that one can also hear in succession. The difference between hearing the chord and hearing the notes in succession consists in the fact that simultaneous notes have *together* a way of sounding that distinguishes *them* from their surroundings and this way of sounding is a way one note can sound.

If we explain what a sensory whole is in terms of ways things look or sound together, we make room for the fact that one can perceive a multitude as unity and yet learn to analyse the unity into its constituents. Consider again the example of hearing the chord. We hear the notes, but to the untrained ear they appear as one because they are only distinguished (and meaningful in the tonal system) together. The untrained listener can only hear them because only together they sound to him in a way that distinguishes them from other sounds. While for the untrained listener the notes only sound together distinct, the trained musician can also direct his attention to the notes that make up the chord. The degree of fusion is lower for the trained musician because the notes have a collective way as well as individual ways they sound to him.

6. Conclusion

How is the apprehension of multitude as a unity to be explained? In *Tonpsychologie* Stumpf tried to explain how we apprehend a multitude by appeal to the notion of a sensory whole. We learn what sensory wholes are by comparing and contrasting chords and similar things with sums. Sensory wholes seem to be nothing other than the unities that created our puzzlement in the first place. So Stumpf's proposal is not helpful.

I propose to take sensory wholes to be a special case of the more general phenomenon that things, in order for us to see (hear) them, must look (sound) to us a certain way. How is the apprehension of multitude as a unity to be explained? By extending the notion that an object looks to a perceiver to be a certain way: If someone is perplexed at the idea that some things can be perceived *as one*, we can point out to the fact that some things are such that they look together distinct from their surroundings to us and that this way of looking is the way one object would look to us. Whenever that is the case, we still see them all, but we 'apprehend them as a unity'.[16]

Notes

1 See Fisette (2015) for an overview over Stumpf's life and work.
2 James (1893, 208) said of his own *Principles of Psychology:* '[I]n my book I am but the humble follower of the eminent Munich Psychologist'. See Jackman, infra, for a discussion of James.
3 All translations are mine. Thanks to Sarah Tropper for comments on the translation.
4 In the context of Stumpf theory, as is also the case for other Brentanians, the notions of 'content' and 'object' can often be used interchangeably.
5 For an overview and analysis of empiricism/nativism for visual perception, see Smith (2000). See also Woodward (1978) for an account of the history of views on space perception. Hatfield (1990 Chs. 4 and 5) gives a broader overview that includes Lotze's work, but does not mention Stumpf at all.
6 Brentano discussed common sensibles, among other places, in Brentano (1874, book II, Chapter 4).
7 See *De Anima* III.1, 425a14–24.
8 See Stumpf (1907, 18). Stumpf (1907, 18–19) provides further arguments against the Unity View.
9 See Stumpf (1890, 61–62).
10 For a recent application of the notion of perceiving things together, see Tye (2009).
11 I adopt these definitions from the definitions of the corresponding predicates. See Oliver and Smiley (2001, 289) and McKay (2006, 6ff.).
12 Husserl seems to have something similar in mind when he talks about 'quasi-qualities' or 'sensory qualities of second-order' (Husserl 1891, 225). For example he said that there is a 'characteristic property of the uniform total intuition of the set that can be apprehended in one glance' (ibid, 227). But there is a distinction between a joint look that some things have together and a look they have.
13 For further discussion, see Siegel (2006, 434).
14 Husserl (1913, 244) argued that some object are only fused if 'no elements stand out' or if they 'merge' into each other. What it means for perceived object to merge, on Husserl's account, is for them to form a series of pairs such that the members of each pair are indistinguishable from each other. But this condition is too strong. For one thing, under this condition, a chord is not a fusion. Husserl himself does acknowledge that there is a kind of fusion which is not 'a blurring into each other in the form of continuity or in another form that nullifies the separation, but it is at least a kind of especially intimate connection' (Husserl 1913, 248). But he says little more on what this other

kind of 'intimate connection' might be. On Husserl and Stumpf on fusion, see Ierna (2009).
15 See Martinelli (2013) for a comparison between Stumpf's and Brentano's conception of tonal fusion.
16 I am grateful to audiences in Göttingen, London, and Sheffield for helpful discussion. Many thanks to Luca Barlassina, Christian Beyer, Bill Brewer, Jorgen Drystadt, Paul Faulkner, Giulia Felappi, Denis Fisette, Miranda Fricker, David Galloway, Dominic Gregory, Chris Hookway, Chris Hughes, Nils Kürbis, Stephen Laurence, Jimmy Lenman, Guy Longworth, Stephen Makin, Eliot Michaelson, Daniel Morgan, David Papineau, Dolf Rami, Nick Shea, and Holmer Steinfath. Special thanks to Sarah Tropper for very detailed comments and discussion and Bob Stern for feedback. Many thanks to Sandra Lapointe for comments that helped me to focus the discussion.

Bibliography

Bain, A. 1855. *The Senses and the Intellect*. London: J.W. Parker and Son, West Strand.
Brentano, F. 1874. *Psychologie vom Empirischen Standpunkt*. Reprint of the 1924 edition. Hamburg: Meiner.
———. 1907. *Untersuchungen zur Sinnespsychologie*, ed. by R. Chisholm. Hamburg: Meiner Verlag, 1979.
Brentano, F. and Stumpf, K. 1867. *Briefwechsel 1867–1917*, ed. by M. Kaiser El-Safti (with the help of T. Binder). Frankfurt am Mian: Peter Lang, 2014.
Dretske, F. 1969. *Seeing and Knowing*. Chicago: Chicago University Press.
Fisette, D. 2015. Carl Stumpf. *Stanford Encyclopedia of Philosophy*. https://plato.stanford.edu/entries/stumpf/
Hatfield, G. 1990. *The Natural and Normative: Theories of Spatial Perception from Kant to Helmholtz*. Cambridge, MA: MIT Press.
Herbart, W. 1825. *Psychologie als Wissenschaft*. Königsberg: August Wilhelm Unzer.
Hume, D. 1739–1740. *A Treatise of Human Nature*, L.A. Selby-Bigge and P.H. Nidditch, 2nd edition. Oxford: Clarendon Press, 1978.
Husserl, E. 1891. *Philosophie der Arithmetik*, Husserliana 12. Den Haag: Martinus Nijhoff, 1970.
———. 1913. *Logische Untersuchungen II/1: Untersuchungen zur Phänomenologie und Theorie der Erkenntnis*. Reprint of the second edition. Germany: Max Niemeyer Verlag, 1980.
Ierna, C. 2009. Husserl et Stumpf sur la Gestalt et le Fusion. *Philosophiques* 36, 489–510.
James, W. 1887. The Perception of Space I. *Mind* 12, 1–30 and 183–211.
———. 1891. *The Principles of Psychology* II. London: MacMillan and Company.
———. 1893. Mr. Bradley on Immediate Resemblance. *Mind* 2, 208–210.
———. 1895. The Knowing of Things Together. *Psychological Review* II, 105–124.
Lotze, R.H. 1852. *Medizinische Psychologie oder Physiologie der Seele*. Leipzig: Weidmann'sche Buchhandlung.
———. 1873. Mitteilung Lotzes. In Stumpf 1873.
Martinelli, R. 2013. Brentano and Stumpf on Tonal Fusion. In D. Fisette and G. Fréchette (eds.) *Themes from Brentano*. Amsterdam: Rodopi, 339–359.
McKay, T. 2006. *Plural Predication*. Oxford: Oxford University Press.

Oliver, A. & Smiley, T. 2001. Strategies for a Logic of Plurals. *Philosophical Quarterly* 51, 289–306.

Siegel, S. 2006. How Does Visual Phenomenology Constraint Object-Perception? *Australasian Journal of Philosophy* 84, 429–441.

Smith, A.D. 2000. Space and Sight. *Mind* 109, 481–518.

Stumpf, C. 1873. *Über den Ursprung der Raumvorstellung*. Leipzig: S. Hirzel.

———. 1883. *Tonpsychologie*, vol. I. Leipzig: Hirzel.

———. 1890. *Tonpsychologie*, vol. II. Leipzig: S. Hirzel.

———. 1892. Psychologie und Erkenntnistheorie. In *Abhandlungen der Königlich Bayerischen Akademie der Wissenschaften*, vol. 19, 2nd part, München: Verlag der K. Akademie in Kommission G. Franz, 465–516.

———. 1906/7. *Psychologie Vorlesungen Wintersemester 1906/7*. Mitschrift von W. Koffka. Unpublished Typoscript.

———. 1907. *Erscheinungen und ihre Psychischen Funktionen*. Berlin: Verlag der Königlichen Akademie der Wissenschaften in Kommission G. Reimer, 3–40.

———. 1919. Spinozastudien. *Abhandlungen der Preußischen Akademie der Wissenschaften: Philosophisch-historische Classe* 4, Verlag der Akademie der Wissenschaften in Kommission Walter DeGruyter u. Co., 1–57.

———. 1924. Carl Stumpf. In R. Schmidt (ed.) *Die Philosophie der Gegenwart in Selbstdarstellung, vol. V.* Leipzig: Meiner, 1–57.

———. 1928. *Gefühl und Gefühlsempfindung*. Leipzig: Verlag von Johann Ambrosius Barth.

———. 1939. *Erkenntnislehre I*. Leipzig: Verlag von Johann Ambrosius Barth. Reprint Paderborn: Pabst Verlag, 2008.

Sully, M. 1891. Review of Tonpsychologie. *Mind* 16, 274–280.

Tye, M. 2009. A New Look at the Speckled Hen. *Analysis* 69, 258–263.

Woodward, W.R. 1978. From Association to Gestalt: The Fate of Hermann Lotze's Theory of Spatial Perception, 1846–1920. *Isis* 69, 572–582.

12

CHRISTIAN VON EHRENFELS ON THE MIND AND ITS METAPHYSICS[1]

Carlo Ierna

1. Introduction

Christian von Ehrenfels's foremost contribution to philosophy of mind is undeniably his seminal 1890 article on *Gestalt* qualities.[2] This work is considered to have been a "watershed" (Smith 1988b, 15) and a "revolution" (Smith 1994, 20). Ehrenfels' notion of *Gestalt* resonated not only with his contemporaries, in the School of Brentano and in phenomenology (see e.g. Heinämaa 2009), but it continues to inform cognitive science (see e.g. Wildgen 2001) and philosophy of mind. In this chapter I will outline some of the influences and background of his conception, briefly discuss his notion of *Gestalt*, explain how it was taken up by others, and then consider how Ehrenfels himself further applied and developed it.[3]

1.1 Ehrenfels in the School of Brentano

Ehrenfels began his studies in philosophy in Vienna in the winter semester of 1879/80, attending lectures by Franz Brentano and the young Alexius Meinong, who had just started teaching there as *Privatdozent* in the previous year. In 1882 Meinong was appointed professor at the University of Graz and Ehrenfels followed him in the winter semester of 1884/1885 in order to write a dissertation "*Über Größenrelationen und Zahlen. Eine psychologische Studie*" ("On Relations of Magnitude and Numbers. A Psychological Study" (Ehrenfels 1885, ed. Ierna 2017a). In 1887 Ehrenfels returned to Vienna to obtain his *Habilitation*, "*Über Fühlen und Wollen. Eine psychologische Studie*" ("On Feeling and Willing. A Psychological Study").[4] Ehrenfels lectured in Vienna from 1891 until 1896, when he was appointed professor at the Charles University in Prague, where he would become a colleague of Anton Marty, one of Brentano's more orthodox students (Fabian 1986b, 21 ff.). Unlike most other prominent students of Brentano,[5] he did not establish a school of his own, though he did influence the views of *Gestalt* psychologists in Berlin, around Stumpf, and in Graz, around Meinong.

Throughout his life Ehrenfels managed to remain on good terms with both his teachers Meinong and Brentano, all the while progressively developing his own ideas in quite original directions.

Ehrenfels shares for the most part the views on "descriptive psychology" Brentano developed in his lectures and in *Psychology from an Empirical Standpoint* (1874). On Brentano's account, "the true method of philosophy is none other than that of the natural sciences" and, as such, the study of mind and consciousness should rely on an interdisciplinary collaboration between philosophy, psychology, and natural scientific investigations into e.g. brain physiology, the mechanical workings of the sense organs etc.[6] Descriptive psychology, as such, deals with mental phenomena, abstracting from causality, merely describing what one finds given in inner experience. Brentano distinguishes inner and outer perception, i.e. he distinguishes the perception of psychical, mental phenomena from the perception of physical, natural phenomena and argues that the domain of descriptive psychology is exclusively the former. Inner perception is also contrasted with introspection, which Brentano rejected (Brentano 1874, 36).[7] According to Brentano, mental acts can be grouped in three major classes: presentations, judgements, and emotions, i.e. what Brentano also calls "phenomena of love and hate" or sometimes "*Gemütsbewegungen*".[8] (Brentano 1874, 260). As judgements stands to logic, emotions stand to ethics (Brentano 1874, 293). For Brentano, the class of emotions would also encompass phenomena related to the will (Brentano 1874, Ch. 8 "*Einheit der Grundclasse für Gefühl und Willen.*" 307 ff.), since there would be a continuity between feeling and striving, affective and conative states, using the following example: "sadness – yearning for the absent good – hope that it will be ours – the desire to bring it about – the courage to make the attempt – the decision to act" (308).

This however is one fundamental point of disagreement with Ehrenfels, who extensively criticized and rejected Brentano's view that will and emotions belong to the same class of mental phenomena (Ehrenfels 1887, 537–548). Ehrenfels argues that the opposition of "love and hate" is not equivalent to that of "pleasure and displeasure" (Ehrenfels 1887, 545) and that the kind of continuity Brentano sees between feeling and willing is not necessary, drawing a line between the mere unpleasant feeling of sadness and the undeniable element of desire and striving in the yearning (547).

Ehrenfels also disagreed with Brentano's view on the intensity of mental phenomena. In 1896,[9] Brentano argued that while, in the case of sensation, the intensity of sense perception, i.e. the mental act as a whole is always equal to that of the sensed content (1907, 65), the case would be different for abstract concepts, and that the corresponding mental acts would lack any intensity (68). Ehrenfels (1898b) had no trouble finding counterexamples to Brentano's theory. If the intensity of the sensed content determines the intensity of the sensation, and if, as Brentano argued, it also determines the intensity of the judgements and emotions that are built on them, then a judgement bearing on a *crescendo* tone would have to become more and more intense as the tone becomes louder and louder (Ehrenfels 1898b, 54). Ehrenfels considered this patently absurd. He brought a similar example to bear on the case of emotions. Imagine that you spend your summer vacation in a cottage next to a brook. In the beginning the sound of the water delights you, but the incessant noise soon starts to annoy you, growing odious, until you get used to it and it becomes entirely indifferent (Ehrenfels 1898b, 55). While the murmuring of the brook does not change in intensity, the intensity of the emotions related to it will run the whole gamut of love and hate.

A third important disagreement relates to ethics and the theory of value. Brentano (1889, 17) considered the good to be an absolute notion: "We call something good when the love relating to it is right. That which can be loved with a right love, that which is worthy of love, is good in the widest sense of the term". This however Ehrenfels rejected (1897, §16, 43–51). Specifically, he disagrees with Brentano's claim that there is an analogue for "correctness" in the case of emotions as in the case of judgements.[10] Ehrenfels extensively criticizes the evidence of inner perception that Brentano adduces for such a possibility. Ehrenfels proceeds by attacking the examples Brentano provides of acts of love whose putative correctness is intrinsically evident (such as love of knowledge, hate of pain, etc.) He argues that, since there are plenty of alternative explanations, Brentano's conclusion, that they would have the kind of intrinsic correctness that would turn them into something absolutely good, is not warranted. Ehrenfels (1897, 50) rather aims to show that an ethical theory is possible without any assumption of an absolute.[11]

2. On *Gestalt* qualities

Ehrenfels's seminal 1890 article "On '*Gestalt*' qualities" begins with the question: "Is a melody (i) a mere sum [*Zusammenfassung*] of elements, or (ii) something novel in relation to this sum, something that certainly goes hand in hand with, but is distinguishable from, the sum of elements?" (Ehrenfels 1890, tr. Smith 1988a, 83).[12] If the answer is (ii) then, according to Ehrenfels, "one has in effect accepted what we call the tonal *Gestalt*" (Ehrenfels 1890, 91). One of Ehrenfels's main arguments in favour of (ii) is that people recognize the same melody when played in different keys. Since the individual sense impressions are different from key to key, a melody cannot be a simple sum of tones (Ehrenfels 1890, 90 ff.). Hence, a melody as a whole is something more: a *Gestalt*.

> By a *Gestalt* quality we understand a positive content of presentation bound up in consciousness with the presence of complexes of mutually separable (i.e. independently presentable) elements. That complex of presentations which is necessary for the existence of a given *Gestalt* quality we call the foundation [*Grundlage*] of that quality.
> (Ehrenfels 1890, 93)

According to Ehrenfels, there is a fundamental distinction between "temporal" and "non-temporal" *Gestalten*. Temporal *Gestalt* qualities develop over time, as in the case of music. Every note in a simple melody is given one by one in succession, as Ehrenfels says: "at most one element can be given in perceptual presentation". Yet, beyond the succession of single notes, we also hear the melody as a whole, remembering previously heard notes, expecting and anticipating developments in the harmonies.[13] The whole is, however, never completely given all at once to the listener. This is only possible in the case of non-temporal *Gestalt* qualities. The latter do not develop over time, and they can be given at once. The elements or foundations of the whole "can be given completely in perceptual presentation" (Ehrenfels 1890, 94). The whole is then completely present all at once alongside all its parts. Most visual *Gestalten*, e.g. paintings, are of this type.

On Ehrenfels's account, virtually any change, process, or movement that has some unity to it, involves a *Gestalt* quality. As a result, *Gestalt* qualities are not necessarily perceptual. For one thing, *Gestalten* are also involved in more abstract contexts. An architect, for instance, who designs a building, initially only has "symbolic presentations" of it, i.e. presentations through signs. He only obtains an intuitive "fulfilment" of these "empty" presentations once he inspects the completed work and sees whether it matches his earlier presentations. On the other hand, such fulfilment may fail. We may fail to acquire the complete presentation of an object, most obviously when the object that is represented symbolically turns out to have incompatible, contradictory properties, such as "round circle". According to Ehrenfels, the process of fulfilment, or its failure, should be understood as characteristic *Gestalten* in inner experience.

In addition to *Gestalten* that are based directly in sensory contents, Ehrenfels think that we can also have *Gestalten* based on other *Gestalten* i.e. "higher-order" *Gestalten*. This occurs, for instance, when we compare and contrast different elementary *Gestalten* (Ehrenfels 1890, 102, 104, 105). Ehrenfels gives a long list of examples. We have higher-order *Gestalten* in the case of actions "expressed by means of common nouns (kindness, service, rivalry, marriage, theft, war, etc.) or verbs (entreat, complain, help, rob, avenge, etc.)" (Ehrenfels 1890, 107). Moreover, on Ehrenfels's account, whenever we group various objects as belonging together by virtue of a common feature, we effectively identify a *Gestalt* as the uniting element. This is the case for

> all designations of human individuals or groups of whatever kind (Hans and Paul, priests, manual workers, Scotsmen, rogues, etc.), as well as most designations for human corporations and institutions (state, authority, the insurance market, etc.), all names of places and territories, and equally all names of animal species.
> (Ehrenfels 1890, 107)

Indeed, Ehrenfels often takes his cue from ordinary language, the assumption being that if ordinary language has provided a name for the phenomenon, it must pick out the unitary character that constitutes a *Gestalt*:

> We have to make do with a few words for isolated examples from the whole range of possible colour changes (e.g. blushing, blanching,

darkening, glowing, etc.). [. . .] Beside the musical temporal qualities already considered we have to recognize also such noise or resonance *Gestalten* as, say, thundering, exploding, rustling, splashing, etc.

(Ehrenfels 1890, 98, 100)

It is no surprise, then, that Ehrenfels would claim that "the larger part of both our everyday and our scientific vocabulary designates *Gestalt* qualities". In practice, all verbs (with few exceptions such as the auxiliaries), all nouns, and all adjectives that refer to "more than a single presentational element" (Ehrenfels 1890, 108) would already constitute a *Gestalt*.

In the history of psychology, when discussing *Gestalt* psychology (or *Gestalt* theory), one usually does not fail to mention Ehrenfels's 1890 article.[14] Most of the time, however, what is lacking is a discussion of Ehrenfels's background, the details of his own theories, as well as his connection to the larger community of psychologists and philosophers of his time.[15] For one thing, while Ehrenfels introduced the concept of *Gestalt* quality in contemporary philosophy and psychology, he himself credits the fundamental inspiration for his 1890 article "*Über 'Gestaltqualitäten'*" ("On '*Gestalt* Qualities'") to Ernst Mach's 1886 *Beiträge zur Analyse der Empfindungen* (*Contributions to the Analysis of Sensations*). Indeed, Mach had argued that we can perceive spatial and tonal "shapes" (*Gestalten*) directly, and that we can notice similarities and equalities among such shapes even when their instances are very different, e.g. when their colors or orientations are different (see e.g. Mach 1886, 43). Mach had pointed out that we can notice the similarity of shapes – understood literally – in geometry, supervening on the equality of the lengths of the sides, of the angles etc. (Mach 1886, 47), and metaphorical "shapes" in music (Mach 1886, 128).[16] This suggests that Mach also had a higher order concept of "shape", i.e. a concept of *Gestalt*. Similar issues had also been considered elsewhere in the School of Brentano. Carl Stumpf, for one, had made similar remarks regarding our ability to compare shapes in different objects:

> Language is quite arbitrary in calling two objects of the same shape [*Figur*] and different color "similar", but not two objects of the same color and different shape [*Figur*]. This is because the shape [*Gestalt*] is in many ways a more important property.
>
> (Stumpf 1883, 115)

More importantly, Brentano, their mutual teacher, had also proposed a generalization of the concept of *Gestalt*:

> The shape [*Gestalt*] of two closed areas is the same when the distances of the borders that stand in the same relation of direction to one another are proportional, i.e. when the relations of magnitude of the distances of the border-points, that are in the same relation of direction to one another, are the same. Here we are dealing with relations of relations,

a situation that, at first quite surprisingly, would even allow to speak of a true sameness of angles and shape in wholly heterogeneous domains if we generalise the concepts of angle and shape [*Gestalt*]. If time were really curved and would turn steadily back on itself, then it would be truly and properly of the same shape [*von gleicher Gestalt*] as a circular line in space.

(Brentano 1884/85b, 58 f.)[17]

While a *Gestalt* is certainly not reducible to a geometrical shape, the way we perceive and compare such shapes can be the basis for a derivative use of the term. Even when the contents of our sensations are very different, we can notice similarities. In other words, we can "see" higher order relational properties that are based on comparisons that go beyond sensory contents. These include relations of similarity, difference, equality, increase etc. as well as relations between parts and wholes. The notion of *Gestalt* was developed to make sense of a range of higher order phenomena, including what is the case when we see a unitary whole instead of a collection of parts, or when we can meaningfully compare wholes whose parts do not match. The ongoing discussions in the School of Brentano concerning mereology as well as higher order objects and relations constituted an important background to Ehrenfels's reception of Mach. In particular, Ehrenfels repeatedly quotes Meinong's 1882 *Hume Studien II: Zur Relationstheorie*.[18] In this book, Meinong discusses such topics as the similarity, difference, and sameness of *Gestalten* when comparing complex objects, including people, landscapes etc.[19] These are topics that Ehrenfels had also tackled in his dissertation, which originated as a commentary to Meinong's *Hume Studien II (see Ierna 2017b, 165)*. In his dissertation, Ehrenfels analyzes comparisons of relations across domains and higher order relations (i.e. relations of relations), showing that relations between spatial magnitudes are no different from relations between temporal magnitudes *(see Ierna 2017b, 177)*. His relevant conclusion is that, in both cases, relations of similarity are altogether independent from their foundations, i.e. from the individual elements that compose them in a particular domain. The conclusion of his dissertation is then that "We can find complexes in the most disparate domains of what we can present, which display a clearly observable similarity in their relations, so that even the most incompatible things can obtain unity and harmony through this relation" (Ehrenfels 1885, 85, ed. Ierna 2017a, 234).[20] In this respect, the 1885 dissertation seems to already anticipate some elementary positions of his 1890 article.

3. *Gestalt* psychology beyond Ehrenfels

The issue that would soon lead to a profound divide between the Berlin and Graz Schools of *Gestalt* psychology was whether Gestalt qualities are the result of a mental act or are passively given: do we actively construct *Gestalten* or do we merely notice them? While Ehrenfels admits that we can actively switch between different *Gestalten* by changing the focus of our attention, we do not actually produce the *Gestalt*, but merely notice it (Ehrenfels 1890, 112 f., cf. Bentley 1902, 275). By focusing on one side of a Necker cube, it seems oriented one way, by focusing on another, in another way. The interpretations are incompatible, yet arise based on the same visual elements. The foundations, the points and lines, are the same, but the higher order *Gestalten* of the cubes are different.

There seem to be two incompatible claims with respect to the nature of *Gestalten*. On the one hand, a *Gestalt* is tied to the specific combination of a set of foundations into a specific whole. The Gestaltqualität is a holistic property, i.e. pertains to the whole and not to the parts. It can be noticed for itself as an additional, higher order characteristic, in the way that we notice a major or minor key in a melody. On the other hand, the same *Gestalt* can arise in multiple instances on the basis of a variety of possible combinations of foundations. The same *Gestalt*, the same melody, can be played in different keys, on different instruments etc. (compare Smith 1988b, 14). The contrast between a *Gestalt* as individual and as general led to many discussions among the early Gestaltists. As Köhler (1961, 2) remarks:

> In the eighties of the past century, psychologists in Europe were greatly disturbed by von Ehrenfels' claim that thousands of percepts have characteristics which cannot be derived from the characteristics of their ultimate components, the so-called sensations. Chords and melodies in hearing, the shape characteristics of visual objects, the roughness or the smoothness of tactual impressions, and so forth, were used as examples. All these "Gestalt qualities" have one thing in common. When the physical stimuli in question are considerably changed, while their relations are kept constant, the Gestalt qualities remain about the same. But, at the time, it was generally assumed that the sensations involved are individually determined by their individual stimuli and must therefore change when these are greatly changed. How, then, could any characteristics of the perceptual situation remain constant under these conditions?

A *Gestalt* quality allows us to see a set of sensory elements as a unitary whole, instead of as a mere sum: a forest or an avenue instead of a bunch of trees. A new kind of whole emerges from the arrangement of simpler elements, not only in single sensory modalities, but also multi-modally, as when a smell and a taste "fuse" together. Ehrenfels considered Gestalten outside of the domain of sensation as well, such as between mind and world, and purely within consciousness itself in inner perception (Ehrenfels 1890, 272 f.). Ehrenfels's theory is of the utmost and encompassing generality: "Almost all of the theoretical and conceptual issues which came subsequently to be associated with the Gestalt idea are treated at some point in the [1890 article], at least in passing" (Smith 1988b, 15). Yet, this also left many sketchy details and unsolved problems, as the conundrum mentioned Köhler's quote above, that were for the most part taken up in the further reception of his work and developments of the idea of Gestalt independently from Ehrenfels.

Ehrenfels's 1890 article got its most important reception, at first, in and through the works of his teacher Meinong.[21] In 1894 Meinong founded the first psychological laboratory in Austria, after Brentano had previously failed to obtain funding to establish one in Vienna in 1874, and his students were among the first to investigate *Gestalt* phenomena experimentally (e.g. Benussi 1904). There are at least two ways in which Meinong contributed to the development of *Gestalt* theory. First, Meinong himself considered the use of the terms "shape" and "quality" misleading. In Meinong's terminology, *Gestalten* are "founded" in their constituents, and the latter are the "founding content" of *Gestalten*. (Meinong 1891, 253).[22] Ehrenfels immediately adopted this new terminology (Ehrenfels 1891, 293). This contributed to stress the fact that *Gestalten* are higher order objects, as a team is a higher order object than the single players. Second, just like Meinong, the members of the Graz School disagreed with Ehrenfels's earlier position.

By contrast, Meinong and his students believed that higher order objects are actively produced by a mental effort, operating on the lower order constituents (Smith 1994, 259 f.). The Gestalt as a whole is actively made out of its founding contents. It is only through a specific activity (referred to as "*Gestaltbildung*" or as a form of "*Vorstellungsproduktion*") that we can add the non-sensory higher order *Gestalt* on top of the primary contents of sensation. Instead of considering the *Gestalt* as a quality given at once together with its foundations, the members of the Graz school considered it to be a separate object. They spoke, not of "*Gestaltqualitäten*", but of "*Gestaltgegenstände*" and referred to the founding contents as *inferiora* and to the founded one as *superiora* (see e.g. Ameseder 1904, 110 ff.). While the (founding) sensory contents were considered "real", the (founded) *Gestalt* was considered "ideal" and the relation between the two, the founding itself, being clearly distinguished from causation. (See e.g. Benussi 1904, 383.)

The other major school of Gestalt psychology was the Berlin School, which developed around Carl Stumpf in the early decades of the twentieth century. Ehrenfels's influence in Berlin was partly through his students. Max Wertheimer attended lectures by Ehrenfels – as well as Marty – at the university of Prague from 1898 to 1901, later transferred to Berlin where he continued to study under Stumpf (King and Wertheimer 2005, 43 f., Ash 1989, 52). Stumpf founded a psychological institute in Berlin in 1900. It is within this institute that Stumpf's students at the time – Wertheimer, Koffka, and Köhler – contributed to further develop *Gestalt* psychology. Their central position was radical holism, hence entirely opposite that of the Graz school. The Berlin School denied that the founding elements of a Gestalt are first given individually and the Gestalt itself would then be the result of an act of combination. On their account, it is not the case that the founding elements are first given individually and then combined to form a Gestalt. What is first is the Gestalt itself. Indeed, they went so far as to deny that individual contents of sensation are given directly, and argued that they should be understood as abstractions from the whole of a perceptual field. A group of sensory contents would not *have* a *Gestalt*, but actually *be* a *Gestalt*.[23] Consider the case of four lines intersecting at right angles to form a square: is the square made from the lines or the lines abstracted from the square? The Berlin group argued for the latter. The "square" or "squareness" is not a property of a group of lines in a specific configuration, the square is what is perceived first and foremost. It is likely that when presented with a suitable drawing, most people, when asked "what is this?", would answer "a square" and not "four lines intersecting at right angles", just like they would describe the following:

---

as "a line" and not as "a one dimensional infinite set of points".

Interestingly, Ehrenfels's notion of *Gestalt* was exported overseas quite early on. In 1891 already *The Monist* had a report on Meinong's article of the very same year, in which Ehrenfels's 1890 work was of course extensively considered.[24] It also had a report on Ehrenfels' s1891 article on the philosophy of mathematics in the next issue, in which the notions of *Gestaltqualitäten* and founded contents were discussed in connection with symbolic numbers.[25] Moreover, in Stout's *Analytic Psychology* (1896) Ehrenfels's 1890 article is cited right at the opening of the third chapter, dedicated to "The Apprehension of Form". In this chapter, Stout discusses "forms of combination", a term that is meant as translation of "*Gestalt*".[26] Ehrenfels's article (and Meinong's reaction) were extensively discussed by Bentley in *The American Journal of Psychology* in 1902, and the reception was overall significant enough to make it possible for Zigler in 1920 to simply refer to Ehrenfels's "Well-known article". While the Graz School and, perhaps even more significantly, the Berlin School are usually associated to developments of the notion of *Gestalt*, Ehrenfels's 1890 article nonetheless was a fixed point in the background, both in German speaking and English-speaking psychology and philosophy of mind.[27]

4. Ehrenfels's own development of Gestalt: the metaphysics of mind

At the closing of his 1890 article, Ehrenfels claims that, ultimately, the concept of *Gestalt* "would yield the possibility of comprehending the whole of the known world under a single mathematical formula" (Ehrenfels 1890, 116). This might come across as both grandiose and unachievable. Nevertheless, Ehrenfels seriously pursued this goal, finding applications for the notion of *Gestalt* in a number of domains, including in the philosophy of mind.[28] It is quite remarkable that, in the latter respect, the relevance of and ontology of *Gestaltqualitäten* to an understanding of mind comes to the fore in Ehrenfels's writings on religion and cosmology. In what follows, I explain how Ehrenfels's application of the notion of Gestalt in cosmology informs his metaphysics of the human mind.

In his *Kosmogonie*,[29] Ehrenfels sketches a cosmology based on the duality of cosmos and chaos.[30] The world is created by the complementary actions of the two principles: the *Gestaltungsprinzip* that "shapes" or "forms" ("*gestalten*" as a verb) the universe,[31] and absolute chaos. In this context, instead of speaking of "temporal" or "non-temporal" *Gestalten* Ehrenfels now speaks of "static" and "kinetic" ones (Ehrenfels 1916; Fabian 1990, 84). As Ehrenfels sees it, "causal chains" (*Kausalstränge*) always give rise to "*Gestalt* sequences" (*Gestaltfolgen*), and hence these terms can be used interchangeably: "All causal powers are *Gestalting* tendencies [*Alle Wirkungskräfte sind Gestaltungstendenzen*]" (Ehrenfels 1916; Fabian 1990, 156).[32] Ehrenfels then proposes a subdivision of *Gestalten* into the following classes: inanimate nature, living organisms, and organic derivatives. The latter would include everything from bird nests and beaver dams to palaces, machinery, and artworks (Ehrenfels 1916, 85). Based on this classification, Ehrenfels distinguishes two kinds of *Gestalt* sequences: autotropic and heterotropic. The former applies to genealogical relations, i.e. beavers generating beavers, humans generating humans. The latter applies to cases where *Gestalten* of one type generate new *Gestalten* of another type, e.g. beavers constructing dams, humans constructing buildings etc. Ehrenfels then points out the universal "kinetostatic tendency", i.e. that all kinetic *Gestalten* have a tendency to generate static *Gestalten* (Ehrenfels 1916, 88). Whenever a sequence of kinetic *Gestalten* comes to an end, it tends to leave behind a static *Gestalt*. For instance, buildings survive their builders and all organic life leaves behind static traces of their existence and activity, ultimately their corpse ("*Tendenz zur Spurenbildung*" Ehrenfels 1916, 90). Using these conceptual resources, all of which are founded in the notion of *Gestalt*, Ehrenfels thus provides an original account for the creation of the world, the origin and evolution of life, and human activity. Newer *Gestalten* are built by, out of, and on top of older ones, leading to *Gestalten* of increasingly higher order or "superimposed *Gestalten*" (Ehrenfels 1916, 102, 136). On Ehrenfels's account everything ultimately emanates from the cosmic *Gestaltungsprinzip*, the principle of order. The latter produces new *Gestalten* blindly, by "emanation", and "flows into them", propagating its drive to create (Ehrenfels 1916; Fabian 1990, 99). This impulse to generate ever further *Gestalten* is the ultimate origin and foundation of every *Gestalt* sequence. However, the human mind forms an exception to the blindness of this process of emanation, because it is capable of purposeful *Gestaltung*.

Let us then look at what makes human consciousness so special in this regard. What are human minds? On Ehrenfels's account, humans are not only multicellular organisms, they are also "multipsychical" (Ehrenfels 1916, 125):

> There can be no doubt that the individual human mind is at the same time also a state [*Staat*], and indeed composed of higher and lower units of consciousness [*Bewußtseinseinheiten*], whose number perhaps is equal to or even surpasses the number of the cells of his body. What each individual calls "his" consciousness, and whose unity is manifested to us in inner perception, is merely the central, ruling consciousness in this state.

From these layers of consciousness in a human mind, Ehrenfels then conjectures that the divine intellect, the mental-like ("psychoid") principle of order, stands to the multi-psychical human consciousness at large, like the individual human stands to his constituent lower units of consciousness. This is what explains his claim that "It is likely, that god thinks with our brains and wills in our willing" (Ehrenfels 1916; Fabian 1990, 142). In human consciousness the *Gestaltungsprinzip* comes to self-awareness and discovers the existence of purposes (Ehrenfels 1916; Fabian 1990, 226 f., 230): by purposeful *Gestalten* humans do god's work and bring meaning into the universe.

Indeed, in his *"Gedanken über die Religion der Zukunft"* ("Thoughts on the Religion of the Future"),[33] Ehrenfels elaborates on this point, further developing the idea of "superposition of units of consciousness". Every individual neuron in my brain, on his account, is in some sense itself both conscious and, at the same time, a partial constituent of my unitary consciousness as an individual human being. Analogously, together humans beings themselves are also partial constituents of "personalities of higher order": there would be literally a *Volksseele* (Ehrenfels 1922b; Fabian 1990, 262). As a consequence, although the human mind is a higher-order *Gestalt*, it is not therefore something abstract and unreal:

> The psychical is something "real" [*Reales*], something "actual" [*Wirkliches*] in the most proper sense of the word. The psychical is not without essence and only seemingly existing, it is something existing, capable of acting [*wirken*], and not just on the psychical itself (in the inner conscious life of each individual), but also [. . .] on the material.
> (Ehrenfels 1916; Fabian 1990, 130 f.)[34]

This is a radical negation of materialist accounts that reduce the mind to a mere epiphenomenon, caused by the material world, but incapable of acting on or affecting it. Ehrenfels, who has little esteem for this view, uses an analogy. If materialism is right, then Immanuel Kant composed his *Critique of Pure Reason* purely mechanically, like an automaton, without any of his acts of consciousness directly influencing his writing (Ehrenfels 1916, 126). Ehrenfels's point is that the sequence of events that led to the composition of Kant's opus magnum cannot be adequately explained exclusively in terms of physical causes and processes. Ehrenfels argues that even if we go along with the "depotentiation of the psychical", we still have to allow for causality in consciousness, since psychical acts have effects and may cause other psychical acts. But, on Ehrenfels's account, one cannot subscribe to the claim that brain chemistry causes smells, sounds etc. and furthermore hopes, fears etc. and reject the idea that perceptual and affective states do not also have neurophysiological effects (Ehrenfels 1916, 128). Instead, Ehrenfels argues for the hypothesis of a "layered mind", where the lowest levels, such as simple physical phenomena as the contents of sensation, might be directly instantiated in the brain and caused by physical stimuli, but the higher levels supervene on the lower levels of psychical acts and would then only be indirectly instantiated or affected by the brain and would rather be due to "pure psychical stimuli" ("*rein psychische Reizung*") (Ehrenfels 1916, 129 f.). Ehrenfels here has in mind the Brentanian account of superposition of mental acts, which Ehrenfels indeed quotes as support: "Let us consider the example of the psychical phenomenon of judging, which presuppose some presentations, without being reducible to mere presentations of processes of presentation" (Ehrenfels 1916, 130). For Brentano there are three main classes of mental acts: presentations, judgements, and emotions. A judgement arises when a positive or negative "quality" is added to a presentation: a judgement is the acceptance or rejection of the existence of the presented (Brentano 1874, 104, 111, 260).[35] Clearly, qualities like acceptance or rejection, the distinctive features of judgements, are not simply themselves presentations or reducible to an aspect of the presentation.[36]

5. Conclusion

By 1916,[37] the discussion of *Gestalt* qualities in psychology had moved on, with the two schools in Graz and Berlin having already produced significant results. In the debates between the two schools, Ehrenfels's own more philosophical and theoretical approach to the theory of *Gestalt* was however mostly disregarded. This might have been a consequence of the growing importance of experimentation and measurement, and the growing opposition to metaphysics. Ehrenfels himself nevertheless continued to consider his proposal in the *Kosmogonie* as a serious scientific hypothesis to be empirically tested (Ehrenfels 1916; Fabian 1990, Ch. 2). It is hard to say whether the analyses of order and chaos in the universe, the effect of the kinetostatic tendency, and the metaphysics of mind he proposes have much to tell us. What is clear, however, is that the underlying questions, the fundamental problems of intentionality, free will, interactionism, higher order objects, and their connections to sensations and/or fundamental physics, were issues then as much as now.

Notes

1. I'd like to thank the editor, Sandra Lapointe, for her extensive and detailed comments and corrections to earlier drafts of this chapter, which have significantly improved the language and exposition.
2. Ehrenfels (1890; reprint in Fabian 1988, 128–155); translation in Smith (1988a, 82–117).
3. For the more general relevance of the notion of *Gestalt* for current debates, see e.g. Epstein and Hatfield (1994), though they take into account nearly exclusively the theories of one particular strand of *Gestalt* psychology, i.e. of the Berlin School as represented by Kurt Koffka and Wolfgang Köhler. Also see Zimmer (2001, 141 f.).
4. Ehrenfels (1887, reprint in Fabian 1988, 15–97).
5. Stumpf established a psychological institute in Berlin, Marty reared the second generation of orthodox Brentanists in Prague, Meinong founded a psychological laboratory in Graz (the first in Austria), Husserl initiated the phenomenological movement, Twardowski captained Polish philosophy. See Albertazzi et al. (1996).

6 Indeed, when he obtained the chair of philosophy in Vienna in 1874, he requested funding for a psychological laboratory. If he had obtained the necessary support from the Austrian government, this would have been the first, anticipating Wundt's by five years.
7 For more details on Brentano's science of consciousness, see Ierna (2014); Dupuy (2009, 99–107), and the contribution of Rollinger in this volume. For the relevance of the descriptive psychology of the School of Brentano in the history of cognitive science and the philosophy of mind more in general, see Albertazzi (2001).
8 See Brentano (1884/85a, 47, 52).
9 Published in Brentano (1907, 51–98).
10 On Brentano's notion of "correct emotion", see Baumgartner and Pasquerella (2004).
11 Ehrenfels was a socially and politically engaged ethical thinker. Among his various pursuits are a proposed reform of sexual ethics, new racial policies (including an endorsement of mixed marriages and races), and the formulation of a new religion on a scientific basis. Though these pursuits had a very limited influence, Ehrenfels's views on religion (just like his philosophy of mathematics), found novel applications for the concept of *Gestalt* quality. For more detailed biographical information, see Fabian (1986b) and Ierna and Rollinger (2015). For a discussion of his proposed reform of sexual ethics, see Dickinson (2002).
12 I use Smith's (1988a) translation, the page numbering also refers to the latter.
13 Ehrenfels (1890, 272 f.) also considered temporal *Gestalten* in the domain of psychical phenomena, such as the rising and falling of emotions as presentations of inner experience.
14 Although, according to Macnamara and Boudewijnse (1995, 401) "in some recent textbooks on the history of psychology Ehrenfels's contribution fades almost to non-existence".
15 E.g. Mandler (2007, 114).
16 For a more detailed account, see Mulligan & Smith (1988).
17 The original text in German.

> Die Gestalt zweier geschlossener Gebiete ist gleich, wenn die Abstände der Grenzen, die in demselben Richtungsverhältnis zueinander stehen, proportional sind, d.h. wenn die Größenverhältnisse der Abstände der Grenzpunkte, die in demselben Richtungsverhältnis zueinander stehen, gleich sind. Man hat es auch hier mit Verhältnissen von Verhältnissen zu tun, ein Umstand, der es, was vielleicht zunächst überrascht, sogar erlauben dürfte, bei verallgemeinerten Begriffen von Winkel und Gestalt von einer wahren Gleichheit der Winkel und Gestalt auf ganz heterogenem Gebiet zu sprechen. Wäre die Zeit wirklich krumm und liefe gleichmäßig sich krümmend in sich zurück, so wäre sie wahrhaft und eigentlichst von gleicher Gestalt wie eine Kreislinie im Raume.

Ehrenfels did not attend this lecture course, though he must have heard Brentano's 1882 "*Alte und Neue Logik*" and transcriptions of lectures were widely copied and circulated within the school.

18 Meinong (1882, reprint in Haller et al. 1971).
19 The broader awareness of *Gestalt* phenomena in the School of Brentano is also underscored by the fact that Edmund Husserl, coming from the same background and having been likewise inspired by Mach and Meinong, also used the term *Gestaltmoment* for higher-order quasi-qualities independently from and possibly prior to Ehrenfels (Husserl 2005). Husserl then switched to "figural moment" in the 1891 *Philosophy of Arithmetic,* citing Ehrenfels's 1890 article only to remark on his priority and independence (Husserl 1891, 236; also see Ierna 2005, 2009). Yet, Husserl ultimately did

think they had both hit on the same phenomenon: "The further question regarding the origin of improper presentations of quantities led to the "quasi qualitative or figural" moments constituted by the "fusion" of the relations of the content, the same, that Von Ehrenfels, led by quite different problems, called *Gestalt*qualities in his well-known 1890 treatise" (Husserl 2002, 295).
20 The original text in German.

> Darum werden sich auf den verschiedensten Gebieten des Vorstellbaren Complexe auffinden lassen, welche gleichwol in ihren Verhältnissen eine deutlich wahrzunehmende Ähnlichkeit zeigen, so daß durch die Relation auch dem scheinbar Unvereinbarsten Einheit und Harmonie verliehen werden kann.

The first page number refers to the original handwritten manuscript of Ehrenfels's dissertation conserved at the archives of the Karl-Franzens-Universität Graz. The dissertation has now been published in Ierna 2017a.
21 Meinong (1891, 1899); compare Smith (1988b, 22). The 1891 article is actually an extensive review of and reaction to Ehrenfels's article.
22 Cf. Bentley (1902, 279), who uses "consolidating" and "consolidated" contents as translation.
23 On this, see Smith (1988b, 13).
24 See *The Monist*, Vol. 2, No. 1 (October 1891), 156–157.
25 See *The Monist*, Vol. 2, No. 2 (January 1892), 317. For the Brentanist philosophy of mathematics, including a discussion of Ehrenfels, see Ierna (2011).
26 Stout (1896, 65 and note), compare Van der Schaar (1996, 313) and Van der Schaar (2013, 131).
27 According to Arnheim (1961, 90), "It has given a name to one of the most characteristic schools of scientific thought in our time and thereby established its existence formally. It is responsible for the word "Gestalt" having acquired citizenship in the English language".
28 Including, but not limited to mathematics and the distribution of prime numbers, see Ehrenfels (1922a, reprint in Fabian 1988, 455–505).
29 Ehrenfels (1916, reprint in Fabian 1990, 69–230).
30 Compare Fabian (1986b, 44 f).
31 Compare Simons (1988, 160).
32 While keeping *Gestalt* untranslated is perhaps not very satisfactory, Focht's translations of "causal lines" and "configuration-sequences" is also quite awkward and obscures the relevant terminological connections.
33 Ehrenfels (1922b, reprint in Fabian 1990, 231–280).
34 Compare Brentano (1874, 7).
35 See also the contribution by Rollinger in this volume.
36 For a more extended discussion of Brentano's theory of judgement and its relation to logic, see Simons (1987, 2004). For a more detailed treatment of the topics addressed in this section, see Ierna 2017c.
37 And certainly by 1948, when Focht's translation of the *Cosmogony* appeared.

Bibliography

Albertazzi, Liliana, editor, 2001, *The Dawn of Cognitive Science. Early European Contributors*. Dordrecht: Kluwer.

Albertazzi, Liliana, Massimo Libardi, and Roberto Poli, editors, 1996, *The School of Franz Brentano*. Dordrecht: Kluwer.

Ameseder, Rudolf, 1904, "Beiträge zur Grundlegung der Gegenstandstheorie", in Meinong, Alexius, editor, *Untersuchungen zur Gegenstandstheorie und Psychologie*. Leipzig: Barth.

Arnheim, Rudolf, 1961, "*Gestalten* – Yesterday and Today", in Henle, Mary, editor, *Documents of Gestalt Psychology*. Berkeley and Los Angeles: University of California Press, 90–96.

Ash, Mitchell G., 1989, "Max Wertheimer's University Career in Germany", in *Psychological Research* 51, 52–57.

Baumgartner, Wilhelm, and Lynn Pasquerella, 2004, "Brentano's Value Theory: Beauty, Goodness, and the Concept of Correct Emotion", in Jacquette, 2004.

Benjamin, A. Cornelius, 1950, "Review of *Cosmogony*. By Christian Ehrenfels. Translated from the German by Mildred Focht", in *The Philosophical Review* 59:3 (July 1950), 389–391.

Benussi, Vittorio, 1904, "Zur Psychologie des Gestalterfassens (Die Müller-Lyersche Figur)", in Meinong, Alexius, editor, *Untersuchungen zur Gegenstandstheorie und Psychologie*. Leipzig: Barth.

Bentley, I. Madison, 1902, "The Psychology of Mental Arrangement", in *The American Journal of Psychology*, 13:2 (April 1902), 269–293.

Brentano, Franz, 1874, *Psychologie vom Empirischen Standpunkte*. Leipzig: Duncker & Humblot.

Brentano, Franz, 1884/85a, Ms. Y 2: *Die elementare Logik und die in ihr nötigen Reformen I*. Vienna: unpublished lecture notes from the Husserl-Archives Leuven.

Brentano, Franz, 1884/85b, Ms. Y 3: *Die elementare Logik und die in ihr nötigen Reformen II*. Vienna: unpublished lecture notes from the Husserl-Archives Leuven.

Brentano, Franz, 1889, *Vom Ursprung Sittlicher Erkenntnis*. Leipzig: Duncker & Humblot.

Brentano, Franz, 1907, *Untersuchungen zur Sinnespsychologie*. Leipzig: Duncker & Humblot.

Chisholm, Roderick, 1986, "Reflections on Ehrenfels and the Unity of Consciousness", in Fabian, 1986a, 136–149.

Dickinson, Edward, 2002, "Sex and the 'Yellow Peril': Christian von Ehrenfels' Program for the Revision of the European Sexual Order, 1902–1910", in *German Studies Review* 25:2, 255–284.

Dupuy, Jean-Pierre, 2009, *On the Origins of Cognitive Science: The Mechanization of the Mind*. Cambridge, MA: MIT Press.

Ehrenfels, Christian von, 1885, *Über Größenrelationen und Zahlen. Eine psychologische Studie*. Graz: original dissertation manuscript, conserved at the archives of the Karl-Franzens-Universität Graz, with a transcription by Reinhard Fabian, published in Ierna 2017a.

Ehrenfels, Christian von, 1887, *Über Fühlen und Wollen. Eine psychologische Studie*. Vienna: Kaiserliche Akademie der Wissenschaften, CXIV:II, 523–634.

Ehrenfels, Christian von, 1890, "Über 'Gestaltqualitäten'", in *Vierteljahrsschrift für wissenschaftliche Philosophie* 14, 249–292.

Ehrenfels, Christian von, 1891, "Zur Philosophie der Mathematik", in *Vierteljahrsschrift für wissenschaftliche Philosophie* 15, 285–347. (Reprint in Fabian 1988, 415–451).

Ehrenfels, Christian von, 1897, *System der Werttheorie. I Allgemeine Werttheorie, Psychologie des Begehrens*. Leipzig: Reisland.

Ehrenfels, Christian von, 1898a, *System der Werttheorie. II Grundzüge einer Ethik*. Leipzig: Reisland.

Ehrenfels, Christian von, 1898b, "Die Intensität der Gefühle: Eine Entgegnung auf Franz Brentano's neue Intensitätslehre", in *Zeitschrift für Psychologie und Physiologie der Sinnesorgane* 16, 49–70.
Ehrenfels, Christian von, 1916, *Kosmogonie*. Jena: Dietrichs.
Ehrenfels, Christian von, 1922a, *Das Primzahlengesetz, entwickelt und dargestellt auf Grund der Gestalttheorie*. Leipzig : Reisland.
Ehrenfels, Christian von, 1922b, "Gedanken über die Religion der Zukunft" (8 articles), in *Prager Presse* 23 April, 7/14 May, 28 May, 4 June, 18 June, 2 July, 16 July, 27 August 1922.
Ehrenfels, Christian von, 1948, *Cosmogony*, Focht, Mildred, translator. New York: The CometPress.
Epstein, William, and Gary Hatfield, 1994, "Gestalt Psychology and the Philosophy of Mind", in *Philosophical Psychology* 7:2, 163–181.
Fabian, Reinhard, editor, 1986a, *Christian von Ehrenfels: Leben und Werk*. Amsterdam/Atlanta: Rodopi.
Fabian, Reinhard, 1986b, "Leben und Wirken von Christian v. Ehrenfels. Ein Beitrag zur intellektuellen Biographie" in Fabian, 1986a, 1–64.
Fabian, Reinhard, editor, 1988, *Christian von Ehrenfels Philosophische Schriften III: Psychologie, Ethik, Erkenntnistheorie*. Munich/Vienna: Philosophia.
Fabian, Reinhard, editor, 1990, *Christian von Ehrenfels Philosophische Schriften IV: Metaphysik*. Munich/Vienna: Philosophia.
Fabian, Reinhard, 1996, "Christian von Ehrenfels", in Albertazzi et al., 1996.
Haller, Rudolf, Rudolf Kindinger, and Roderick Chisholm, editors, 1971, *Alexius Meinong Gesamtausgabe*. Graz: Akademische Druck- und Verlagsgesellschaft.
Heinämaa, Sara, 2009, "Phenomenological Responses to Gestalt Psychology", in Heinämaa, Sara and Reuter, Martina, editors, *Psychology and Philosophy. Inquiries into the Soul from Late Scholasticism to Contemporary Thought*. Dordrecht: Springer, 263–284.
Husserl, Edmund, 1891, *Philosophie der Arithmetik*. Halle-Saale: Pfeffer-Stricker.
Husserl, Edmund, 2002, *Logische Untersuchungen (Ergänzungsband: Erster Teil)*. Melle, Ullrich, editor, Husserliana XX/1. Dordrecht: Kluwer.
Husserl, Edmund, 2005, "Lecture on the Concept of Number (WS 1889/1890)", ed. & tr. Ierna, Carlo, in *The New Yearbook for Phenomenology and Phenomenological Philosophy* 5, 278–309.
Ierna, Carlo, 2005, "The Beginnings of Husserl's Philosophy (Part 1: From *Über den Begriff der Zahl* to *Philosophie der Arithmetik*)", in *The New Yearbook for Phenomenology and Phenomenological Philosophy* V, 1–56.
Ierna, Carlo, 2009, "Husserl et Stumpf sur la Gestalt et la fusion", in *Philosophiques* 36/2, 489–510.
Ierna, Carlo, 2011, "Brentano and Mathematics", in *Revue Roumaine de Philosophie* 55/1, 149–167.
Ierna, Carlo, 2014, "La science de la conscience selon Brentano", in Niveleau, Charles-Edouard, editor, *Vers une philosophie scientifique. Le programme de Brentano*. Paris: Démopolis, pp. 51–69.
Ierna, Carlo, editor, 2017a, "Christian von Ehrenfels, *Über Größenrelationen und Zahlen. Eine psychologische Studie*", in *Meinong Studies* 8, pp. 185–234.
Ierna, Carlo, 2017b, "On Ehrenfels' Dissertation", in *Meinong Studies* 8, pp. 163–184.
Ierna, Carlo, 2017c, "Die Gestalten und das Gestalten der Welt", in *Meinong Studies* 8, pp. 53–68.

Ierna, Carlo, and Robin Rollinger, 2015, "Christian von Ehrenfels", in Zalta, Edward, editor, *The Stanford Encyclopedia of Philosophy*. Stanford: The Metaphysics Research Lab.
Jacquette, Dale, editor, 2004, *The Cambridge Companion to Brentano*. Cambridge: Cambridge University Press.
King, D. Brett, and Michael Wertheimer, 2005, *Max Wertheimer and Gestalt Theory*. New Brunswick, NJ: Transaction Publishers.
Köhler, Wolfgang, 1961, "Gestalt Psychology Today", in Henle, Mary, editor, *Documents of Gestalt Psychology*. Berkeley and Los Angeles: University of California Press.
Mach, Ernst, 1886, *Beiträge zur Analyse der Empfindungen*. Jena: Gustav Fischer.
Macnamara, John, and Geert-Jan Boudewijnse, 1995, "Brentano's Influence on Ehrenfels's Theory of Perceptual Gestalts", in *Journal for the Theory of Social Behaviour* 25.4, 401–418.
Mandler, George, 2007, *A History of Modern Experimental Psychology From James and Wundt to Cognitive Science*. Cambridge, MA: MIT Press.
Marty, Anton, 1892, "Anzeige von William James: *The Principles of Psychology*", in *Zeitschrift für Psychologie und Physiologie der Sinnesorgane* 3, 297–333.
Meinong, Alexius, 1882, "Hume Studien II. Zur Relationstheorie", in *Sitzungsberichte der philosophisch-historischen Klasse der Kaiserlichen Akademie der Wissenschaften in Wien*, Band 101, Wien, 573–752.
Meinong, Alexius, 1891, "Zur Psychologie der Komplexionen und Relationen", in *Zeitschrift für Psychologie und Physiologie der Sinnesorgane* II, 245–265.
Meinong, Alexius, 1899, "Über Gegenstände höherer Ordnung und deren Verhältnis zur inneren Wahrnehmung", in *Zeitschrift für Psychologie und Physiologie der Sinnesorgane* XXI, 182–272.
Mulligan, Kevin, and Barry Smith, 1988, "Mach and Ehrenfels: The Foundations of Gestalt Theory", in Smith, 1988a, 124–157.
Rollinger, Robin, 1999, *Husserl's Position in the School of Brentano*, Phaenomenologica 150, Dordrecht: Kluwer.
Simons, Peter, 1987, "Brentano's Reform of Logic", in *Topoi* 6, 25–38.
Simons, Peter, 1988, "Gestalt and Functional Dependence", in Smith, 1988a, 158–190.
Simons, Peter, 2004, "Judging Correctly: Brentano and the Reform of Elementary Logic", in Jacquette, 2004, 45–65.
Smith, Barry, editor, 1988a, *Foundations of Gestalt Theory*. Munich/Vienna: Philosophia.
Smith, Barry, 1988b, "Gestalt Theory: An Essay in Philosophy", in *Foundations of Gestalt Theory*. Munich/Vienna: Philosophia, 11–81.
Smith, Barry, 1994, *Austrian Philosophy: The Legacy of Franz Brentano*. Chicago and Lasalle, IL: Open Court.
Stout, George Frederick, 1896, *Analytic Psychology*, London: Swan Sonnenschein.
Stumpf, Carl, 1883, *Tonpsychologie*. Vol. 1. Leipzig: Hirzel.
Van der Schaar, Maria, 1996, "From Analytic Psychology to Analytic Philosophy: The Reception of Twardowski's Ideas in Cambridge", in *Axiomathes* 3, December 1996, 295–324.
Van der Schaar, Maria, 2013, *G.F. Stout and the Psychological Origins of Analytic Philosophy*. New York: Palgrave Macmillan.
Toccafondi, Fiorenza, 2009, "Stumpf and Gestalt Psychology: Relations and Differences", in *Gestalt Theory* 31:2, 191–211.

Wildgen, Wolfgang, 2001, "Kurt Lewin and the Rise of 'Cognitive Sciences' in Germany: Cassirer, Bühler, Reichenbach", in Albertazzi, Liliana, editor, *The Dawn of Cognitive Science. Early European Contributors*. Dordrecht: Kluwer, 299–332.

Zigler, M. J., 1920, "An Experimental Study of Visual Form", in *The American Journal of Psychology* 31:3 (July 1920), 273–300.

Zimmer, Alfred, 2001, "Christian von Ehrenfels", in Albertazzi, Liliana, Dale Jacquette, and Roberto Poli, editors, *The School of Alexius Meinong*. Aldershot: Ashgate, 135–143.

13

EDMUND HUSSERL

From intentionality to transcendental phenomenology

Paul M. Livingston

In his 1874 *Psychology from an Empirical Standpoint*, Franz Brentano, resurrecting medieval terminology, famously defined *intentionality*, or *directedness toward an object or content*, as the characteristic and defining feature of the "mental":

> Every mental phenomenon is characterized by what the Scholastics of the Middle Ages called the intentional (or mental) inexistence of an object, and what we might call, though not wholly unambiguously, reference to a content, direction toward an object (which is not to be understood here as meaning a thing), or immanent objectivity. Every mental phenomenon includes something as object within itself, although they do not all do so in the same way. In presentation something is presented, in judgement something is affirmed or denied, in love loved, in hate hated, in desire desired and so on.
> This intentional in-existence is characteristic exclusively of mental phenomena. No physical phenomenon exhibits anything like it. We can, therefore, define mental phenomena by saying that they are those phenomena which contain an object intentionally within themselves.
> (Brentano 1874[1995]: 88–89)

On Brentano's view, mental phenomena are thus universally characterized by intentional directedness. This directedness or reference is also understood as the phenomenon's "immanent objectivity," its "includ[ing] something as object within itself." Despite the diversity of the activities and states of our mental life, including perception, judgment, and imagination, as well as emotional states such as love and hate, all of them can thus be structurally understood in terms of this directedness toward "something" that is the object or content of the relevant act in each case.

Thirty-nine years later, in his 1913 "General Introduction to Pure Phenomenology", the first book of his *Ideas Pertaining to a Pure Phenomenology and to a Phenomenological Philosophy*, Edmund Husserl would articulate the "principle of all principles" underlying the systematic theory and *praxis* of "transcendental" phenomenology:

> No conceivable theory can make us err with respect to the *principle of all principles: that every originary presentive intuition is a legitimizing source of cognition*, that *everything originarily* (so to speak, in its 'personal' actuality) *offered* to us *in 'intuition' is to be accepted simply as what it is presented as being*, but also *only within the limits in which it is presented there*. We see indeed that each <theory> can only again draw its truth itself from originary data. Every statement which does no more than confer expression on such data by simple explication and by means of significations precisely conforming to them is . . . actually an *absolute beginning* called upon to serve as a foundation, a *principium* in the genuine sense of the word.
>
> (Husserl 1913[1983]: 43–44).

In this essay, I trace the development of Husserl's project over the last years of the nineteenth century, following its trajectory from his teacher's resurrection of the idea of intentionality to the guiding principle of "legitimizing" presentation articulated in *Ideas*. As we shall see, this development would lead Husserl to augment or wholly replace many of the most central elements of Brentano's own method in *Psychology from an Empirical Standpoint* on the way to his understanding of "pure" or "transcendental" phenomenology as a comprehensive foundation for philosophical and scientific research. As Husserl comes to understand it, phenomenology is not primarily a "psychological" method, nor is it essentially "empirical", and it by no means limits itself, in the scope of its systematic study of phenomena, to those which Brentano would have characterized as "mental". Nevertheless, Husserl's development of it can be understood as a direct outcome of his consideration of the consequences of one central and guiding idea from Brentano, namely the idea that what is distinctive of mental states is the intentional *presentation* of their objects.[1]

Over the course of his career, and in considering diverse subject matters ranging from mathematics and logic, to ontology, semantics, and the theory of value, Husserl adds at least three crucial ideas to Brentano's conception of intentionality. First, he draws the essential distinction among *modes* or *ways* of presenting or being presented that leads him, in the quotation earlier, to seek a source for all "legitimating" cognition in *intuition* – or the "proper", "direct", or "authentic" *having* of a (presented) object or phenomenon. Second, he develops a new conception of the "evidence" with which intuitive acts thus give their objects, and a correlative conception of the possibility that we can know these acts *themselves* in reflecting on them. And third, he develops an idea of the truth and validity of a *theory* as such, according to which such truth and validity always depends ultimately upon the intuitive and evidential givenness of the theory's objects. With this, as we shall see, Husserl was able to develop the idea of phenomenology as a foundational discipline, exhibiting, on the one hand, the universality and objectivity of logic, and on the other, the concern with the phenomena of consciousness that already characterized psychology in its Brentanian and other early forms.

1. Brentano and the *Philosophy of Arithmetic*

When Brentano described intentionality as the characteristic feature of mental phenomena, he also invoked an exhaustive distinction between these phenomena and what he called "physical" ones. The distinction as Brentano uses it, however, does not correspond to the distinction between mind and matter or indeed to any familiar mental/physical distinction. Brentano gives as examples of mental phenomena acts of perception, as well as judgments, recollections, inferences, etc. Physical phenomena, on the other hand, are (for instance) "a color, a figure, a landscape which I see, a chord which I hear, warmth, cold, odor which I sense; as well as similar images which appear in the imagination" (Brentano 1874[1995]: 79–80). The basis for the distinction is that "mental" phenomena are always *presentations*, or phenomena "based on" presentations, in the sense of *acts* of presenting (rather than the content or object presented), whereas physical phenomena need not be; given this, Brentano argued, mental phenomena could be known by means of "inner perception", whereby they could be perceived with "immediate" and certain "evidence", whereas "physical phenomena", as merely intentional objects, do not possess "actual existence" at all, and thus are believed to exist only as the result of a highly dubious "blind compulsion" (Brentano 1874[1995]: 97–98). Hence, what it means for an intentional object to be "objective" is no more (and no less) than that it is effectively *presented* in consciousness.

Brentanian psychology played a crucial role in Husserl's early work in the philosophy of mathematics. In *Philosophy of Arithmetic* (Husserl 1891[2003]), Husserl's first book, the task as Husserl conceives of it is to clarify the "psychological constitution" of concepts having to do with quantities, including the concepts of number, unity, and multiplicity. He assumed that he would thus illuminate the psychological basis of enumeration, numerical judgment, and arithmetic calculation (Husserl 1891[2003]: 14). The first part of the book offers an analysis of presentations of *multiplicities* or groups (Husserl 1891[2003]: 16). Roughly, on Husserl's account, the concept of multiplicity is the product of a twofold process: (i) a kind of abstraction on particular groups followed by (ii) a reflection on the *differences* between members of such groups that produces what Husserl takes to be the "schematic forms" of (at least the smallest) whole numbers (Husserl 1891[2003]: 18–22; 52–57). This process, however, presupposes the *unity* of the group or multiplicity presented, and Husserl thought he needed to account for the latter. What binds the elements of an arbitrary group in such a way that they can be counted at all? Part of Husserl's answer relies on Brentano's distinction between "physical" and "mental" (or "psychical") phenomena. According to Brentano, relations between physical phenomena are relations between the *objects* presented rather than between the *presentations* of these objects, i.e. the mental acts of which they are the content. In the case of "psychical" phenomena, on the other hand, the relation is purely psychological in the sense that its terms are the mental acts themselves: for example, the kind of "combination" that occurs when several contents are united as the subject matter of a unitary act of judgment is one such "psychical" relationship (Husserl 1891[2003]: 72). Husserl then argues that when we combine "things" into arbitrary totalities that can be counted – what Husserl takes to be the psychological basis for concept of number – we rely on the second type of relation, i.e. a relation between mental phenomena. The decisive consideration here is the complete *arbitrariness* of the things that can be grouped together into a determinate multitude and counted. For instance, it is possible to form a presentation of the plurality composed of *redness*, *the moon*, and *Napolean*, counting them as three, although these are (as "primary contents") obviously completely diverse presentations (Husserl 1891[2003]: 77).[2] On Husserl's account the "generic concept" of (cardinal) number rests on the concept of an arbitrary multiplicity, and the concept of multiplicity in turn rests on the general concept of an arbitrary "something" which permits the formation of the number concepts as "one", or "one and one", or "one and one and one," and so on (Husserl 1891[2003]: 84–85).

This argument which is developed in part I of *The Philosophy of Arithmetic*, is meant to explain, using the resources of Brentanian psychology, how number concepts can be (as he puts it) "authentically" presented. Husserl distinguishes between presentations whose objects, in this case a multitude, can themselves be presented to consciousness directly and merely "symbolic" presentations. Husserl needs the latter concept if he is to make sense of most of mathematics, since most of mathematics relies on number-presentations and concepts of numerical operations which are *not* given authentically (Husserl 1891[2003]: 191). These are, for instance, presentations of larger numbers and of the infinite, as well as the general techniques of arithmetic *calculation*, which have algorithmically unlimited scope. In calculating with these numbers, Husserl argues, the mathematician does not work with the concepts of the corresponding multitudes themselves as they are authentically given. Rather, she works with *symbolic* presentations, presentations that make essential use of signs to present (in an "inauthentic" but nevertheless determinate manner) the concepts of the corresponding magnitudes.

For Husserl, the development and practice of arithmetic as a calculative technique rests ultimately on the symbolic presentations of an unlimited number system that itself allows the construction of unlimited new number concepts (1891[2003]: 247). This construction is a "logical technique" which Husserl says – like all "logical technique" – overcomes the natural limitations of our mental abilities by constructing the signs for numbers systematically and in rigorous "logical" parallel to the conceptual formations for which they stand (Husserl

1891[2003]: 248, 252, 287). With this, it also becomes possible to develop the concepts and symbolization of higher types of operations, for instance algebraic ones such as exponentiation. However, in order for the results to underwrite a complete theory of "symbolic number determinations," Husserl concludes by acknowledging, it would be necessary to develop (in addition to the theory of the symbolic presentation of whole numbers developed here) not only a logical theory of the symbolism of other types of numbers (for instance negative, fractional, and real ones) but indeed a general "logical" technical theory of all possible operations, allowing *all* unknown quantities (that could nevertheless be symbolized) to be "calculated out at any time" (Husserl 1891[2003]: 299). The execution of such a theory still lies very much in the future for the author of the *Philosophy of Arithmetic*, and the reader is referred to a second book of the work which in fact never appeared. But the idea nevertheless captures what would later come to be known as *completeness*, a feature to which, as he argues, all "logical techniques" as such essentially aspire (Husserl 1891[2003]: 236).[3]

With this account of the basis of number concepts and the technique of arithmetic in authentic and inauthentic presentation, Husserl thus develops an account of their "psychological constitution". What's interesting about Husserl's psychological theory is that it needs to be complemented by an account of the recursive *techniques* by virtue of which they can be extended beyond the finite limitations of our actual presentative abilities. In this sense, Husserl's psychology needs his logic. Both the psychology and the logic, however, liberally draw on the idea of intentional *presentation* that Husserl inherits from Brentano: both the reflective acts of abstraction that generate the concepts of small numbers, and the regular symbolism that allows the construction of arbitrarily large ones, are understood essentially as *acts* of presentation to consciousness. What appears problematic about this conception, though, is the fact that it seems to compromise the apparent *objectivity* of judgments about number, at least if the objectivity of judgment is a matter of its truth being independence from psychology or the activities of any individual subject.

This objection was, at any rate, at the basis of Gottlob Frege's highly critical and often acerbic 1894 review of Husserl's work (Frege 1894[1972]). In his own *Foundations of Arithmetic*, published 10 years earlier, Frege had conceived of judgments about number and arithmetic as judgments about objective matters, existing in themselves and quite independently of any human subjectivity. Seeking a purely logical basis for the definition of number, Frege objects strenuously to the "psychologistic" logicians who, denying this objectivity or neglecting it, instead explain number and logic in terms of psychological processes, subjective phenomena, or internal presentations. In the review, Frege objects particularly to the tendency evident in Husserl's account whereby "everything becomes presentation" (Frege 1894[1972]: 323–324). Frege argues that Husserl's account of the presentational basis for small numbers in presented totalities or groups involves, contradictorily, that the items that make up these totalities be presented both as *distinct* (in order to be countable) and also (in some sense) *the same* (in order to be unified in the presentation of the counted totality itself). Husserl can sustain the apparently contradictory position only by appealing to the psychological activity of abstraction, whereby (on Husserl's account as Frege reads it) one can retain the distinctness of the objects themselves while nevertheless "cleansing" them of all "bothersome particularities and differences" (Frege 1894[1972]: 323). This has the effect of completely blurring the distinction between presentations and the objects they present, as well as insinuating that the act of abstraction, when performed on the presentation of a totality, is somehow itself capable of changing what is presented itself (Frege 1894[1972]: 324). Finally, Frege objects on similar grounds to Husserl's account, in part II of *The Philosophy of Arithmetic*, of the symbolic presentations purportedly characteristic of arithmetic calculation generally and running in logical parallel to the corresponding "real" presentations. What goes missing in this account, Frege suggests, is exactly the objects that either kind of presentations would be presentations *of*: the "very thing" that we indeed seek to present to ourselves either in real or symbolic forms (Frege 1894[1972]: 336).

As we shall see in more detail below, Husserl's *Logical Investigations* of 1900–1901 begins with a "Prolegomena to Pure Logic" that aims to clarify the idea of pure logic in part by means of a strong and univocal critique of psychologism about logic. And Husserl would himself later repudiate the *Philosophy of Arithmetic* as an immature work, not yet reflecting his "breakthrough" to the proper methods of phenomenological analysis and clarification. These two facts have often produced the impression that Frege's review was decisive in producing Husserl's anti-psychologistic position in the *Logical Investigations*; in fact, though, as some recent commentary has emphasized, matters are significantly more complicated than this.[4] First, Husserl sought to give an account only of the "psychological constitution" of number concepts and the technique of arithmetic. Such an account is "psychologistic" in a sense that is objectionable from a Fregean perspective only if it attempts to *reduce* logic or numbers themselves to psychological acts or activities, and it is not clear (despite the admitted existence of some suggestions in this direction) that Husserl intended to perform either of these two types of reduction.[5] Second, as we have seen, the "psychological constitution" of basic number concepts is here attributed to their formation in relation to everyday judgments about groups, and these judgments (as Husserl sometimes indeed emphasizes) have important "logical" aspects related to their possible truth as well as simply psychological ones. Logic is itself treated as a regular *technique* of extending these judgments by means of symbolism, a technique which is not to be understood simply in terms of the idiosyncratic activity of any individual reasoner. While Husserl, in this early work, certainly does not always distinguish clearly enough the logical and the psychological aspects of his account of what is involved in number judgments and calculations, many aspects of it are not clearly "psychologistic" in the sense to which Frege objects. Finally, and most decisively for the future of his development of the phenomenological method, it is noteworthy that Husserl never, even in the context of his later repudiation of the project of his early work, abandons the central idea of clarifying the sense and structure of phenomena by means of a consideration of intentional *presentation*. In fact, the conception which Frege repudiates as committing a devastating and theoretically fatal confusion of psychological act with object presented is not at all abandoned, but rather strengthened, universalized and articulated in vastly more theoretical detail (and indeed in a way broadly consistent with Frege's own arguments against psychologism) in Husserl's subsequent work.

2. 1889–1895: development of presentation, intuition, and content

In an 1889 letter to Brentano, amidst praise of his teacher and his work on "descriptive psychology", Husserl alludes to the difficulties that still remained for him in developing, as he still hoped to do, a general theory of arithmetic on the basis of the idea of presenting (Husserl 1889[2015]: 71). At the time he wrote the letter, Husserl still anticipated completing the work of a general theory of arithmetic, including all varieties of number and an analysis of the continuum. But this "arithmetica universalis" never appeared, and already in the letter Husserl here expresses a degree of doubt as to whether Brentano's distinction between proper (or "authentic") and improper ("symbolic") presentation is itself adequate to the task. Whether for this reason or for reasons relating to the developments being made of Brentano's views by other prominent students of his (including Stumpf, Meinong, and Twardowski), Husserl would soon develop the theory of presentation further by introducing a number of key distinctions, going beyond those suggested by Brentano himself, about the content, objects, and internal structure of the varieties of intentional acts.

In the 1894 article "Psychological Studies in the Elements of Logic" (Husserl 1894[1994]), Husserl begins by noting that presentational acts of consciousness have, in general, a *complex* structure that can be further explicated in terms of a distinction between their *independent* and *dependent* parts (or "moments"). For example, a presentation of a *perceptible thing* (such as a table or house) has a kind of "natural" unity, such that its parts or aspects can be varied imaginatively while it still retains its identity (for instance, one can imaginatively vary its colors, or imagine it as somewhat smaller or larger than it actually is). This is not so, however, for other kinds of intuitable contents, such as the colors or shapes themselves: here variation of this kind suffices to destroy the identity of the intuited particular (Husserl 1894[1994]: 139). Husserl puts the point by characterizing the first kind of content as exhibiting a kind of "independence" of its elements, whereas the second kind does not. Moreover, where contents are "dependent" on other contents in this sense, variation in the latter *necessarily* alters the former, and it is possible, Husserl suggests, to be aware of this necessary connection. The necessity of such linked variation of aspects of contents can furthermore be fully (self-)"evident", in the sense that its distinction from any kind of contingent or causal relation is itself directly apparent to consciousness (Husserl 1894[1994]: 140–142). With this in view, it is also possible, Husserl argues, to clarify the distinction between the "abstract" and the "concrete" in terms of the distinction between dependent and independent parts of presentations generally (Husserl 1894[1994]: 144–147).

In the second part of the essay, Husserl seeks further to clarify the structure of presentations by considering the ways in which they "give" their objects, with varying degrees and kinds of evidence or fullness. Here, he introduces a second crucial distinction, that between the actually *intuited* content of a presentation and its broader "intended, complete content" (Husserl 1894[1994]: 149). Whereas every intentional presentation has, as such, a full content in the sense of the totality of what it intends (or presents, in one sense of the term), it is generally only a very limited part of this full content that is actually "given" in the sense of intuition, or of a proper and direct "having" of the presented *object* itself. The distinction is perhaps clearest in the case of perception. When, in the course of life, we take ourselves to perceive an ordinary object, say a tree, we presuppose and envision the total content of our intentional act as intending the full object itself as it exists independently of us and outside our own consciousness. However, what we actually *intuit*, at any particular moment, in a direct way is much more limited: it is only an aspect of the object from one viewpoint, under particular light conditions, at a particular time, etc. (Husserl 1894[1994]: 149–150). The full or complete content of the intentional act thus *intends* more than is in fact *fulfilled* by actual intuitive "having". In the flow of our temporal experience of a perceived thing, our intuitions tend successively to "fulfill" the intended content more and more, but do not ever give the thing itself in its *complete* fullness and with complete evidence. By contrast with presentation by means of images, signs, or concepts, intuition is thus to be understood as "setting before" us directly something in an "authentic sense", whereby this setting forth itself provides the substrate for the mental act (rather than the opposite relation, which rather characterizes non-intuitive presentation) (Husserl 1894[1994]: 150). The distinction resembles the one between "authentic" and "symbolic" presentations that Husserl had earlier drawn from Brentano. But it is not the same distinction, for here it is not a question of distinguishing merely symbolic presentations that go proxy for their objects from those that actually present these objects themselves. Rather, the idea of a presentation that goes beyond what it actually "gives" is here applied to intentional presentations generally, including not only conceptual ones but *also* most elements and aspects of the "content" of perceptual experience itself. With the distinction as he develops it in 1894, Husserl can accordingly distinguish much more clearly between the "content" of an intentional act in general, on the one hand, and what it actually *presents*, in the sense of authentic intuition, on the other. Accordingly, Husserl no longer runs together, as he and Brentano both earlier had, the "content" and the "object" of an intentional act generally. Rather, it is possible in each case to distinguish the "content" in the sense of the maximal and total intention – what is *meant* in the intentional act as a whole and as such – from the (typically much more limited and sometimes non-existent) "object" that it actually intuitively gives (Husserl 1894[1994]: 151).

These distinctions, and especially the last one, are at the center of the conception of "intentional objects" that Husserl develops in the posthumously published 1894–1895 article of the same name (Husserl 1895[1994]). Here, Husserl takes up a problem about the existence of the objects of intentional or presentational states that had been noted as early as 1837 by Bolzano, and would (with decisive consequences for the development of what became called the "analytic" tradition) be taken up a few years later by Russell, responding to Meinong.[6] This is the problem of "so-called objectless presentations" – presentations, that is, which apparently "present" an object that does not exist, including both possible but nonexistent objects such as "the present King of France" and impossible ones such as a "round square." Such presentations have a determinate sense and appear to attribute specific properties to something to which they seemingly therefore correspond. But if we then indeed treat them as having objects, we almost immediately fall into the contradiction that these objects are said at once to exist and not to exist. (Husserl 1895[1994]: 347). Husserl considers a line of approach to the problem that had recently been attempted by Twardowski and is also closely connected (Husserl says) with Brentano's own approach. This is to ascribe to the "objects" of presentation a kind of "merely intentional" existence that consists simply in "mere being-represented." Although such "intentional" existence is, on this picture, a *kind* of existence (as it were, "immanent" existence in the presentation), it falls short, on this view, of the "true" existence that is asserted of something in an affirmative existential judgment about it. The problematic objects apparently referred to by presentations such as "round square" can then be treated as "merely intentional" existents in this sense (Husserl (1895[1994]: 349–350).

Armed with the distinctions he had worked out about the content and objects of intentional acts, Husserl finds this conception, however, wholly untenable. First, he says, if the object of a presentation is *literally* contained within it, or immanent to it, then the existence of the object is every bit as genuine as that of the presentation itself. There is then no good reason to "downgrade" it and regard it as only a "modified", non-genuine, or second-class existence (Husserl (1895[1994]: 351). When contents *are* in fact immanent to conscious presentations, they are *just as such* existences in the full and unmodified sense of the term. For instance, if I am able to focus on a color and *intuitively* present it to myself, then this color exists every bit as much as anything in the world. But second and most decisively, although there is admittedly a sense in which an impossible object such as a "round square" can be said to be *intended* in a presentation according to its content, to say so is *in no sense* to acknowledge the actual or even possible existence of such an object. For it is in no way possible to maintain that such an object could *ever* be *intuitively* given "in," or with, the presentation itself. Indeed, Husserl emphasizes that the generalities of logic and mathematics, which establish (for instance) the incompatibility of squareness and roundness, are indeed *full* generalities, and as such should not and cannot be denied for the purposes of a (putatively) special domain of "merely intentional" existents. For these generalities, after all, "take no cognizance of the distinction between that which occurs and is valid within the subjective lived experiences of men and that which otherwise occurs and is valid in the world" (Husserl (1895[1994]: 352).

With this, Husserl clearly and decisively rejects Brentano's way of talking of the general intentional "inexistence" of objects in intentional acts. Whereas acts may indeed have the intuitive giving of real objects as (some of) their real immanent parts, there is no good reason to suppose that presentations in general "contain" the objects corresponding to the contents they present. What, though, is then the sense of talking of these "contents" themselves? What is meant by saying that something is "presented" in a presentation is, Husserl suggests, not indeed that that "something" exists in any sense, but that the presentation has an *ideal* content that involves its being *just this* presentation (Husserl (1895[1994]: 353). This possession of a content is a matter, Husserl argues, of the *logical* rather than the *psychological* function and structure of the presentation itself. Seen this way, the logical "content" of the presentation is understood in terms of its possible application to objective situations and states of affairs, and not in terms of any aspect of its psychological structure as lived or experienced act. Indeed, it is reasonable to assume that one and the same content (in the *logical* sense) can be shared by a number of distinct acts which have little or nothing *psychologically* in common (Husserl (1895[1994]: 353). From this perspective, Husserl argues, it is now possible to develop a systematic account of the *general logical* laws and relations that govern thought in *any* possible domain and without respect to specific existential assumptions. Assertions involving names for seemingly nonexistent objects, such as "Zeus is the highest of Olympian gods", are to be seen as actually having the structure of *hypothetical* judgments premised on the corresponding existential assertion (i.e., that of the existence of Zeus) or on the assertion of the truth of the relevant (perhaps fictional or mythological) context (Husserl (1895[1994]: 357–359).[7] Transformed in this way, these judgments can now be seen as not, in fact, "about" the (seeming) objects, but rather "about" the contents of presentations, and as such governed by the *general* logical laws that govern all inference and deduction in any domain whatsoever (Husserl (1895[1994]: 362–364). For example, the judgment seemingly "about" Zeus does not require Zeus himself as an object, but is simply understood as relating the *content* of the claims of Greek mythology to what they logically entail. Neither these claims nor their logical consequences are treated as true, but *that they have* the logical consequences they do is a legitimate matter for purely *logical* investigation. With this, the logical laws governing objective contents take on once more the generality that characterizes, for instance, axioms in mathematics. Moreover, it is possible to consider the articulation of logical contents through their consequences to hold with full generality, as having the formal scope of the (one) world, in general, without restriction to particular domains or to the condition of the assumed existence of *any* contingent existence at all (Husserl (1895[1994]: 363).[8]

3. The *Logical Investigations* (1900–1901)

Over the course of the 1890s, Husserl thus developed the idea of intentional presentation by means of a series of articulating distinctions that also provide the basis for clarifying the relationship between content and object, the presentational basis of evidence and of knowledge, the objectivity of logical content, and the relationship between psychology and logic. These articulations would provide many of the most significant elements of the structure and method of the work that Husserl termed, in its second (1913) edition, his "break-through" to the project of phenomenology, the *Logical Investigations* of 1900–1901 (Husserl 1913[1970]: 43). In the introduction to the second volume of the *Investigations*, Husserl describes the task of a "pure phenomenology of the experiences of thinking and knowing" as exclusively concerned with "experiences intuitively seizable and analysable in the pure generality of their essence" (Husserl 1913[1970]: 249). Thus understood, Husserl says, pure phenomenology is a field of "neutral researches" standing at the root of various distinct sciences. On the one hand, it is an "ancillary" to psychology conceived as an empirical science, proceeding by means of an intuitive clarification of the *essential content* of those experiences, especially those of "presentation, judgement and cognition" which empirical psychology treats rather as "real events in the natural context of zoological reality" (Husserl 1913[1970]: 249).[9] On the other, in "laying bare" the underlying *sources* for the concepts and ideal laws of pure logic, phenomenology grounds both a proper "understanding" and an "epistemological critique" of pure logic itself, on which all "objective meaning" and the "theoretical unity of all cognition" ultimately depend (Husserl 1913[1970]: 249–250).

As Husserl further explains in the first volume of the *Logical Investigations*, titled "Prolegomena to Pure Logic," the idea of such a "pure" logic thus takes into consideration not only the narrower concerns of a formal symbolism or a logical calculus, but also the more "epistemological" issues concerning the intuitive basis of cognition, the "semantic" issues concerning the general forms of possible *meanings* and *senses*, and the ultimately "metaphysical" question of the most general categories of objectivity, categories such as "Object, State of Affairs, Unity, Plurality, Number, Relation, Connection, etc." (Husserl 1913[1970]: 237). The idea of a pure logic is thus, Husserl suggests drawing on ideas suggested by Leibniz and Bolzano, that of a *mathesis universalis* or pure theory of the unitary *form* of any possible objective theory as such (Husserl 1913[1970]: 218–220, 223–224, 234–236). The idea of such a pure theory of theories itself points to a series of interrelated maximally general and formal concepts of meaning, truth, evidence, and objectivity, and the task of phenomenology with respect to these is to track down the actual "origins" of these concepts in phenomenologically clarified experience, including above all their basis in actually *intuitive* presentation (Husserl 1913[1970]: 237–238).

The "Prolegomena" as a whole seek to clarify the idea of such a general theory of theories by way of an argument in two main parts. The first and larger part is primarily negative, directed critically against psychologism, historicism, and empiricism about logic. Husserl begins by considering the sense in which logic is "normative", governing how we *should* think or reason rather than how we actually *do* think, and concludes that this ideal normativity demands that we must separate the concern of logic from any species of *causal* relation or process. Nevertheless, logic as characterized by this kind of normativity is not to be conceived simply as a kind of technique – here Husserl rejects the conception of logic as a method for extending human cognition beyond its natural limitations that he had advanced in *Philosophy of Arithmetic* – but rather as grounded in a prior *theoretical* discipline that is actually descriptive, the pure "theory of theories" itself (Husserl 1913[1970]: 87–89). Husserl proceeds to give a battery of more or less devastating arguments against psychologism in various forms. A first argument turns on the normative status of logic itself: since psychology concerns itself with, at most, causal regularities, it has nothing to say to account for the basis of this normativity, and thus cannot be a foundation for logic (Husserl 1913[1970]: 92–93). More strongly and decisively, however, the results of psychological analysis and explanation can only ever be known inductively, and as such are only probable and cannot be known with certainty. The laws of logic can, however, be so known (Husserl 1913[1970]: 101–102). Even more generally, psychological logicians have confused the laws of logic themselves – which govern the field of possible *contents* rather than that of possible *acts* – with the acts of judgment in which we come to know them (Husserl 1913[1970]: 102–103). The ultimate result of this confusion can only be, Husserl goes on to argue, a subjective and "skeptical" relativism about logic itself Husserl 1913[1970]: 135–138; 145–147). For psychologism, in treating the laws of logic as conditioned by the *empirical* and *factual* conditions under which they are known by individual subjects, treats them as *relative* to these very facts. In this, subjectivist psychologism is ultimately self-refuting in that it denies the very (universal and objective) conditions for the existence and meaningfulness of any content-bearing theory whatsoever (Husserl 1913[1970]: 135–139).

In drawing the distinction between psychology and logic in the specific way that he does here, Husserl thus deploys a conception of *ideal content* that draws both on Bolzano's account of an objective science – as a deductively structured collection of truths "in themselves" the form of an ideal theory of scientific knowing and on the idea, also originating in its contemporary form with Bolzano (and his contemporary, Herbart) and further developed by Lotze, of the ideal *content* of a sentence, as distinct from the conditions or reality of the act or activity of judging or asserting it. The attitude of "realism" about logically (or phenomenologically) articulated contents that follows from this is defended in the second, briefer part of the "Prolegomena", and further provides a basis for much of the work of the specific investigations that follow. Still, it is important to note that this realism about content is significantly tempered, throughout the work, in at least two ways. First, Husserl here treats ideal meanings as general *species* or *types* of a certain aspect of individual acts that instantiate them. There is thus a sense in which the attitude of "realism" about their existence does not go beyond realism about specific intentional acts themselves. Second, Husserl insists that the forms and relationships of ideal content are in each case always to be concretely demonstrated through phenomenological reflection and ultimately through concrete *intuitive* demonstration in experience. To demand such a demonstration in each case is not, as Husserl repeatedly emphasizes, to once again place the ideality of content on a "subjective" basis. It is only to point to the need for, and the possibility of, a clarification of the structures and relationships of ideal content, which also (as he argues) yield the most general account of the way in which actual and possible cognition is structured in what is ultimately given in intentionally presenting experience.

With this task in view, the work of the several separate investigations falls into place as jointly articulating the phenomenological basis for meaning, cognition, judgment, and presentation as such, through considerations that interweave (what we would today discuss as) epistemology, semantics, ontology, and the "philosophy of mind". Investigation I considers the nature of linguistic expression and its relationship with the broader concepts of meaning and sense as such, developing a doctrine of sense in general as intimately linked to (phenomenologically illuminated) content, prior to its possible expression or communication. Investigation II moves to the prior ontological question of the form of the unity of species and general types, arguing at length against early modern theories of "abstraction", which fail (as Husserl argues) because of their primarily nominalist orientation. Investigation III gives a detailed mereological theory of wholes and parts, developing the suggestions about the dependency structure of acts and contents that were already sketched (as we saw previously) in the 1894 "Psychological Studies in the Elements of Logic," and Investigation IV applies this structure to develop a "pure grammar" of relations of "dependent" and "independent" meanings within larger meaningful wholes.

It is in Investigations V and VI, however, that the specific structure of intentionality and its implications for cognition, considered as a matter of the synthesizing "fulfillment" of certain intentions by means of actual intuitive presentations, are most deeply and exhaustively developed. Whereas Investigation V undertakes a sustained analysis of the nature and possible ambiguities of intentional "presentation," moving substantially on the ground of the essays from the 1890s that we have already discussed, the sixth and final investigation finally develops in detail the relationship between intentional presentation generally, and its possible fulfillment by means of "concretely giving intuitions", which is, according to Husserl, at the basis for all possible cognition. Here, indeed, *truth* is itself treated as a matter of the "synthesis of fulfillment" whereby a merely intending act is supplied with adequate fulfillment by an intuition of what it itself intends, producing thereby "*the full agreement* of what is meant with what is *given as such*" (Husserl 1913[1970]: 765). The requirement that all actual cognition thus be traced back to its intuitive fulfillment here leads Husserl also to one of the most radical and subsequently controversial innovations of the work: the invocation of the distinctive possibility of an essentially *non-sensuous* form of intuition capable of giving, in intuitive experience, syncategorematic as well as universal structures and types.[10] This "categorial" intuition, although (as Husserl argues) abstractively *founded* in each case on sensuous contents, is itself essentially non-sensuous in that it presents items that do not have a sensory form but nevertheless can be known, and so must be able to be given in an actually intuitive way.

Most generally, Husserl thinks that there must be some way in which the meaningful structures underlying such formal words as "'the', 'a', 'some', 'many', 'few', 'two', 'is', 'not', 'which', 'and,' 'or', etc." can come to intuitive presentation so as to underlie our actual knowledge of these meanings (Husserl 1913[1970]: 774). Although the possibility of such an intuition of categorial structure is indeed always abstractively grounded in the presentation of concrete states of affairs with some sensuous content, a categorical intuition, in Husserl's account, is the intuition – the "actual givenness" – of something that is not itself sensuous and indeed as such "absolutely imperceptible" (Husserl 1913[1970]: 781). Through a closely related form of "abstractive intuition", moreover, Husserl argues that it is possible to have in intuition the *universal* types of given sensible objects. In such "Ideational Abstraction," in particular, the "Idea" or "Universal" corresponding to a thing is brought to consciousness (Husserl 1913[1970]: 799–800).

4. After the *Logical Investigations*

By his own later account Husserl had achieved in 1900–1901 what he took to be the essential "break-through" to a conception of phenomenology as a foundational and critical field of research with respect to the various special empirical and formal sciences. Nevertheless, what the phenomenological "method" is supposed to be remains in many ways uncertain in the first edition of the *Investigations*: the various specific investigations are *thematically* united, as we have seen, by an idea of pure logic as the pure theory of theories, but there is no single articulation of the proper method of phenomenological reflection, beyond the general requirement that cognition be founded in "intuitional evidence". Moreover, it is not clear that Husserl had a clear conception of what is distinctive of his "phenomenology": the term is used only a few times in the first edition, and Husserl often still describes his project, in Brentanian terms, as one of "descriptive psychology".

In the years following the publication of the *Logical Investigations*, Husserl would continue progressively to articulate and develop the methodology of phenomenology in many ways. Beginning around 1906, Husserl suggested the methodology of *epoché*, or "bracketing", as a general phenomenological technique comprising also many possible variations and distinct possibilities of illumination. Most generally, in the phenomenological *epoché*, assumptions about the *actual existence* of external objects are bracketed or put in parentheses: the phenomenological investigator makes no use of these assumptions of existence, characteristic of the "natural attitude", in order to turn explicitly and directly to the underlying presentational experiences themselves. In connection with the argument of *Ideas* I (published in 1913), according to which it is possible thus to "bracket" the entirety of the natural world, Husserl began to describe the phenomenological project as a "transcendental" one, in a sense related to that of Kant's "transcendental idealism." Here, Husserl suggests that the clarification of the essential and constitutive structures of a "transcendental subjectivity" set off against the world as a whole allows the determination of the structures characteristic of its phenomena. Husserl also here develops the general idea of a "noetic-noematic" correlation, a distinction many have taken to refine Husserl's views on the content of presentation, and which allows him to contrast the (noetic) character of temporal acts and the atemporal structure of "noematic" contents. In other works, Husserl would also develop the phenomenology of the consciousness of time, the idea of a "genetic" phenomeology of sense-constitution, the idea of a pre-theoretical "lifeworld" of everyday experience to which all determinate structures of meaning must ultimately be traced, the sense and constitution of intersubjectivity and objectivity on the basis of transcendental subjectivity, and (in his last, unfinished work, *The Crisis of European Sciences*) the theme of the historical teleology of reason and phenomenology's role as critical, rational reflection on this cultural meaning.

Through all of these developments, however, one aspect of phenomenology remains constant: phenomenology is a basic seeing of what is presentatively given in consciousness itself. After Husserl, this phenomenological approach would lead philosophers such as Sartre, Merleau-Ponty, and Heidegger to even more radical developments of the theme of presence and presentation, in some cases (as with Heidegger) leading even to a basic critique of the prominence accorded by Husserl to consciousness itself. Meanwhile, the largely (but not wholly) independent development of what would become known as "philosophy of mind" in the twentieth-century analytic tradition, chiefly from sources in logical positivism and ordinary language philosophy, often ignored or repressed the deep phenomenological implications, as well as presuppositions, of its own analyses.[11] Still, the phenomenological focus on the theme of "presence" and the requirement for demonstration in presence as a precondition for both cognition and objectivity is not obviously wrong or misguided, and retains an important bearing on foundational questions in the philosophy of mind as well as metaphysics today. In these contexts, where theorizing is still often determined by methodologies of formal-linguistic or empiricist analysis that leave the topic of the meaning of presence itself to one side, a further investigation of the theme may still have much of value to contribute.[12]

Notes

1 In this essay, I generally translate "Vorstellung" as "presentation" rather than (the perhaps more usual) "representation".
2 Emphasis in original.
3 For more on this idea of completeness, as it determined the early Husserl's research into the idea of a theory of "pure manifolds" and as related to the conceptions advanced by Dedekind and Hilbert and at issue in Gödel's 1931 incompletenesss results, see Hartimo (2007).

4 Commentators who have helpfully discussed the episode and its implications include Mohanty (1982), Mohanty (2008: 36–39), Smith (2013:17–18), Willard (2003:xxxvi–xxxviii), and Hill (2000).
5 Cf. Mohanty (2008: 3–4).
6 Husserl's reference is to Bolzano's 1837 *Wissenschaftslehre*. In fact, though, the problem has a much longer history, going back at least to the investigations of Plato into the nature of falsehood and non-being in dialogues such as *Sophist* and *Theaetetus*. Husserl also notes (Husserl 1895[1994]: 346) the history of Scholastic disputes over the same issue.
7 The position bears comparison to Saul Kripke's (much more recent) account of (seeming) reference in fictional works in Kripke (1973), especially lectures I and II.
8 This clearly anticipates Husserl's later development of the technique of *epoché* (see section IV, as follows).
9 Here and elsewhere, I translate "Erkenntnis" as "cognition" rather than "knowledge".
10 For a discussion of one of the historically significant controversies to which the discussion led, Husserl's polemic with the logical empiricist Moritz Schlick, see Livingston (2002).
11 For an analysis of this historical (and still current) situation, see Livingston (2004).
12 I would like to thank Sandra Lapointe for providing many very helpful comments and suggestions on an earlier draft of this paper, which have contributed essentially to producing its current form.

Bibliography

Bolzano, B. 1837 [1973]. Theory of Science, ed. By Jan Berg. Dordrecht: D. Reidel. Originally published in German as Wissenschaftslehre. Versuch einer ausführlichen und grösstentheils neuen Darstellung der Logik mit steter Rücksicht auf deren bisherige Bearbeiter, 4 volumes (Sulzbach: J. E. v. Seidel, 1837).

Brentano, F. 1874 [1995]. *Psychology From an Empirical Standpoint*, A. C. Rancurello, D. B. Terrell, and L. McAlister (trans.). London: Routledge. Originally published in German as *Psychologie vom Empirischen Standpunkte* (Leipzig: Duncker & Humblot, 1874).

Frege, G. 1894[1972]. "Review of Dr. E. Husserl's *Philosophy of Arithmetic*". E. W. Klugge (trans.) *Mind* (new series) 81(323): 321–337. Originally published in German in *Zeitschrift für Philosophie und Philosophische Kritik*, 103: 313–332 (1894).

Hartimo, M. J. 2007. "Towards Completeness: Husserl on Theories of Manifolds 1890–1901". *Synthese*, 156: 281–310.

Hill, C. O. 2000. "Frege's Attack on Husserl and Cantor". In C.O. Hill and G.E.R. Haddock, eds. *Husserl or Frege? Meaning, Objectivity, and Mathematics*. Chicago: Open Court.

Husserl, E. 1889 [2015]. "A Letter from Edmund Husserl to Franz Brentano from 29 XII 1889". C. Ierna (trans.) *Husserl Studies*, 31: 65–72.

Husserl, E. 1891 [2003]. *Philosophy of Arithmetic: Psychological and Logical Investigations*. D. Willard (trans.). Dordrecht: Kluwer. Originally published in German as *Philosophie der Arithmetik*. (1891).

Husserl, E. 1894 [1994]. "Psychological Studies in the Elements of Logic". D. Willard (trans.) Originally published in German, *Philosophische Monatshefte*, 30: 159–191. In R. Bernet, ed., *Early Writings in the Philosophy of Logic and Mathematics*. Berlin: Springer.

Husserl, E. 1895 [1994]. "Intentional Objects". D. Willard (trans.) In R. Bernet, ed. *Early Writings in the Philosophy of Logic and Mathematics*. Berlin: Springer.

Husserl, E. 1913 [1970]. *Logical Investigations*. J. N. Findlay (trans). London: Routledge. Originally published in German as *Logische Untersuchungen* (Halle: Max Niemeyer, 1900–1901 and 1913).

Husserl, E. 1913 [1983]. *Ideas Pertaining to a Pure Phenomenology and to a Phenomenological Philosophy: First Book*. F. Kersten (trans.). Dordrecht: Kluwer. Originally published in German as *Ideen zu einer reinen Phänomenologie und phänomenologishen Philosophie, I. Buch: Allgemeine Einführung in die reine Phänomenologie*. (Halle: Max Niemeyer, 1913).

Kripke, S. 1973 [2013]. *Reference and Existence: The John Locke Lectures*. Oxford: Oxford University Press.

Livingston, P. M. 2002. "Husserl and Schlick on the Logical Form of Experience". *Synthese*, 132:2: 239–272.

Livingston, P. M. 2004. *Philosophical History and the Problem of Consciousness*. Cambridge: Cambridge University Press.

Mohanty, J. N. 1982. *Husserl and Frege*. Bloomington: Indiana University Press.

Mohanty, J. N. 2008. *The Philosophy of Edmund Husserl: A Historical Development*. New Haven: Yale University Press.

Smith, D. W. 2013. *Husserl*. Second Edition. London and New York: Routledge.

Willard, D. 2003. "Translator's Introduction" to Husserl (1891[2003]).

14

NATORP'S TWO-DIMENSIONAL MIND

Alan Kim

1. Introduction

Until the nineteenth century, it was philosophy that made the mind its business, investigating the nature of sense-perception, thought, memory, will, and how all these together – as *psychē, anima* – were related to body. From the outset, the soul had seemed different from and opposed to the body. Only bodily things were measurable and calculable; measurement was the *sine qua non* of empirical science; hence, as late as Kant, the very possibility of a distinct, empirical science of soul or mind was denied. However, in the early nineteenth century, throwing Kantian caution to the wind, experimentalists found ways of subjecting the mind, particularly as sensate, to indirect measurement.[1]

With philosophy's monopoly on mind broken, many believed that psychology would supplant philosophy altogether. Thinkers like J. S. Mill sought to reduce "philosophical" problems to psychological ones, and make the conscious subject the foundation of all thinking. Most importantly, psychologizing philosophers tried to reduce logical laws to psychological ones, demoting the apodictic and *a priori* to the *a posteriori* and merely probable. The trend towards psychologism was especially marked in post-Hegelian German philosophy, and it was in Germany, too, that the anti-psychologistic reaction formed. The rise of Neo-Kantianism in the 1870s must be seen in that context.[2] While Frege and Husserl are the best known antagonists of psychologism, the Marburg Neo-Kantian,[3] Paul Natorp (1854–1924), led the charge in his 1887 article, "Ueber objective und subjective Begründung der Erkenntniss [On the objective and subjective grounding of knowledge]", where he outlines his "philosophy of mind".

Of course, to speak of a Neo-Kantian philosophy of mind is to commit anachronism and pleonasm together. Natorp and the Marburgers would not have recognized a philosophical discipline focusing on the mental, because this would cast philosophy's net both too wide and too narrow: too wide in that for them all philosophy essentially concerns the mental and thus mind; too close in that the mental, construed as the phenomena of the human mind, only captures one, in their view secondary, aspect of the properly philosophical approach to mind. Natorp's "philosophy of mind" consequently cuts across disciplinary lines in unexpected ways. It is especially for this reason that Natorp's view of the mental – specifically consciousness (*Bewusstsein*) – should interest contemporary philosophers of mind: not because he has proposals regarding, say, the Hard Problem, but because he articulates a radically unorthodox view of how mind – the putative object of philosophy – should be conceived in the first place.

My task is complicated by the fact that there exists no ready German equivalent for the English, "mind": it can translate "*Geist*", "*Seele*", "*Bewusstsein*", "*Psyche*" depending on context.[4] For his part, Natorp speaks less of mind or mental faculties, and more of the mind's activity, *Denken*, thinking. In particular, his theory of the mental revolves around what he takes to be the two dimensions of thinking: consciousness and knowledge.[5] "Consciousness" (*Bewusstsein*) corresponds to what we usually call "mind", and names thinking as a *psychological* process; I therefore refer to it as "Þ$_\psi$" (read: "Thorn-sub-Psi"). "Knowledge" or "knowing" (*Erkenntnis*, *Erkennen*) is for Natorp a special kind of thinking, epitomized by *science*; I abbreviate it as "Þ$_\Sigma$" (read: "Thorn-sub-Sigma"). The relation of Þ$_\Sigma$ to Þ$_\psi$ is my theme.

2. Þ$_\psi$: Mind as psyche

Like its Latin relatives, *cōnscientia*, *cōnsciō*, and *cōnscius*, "consciousness" is an ambiguous term. On the one hand, it may connote bare responsiveness, a sensate state compatible with disorientation, numbness, or inebriation. One is conscious, but not conscious of anything in particular. Let us call this "minimal consciousness". On the other hand, consciousness usually seems to involve cognition, as its root, *sciō* (to know) indicates a consciousness-*of* some thing, some apparent feature of the world *beknownst*[6] to me. This latter sense is amplified by the prefix[7] 'con-' that gives the term 'consciousness' the literal sense of "joint knowledge" or "knowing in common":[8] it implies an awareness of appearances perceived in or as a common world. Where minimal consciousness is mere phenomenal awareness, cognitive consciousness is awareness of determinate phenomena or "objects". Having objects, such consciousness is intentional; let us therefore call this more robust notion "intentional consciousness". For Natorp, it is intentional consciousness that forms the basis of "experience" (*Erfahrung*), in virtue of its *objective* intention. By contrast, "minimal consciousness" exemplifies the limit-case of what he calls "*Erlebnis*", i.e., consciousness in its lived,[9] subjective immediacy.

Following Kant, one important problem for Natorp was to provide a philosophical account of the possibility of *objective experience*: how can my mental representations (*Vorstellungen*) reveal something beyond their subjective immediacy, i.e., some "object" in the world? This is why, for Natorp, a philosophy of mind (as intentional consciousness) is a philosophy of experience. Experience is first and last realized in a conscious psyche, but to the extent that it is objective-intentional, experience always points beyond that psychic realization.[10] In the Kantian spirit, he considers his task to be the excavation of the transcendental source that underwrites the objectivity of experience.

While Natorp's philosophy of mind is not mainly concerned with the psychological, subjective dimension of representations, he nevertheless does have views on the psyche. If the "objective" tends to the common world beyond the mind itself, Natorp by contrast interprets consciousness "as such" as the subjective aspect of any mental representation. For example, the representation of a tree will involve a subjective component of visual (and perhaps auditory or tactile) *sensa*, plus a unifying concept that isolates just these *sensa* from all others, determining them as *a* tree, which is at the same time *this* tree – the tree of which I am conscious as an object in the common world. The intended tree, on the one hand, is *erfahren* objectively as this determinate thing; it is public and can be pointed out to another with whom I "jointly" cognize it. The *sensa*, on the other hand, are subjectively *erlebt*, private, and cannot be pointed out to another. Thus, the lived subjective aspect of the conscious representation is the phenomenal appearing, or what Natorp calls "*Erscheinung*" or "*phainesthai*".[11]

This phenomenal appearing is a precipitate distilled from the *objective* representations of everyday intentional consciousness. For one is never aware of one's purely subjective stream of appearances, a continuous, indeterminate flow of *phainesthai*. Rather, what one is aware of is a parade of *phainomena*.[12] The plural, "phenomena", already indicates the articulation of the phenomenal flux into discrete unities that are in some way determined. Thus, all experience is the product of an appearing (*Erscheinung*) subjectively "given", on the one hand, and, on the other hand, an articulating, determining, and hence "objectivating" function. The subjective appearing taken for itself constitutes consciousness as lived awareness; it is the "chaotic"[13] material that gets formed through an activity: its conceptual determination[14] into *objects-of* consciousness, viz., the representations that we always intend as lying "beyond" the immediacy of our conscious minds.

In sum, the mind, construed as consciousness, has an ambiguous[15] nature. As consciousness-of or "intentional consciousness", it is of objects, and in this sense objective. But this is not the *living* sense of consciousness as awake, alive, and sensate. This latter captures the immediately lived awareness (*Erlebnis*) that is my individual subjectivity. Waking awareness just is mere *phainesthai* (i.e., it is not "of" the flux of appearing): it is appearing-as-being-appeared-to, and thus the matter of the hylomorphic compound we call *a* conscious representation.[16] Hence, subjectivity can only be seen in or through such a hylomorphic compound, but never purely in itself.[17] What is alive or "animate" in the *anima* or *psychē* can only be *lived out* (*erlebt*), never determined, articulated, captured "as such", since subjectivity *is* the continuum of appearing, whereas objectivity minimally implies discrete unities.[18]

In its immediacy, pure subjective appearance may be considered "given" (*gegeben*). Indeed, another way to conceive *Erscheinung* as representational "matter" just is as "givenness", the datum the representing function has to work with and operate upon. Conversely – and this is key to Natorp's philosophy – this means that what is objective and (already) cognized (*erkannt*) as some *thing* in intentional consciousness, is never immediately given. An object (*Gegenstand, Object*), Natorp writes, is not that which stands over against the knower, but rather, "in the first place, that which *knowledge* sets over against *itself*" – as a goal to be achieved.[19] In other words, if subjective appearance is given (*gegeben*), it nevertheless brings along with it the task (*Aufgabe*) of objectivating it, of cognizing and understanding the object in or through the subjective, just as matter in general calls on us to constitute a thing "in" it (like molding clay) or "out of" it (like working wood).[20] The object is not a gift (*Gabe*), but a task (*Aufgabe*).[21]

To be clear: a representation's phenomenal content, its *phainesthai* or *Erscheinung*, is indeed immediately given;[22] but as the mere matter of the representation, it is nothing, not even "a" representation. By contrast, the *phenomena per se* – as articulated in and to the mind – have already undergone individuation,[23] determination, in short, objectivation.[24] Therefore, in thinking or intending them, the ego does not passively receive them as given, ready-made, but rather has always already had a hand in constituting them, seeking and finding targets in the flux to apprehend and comprehend. Just as consciousness exhibits an ambiguous nature, flickering between the subjective and objective, the immediate awareness and absorption in appearance, on the one hand, and a cognitive distance, on the other – so, too, the intentional object again displays material and formal aspects: as apparent to the mind, it remains subjective and *doxastic*; but taken as a representation *of* some thing *in* the appearing (like the pot that is *in* – not "behind" or "beyond" – the clay),[25] it is *objective*.[26]

It is this insight into what he takes to be the absolute givenness of the subjective and the absolute task of the objective that motivates Natorp's critique of all (allegedly) scientific psychologies, both empirical (e.g., Wundt or Külpe's) and pure (e.g., Husserl's): psychology misapprehends and distorts its theme (*psychē*) by objectivating it in *logoi* (objective accounts or "science").[27] He writes:

> Subjectivity as such does not want to let itself be grasped at all in its immediacy. It can only be grasped – to the extent that it is graspable [at all] – in concepts; for there is absolutely no other organon of knowledge [than the concept]; yet, grasped by a concept, subjectivity is already no longer the absolutely immediate and subjective, but always already somehow objectivated.[28]

As a (putative) science, psychology aims at the objective determination of *the* subjective. But if its task is to grasp the subjective as such, then in *objectivating* the subjective it destroys the very "subjective content" that it strives to grasp *as* subjective. Instead, psychology *nolens volens* transmutes the subjective into its very opposite, an object. As Natorp sees it, living consciousness or *Erlebnis*, *psychē* eternally eludes *logos*, determination, and hence being *objectively* known. More on this in Section III.

3. Þ$_\Sigma$: Mind as knowing-thinking (*erkennendes Denken*)

Let us take stock: cognitive consciousness, as opposed to minimal awareness, is of representations. These have two aspects: subjective-phenomenal, and intentional-conceptual. As concepts work the chaotic phenomenal matter, they *intend* objectivity; through concepts, consciousness strives for penetrating insight into the "basic unified form"[29] of an object appearing, mediately, in the phenomenal flux that is immediate subjectivity.[30] Finally, the fact that cognitive consciousness seeks insight into the phenomena shows that it essentially aims at knowledge. However, as dominated by the ebb and flow of the subjective, it remains doxastic and falls far short of its intended goal. Because representations in individual consciousness are ever wavering (despite their objective intention), Natorp claims, we have developed a method of stabilizing the *doxa*, thus achieving, as far as possible, the cognitive aim implicit in even the barest flicker of a thought. The exercise of this method is called "science"[31] or "*Wissenschaft*",[32] and therefore represents the highest, paradigmatic form of thinking – *Wissen* or, as Natorp calls it, *Erkennen, Erkenntnis*. It is his theory of scientific thinking (Þ$_\Sigma$) (or "knowing-thinking") that concerns us in this section.

For the Marburgers, the exact sciences serve as exemplars of objectivation, because their explicit, self-declared goal is objectivity. Thus, philosophy's task is to trace and clarify their conditions of possibility – what Natorp calls "transcendental logic". But first, we require a correct grasp of what Þ$_\Sigma$ does. All *Erkennen* aims at the "object", seeking to move from the immediacy of lived subjective experience to that which this experience is *of*, something intended.[33] The common view, according to which this object exists beyond and independently of the individual knowing subject,[34] is on Natorp's view wrong.[35] Rather, on his account, science is not concerned with objects as things apparently given to us or immediately received by us through the senses, but rather with the "objective truth" or "objectivity" lying beyond the sensed thing. This objectivity is never given. Instead, like the object of a game, is an objective to be achieved – it is a task (*Aufgabe*).

What does thinking strive for in pursuing objectivity? For Natorp, "thinking means determining"[36] and "determining is thinking".[37] Determination, in turn, is a delimiting, unifying operation upon a manifold, where "manifold" means a relatively indeterminate plurality. The manifold is given as in some respect indeterminate, thus challenging thinking to its task: to determine a unity within that manifold. It is this unity, then, that is the object "appearing in" the manifold. Thus thinking, conceived as the determination of the indeterminate, essentially involves two correlative notions, viz., the manifold, on the one hand, and, on the other, the "synthesis" or unification of that manifold. Thinking cannot take place without some material upon which to operate; this material is provided or given as the manifold.

Distinctions between determination and indeterminacy, synthesis and manifold, provide the basic structure of Natorpian thinking. This structure, as we saw in Section I, is already operative in the generation of doxastic unities, the conscious representations of the everyday world. These representations, while *quasi*-objective, nevertheless manifest all manner of inconsistency and, thus, residual indeterminacy. The world of everyday individual consciousness (*Erlebnis*) is Plato's realm of opinion (*doxa*), and it is upon this doxastic, *relative* indeterminacy that *Erkennen* (Þ$_\Sigma$) goes to work.[38] Now here, too, in Þ$_\Sigma$, the motif of determination recurs. Only now, instead of directly working the chaotic[39] phenomenal manifold, as did Þ$_\psi$, Þ$_\Sigma$ takes as its matter the doxastic manifold of everyday consciousness. Thus, we see that *Erlebnis* and *Erfahrung*, *doxa* and *epistēmē*, Þ$_\psi$ and Þ$_\Sigma$ occur along a spectrum of relative subjectivity and objectivity.[40]

Science (Þ$_\Sigma$) explicitly determines objects, whereas consciousness (Þ$_\psi$) implicitly[41] does so. On Natorp's view, because science is the paradigm of objective knowledge, it is with a view to it that we might best observe to what thinking-as-determining really amounts.[42] Science aims to reveal the systematic order and unity of the phenomenal world: it strives for a complete, objective account of the phenomena, of the world and its contents as objects.[43] How does it achieve this aim, and what are the preconditions of its activity?

For scientific thinking, "determination" means discovering unity within the phenomenal plurality or manifold. Plurality gets determined by being related to a unifying principle; being considered with respect to such a principle just is what it means for the plurality to be determined.[44] Now, since all that is given is the phenomenal manifold, but not its determining principle, the latter must find its origin (*Ursprung*) in thinking itself. Natorp calls the principle produced or "posited" by thinking, "law" (*Gesetz*).[45] His appeal to the familiar notion of a natural or scientific law seems plausible, since such a law is in fact a single principle unifying an infinite variety of phenomena. It is by reference to that law that they may be thought as cases or instances *of* that one law, thus forging a systematic unity out of what were previously unrelated particulars.[46] But by interpreting laws literally as "posits", Natorp is also making the stronger, stranger claim that these scientific laws are spontaneously legislated by thinking itself.[47]

This claim highlights the Kantian underpinnings of Marburg philosophy: it is the *a priori* categories of the Understanding that rule the phenomena given in intuition, making them comprehensible as objective experience.[48] The Marburgers radically modify Kant's architectonic by relativizing[49] the categories, on the one hand, and by ridding intuition of its receptive character, on the other. However, both Kant and the Marburgers agree that experience (*Erfahrung*) of objects is constituted within a conceptual or categorial framework that makes such experience possible, and that therefore must be prior to experience. Instead of being given in experience, the framework lays the groundwork of (objective) experience. Thus, for thinking to think any*thing*, to determine any objectivity, it must first "spontaneously", from and out of itself, posit or "set" (*setzen*) the categorial infrastructure to which the phenomena can be related. In German, what has been posited (*gesetzt*) is a *Gesetz* – and "*Gesetz*" is the German word for "law". Thus, the "laws of science" turn out to be just those posits (*Gesetze*) laid down in thinking.

A law then serves as the foundation or grounding (*Grundlage*; *Grundlegung*), or, as I said, as the framework or infrastructure in which the phenomenal manifold finds a stable frame of reference. Relating the manifold to these laws allows us to think (not "see") what is objective in the phenomena, viz., the law of which they are particular cases. It is the phenomenon *as* instance of a law that is, then, the "determined object".[50]

Unfortunately, Natorp's presentation can be quite obscure and misleading. First, he sometimes seems to suggest that the object *is* the law. But his considered view must be that law is what makes thinking a particular object possible, namely as the one, determinate thing given to me only in and as fluctuating appearance. Surely it is not the law that is so given, since on his view law is not given at all, but legislated in thought so as to make sense of *Erscheinung* in the first place. Thus, the ultimate end of scientific thinking is "the object": an intelligible unity in the sensible manifold, or what Natorp often calls "the X of knowledge".[51] The law, for its part, is sought as the means by which the X may be determined and in that sense "found".

Second, while law as posit seems to connote fixity, this cannot be Natorp's position. He talks of relating the manifold to the law in order to determine cases of the law (i.e., objects) in the manifold, which suggests that the law is a mere point of reference with respect to which thinking orients itself. But again, on Natorp's considered view, the law cannot be inert. Rather, it is a dynamic function of think*ing*; it *is* what think*ing*, as such, *does*.[52] Thinking does not first posit a law, and then refer the manifold back to it. Rather, thinking, *as* it thinks, posits a function that at once and in the same move[53] unifies the manifold. Thus, the law itself is the synthetic "relating";[54] *it* generates the objectivities. (As Natorp bluntly states: "Thinking in general [just] means relating".)[55] Here, Natorp draws on Lotze's famous distinction: things *are* (have being or *Sein*), whereas laws *are valid* (they "hold" or *gelten*, have *Geltung*).[56] For his part, Natorp gives this *gelten* the active sense of governing the manifold, constituting and generating the objective cases that fall under the law. Take the function, $f(x) = y^2$. It determines a manifold, namely the points on a Cartesian plane, by legislating a relation among points with respect to the (previously laid down) x- and y-axes. The relation defined by the function synthesizes a parabola; the function, while not a curve of any kind, constitutes the parabola by determining a relation within the manifold, "doing" this all at once, not in sequence.

His notion of legislation is liable to a third possible misinterpretation. "Laying down the law" sounds as if thinking constructs frameworks by fiat.[57] This is not the case. Rather, because one only *truly* thinks (P_Σ) insofar as one is guided by a rule, legislation must itself always follow some sort of rule. For Natorp, all thinking-as-legislation is governed by the basic "law of lawfulness", the categorical imperative of thinking that stands so to say as its constitution.[58] This imperative (Natorp here again uses a Kantian notion) requires that thinking, in order to hold (*gelten*) as such, be able to justify the legitimacy of its statutes. Concretely, this means being able to anchor any challenged law in other, unchallenged laws, thus showing the transcendental *Rechtsgrund* and legitimacy of the law in question.[59]

Interestingly, Natorp's characterizes laws as hypotheses. Here, he draws on etymology: the Greek, ὑπό-θεσις (*hypo-thesis*), comes from the verb, ὑπο-τίθημι (*hypo-tithēmi*), which literally means, "to place or set under or below", from *hypo-* (under) and *tithēmi* (to place, set). "Hypothesis" echoes the German words, *setzen* (set, place) and *legen* (lay, place), from which Natorp derived his idiosyncratic conception of *Gesetz* (law) as *Grundsatz*[60] or *Grundlegung*: a hypothesis is what is laid down as the ground of determination, i.e., as the law of further determination. Natorp relies here on Plato's famous description of philosophical hypotheses at the end of *Republic* VI.[61] On the one hand, the mathematical sciences lay down hypotheses (e.g., axioms) as if everyone knew what they meant, and then descend to the theorems they entail.[62] By contrast, dialectic lays down hypotheses as "stepping-stones [*epibaseis*]" by which reason ascends to the highest, "unhypothetical" principle of all thought.[63] This image, together with Socrates's description of his "method of hypothesis" in the *Phaedo*,[64] forms the basis of Natorp's conception of thinking as ascending and descending hypothetically over a scaffolding of laws.

For Natorp, then, $Þ_Σ$ consists, first, in the positing of hypotheses, and then in either descending from a hypothesis to a determined object, or in ascending from a hypothesis to its higher grounds or justification. The hypothetical process as a whole tends both towards ever-greater scope as well as ever-finer resolution of the phenomenal manifold.[65] More precisely, it *pursues* a perpetually receding horizon of total objectivation – complete knowledge – of nature as that which appears in and through phenomena. It is this "*pursuit*" that Natorp calls "method", appealing to one of meanings of the Greek word, *methodos*:[66] the "hypothetical method" is not a way *of* making and testing conjectures. Rather, the very act of hypothesizing *is* "method" in the sense of a pursuit or prosecution of the "objective", the "delimitation of the unlimited".[67] This pursuit, which is the essence of scientific thinking, is in principle infinite. The hypotheses that constitute it, Natorp says, are like the instantaneous standstills that my foot must make as I walk, but only to push off and take the next step: "the stand [of the hypothesis] must always again be left behind".[68]

This means that the objectivity determined in light of a given hypothesis only has objective validity for the very moment of its determination, namely as the provisionally achieved goal of the last step, the one just taken. But the object just determined now provides the starting point (*epibasis*) for the next step, for all further determination of an object is only possible on the basis of an already (relatively) determined object.[69]

> Thus there can be no further talk of any "factum" in the sense of complete or perfect knowledge; rather, all knowledge [*Erkenntnis*] that closes a gap in our previous knowledge [*Wissens*] will produce new and greater problems. Indeed, following Spencer's analogy of a sphere whose radius increases towards infinity, as the comprehensive scope [*Umfang*] of the

knowledge we have gained increases (represented by the increase of [the sphere's] volume), [so too] will the extent [*Umfang*] of new questions yet to be solved increase (represented by . . . the surface of the sphere).[70]

This "method" or "process" is "everything":[71] that is, science as the paradigmatic species of thinking illustrates its active and spontaneous essence – it is not a static "body of knowledge", but a pursuit in constant motion: hence "all fixed 'being' must resolve itself into a 'going' [*Gang*], a *motion* of thinking".[72]

We thus arrive at perhaps the most paradoxical aspect of Natorp's conception of thinking. Surely all this talk of its "activity" and "motion" must pertain to the *conscious "thought-processes"* (P_ψ) of the thinking individual's *mind*. But as Natorp sees it, this is not the case. Thinking (P_Σ) as described previously is not a psychological process, for "knowledge sets the object up over against itself as *independent* of the subjectivity of [psychological act] of knowing".[73] What sense can we can give such "thinking" that is, to borrow Dummett's phrase, "extruded from the mind"?[74] Natorp's conception of thinking as an anonymous process independent of a particular thinker is not as strange as it seems, if we think of thinking like a craft (*technē*), e.g., house-building; or an activity, like baseball-playing. On the one hand, it is tempting to say that such crafts or activities consist in the actions of workers lifting, digging, riveting, and hammering, or players throwing, catching, hitting, and sliding. But the craft or activity is not to be reduced to a sum of concrete actions. Rather, house-building and baseball-playing are prior to house-building-motions or baseball-playing-motions, for it is only with respect to house-building and baseball-playing that such motions might even be identifiable as such. It is only because there is a type of process called "house-building" that there are individual house-builders, only because there is a process called "the game of baseball" that there are individual baseball-players. Likewise, for Natorp, it is only because there is a type of process called "thought-thinking" that there are individual thinkers. Further, the craft of house-building and the activity of baseball-playing are both constituted by their respective ends, viz., houses and (baseball) victories, even if there are no house-builders or baseball players to assume those goals as their own. As Aristotle says, "craft does not deliberate".[75] Similarly, thinking (P_Σ) is constituted by *its* goal, objectivity, even if there happens to be no thinker (P_Σ) on hand. Hence, thinking as a "craft"[76] is not a concrete psychological or neurological event, but rather the process of object-determination as such. In this sense, thinking does not think, any more than baseball plays baseball.

In sum, this process of thinking (P_Σ), on Natorp's view, has several distinct moments. First, it lays down laws; this is equivalent to risking a hypothesis.[77] These laws are the *a priori* conditions of possibility of the objective experience that pertain to science. Second,[78] in experience itself, the law synthesizes a unity, i.e., an objectivity (objects or ensembles of objects) in a given manifold. This determination-via-laws is the "descending" moment of thinking. Third, should a particular law be challenged, thinking secures its legitimacy by "ascending" to higher, unchallenged laws, to demonstrate and justify the challenged law.

Although categorial functions (and especially the *Urgesetz* that there *be* law at all) can be seen as absolutely foundational, on Natorp's view, the hypotheses of scientific objectivity are, for their part, only ever *relatively* so. They function as *a priori* constitutive laws in relation to the objects constituted with reference to them. But, on the one hand, such objects, as we saw above, are only provisionally, if not partially determined,[79] for they always give rise to new and unsuspected areas of indeterminacy, and the apparent determinacy of the object reverts to being a task for descending thought. On the other hand, the laws themselves may be criticized, challenged, and compelled to change, as the history of scientific crises and revolutions amply demonstrates. Thus, thinking ($Þ_\Sigma$) is in every way fluid and dynamic for Natorp. On the grand scale, the transcendent Atlantean fixity associated with the concept of law dissolves into a historically evolving series of law-structures subtending the scientific worldviews of passing epochs. But these law-structures themselves, as interrelations of functions, are internally active and generative, as well. Thinking spontaneously hypothesizes or legislates objectivating laws or functions, which, for their part, are generative of the objects, the things "visible" (i.e., intelligible) within a particular worldview. Thinking, therefore, manifests itself for Natorp as an infinite and eternal pursuit of objectivity. This pursuit, though endless, is far from fruitless, for the dominion of justified laws and legitimate objects constantly grows. Nevertheless, as thought's empire expands, so too does the horizon of the undetermined, calling forth ever new effort.

4. $Þ_\Sigma$ and $Þ_\psi$: thoughts in mind

It should now be clear that, for Natorp, an investigation that begins and ends with mind must be misguided. In virtue of its subjective immediacy, consciousness may *seem* clearer and more knowable to us, but this is an illusion. In fact, Natorp argues, this immediacy is not cognizable at all, for

> [t]he stage of *pure* subjectivity would be identical with that of absolute indeterminacy. We may reason back to such a stage as to an original Chaos, but cannot grasp it in itself. The *constructive* objectivating achievement of knowledge [$Þ_\Sigma$] comes first.[80]

What truly is epistemically accessible, then, is the objective content "present[ing] itself in the subjective course of cognition",[81] especially in scientific *Erkennen*.[82] The subjective can only be expounded in relation to and therefore after the objective.[83] Hence, any account of the subjective psyche – any psychology – cannot precede, but must instead take its point of departure in objective knowledge. Or as Natorp says elsewhere: "Subjectivation becomes the problem of *psychology* only after, not before [objectivity]; for the object-relation of any kind always precedes as a founding [process] any and all subject-relation".[84]

As we saw at the end of Section I, the appearing that *is* subjectivity can never be conceptually grasped – i.e., objectivated – without immediate distortion. Hence, "critical psychology" represents the second-best option: starting with the synthesized objectivities of some phase of knowledge, we perform a "*Reflexion*",[85] and reverse the objectivating process to reveal its hyletic precursors.[86] On the basis of objectivation,

> we *reconstruct*, as far as possible, the stage of original subjectivity, which would not be accessible to any knowledge by any other path than this *reconstructive* one, which takes as its starting point the already completed objective construction.[87]

Critical psychology, then, looks not at the active methods of carding, spinning, or weaving, but at the worked-over fleece, yarn, or warp. If thinking ($Þ_\Sigma$) constitutes the world of *Erfahrung* by objective determination, then it is by subjective reconstruction that critical psychology reconstitutes the inner world of *Erlebnis* ($Þ_\psi$).

Critical psychology is the Penelopean project of undoing the knots and nodes at which determinate objects have been stitched into the tapestry of experience in order to reconstruct the antecedent stage of relatively indeterminate *Erlebnis*.[88] I stress the word "relatively" to indicate the narrow limits within which such an enterprise is possible. On Natorp's account of objectivation, the sensible manifold is the extreme pole of indeterminacy. Hence, the theoretical limit of any psychological reconstruction must be this extreme, Natorp's "original Chaos", or James's "blooming, buzzing confusion".[89] Practically speaking, however, it is impossible to undo objectivation that far,[90] since it would take us into primitive regions where our very project would not just appear meaningless, but indeed no longer even be articulable. Thus, the stratum of consciousness we may expect Natorpian psychology to expose cannot lie far beneath the surface of the doxastic everyday,[91] i.e., in a realm already saturated by symbols, language, and culture.

Take an example: you are reading this text. Reading printed words is an everyday mode of consciousness in which, without conscious effort, a manifold of marks seems to morph spontaneously into words, phrases, sentences, which you see as already constituted. As such they present a further task (*Aufgabe*) of determination, e.g., the interpretation of their meaning. Hence, the words we read are doxastic objects of everyday consciousness. The Natorpian psychologist stops right here, refusing to ascend "thinking-ly" to the determinative interpretation of the word-groupings (sentences, paragraphs, the essay as a whole); instead he dwells on the individual word's sensible appearance, trying to see past its familiar *Gestalt* into its *Gestalt*-elements: the concatenation of its syllables, letters, and the latter's forms.[92] Thus, an earlier phase of objectivation is subtly brought to light, that phase where as children we learned not only how to assemble letters into words, but even before that, to form those letters from lines, curves, and dots. This process might temporarily revive the *Erlebnis* of indeterminate gazing that we all must have engaged in before we learned to see letters, words, sentences, before the manifold of the printed page became progressively determinate and meaningful.[93]

5. Conclusion: Natorp and Husserl

While Natorp's theory of thinking includes some trenchant attacks on physicalism and psychologism that may be out of style, his critique of phenomenological approaches is likely to interest contemporary philosophers of mind, theorists of qualia, "phenomenology" of consciousness, and subjective "experience".

As we have seen, Natorp's conception of P_Σ turns on a radical resolution of the hoary subject-object dichotomy: "the subject", on his view, is really *subjectivity*, the phenomenal flow of *Erlebnis*; "the object" is really *objectivation*, the progressive determination of flux into *Erfahrung*. Objects are not given, but are "intended", i.e., *aimed at*, and then infinitely constructed; what *is* given – the matter or hylic flow – is as such indeterminate and thus beyond our immediate grasp. Natorp's approach thus preserves subject and object as distinct and irreducible (unlike the reductionist monists), but also as essentially unified (unlike the dualists): coordinated moments of the single process of cognition.[94] This is the theory underlying his reviews of Husserl's *Prolegomena* and *Ideas*,[95] in which Natorp expressed criticisms that he and Husserl discussed privately over the course of a correspondence spanning thirty years.[96] Each often assured[97] the other that their differences were not as great as they seemed – but they may have been greater than either wished to admit.

Natorp's criticisms boil down to this: Husserl's ill-chosen terminology[98] works against his true aims, causing him to *Platonize*.[99] As Natorp argues in *Platos Ideenlehre*, Plato's recurrent metaphors of noetic vision clandestinely misled others (and perhaps sometimes himself) into a static,[100] "substantial" interpretation of the forms. And just as this generated the absurdities of separation for which Aristotle chides Plato, so, too, Natorp argues, Husserl's "ideal species"[101] of logical notions, e.g., representations, concepts, judgments, conclusions, proofs are but inert abstractions from psychological acts.[102] Their abstract nature makes it hard for Husserl to motivate, in turn, their downward, normative force on actual thinking.[103] According to Natorp, Plato himself decisively rejected the abstractive-substantive interpretation of separate forms by showing them to be functions determining the sensible manifold.[104] Natorp argues that this should also be Husserl's strategy, avoiding reference to the "formal" and "ideal", or to "species", and later, "essence [*Wesen*]", "*eidos*", or (especially) "eidetic intuition [*Wesensschau*]". These terms mislead us into thinking of the norms of objectivity as themselves being objects; instead, as Natorp sees it, talk of "law" helps guard against confusing a norm and a case determined by it.

Phenomenology styles itself the science of consciousness, the science Husserl conceived as foundational to all other sciences. For Natorp, this raises two important problems. First, the claim that consciousness should be the foundation of science is misguided: "any recourse to the subject and its faculties is completely foreign to objective science".[105] As Natorp sees it, in upholding the opposite, Husserl joins the rank of those who think it "obvious that the true foundation of knowledge [*Begründung der Erkenntniss*] is to be sought in the relation to the subject, i.e., in subjective 'consciousness [*Bewusstsein*]'".[106] Worse, Husserl's interpretation of consciousness as "intentionality" ought to be seen to lie at the root of Husserl's various terminological (and conceptual) confusions. On Husserl's view, the mental phenomena constituting consciousness essentially differ from physical phenomena in that they "in-tend" or "stretch out towards" an object.[107] As Franz Brentano, Husserl's teacher, put it, consciousness is always consciousness *of* something. Thus, phenomenology presupposes a relation between two distinct *relāta*: the subject and the object.

Natorp argues that on this view of intentionality, the object seems to enjoy an existence independent of the subject: subject and object somehow exist before entering into the intentional relation, just as visible objects exist whether or not someone is looking at them, but become seen (objects) just as soon as some subject sees them. In other words, according to Natorp, Husserl conceives the object as given to the subject, and the subject's *intentiō* as a receiving "of" the object "as such": the phenomenon simply as it appears.[108] Here lies the bone of contention. For Natorp, an appearing (*phainesthai*) is not a kind of object: it is *subject* (*-ivity*). Objects are not given as things that already "stand-over-against" the subject as *Gegen-stände*, but as tasks, goals, objectives. In his discussion of Husserl's "*Philosophie als strenge Wissenschaft* [Philosophy as Rigorous Science]" (1910–1911), Natorp says: "*experienced* immediacy [*das erlebte Unmittelbare*] is not also *known* immediately – or even thought".[109] Husserl seems to agree at least in the case of adumbrations of sensible phenomena, but "eidetic intuition" seems to imply immediate experience (*Erlebnis*) of ideal objects "as such".[110] While this idea is foreign to Husserl's early work, by 1911, Husserl does hold that phenomenology itself is a rigorous science, standing above all others (including empirical psychology), precisely because it achieves the immediate grasp, in "apodictic evidence", of the essences or ideal species of all mental representations and operations, including those of logic.[111] But if, as Natorp claims, the very notion of such an intuition is incoherent, then phenomenology and philosophy must give up the mantle of science, and content themselves with the status of *critique*.[112]

For his part, Natorp argues that intentionality cannot be a "stretching-forth towards a separate, independent object", but must rather mean the "striving-forth *towards* the complete, lawful determination of appearance", the pursuit of an object.[113] On Natorp's view, Husserl fails (at least in *Ideas* [1913]), to appreciate (or at least clearly *express*)[114] how, rather than immediately grasping objects, the activity of categorial functions progressively constitutes them.[115] Natorp thus argues that Husserl is unable to countenance a generative transcendental logic, inadvertently remaining stuck in a sterile "formal logic".

Already in his 1901 review of the first volume of Husserl's *Logical Investigations*, the *Prolegomena to Pure Logic* (1900), Natorp argued that Husserl's views were confused. Why, Natorp asks, does Husserl insist on the formal as opposed to the material (i.e., objectivating) character of logic? This is especially odd, Natorp argues, since when Husserl seeks to prove the objective validity of logical laws, he does not confine himself solely to traditional, "formal" logic, but includes all of pure mathematics. But pure mathematics, Natorp claims, is a material part of the sciences. Hence, he argues that Husserl's actual use of "formal" goes beyond the traditional sense, and "in both scope and content" is equivalent to the "'pure' and 'objective' – in short, to the *transcendental*".[116]

Because he thus confuses the formal and the transcendental, Natorp argues, Husserl also fails to resolve the "*opposition* between the formal and material, the apriori and the empirical, and thus also between the logical and psychological, the objective and the subjective: in a word – in *Husserl's* words – between the ideal and the real".[117] Material, empirical, psychological "reality" paradoxically persists as an irrational remainder; Husserl never demonstrates the "inner, cognitive, and thus *logical*" connection between the material and formal in the object, contenting himself with the "stark, pure *separation* of the two".[118]

By contrast, Natorp understands idealism's aim to be the *grounding* of the real in the ideal: to show, through a "transcendental logic" how the *real object* comes about.[119] Kant, says Natorp, "built up the whole concept of the object from the formal elements of knowledge [*Erkenntnis*], [from] the logical in the most deepest sense".[120] The result is that "the opposite side of the objective – the subjective – reveals itself as the *quasi-object* of psychology, i.e., just *as* the mere opposite side of the objective, its mirror image, its '*reflexion*', as it were".[121]

Husserl proved highly receptive to Natorp's criticisms, and often reported to the latter how far he had advanced from previous positions.[122] For example, by 1908 Husserl had come to think that the application of the label, "descriptive psychology" to phenomenology was inapt.[123] Then, in 1909, Husserl tells Natorp that he has "considerably" revised his views regarding the relation between (i) Natorp's transcendental and his own phenomenological methods; (ii) Natorp's critical psychology and his own phenomenology; and (iii) their respective conceptions of "pure logic".[124] Yet, it is striking that despite his movement in Natorp's direction, Husserl nevertheless maintains the distinctions between their respective philosophies.[125]

> My – in no wise psychological – *problems* are not congruent with those of the Marburg Circle. And my *transcendental*-phenomenological method (not psychological: neither genetic nor descriptive psychology) differs, in both aim and essence, from the transcendental-*logical* [method] in your sense.[126]

Or, as he wrote Natorp years later: "Your conceptual manner of forming thoughts, your manner of objectivating in a logical-theoretical way – is foreign to me".[127] In 1909, even after adopting Natorp's talk of "constitution" of objectivities and proclaiming himself to be an "honest idealist", he still maintains that phenomenologists "work . . . as it were from the bottom up".[128] By contrast, the Marburgers, with their "completely different problematic and method", have "worked up firm formulations of the highest epistemological problems, which are their starting points and towards which all further work is oriented".[129] Husserl expressed the hope that their divergent approaches to mind, which "must somehow hang together, in an obscure yet close kinship", would one day be "reconciled" in both method and substance.[130]

"From the bottom up": i.e., starting with "consciousness", *Erlebnis*, psyche. Indeed, these too are Natorp's concern – but from the top down.[131] So he might have replied: to be sure, we all start at the bottom – but to *see* the valley, you must climb the mountain; to *know* the phenomena, you must first receive their law.[132]

Notes

1. See my (2009).
2. I treat this in detail in Ch. 2 of my (2010).
3. The other major members of this school are its founder, Hermann Cohen (1842–1918) and its last luminary, Ernst Cassirer (1874–1945).
4. Further possibilities are *"Vernunft", "Verstand", "Gemüt"*, which all play important roles in eighteenth- and nineteenth-century philosophy.
5. "Erkenntnis" is often translated by "cognition". However in the context of Natorp's theory, it is preferable to use "cognition" to mean the psychological instantiation of knowing-thinking. But that is precisely not what Natorp means by Erkenntnis – knowledge is not in itself psychological, and this is a central if problematic aspect of his theory.
6. The German word "*be-wusst*" (< *wissen*, "to know") may connote both subjective awareness and objective "beknownst-ness" (see Kim, 2015b, n. 66).
7. *Com-* (with, together with).
8. Compare Latin *cōnscientia* with *scientia*.
9. As the root verb, (*er-*) *leben* ("to live") suggests.
10. Natorp (1887: 267).
11. Natorp (1887: 273); Greek middle-passive infinitive, φαίνεσθαι, "to appear".
12. Natorp (1887: 283); cf. Natorp (1921a: 469); Natorp (1912b: 37, 38, 76, 99, 103, 190, *et passim*); Kim (2007: 167–168).
13. Natorp (1887: 283).
14. Cf. Natorp (1887: 283, 285).
15. I say "ambiguous" and not "two-fold". It is not two distinct aspects we are talking about, but rather a wavering and confusing flickering between awareness and awareness-*of*, between subjectivity and objectivity.
16. Cf. Kim (2007: 165).
17. Natorp (1887: 274).
18. The phenomenon prior to reduction to law is "the most concrete expression of subjectivity" (Natorp (1887: 273).
19. Natorp (1887: 268). Note that Natorp speaks of knowledge, not the knower; and that the object does not "appear" (is not "given") over against knowledge, but that it is that which knowledge itself sets over against itself.
20. Natorp (1888: 43, 51, *et passim*; Natorp, 1912b: 69, ff.
21. Natorp, 1887: 282; cf. esp. 283): the object is given, but *only* as an *X*-to-be-determined; (1912b: 200; 203).
22. Cf. esp. Natorp (1887: 273): "Subjectivity means the relation of the represented [*repraesentātum*] to the representing [subject: *repraesentāns*] insofar as the former is represented by the latter, i.e., insofar as the former constitutes the *content* of the latter's subjective *Erleben*; in other words, [subjectivity] means the *immediate relation to the ego*". Cf. Twardowski (1894: 12, ff.); Natorp (1901: 276; 1912a: 208).

23 Natorp (1887: 279).
24 On content (*Inhalt*) as opposed to activity (*Thätigkeit*), cf. esp. Natorp (1887: 260).
25 *Doxa* in Plato, Natorp writes, indicates "material givenness, not forming, shaping act [*materiale Gegebenheit, nicht formender Akt*]" (Natorp, 1921a: 475).
26 Cf. Natorp (1887: 266; 280–281).
27 Kim (2007: 160–161); Natorp (1912b: 43); Natorp (1887: 259).
28 Natorp (1887: 283).
29 Natorp (1887: 273).
30 Natorp (1887: 283).
31 "Science" derives from the Latin *scientia*, which in turn stems from *sciēns* (knowing, understanding), the present participle of *sciō* (I know, understand).
32 "*Wissen*" (to know), cp. English "wit", Latin "*videō*" (to see), and Greek "*idea*".
33 Natorp (1912a: 203).
34 Cf. Natorp (1887: 259).
35 Natorp calls the benighted view "dogmatism", i.e., the view that things or objects are given to the scientist in experience, who, in turn, brings order to them. This view, which Natorp traces back to Aristotle and attributes to modern-day positivists, is most lucidly refuted by Cassirer (1910).
36 Natorp (1912b: 203).
37 Natorp (1912b: 205).
38 This is readily illustrated in Plato's ethical dialogues, where the *skopos* or "objective" of the dialogue, say, "virtue" or "justice", is already roughly determined within a system of other concepts, but only at the level of *doxa*. The interlocutor's grasp of the targeted value, in spite of his self-assessment, is far from thoughtful in the strict sense of "thinking". Instead, it is subjective just insofar as it has been passively received, and not positively taken up as a task for examination and further determination. Socrates forces the task on the interlocutor by removing the latter's *doxa* into the objective realm, demanding an account of its *relation* to other deeper *Grundsätze* or propositions to which the interlocutor is committed, wittingly or not, as a participant in the dialogue itself. The discussion below of hypothetical ascent and descent can readily be transposed from the "scientific" to this ethical context.
39 Natorp (1887: 283).
40 Cf. Natorp (1887: 274–275, 269). My account tries to fill the explanatory gap identified at Dahlstrom (2015: 246). Cf. Kim (2007: 165, f.).
41 Everyday doxastic intention of independent objects happens "naively" and "completely without reflection", so that the object "*appears* there from the outset and [as] given" (Natorp, 1887: 269).
42 Other kinds of objectivation are not parasitic on or approximations of science: ethical, political, and aesthetic objectivities have their own "equal right" over against the theoretical ones generated by science. Nonetheless, on Natorp's view, the process of objectivation is clearest in science, and therefore an appropriate starting point for reflection on the nature of thought. Cf. Luft (2015: 222).
43 "Science strives, at least since Galileo, to make true this sense of 'object'; in the reduction to the law, it fulfills the objectivation of the appearance/phenomenon" (Natorp, 1887: 272; cf. 276).
44 Cf. Natorp (1921a: 208).
45 Natorp (1887: 276–277; 273).
46 Subsumption of cases under a law: Natorp (1921a: 155).
47 The understanding is "the author, and not merely the interpreter of nature (viz., the nature of the natural sciences)" (Natorp, 1912b: 199). Cf. Natorp (1921a: 317).
48 Cf. esp. Kant (*KrV*, A76–79/B102–105; A92/B125).
49 The details lie beyond our scope; cf. my (2010: 79, ff.); Friedman (2008: 239–240).

50 Cf. Plato (*Rep.* VI, 511c1–2).
51 Cf. e.g., Natorp (1887: 282, *et passim*).
52 Cf. esp. Natorp (1910: 67, ff.).
53 Just as in an attack in chess, there are not two separate moves – first, the placing (*setzen*; positing) of the knight, and then, distinctly, say, checking the king. Rather, *in* posting the knight, the king is checked.
54 "Setzen heisst beziehen [to posit is to relate]" (Natorp, 1921a: 272).
55 Natorp (1910: 67).
56 Cf. 1921a: 201.
57 Natorp (1921a: 216).
58 Natorp (1921a: 194–195).
59 Cf. esp. Natorp (1912b: 197).
60 Natorp (1921a: 196–197).
61 Natorp (1921a: 216).
62 *Rep.* VI, 510cd.
63 *Rep.* VI, 511b.
64 Cf. esp. Natorp (1921a: 157).
65 Natorp (1921a: 317–318).
66 Natorp (1912a: 199); cf. my (2010)
67 Natorp (1910: 13). Cf. Natorp (1918: 19).
68 Natorp (1912a: 203; cf. 207).
69 Natorp (1887: 284).
70 Natorp (1910: 14; cf. 1912a: 202–203). This differs from Friedman's rendering of Cassirer's philosophy, in which "an ideally complete mathematical representation of the phenomena" is ever more closely approximated (Friedman, 2005: 80). Rather, for Natorp, the realm of phenomena itself continuously expands.
71 Natorp (1910: 14).
72 Natorp (1912b: 199).
73 Natorp (1887: 269).
74 Dummett (1994, Ch. 4, "The Extrusion of Thoughts from the Mind").
75 *Physics*, II.8, 199b28.
76 E.g., Plato's *dialektikē technē* (*Phaedrus* 276e) and *peri tous logous technē* (*Phaedo* 90b), to which Natorp appeals (Natorp, 1921a: 55, 66, 133, 153, f.).
77 Natorp (1912b: 203).
78 In logical, not temporal order.
79 Natorp (1921a: 282).
80 Natorp (1887: 283).
81 " *im subjektiven Verlauf des Erkennens*"; Natorp says this what Husserl is trying express, all too metaphysically, when he says the "ideal" "realizes" itself in the lived experience of the psyche (Natorp, 1901: 281).
82 Cf. Husserl's assessment of the difference between his "Göttinger" and Natorp's "Marburger" approaches (HN 18Mar09; *Briefwechsel*: 110).
83 Natorp (1917: 241; 243).
84 Natorp (1912a: 208).
85 Natorp (1917: 240; 1921a: 465; 1912b: 289, *et passim*).
86 Natorp (1921a: 465).
87 Natorp (1887: 283). He repeats the point years later; see Natorp (1912b: 289; 1917: 246).
88 At any stage of objectivation, the object is an object only *at* the attained stage, "but no longer for every higher [stage], and not yet for every lower stage" (Natorp, 1912a: 208).
89 James (1890: 488).

90 Here I diverge from Dahlstrom (2015: 246).
91 What Natorp calls "gemeine Vorstellung" (Natorp, 1887: 284).
92 The term, *Gestalt*, here is mine. Cf. Natorp (1912a: 197) ("*Buchstabieren der Erscheinungen*"), Natorp (1921a: 317); Menn (1998).
93 An *Erlebnis* we can reproduce in a way for ourselves by gazing at a script unintelligible to us. Still, although Arabic or Mongolian appears to this writer as mutely sensible, yet it is precisely because I recognize these scripts as *apparently* saying something that they can even appear "mute" to me. To the infant the words on a page are simply other marks, if anything, *less* meaningful than whatever pictures they may accompany; my daughter used to try to dust them away.
94 The hidden advantage of taking science as a starting point is that both idealists and physicalists assent, in their own way, to the validity of *Wissenschaft*.
95 Natorp (1901, 1917), respectively. Cf. Natorp (1912b: 280, ff.).
96 1894–1924, contained in *Husserliana Dokumente* III, vol. 5: "Die Neukantianer" (Husserl, 1994: 39–165).
97 E.g., HN 18Mar09 (*Briefwechsel*: 110–111); Natorp (1917: 226, 236, 241).
98 Natorp (1917: 226).
99 Natorp (1901: 282–283). The charge is repeated at Natorp (1917: 231).
100 Natorp (1917: 230–231).
101 Cf. Natorp (1917: 239).
102 Natorp (1901: 275–276). Cf., e.g., *Prolegomena*: §§66, 67.
103 Cf. Natorp (1901: 274).
104 In the *Parmenides*; Natorp (1921a: 245–247). Cassirer lucidly treats this distinction between substantial and functional notions of "concept" in his (1910).
105 Natorp (1887: 265).
106 Natorp (1887: 261); cf. Natorp (1921a: 238).
107 From Latin, *intendō*, "to stretch out, reach forth, extend". That which does the stretching is the intentional subject (*intentiō*); that towards which it stretches is the intentional object (*intentum*). Unlike Brentano, Husserl does not hold all consciousness to be intentional, e.g., feelings and moods. The point does not affect Natorp's argument, since for him, feelings pertain solely to subjectivity.
108 Cf. esp. Natorp (1917: 228).
109 Natorp (1912b: 289). Again: "the 'immediacy' of pure consciousness is never already *cognized* [known, *erkannt*] immediately as such; it is not even *cognizable* [*erkennbar*]" (Natorp, 1917: 237).
110 Natorp (1912b: 289).
111 Natorp (1901: 275–276).
112 "Das eigentliche Arbeitsfeld des Philosophen aber ist und bleibt – die *Erkenntnisskritik*" (Natorp, 1893: 611).
113 Natorp (1917: 241; 237).
114 Cf. esp. Natorp (1917: 236).
115 Natorp (1917: 233).
116 Natorp (1901: 282).
117 Natorp (1901: 282).
118 Natorp (1901: 282).
119 Natorp (1901: 283).
120 Natorp (1901: 283).
121 Natorp (1901: 283).
122 E.g., HN 23Dec08, *Briefwechsel*: 103. But see Fink (1933).
123 HN 23Dec08, *Briefwechsel*: 103.
124 HN 18Mar09, *Briefwechsel*: 108–109.
125 As does Natorp, e.g., at Natorp (1917: 225).

126 HN 23Dec08, *Briefwechsel*: 103.
127 HN 1Feb22, *Briefwechsel*: 149.
128 HN 18Mar09, *Briefwechsel*: 110. Cf. *Prolegomena*: 228.
129 HN 18Mar09, *Briefwechsel*: 110.
130 HN 18Mar09, *Briefwechsel*: 110–111.
131 The image brings to mind Heraclitus's saying, "the way up and down is the same" (Fr. 60) – quoted by Natorp in a similar connection (Natorp, 1921a: 465); cf. Natorp (1921b: 165).
132 "The point is not to *experience* – our *experience* [unser Erleben zu – *erleben*]; why would we then need a *science*, a *method*?" (Natorp, 1917: 237; cf. 1912a: 198).

Bibliography

Calvo, P., and Symons, J., eds. 2009. *The Routledge Companion to Philosophy of Psychology*. New York: Routledge.
Cassirer, E. 1910. *Substanzbegriff und Funktionsbegriff*. Berlin: Bruno Cassirer.
Dahlstrom, D.O. 2015. "Natorp's Psychology". In de Warren and Staiti, 2015: 240–260.
De Warren, N., and Staiti, A., eds. 2015. *New Approaches to Neo-Kantianism*. Cambridge: Cambridge University Press.
Dummett, M. 1994. *Origins of Analytical Philosophy*. Cambridge, MA: Harvard University Press.
Fink, E. 1933. "Die phänomenologische Philosophie Edmund Husserls in der gegenwärtigen Kritik." *Kantstudien*, vol. xxxviii: 321–383.
Friedman, M. 2005. "Ernst Cassirer and the Philosophy of Science." In Gutting, G., ed., *Continental Philosophy of Science*: 71–83. Oxford: Blackwell.
———. 2008. "Ernst Cassirer and Thomas Kuhn: the neo-Kantian tradition in history and philosophy of science." *Philosophical Forum* 39(2): 239–252.
Husserl, E. 1900. *Logische Untersuchungen: Prolegomena zur reinen Logik* [*Prolegomena*]. Tübingen: Niemeyer.
———. 1913. *Ideen zu einer reinen Phänomenologie und phänomenologischen Philosophie*. = *Hua* vol. iii. The Hague, 1950: Nijhoff.
———. 1994. *Husserliana: Dokumente* III (*Briefwechsel* [correspondence]), vol. 5: "Die Neukantianer [the Neo-Kantians]". Schumann, K., ed. Dordrecht: Kluwer.
James, W. 1890. *The Principles of Psychology*. New York: Holt.
Kant, I. 1998. *Kritik der reinen Vernunft*. Hamburg: Meiner.
Kim, A. 2003, 2016. "Paul Natorp". *Stanford Encyclopedia of Philosophy*. http://plato.stanford.edu/entries/natorp/
———. 2007. "Recollecting the Soul: Natorp's Construction of a Platonic 'Psychology'". *Internationale Zeitschrift für Philosophie*, vol. xvi, no. 2: 159–174.
———. 2009. "Early Experimental Psychology". In Calvo and Symons, 2009.
———. 2010. *Plato in Germany: Kant – Natorp – Heidegger*. Sankt Augustin: Academia.
———. 2015a. "Neo-Kantian Ideas of History". In de Warren and Staiti, 2015: 39–58.
———. 2015b. "Johann Friedrich Herbart". *Stanford Encyclopedia of Philosophy*. http://plato.stanford.edu/entries/johann-herbart/
Luft, S. 2006. "Natorp, Husserl und das Problem der Kontinuität von Leben, Wissenschaft und Philosophie". *Phänomenologische Forschungen*, vol. 6: 99–134.
———. 2015. "The Philosophy of the Marburg School: From the Critique of Scientific Cognition to the Philosophy of Culture". In de Warren and Staiti, 2015: 221, ff.

Menn, S.P. 1998. "Collecting the Letters". *Phronesis*, vol. xliii, no. 4 (November): 291–305.
Natorp, P. 1887. "Ueber Objective und Subjective Begründung der Erkenntniss [On the Objective and Subjective Grounding of Knowledge]". *Philosophische Monatshefte*, vol. xxiii: 257–286.
———. 1888. *Einleitung in die Psychologie nach kritischer Methode*. Freiburg: Mohr.
———. 1893. "Zu den Vorfragen der Psychologie". *Philosophische Monatshefte*, vol. xxix: 581–611.
———. 1901. "Zur Frage der logischen Methode. Mit Beziehung auf Edm. Husserls 'Prolegomena zur reinen Logik'". *Kantstudien*, vol. vi: 270–283.
———. 1910. *Die logischen Grundlagen der exakten Wissenschaften*. Leipzig: Teubner.
———. 1912a. "Kant und die Marburger Schule". *Kant-Studien*, vol. xvii: 193–221.
———. 1912b. *Allgemeine Psychologie nach kritischer Methode*. Tübingen: Mohr. Reprinted 1965, by Bonset (Amsterdam).
———. 1917. "Husserls 'Ideen zu einer reinen Phänomenologie'". *Logos*, vol. vii, no. 3: 224–246. Originally appeared 1912 in *Die Geisteswissenschaften*, vol. i: 420, ff.
———. 1918. *Hermann Cohens philosophische Leistung unter dem Gesichtspunkte des Systems*. Berlin: Union Deutsche Verlags-Gesellschaft.
———. 1921a. *Platos Ideenlehre: Eine Einführung in den Idealismus*. 2nd ed. Hamburg: Meiner.
———. 1921b. "Paul Natorp". In *Die Philosophie der Gegenwart in Selbstdarstellungen*, Schmidt, R., ed. Leipzig: Meiner: 151–176.
———. 1981. "On the Objective and Subjective Grounding of Knowledge". Translation of Natorp (1887). Phillips, L., Kolb, D., trans. *Journal of the British Society for Phenomenology*, vol. 12, no. 3 (October): 245–266.
Twardowski, K. 1894. *Zur Lehre vom Inhalt und Gegenstand der Vorstellungen. Eine psychologische Untersuchung*. Vienna: Hölder.

INDEX

abstraction(s) 38, 62, 72n8, 141, 179, 188, 191, 204, 221, 234, 236–237, 244–245, 260: "Ideational" 245; process of 188, 191, 237; theories of 244
affects 117, 147, 150, 152, 155, 192
âme 1
aphasia 148, 156–163, 164n20; conduction 157–158
a priori methods 7–8
Aquinas 188
Aristotelian tradition 26, 40n13, 49, 97, 182, 200
Aristotle 168, 174, 182, 188, 200, 257, 260, 264n35; doctrine of 'common sensibles' 200, 202, 211n6
assumptions 195, 245; theory of 190
attitude(s) 16, 44, 46, 49, 54, 129, 137, 188, 192
Augustine 188
Austria 2, 4, 44, 65–66, 72–73n22, 187–188, 195n2, 221, 225n5, 226n6
Austro-Hungarian Empire 44, 66, 191
Avenarius, Richard 87, 90, 92

Baumann, Johann 69–70, 73n37; theory of the will 69–70
Beneke, Friedrich Eduard 5
Benussi, Vittorio 191; and Graz Gestalt theory 191
Bergson, Henri 154
Berlin 16, 17, 18, 214, 221, 225n5
Berlin School 219, 221–222, 225, 225n3
binocular: rivalry 100–102, 107; vision 82–83, 88, 111
Bois-Reymond, Emil du 113n7
Bolzano, Bernard 3–4, 9–11, 12, 20n4, 21n10, 21n12, 42–55, 56n7, 56n12, 56n13, 56n15, 56n16, 57n17, 57n20, 57n21, 57n22, 57n24, 57n26, 58n27, 58n28, 58n29, 58n30, 58n32, 58n34, 179, 189, 240, 242–243, 247n6; *Athanasia* 42, 43, 50; *On the Concept of an Organism* 43, 50; *Paradoxes of the Infinite* 43, 57n23; and philosophy of mind and action 43, 55; *Theory of Science* 11, 42, 45, 54; *see also* judgement; metaphysics; objectuality; representation
Boskovich, Ruder 57n24
Bradley, Francis Herbert 139, 144n21
brain 152–153; brainstem 148, 151, 156; Broca's "motor center" 157–159; cerebellum 150–151, 154; cerebral cortex 150; cerebral ganglia 151; cerebral peduncle 151; cerebrum 153, 162; cortex 150–151, 153–162; cortical centers 163n5; cortical fields 163n5; medulla oblongata 150; midbrain 148, 154; neocortex 153; parietal lobes 159; pons 151; spine/spinal cord 150–153, 156; tegmentum 151; temporal lobes 159; vascularization of 153; Wernicke's center 159, 162
brain fields 148, 161, 162
Brentano, Franz 4, 10, 12, 15–19, 39, 43–48, 56n6, 56n7, 56n15, 56n16, 66, 70, 72n20, 74n40, 88, 107, 114n30, 147–148, 152–157, 161–162, 163n1, 164n15, 168–183, 183n3, 183n5, 183n6, 183n7, 183n8, 186–190, 192–193, 198–199, 200, 210, 211n4, 211n6, 212n15, 214–216, 218–219, 221, 225, 226n7, 226n10, 226n17, 232–234, 238–241, 245, 261, 266n107; act psychology of 147–148, 152, 156, 161–162; definition of logic 169–170;

INDEX

definition of philosophy 168–171, 181; definition of psychology 171, 180–182; early philosophy of mind of 171, 177, 179, 181, 183, 183n6, 183n9; inexistence theory 189; "intentional inexistence" 88, 232, 241; and mental phenomena/acts 175–180, 187–188, 232, 234–235; metaphysics of 171; phenomenology of 4; "Psychognosy" lectures 176; *Psychology from an Empirical Standpoint* 4, 16, 44, 56n6, 70, 163n1, 171, 174–177, 180, 183n6, 187–188, 215, 232–233; "reism" 168; School of 66, 214, 218–219, 226n7, 226n19; tripartite classification of mental acts 48; Würzburg lectures on immortality 181; *see also* consciousness; emotion(s); intentionality; judgement(s); love and hate; perception(s); phenomenology; presentation(s); "psychognosy"; psychology; representation(s); sensation(s)

Breuer, Josef 156, 161

Britain 2, 5

British empiricism 67, 179, 187

British empiricists 179, 187

Brücke, Ernst 147–149

Carnap, Rudolf 4, 93

Cartesian 29, 153, 182, 255; doubt 188; epistemology 18; post- 10, 52

causality 13, 53, 58n32, 128, 215, 224; law of 104

central nervous system 83, 86, 147; *see also* nervous system

Charcot, Jean-Martin 15, 149, 152–153, 161

Christianity 117

Claus, Carl 148

Clifford, W. K. 87

cognition(s) 1, 23–26, 29–30, 38, 39n3, 89, 98, 136, 143n7, 148, 157, 190, 193, 195, 233, 242–244, 246, 247n9, 250, 258, 260, 263n5; and objectives 193, 195; self- 25, 39n4; theory of 11, 44

cognitive science(s) 5, 15, 149, 165n27, 214, 226n7

conduction aphasias, Meynertian-Lichtheimian thesis of 157, 160–161; and paraphasias 157

conscious, the 67

consciousness 10, 11, 14, 15, 16, 23, 27–30, 32–35, 38, 39n6, 40n10, 43, 46, 55, 64, 67, 72n8, 73n31, 74n40, 79, 88–89, 102–108, 114n29, 148–150, 152–156, 162, 164n25, 201, 215, 216, 220, 223–224, 234, 236, 238, 245–246, 250–252, 260, 266n107; Bretanian theory of 19, 44–45, 172–173, 175–177, 180, 182, 226n7, 261; cognitive 250, 253; empirical 24, 30–31; higher-order thought (HOT) theories of 120, 122, 131n15; individual 254; inner 180; intellectual 38; intentional 250–252; linguistic nature of 121–122, 128; minimal 250, 253; for Natorp 250–254, 258–259, 263; Nietzsche and 117, 118–130, 130n7, 131n15, 131n16; non- 153; objective 251, 252; perceiving 38; phenomenology of 260; presentational acts of 238; pure 266n109; qualitative 123; reflective 130n5; self- 14, 25–26, 32, 34–35, 38, 50, 57n20, 119, 120–122, 128–130; sensory 38, 122; subjective 252, 261; threshold of 64, 67, 154–156; "unconscious" 180; unitary 224; units of 223; unity of 182; visual 108

constructivist 3

continuist-contiguist debate 163n8, 164n18, 164–165n25

cortico-centrism 148, 150–151, 153, 157, 162

Cuvier, Georges 97

Darwin, Charles 61,182

Darwin, Erasmus 182

Darwinian biology 148

Darwinism of mental capacities 160, 163n2

Derrida, Jacques 148, 162–163, 163n7; *Mal d'archive* 148

Descartes, René 34, 102, 104, 170, 181, 182, 192; *Optics* 102; *see also* Cartesian

desire(s) 25, 30, 48–49, 55, 56n13, 56n16, 126, 138, 144n12, 193–195, 232; and desideratives 56n13, 193–195

determinism: physical 156

Dostoevsky, Fyodor 117

Dretske, F. 108, 112, 208

dualism 13, 14, 17, 88, 118, 150, 182, 186, 260; a- 130n4

Dubois-Reymond, Emil 12

INDEX

Ehrenfels, Christian von 16, 17–18, 21n14, 82, 183n3, 193–194, 214–226, 226n13, 226n14, 226n17, 226n19, 227n20, 227n21, 227n25; "*Gedanken über die Religion der Zukunft*" ("Thoughts on the Religion of the Future") 224; "On '*Gestalt*' qualities" ("Über 'Gestaltqualitäten'") 216, 218, 222–223; *Kosmogonie* 222, 225, 227n37; *see also* Gestalt qualities
emotion(s)/feeling(s) 1, 5, 6, 17, 48, 56n13, 70–71, 74n41, 74n42, 74n43, 74n46, 170, 180, 192–195, 226n13; Brentanian 215–216, 225, 226n10; cognitive theory of 70; and dignatives 56n13, 193–195; *see also* love and hate
empirical methods 6–8
empiricism 3, 89, 149, 200–202, 204, 211n5, 243; British 67, 179, 187; doubt 188
English positivists 117
epiphenomenalism 128–130, 131n14
epistemology 9, 11, 44, 170, 171, 190, 198, 244
esprit 1
Europe 2, 15, 60, 220
evolution 61, 80, 161, 223
existentialism 2
Exner, F. 47
Exner, Sigmund 147, 162, 163n8
experience(s) 24, 28, 39n2, 49, 70, 72n20, 73–74n38, 88–89, 92, 98–100, 103, 105–113, 114n25, 114n36, 121–122, 130, 133–143, 143n9, 145n32, 152, 168–169, 173–174, 181–182, 186, 188, 204, 207, 241–242, 243, 246, 250–251, 253–254, 257, 259, 264n35, 265n81, 267n132; conscious 124, 130; immediate 261; inner 25, 169, 174, 215, 217, 226n13; intuitive 245; mystical 144n14; objective 250–251, 254, 257; perceptual 107–110, 112–113, 119, 122, 134, 141, 239; phenomenal 96, 107–108, 110–111; philosophy of 250; plasticity of 111–112; presentational 245; sensorimotor approach to 107–108, 112; sensory 107, 108; subjective 253, 260; temporal 239; veridical 189; visual 108, 110, 112
externalism 108, 112

Fechner, Gustav Theodor 5, 12, 13, 64, 67, 77–80, 86, 113n7, 192; *Elemente der Psychophysik* 77

Feuerbach, Ludwig 2
Fichte, Johann Gottlieb 2, 9, 10, 23, 29–38, 39n8, 39–40n9, 40n10, 40n11, 113, 113n6, 114n20, 114n31; *Grundlage* 30–32, 34
Flechsig, Paul 151, 163n5, 164n14, 164n17
Fliess, Wilhelm 162, 164n24
force-shells: Kant-Boskovich theory of 57n24
free will 35, 148, 151, 155, 226
Frege, Gottlob 3, 5, 11, 42, 56n16, 149, 160, 189, 236–238, 249; *Foundations of Arithmetic* 236–237
French moralists 117
Freud, Sigmund 4, 12, 15, 56n8, 67–69, 72n17, 73n26, 73n30, 113n7, 117, 131n11, 147–163, 163n1, 163n5, 163n7, 163n8, 163n9, 163n11, 163n12, 164n14, 164n15, 164n17, 164n20, 164n21, 164n23, 164n24, 164–165n25, 165n26, 165n27; *On Aphasia (Zur Auffassung der Aphasien)* 15, 147, 149, 156–163; "Dora" case 148; "*Das Gehirn*" ('The Brain') 15, 147, 149–156, 162, 163n12; *The Interpretation of Dreams* 164n14, 164n17; *Project for a Scientific Psychology* 147–148, 154, 156, 162, 165n26, 165n27; psychoanalysis 39; "talking cure" 155, 156
Fries, Jakob Friedrich 5, 7, 10, 12, 39
Frith, Chris 130
functionalism 148; Fechnerian 78

Galileo 264n43
Gall, Franz Joseph 150, 157, 164n13
Geist 1, 32, 36, 50, 57n20, 97, 113n2, 113n6, 186, 250
Gemüt 1, 23–24, 50, 263n4
German Idealism/idealism 9–10, 23, 39, 40n15, 65, 72–73n22, 113n6; post-Kantian 3, 9–10
Germany 2, 12, 65, 187, 249
Gesetz (law) 254–258, 260
Gestalt cosmology 222–223
Gestalt qualities 214, 216–225, 225n3, 226n11, 227n19, 227n32, 259, 266n92; kinetic 223; non-temporal 216–217, 223; sequences of 223; static 223; temporal 216–217, 223, 226n13; theory of 18, 191, 218, 221, 225
Gestaltungsprinzip (principle of order) 223–224

271

God/god 10, 24, 36, 178, 179, 181, 183n5, 224
Goethe, Johann 72–73n22
Graz 16, 18, 78, 188, 190–192, 214, 219, 225n5
Graz School 221–222, 225, 225n3
Great War 194; Allies 194; Central Powers 194
Grice, H. Paul 11

Hall, Marshall 150; "The Reflex Function of the Medulla Oblongata" 150
Hanslick, Eduard 70–71, 73n24, 74n42, 74n43, 74n46; *On the Musically Beautiful* 70–71
Hartnack, Edmund 151
Hegel, Georg Wilhelm Friedrich 2, 9–10, 12, 23, 33, 36–39, 40n13, 65–66, 72–73n22; *Encyclopedia of Philosophical Sciences* 36; *Philosophy of Spirit* 37; post- 65, 249
Heidegger, Martin 4, 16, 246
Helmholtz, Hermann von 4, 12–13, 39, 63, 77, 80, 83–85, 88, 96–113, 113n6, 113n7, 113n10, 114n21, 114n22, 114n24, 114n25, 114n27, 114n28, 114n34, 114n36, 147, 148–149; adverbial theory 109–110, 114n35; *The Doctrine of the Sensations of Tone* 96; doctrine of "unconscious inference" 83–84, 88; *Handbook of Physiological Optics (Handbuch der Physiologischen Optik)* 13, 83, 96–97, 103; and physiological psychology 96; and plasticity of experience 111–112; sign theory 96, 114n12, 114n17; "unconscious inferences" 104–105, 111, 114n30; *see also* intuition(s); perception(s); representation(s); sensation(s)
Herbart, Johann Friedrich 7, 10, 12, 13, 39, 60–71, 72n10, 72n12, 72n17, 72n20, 72n21, 72–73n22, 73n26, 73n28, 73n35, 73n37, 73–74n38, 74n40, 74n41, 74n42, 74n46, 77–78, 86, 104, 113n7, 114n29, 154–155, 164n21, 201, 243; philosophy of mind 66–67; *Psychology as Science (Psychologie als Wissenschaft)* 67–68, 70, 77
Herbartianism 65–66, 73n24
Hering, Ewald 80, 83–84, 86, 111–112; *Beiträge zur Physiologie* 83; *Die Lehre vom binocularischen Sehen* 83; nativist cyclopean theory of 83–84, 111

Hilbert, David 3, 246n3
historicism 243
Höfler, Alois 16, 45, 183n3, 188–189
homuncular fallacy 14–15, 124, 127
homunculus theory 148, 153, 159, 162
Hughlings Jackson, John 152–153, 155, 160, 161; theoretical armature of 152
humanism 72–73n22
Hume, David 178, 181–182, 187–188, 194, 202–204; 'distinction of reason' 202–203; theory of relations 188; *Treatise* 202; *see also* Meinong
Husserl, Edmund 1–2, 4, 11, 16, 17, 18–20, 27, 43, 46–48, 56n15, 149, 174, 179, 183n3, 190, 192, 198–199, 209, 211n12, 211–212n14, 225n5, 227n19, 232–246, 246n3, 247n6, 247n8, 247n10, 249, 252, 260–263, 265n81, 265n82, 266n107; completeness 236, 246n3; *The Crisis of European Sciences* 246; "General Introduction to Pure Phenomenology" 233; and ideal content 243–244; *Ideas* 1, 18, 19, 245–246, 260, 261; *Ideas Pertaining to a Pure Phenomenology and to a Phenomenological Philosophy* 233; and "intentional" existence 240; *Logical Investigations* 4, 19, 47–48, 149, 237, 242, 245, 261; phenomenological method 27, 174, 225n5, 237; "*Philosophie als strenge Wissenschaft* [Philosophy as Rigorous Science]" 261; *The Philosophy of Arithmetic* 226n19, 234–237, 243; "Prolegomena to Pure Logic" 237, 242–243, 260, 261; "Psychological Studies in the Elements of Logic" 238, 244; "theory of theories" 242–243, 245; *see also* intentionality; judgement(s); phenomenology; presentation(s); psychology
hysteria 148–149, 157–158, 161–163

I, the 30–36, 38, 39–40n9, 68, 73n31, 128, 181
Idealism 3, 9–10, 39, 77, 92, 113n6, 262; German 9–10, 40n15, 65, 72n22, 113n6; Hegelian 12; post-Kantian 2, 9; post-Kantian German 3, 9–10; transcendental 246
Idealists 9–10, 23, 38, 43,144n21, 266n94; Absolute 139; German 10

ideas 21n10, 47, 104, 128, 136, 143–144n9, 147, 152, 154–155, 170, 178–179, 188, 193–195, 200, 207; abstract 188, 189; and things 193, 195
ideation 63, 153; passive 160
immanentism 47
immortality 24, 25, 43, 50, 168, 172, 181, 182; *see also* soul, the
Intellectualism 139, 144n21
intentionalism 108; contemporary 96
intentionality 1, 16, 19, 44–47, 69–70, 107, 124, 156, 194–195, 226, 261; Brentanian theory of 19, 45–46, 70, 107, 114n30, 168, 176–177, 183n7, 186, 188, 232–234; Husserlian 233, 239–240, 244, 261; theory of 16, 44
interactionism 156, 162, 164n23, 226
intuition(s) 26, 98–99, 102–103, 109–111, 144n16, 149, 164n21, 200, 233, 239, 244–245, 254; "abstractive" 245; authentic 239; "categorial" 245; categorical 245; "eidetic" 261; Husserlian 244–245, 260, 261; "ideal" 174; intuitive image 105–106; *nonsensuous* form of 245
Italy 191

James, William 15, 60, 85, 88–89, 92–93, 133–143, 143n7, 143–144n9, 144n10, 144n12, 144n15, 144n17, 144n22, 144n23, 145n25, 145n28, 145n32, 145n33, 149, 198–199, 205, 207, 211n2, 259; and concepts/models 133–143, 144n18, 145n28, 145n32, 145n33; 'instrumentalism' 135; 'The Knowing of Things Together' 207; knowing things together 207–208, 211n10; 'metaphorical' form of understanding 136; *A Pluralistic Universe* 134, 137, 139; *Pragmatism* 140, 144n10, 145n28; *The Principles of Psychology* 85, 133, 145n32, 211n2; radical empiricism 89; and ?rejection of logic' 136–142, 144n11, 144–145n24; *Some Problems of Philosophy* 134; *The Will to Believe* 140, 144n10; *see also* monism
judgement(s) 1, 45, 49, 56n13, 57n17, 105, 190–191; affirmations 174; analytic 179; Bolzanian 43, 46–48, 55, 56n13; Brentanian 43–44, 46, 48, 170–171, 174–177, 179, 180, 183n8, 188, 192, 215–216, 225, 227n36, 232, 234; Husserlian 234–237, 241–244, 260;

hypothetical 241; and logic 170–171, 179, 215, 227n36; objectivity of 236; negations 174; numerical 234–237

Kant, Immanuel 1–4, 7, 9–10, 12, 20, 20n4, 23–26, 29–30, 32–34, 37–38, 39n2, 39n4, 39n5, 43, 56n7, 57n24, 60–61, 63, 65, 66, 68, 71n3, 73n35, 86, 96–98, 104, 113, 113n6, 117, 120, 164n21, 224, 246, 249, 250, 254, 255, 262; anti- 20n4; 'cognitive psychology' of 10; *Critique of Judgement* 61; *Critique of Pure Reason* 1, 3, 7, 24–27, 38, 39n2, 39n4, 164n21, 224; as "philosopher of the revolution" 66; post- 2–3, 9, 10, 12, 20n4, 42; theory of categories 179; transcendental idealism of 246; transcendental unity of apperception 98
Kierkegaard, Søren 2, 5
knowledge 250, 252–253, 256–257, 263n5, 263n19; vs. consciousness 250; objective 254, 258
Koffka, Kurt 18, 198, 221, 225n3
Köhler, Wolfgang 18, 198, 220–221, 225n3
Külpe, Oswald 252

Lamarck, Jean-Baptiste 61
Lange, Friedrich Albert 5, 63, 65, 171
Leibniz, Gottfried 10, 21n12, 57n24, 65, 104–105, 120, 242
Lenin, V. I. 92–93; *Empiricism and Empiro-Criticism* 92–93
Lichtheim, Ludwig 157–160, 162, 164n20; "house diagram" 157–158
Lindner, Gustav Adolf 67–68; *Textbook of Empirical Psychology* 67
localizationism 148, 157, 159–161
Locke, John 67, 73n28, 169, 170, 187–188
logic 240, 242–243, 261; conceptual 140–142; formal 66, 261–262; of identity 137, 141, 145n25; laws of 243, 249; pure 237, 242, 245, 262; transcendental 253, 261–262
Logical Empiricists 2
logical positivism 246
Lotze, Hermann 5, 77, 81, 97–99, 102, 105, 113n7, 139, 198–200, 211n5, 243, 255; *Medical Psychology, or Physiology of the Mind* 97, 105

love and hate: Bretanian 48, 170, 175–177, 179–180, 188, 192, 215–216, 232; and ethics 170–171, 180, 215
Lovejoy, Arthur 91–92; *Revolt Against Dualism* 91–92

Mach, Ernst 4, 10, 12–14, 18, 56n5, 68–69, 73n31, 73n32, 73n35, 77–93, 218–219, 226n19; *Beiträge zur Analyse der Empfindungen (Contributions to the Analysis of Sensations)* 68, 77, 82, 85, 86, 87, 88, 218; "bilocation", problem of 91–92; *Erkenntnis und Irrtum* 87, 88–89; "error of introjection" 86; *Geschichte und Wurzel des Prinzips der Erhaltung der Arbeit* 87; "headless body" picture 90; *Lectures on Psychophysics* 13; Mach Card 83–84, 88; monocular depth sensations 82–84; monocular stereoscopy 83–84; 'neutral monism' 13–14, 86–89; philosophy of mind 86, 88, 92; Problem of Introjection 90–91; and sensations of form and symmetry 80–82; sensations of innervation 84–86; "Vorträge über Psychophysik" 77, 80, 86; *see also* Mach Band phenomenon
Mach Band phenomenon 78–80, 82
Marburg Circle 262
Marburgers 249, 253, 254, 262, 265n82
Marty, Anton 16–18, 47, 88, 183n3, 214, 221, 225n5
Marx, Karl 2
Marxism 2, 14, 92
materialism 14, 15, 17, 92, 147, 153, 182, 224; Marxist 92
materialist reductionism 153
Maudsley, Henry 5
mechanism 15, 147
Meinong, Alexius 4, 16–17, 18, 45, 46, 48, 56n13, 57n17, 183n3, 186–195, 214–215, 219, 221–222, 225n5, 226n19, 227n21, 238, 240; *Über Annahmen (On Assumptions)* 190; *On Emotional Presentation* 193; 'Über Gegenstandstheorie' ('On the Theory of Objects') 190; *Hume-Studien* 187–188, 219; 'On the Meaning of Weber's Law' 191; 'On Objects of Higher Order and their relation to Inner Perception' 189; object theory 187–188, 190, 193–195; *Über philosophische Wissenschaft und ihre Propadeutik (On Philosophical Science and its Propadeutics)* 187, 188; philosophy of mind of 186–188; *Psychological-Ethical Investigations in Value Theory* 192; 'For Psychology and Against Psychologism in General Value Theory' 192; theory of assumptions 190; *Theory of Object* 17; '*see also* assumptions; cognitions; desires; emotion(s); ideas; value theory
memory chain 154
Menger, Carl 192
Merleau-Ponty, Maurice 246
metaphysics 9, 24, 42–43, 64–66, 72n20, 157, 169, 181–182, 186, 190, 198, 225, 246; Aristotelian 49; Bolzano's 53; Brentanian 171, 183n5; Ehrenfels's 222, 225; Lichtheim's 159; of mind 17–18, 43, 53, 159, 222, 225; Nietzsche's 117; post-Cartesian dualistic 52–53; of substance 43
Meynert, Theodor 15, 147–162, 163n5, 164n15; materialist reductionism of 153, 164n15; separate "pathways" thesis 151, 158
Meynert-Wernicke thesis 157, 161
Middle Ages 176, 232
Mill, John Stuart 5, 114n28, 171, 181–182, 249
mind, the 1, 24–25, 118, 171, 183n5, 223–224; conscious 14, 118, 123; Bretanian theory of 44; embodied 147; "layered mind", hypothesis of 224; mechanistic theory of 67; metaphysics of 159, 222, 225; nature of 130n3; theories of 43, 54; unconscious 118, 130; *see also* philosophy of mind; study of mind
mind and action: theory of 123; *see also* philosophy of mind and action
mind-body problem 17, 52, 118, 130n3, 186
mind-body relationship 164n23
mind-brain parallelism 148, 152
monad 14, 57n24; primary 104–105
monadology 13–14, 21n12; Herbartian psycho- 80, 86; psychophysical 77
monism 186; metaphysical 139; neutral 13–14, 43, 56n5, 88, 92–93; reductionist 260; substance 50, 52
Moore, G. E. 2, 3, 5, 16
movement 37, 52, 64, 80, 85, 112, 149–152, 155, 158; conscious voluntary

INDEX

(intentional) 85, 112, 149–156, 164n15; reflex arc 150; unconscious involuntary (reflexes) 85, 149–156, 164n14, 164n15; *see also* free will
Müller, Johannes 12, 39, 77, 97–98, 100, 103, 109, 113n7, 150; *Handbook of Human Physiology* 97; "Law of specific nerve energies" (LoSNE)/"Müller's law" 103, 114n19; rational organizing force 98
multi-layered refraction microscope 151
multiplicity 160, 199; arbitrary 235; concept of 234–235; -ies 234
Münsterberg, Hugo 85
mysticism 133, 142, 144n15

nativism 96, 111–112, 115n39, 200, 202, 211n5
Natorp, Paul 19–20, 249–263, 263n5, 263n19, 263n22, 264n25, 264n35, 264n42, 265n70, 265n76, 265n81, 265n82, 266n91, 266n107, 267n131; and *Gesetz* 254–258, 260; "Ueber objective und subjective Begründung der Erkenntniss [On the objective and subjective grounding of knowledge]" 249; philosophy of mind 249–251; *Platos Ideenlehre* 260; *see also* consciousness; knowledge; representation(s)
naturalism 14, 40n13, 113, 118, 133, 143, 148, 149; neurological 163n11; non-reductive 118
neo-Kantian 18, 63; -ism 20, 63; philosophy of mind 249; psychologistic 20n8
nervous system 87, 99, 102, 109, 147–149, 153, 156
neurology 15, 147, 149, 154, 156, 162, 165n27; materialist 164–165n25
neurophysiology 15, 147, 148
neurotransmitters 163n8
Newton, Isaac 60–61, 64–65, 77
Nietzsche, Friedrich 2, 4, 14–15, 61, 69, 73n36, 73n37, 117–130, 130n1, 130n3, 130n4, 130n8, 131n13, 131n15, 131n16; *Beyond Good and Evil* 61, 117, 122; and drives 123–129, 131n11, 131n12; *Ecce Homo* 130; Falsification Claim (FC) 120–122; *Gay Science* 119, 120, 122, 128, 129, 131n13; *Genealogy of Morals* 73n36; naturalism of 117–118; *Thus Spoke Zarathustra* 118; *Twilight of the Idols* 128; *see also* consciousness
nominalism 179; conceptualist 188
North America 2

objectivation 252–253, 256, 259–260, 264n42, 264n43, 265n88
objectivity 9, 133, 234, 236, 242, 246, 251, 253–254, 256–258, 263n15; immanent 176, 232; norms of 260; scientific 258
objectuality: Bolzanian 45–46
ontology: Bolzano's 43, 46, 49–51; Brentano's 17, 171, 183n5; Ehrenfel's 222; Husserl's 19, 233, 244; Meinong's 17
opthalmoscope 102

panpsychism 17, 77, 86
Panum, Peter Ludwig 111, 112
paraphasia 157, 159
Peano, Giuseppe 3
Peirce, C. S. 142, 144n11
perception(s) 1, 13, 24, 98–100, 102, 104–111, 113n7, 122, 127, 144n15, 148, 154, 155, 177, 179–182, 201–204, 207, 209, 223, 239; Brentanian 215, 234; empirist theory 111–112; inner 44, 171, 173, 179–180, 182, 215–216, 220, 223, 234; nativist theory 111; objective 107; outer 215; projection or copy theory of 100, 102; of space 211n5
periodicity 156, 162, 164–165n25
Petzoldt, Josef 92
phenomenalism 164n23, 188; epi- 128–130
phenomenological movement 225n5
phenomenology 2, 17, 18–20, 194–195, 214, 233–234, 242, 245, 260–262; Brentanian 4, 15–16, 172; and *epoché*/"bracketing" 245–246, 247n8; Husserlian 39, 174, 198, 242, 245–246, 261–262; Natorp's 262; pure 174, 233, 242; 'transcendental' ("pure") 16, 18, 242, 246, 262
phenomenon(a) 1, 251–254, 256; mental (psychical) 14, 17, 19, 44, 46, 48, 49–50, 60–61, 67, 71, 170–173, 175–177, 180, 183n6, 187–189, 215, 232, 234–235, 261; physical 175–177, 188, 225, 232, 234–235, 261; subjective 236
philosophical propaedeutic 65–66

INDEX

philosophy: analytical 2–4, 20n2, 42, 240, 246; Austrian 72n12; of cognitive sciences 5; idealist systematic 2; Marburg 254; natural 97; neuro- 5; Polish analytical 16; post-Cartesian 10; post-Hegelian German 249; as science of phenomena 17; of spirit 37; transcendental 12, 171; *see also* philosophy of mind; philosophy of nature; Western philosophy

philosophy of mind 1, 3, 4, 6–7, 10–11, 16, 23, 36, 39, 39n5, 40n12, 40n13, 44, 92–93, 117, 149, 186–187, 199, 214, 222, 226n7, 244, 246, 249; Bolzano's 42–55; Brentano's 147–148, 168–183, 183n6, 183n9, 226n7; contemporary 1, 16, 93; Ehrenfels's 214; Freud's 147; Helmholtz's 113; Herbart's 66; Mach's 86, 88, 92; Meinong's 186, 188; Natorp's 249–251; neo-Kantian 249; Nietzsche's 117–130; post-Fichtean 34; *see also* philosophy of mind and action; philosophy of mind and language

philosophy of mind and action 11, 42–55
philosophy of mind and language 11
philosophy of nature 36–37, 39
phrenology 150, 157, 164n13
physicalism 14, 118, 260
Plato 139, 142, 247n6, 254, 256, 260, 264n25, 264n38, 265n76; *Phaedo* 256; *Republic* 256; *Sophist* 247n6; *Theaetetus* 247n6; *see also* Platonism
Platonism 42, 179; logical 11
plurality 203, 210, 235, 242, 253–254
pragmatism 15, 144n22
Prague 16, 18, 44, 66, 80, 83, 85, 214, 221, 225n5
presentation(s) 44, 48, 62–65, 67–70, 73n29, 74n40, 170, 172, 175–179, 181, 189–190, 200–201, 204, 215–217, 225, 226n13, 227n19, 233–237, 239–241, 244, 246n1; "abstract"/"conceptual" 178–179, 239; and aesthetics 170–171; "authentic" (proper) 178, 235–236, 238–239; Brentanian 170–172, 175–181, 188, 215, 225, 232, 234–236, 238–239; "concrete" 239; conscious 73n29, 240; dark 73n29; dependent 239; "fantasy" 178; Husserlian 235–242, 244–246; improper 227n19; inauthentic 236; independent 239; intentional 236, 238, 239, 242, 244; internal 236; intuitive 242, 244–245; non-intuitive 239; numerical 235–237; real 237; "so-called objectless" 240; symbolic (improper) 217, 235–239

properties: collective 207–210; distributive 207–208, 210; objective 102; qualitative 201
Prussia 66
Psyche 20, 97, 186, 250, 251, 252, 263, 265n81; subjective 258
psychiatry 147; pathoanatomical 163n5
psychoanalysis 15, 39, 67, 117, 147, 149, 155, 165n27
psychognosy" 172–176, 180–181; psychognostic theory of mental acts 175
psychologism 11, 19, 149, 192, 237–238, 243, 249, 260; anti- 11–12, 20, 237, 249; subjectivist 243
psychology: act 147–148, 152, 156; associationist 178; Brentanian 234–235; cognitive 10, 13, 23–24, 63, 70, 191; critical 259, 262; 'descriptive' 4, 15–16, 17, 171–172, 177, 186, 215, 226n7, 238, 245, 262; empirical 12, 16, 21n10, 39, 66, 162, 181–182, 187, 242, 252, 261; experimental 12–13, 15, 17, 39, 65, 149, 187; faculty 12, 61–62, 68, 113n2; genetic 171–173, 175, 262; *Gestalt* 82, 218, 219, 221, 225n3; Herbartian 64, 65, 72n20; Husserlian 236; intentionalist 162; introspective 85; moral 117; Natorpian 259; physiological 17, 86, 96–113, 172; post-Kantian 23; pure 98, 113n6, 172, 252; rationalist 154; scientific 60, 64, 67, 148–149
psycho-physical parallelism 86, 147, 162
psychophysics 64, 67, 80, 86, 88, 172, 186, 192
psychophysiology 15

Quine, W.V.O. 42, 138, 144n13

rationalism 43; anti- 142; German 56n7; ir- 133, 142
rationality 15, 43, 49, 53, 54–55, 65, 137, 140–142, 144n23, 145n25; ir- 133, 144n10
realism 3, 189, 195, 243–244; direct 96; epistemological 47; spatial 100

276

INDEX

reductionism 153, 164n15; materialist 153; physical 149–150; psychical 150
Reinhold, Karl 9, 10, 23, 26–34, 38, 39n6, 39n7, 39n8; *Attempt at a New Theory of Human Representation* 27, 29
relativism 171, 243
representation(s) 1, 12, 24–35, 38, 39n2, 39n6, 40n10, 45–49, 56n7, 56n12, 58n29, 71, 74n43, 96–100, 102–108, 110–112, 114n24, 114n29, 120, 144n22, 147, 154, 159–160, 164n21, 246n1, 251–254, 261; Bolzanian 43, 46–48, 51, 56n12, 57n17, 58n29; Brentanian 43, 47; conscious 26, 120, 154, 251, 253–254; highways 160; Husserlian 260, 261; mental 108, 250–251, 261; for Natorp 251, 253; objective 45–47, 96, 104, 107–108, 251; powers of 51, 57n26; subjective 45–48; unconscious 26, 154; *see also* perception(s)
representationalism 108, 112
representationality 30–31, 33–34, 39n7
repression 67–69, 131n12, 155
Roman Catholic Church 72–73n22
Royce, Josiah 139
Russell, Bertrand 2–5, 16, 88, 92–93, 139, 192, 240; *Mind* 192; *The Principles of Mathematics* 192; *see also* monism
Ryle, Gilbert 4, 62

Sartre, Jean-Paul 246
Schelling, Friedrich 2, 9–10, 23, 33–39, 40n11, 40n12, 113n6; *System of Transcendental Idealism* 33, 34
Schopenhauer, Arthur 5, 65, 69–71, 72n21
Seele 1, 38, 50, 57n20, 97–98, 102, 113n2, 113n6, 250
semantics 3, 4, 233, 244
sensation(s) 1, 13, 24, 47–49, 68, 73n31, 79–93, 96, 98–100, 102–113, 113n7, 114n16, 114n24, 122, 124, 148, 150, 170, 175, 177–179, 192, 200, 202, 205–206, 219–222, 224–225; Brentanian 215; conscious 162; "copy" theory of 100; discrimination threshold 192; illusory 114n22; passive 153; pure 109; subjective 106–107, 112
Siegel, Susanna 110, 112; thesis of cognitive penetrability 110, 112
Socrates 139, 256, 264n38
Sömmerring, S. T. 24; *On the organ of the soul* 24

soul, the 1, 24–25, 38, 42–43, 48, 50, 52–53, 57n22, 63–64, 72n20, 102, 168, 171, 181–183, 183n6, 186, 200, 249; Aristotelian 182; Cartesian 182; immortality of 50, 57n22, 63
spatial properties 112, 199–205
Spencer, Herbert 153, 160, 256
spirit 1, 9, 32, 36–37, 39, 57n20, 97
Stahl, Ernst 97
Steinbuch, Johann Georg 100
stereoscope 100–102; stereoscopic parallax 102
Stout, G. F. 4, 5, 16, 222; *Analytic Psychology* 4, 222
study of mind 1, 4–8, 10–12, 15, 16, 17, 19, 20n6, 60, 63, 65, 215; neo-Kantian perspective on 19; philosophical 7; psychological 7
Stumpf, Carl 16, 17–18, 183n3, 190, 198–211, 211n4, 211n5, 211n8, 211–212n14, 212n15, 214, 218, 221, 225n5, 238; *Erkenntnislehre* 198; *Gefühl und Gefühlsempfindung* 198; and *Gestaltpsychologie* 198; *On the Psychological Origin of the Idea of Space (Über den psychologischen Ursprung der Raumvorstellung)* 198; *Sachverhalte* (states of affairs) 190; *Tonpsychologie* 198–199, 204, 205, 210; *see also* spatial properties; unity
subjectivist 3, 193, 243
subjectivity 34, 37, 236, 246, 251–254, 257–260, 263n15, 263n18, 263n22, 266n107; pure 258
Sully, M. 206, 209
synapse 147, 162, 164n18, 164–165n25

Tarski, Alfred 42
theology 171, 181
thinking 1, 10, 13, 25, 26, 32, 34, 36, 38, 84, 86, 90, 119, 134, 136, 145n28, 170–171, 177, 181, 186, 200, 203–204, 242; for Natorp 250, 252–260, 263n5, 264n38
Tourtual, Caspar Theobald 100
Tristan chord 204–205
truth 11, 19, 21n10, 33–34, 39n3, 45, 50, 73n36, 108, 124, 133, 136–140, 142–143, 143n10, 144n22, 144n23, 145n32, 169–170, 172, 182, 183n8, 190, 233–234, 236–237, 241–244, 253; absolute 143, 145n32; objective 253

Twardowki, Kasimierz (Kasimir) 16–17, 45–46, 66, 183n3, 189–190, 225n5, 238, 240; *On the Content and Object of Presentation* 45, 46, 189

unconscious, the 15, 39, 67, 89, 117–118; theory of 67
unity 18, 24, 68, 73n31, 73n38, 77, 182, 183n6, 198–199, 203–211, 211n8, 217, 219–220, 223, 234, 242, 244, 251, 253–255, 257; of consciousness 182; 'degrees of fusion' 209–210, 211–212n14, 212n15; doxastic 253; within manifold 253–255, 257; multitude as 205–206, 209–211; "natural" 238; plurality in 203, 210; within plurality 254; sensory whole 199, 205–211; transcendental 98; View 211n8
utilitarianism 58n34

value-objectivism 194
value theory 17, 192–193, 216, 233; impersonal values 194; subjectivistic 193
Vienna 2, 16, 44, 66, 73n24, 77, 147, 169, 172, 181, 183n3, 187, 188, 191, 192, 193, 214, 221, 226n6; University of 163n2
Vienna Circle 66, 93

Villaret, Albert 149; *Handwörterbuch der gesamten Medizin* (Comprehensive Dictionary of Medicine) 149
volition(s) 34, 48, 54, 62, 170, 173, 180
von Brücke, Ernst Wilhelm 15

Ward, James 5, 16
Watteville, Armand 159
Weber, Ernst 113n7, 192; fraction of psychophysics 80
Weber-Fechner effect 80
Weber's Law 191–192
"web of belief" approach 134, 138–139, 144n12
Wernicke, Carl 157, 159, 161, 162
Wertheimer, Max 18, 221
Western philosophy 2–4; analytical 2–4; continental 2–4
Wheatstone, Charles 100–101
Witasek, Stephan 191
Wittgenstein, Ludwig 2, 72n12, 145n28, 190; *Philosophical Investigations* 72n12
Wolff, Christian 65
Wundt, Wilhelm 5, 12, 60, 77, 81, 85, 97, 113n6, 148–149, 226n6, 252; complex local sign theory 81; *Outline of Physiological Psychology* 97

Zimmermann, Robert 45, 66; "Philosophical Propaedeutic" 66